I LOVE THE 90S
ESSAYS

ELEXUS JIONDE

INTELEXUAL MEDIA

INTELEXUAL MEDIA BOOKS

I Love The 90s: Essays

Copyright © Elexus Jionde 2025

All rights reserved

ISBN 978-0-9996710-4-7(Hardcover)
ISBN 978-0-9996710-5-4(Paperback)

This book may be purchased in bulk for promotional, educational, and business uses. Contact info@intelexualmedia.com

First Edition: August 2025

For Mother, who birthed me on a day filled with Clinton scandals and historic moments.

CONTENTS

Welcome To The 90s... Again 1
A 90s Baby 2
On The Spice Girls 13
90s Food 27
On King of The Hill 51
90s True Crime 72
90s Serial Killers 108
90s Halloween 120
On Boy Meets World 134
90s Christmas 153
On Moesha 162
90s Style 176
On The X-Files 206
90s Scandals 224
Notes on Methodology and Sources 243
Bibliography
Index
Acknowledgements

I LOVE THE 90S

ESSAYS

ELEXUS JIONDE

INTELEXUAL MEDIA

Welcome To The 90s... Again

It's enticing to look back on the past and simplify it. For many, it's preferable to tracing history's most complex details. As explored in *Lexual Does The 90s*, the decade was as fun and fabulous as it was scandalous and scary. When researching and writing, it became clear to me just how much of my earliest understandings of the world were underscored by nineties trends and news. Though I am technically a 2000's baby because I was born in 1994, I was still influenced by the era of Clinton.

I was a precocious five year old when the decade ended, and I have firsthand memories. But I also came of age in the early 2000s on an endless diet of nineties re-runs and second-hand books culled from thrift stores for two quarters a pop (a dollar if hardback). I baked cakes with my nana to the sound of *Inside Edition* and *Entertainment News* commemoration specials that provided information on the happenings of nineties icons and has-beens. I didn't have all the context though.

While I could have dove into popular nineties fixtures like *The Simpsons*, Beanie Babies, and *Buffy The Vampire Slayer*, instead, every topic in this book was a fragment of my childhood, leaving a mark on me in some fashion. How did global politics, the economy, race, and misogyny impact pop culture, food, style, and holidays? How did region and location affect individual priorities and perspectives? How were American fears represented in media? And, most importantly-- how do our best memories of the nineties obscure the worst parts of the nineties?

Take off your kiwi-strawberry tinted glasses and tell the truth: the nineties were great, but it was complicated.

A 90s Baby

I entered the world on January 26, 1994, at Carolinas Medical Center in Charlotte, North Carolina. My mother spent a cruel 72 hours in labor while a rotation of talk shows and CourtTV programs beamed from the television. Supportive family members waited nearby. When I was taken home, it was to West Charlotte, which would serve as a home base for me throughout my childhood. It was my home base because it was where my nana lived. But my mother and I lived on every side of the Queen City at some point during my upbringing.

My memories of Charlotte in the nineties are steeped in tobacco smoke, Bronner Brothers hair grease, and electric blue Kool-Aid. Like everyone else, how I view the world is shaped by how and where I was raised. My hometown, like yours, is the foundation on which my life was built. My perception of America and the nineties may not end with Charlotte, but it certainly began there.

The City That Raised Me at the End of History

Between 1990 and 2000, the city of Charlotte added 66 square miles of land to its map through annexations. As documented by Chuck McShane in *Charlotte* magazine, there was an influx of 145,000 new residents, bringing the Queen City's population to 541,000. Most of these newcomers came from Ohio and small towns across North Carolina, though more and more were arriving from urban areas like New York. This is why my fancy, well-dressed New York cousins made frequent visits down South to survey the land during holidays. I also saw tons of Ohio State pride growing up, so it's no wonder I fell in love with my alma mater long before ever stepping foot in the Buckeye State. Charlotte's OSU alumni chapter even honored me with a scholarship and a trip to a Buckeyes basketball game when I was in high school.

When the nineties began, Charlotte was in the middle of trying to become more worldly. Charlotte Douglas International Airport, poised to one day become the 11th busiest airport in the country, expanded by 80,000 square feet and added direct routes to Germany and London. In 1991, the Museum of the New South was opened as a "museum without walls," featuring traveling and pop-up exhibits before eventually settling into a permanent location in 1996. Five years later, it was renamed in honor of Family Dollar founder Leon Levine and moved into a 40,000-square-foot building filled with interactive exhibits. It was there that my love of history, storytelling, and archives blossomed as a child. I'd eventually return to the museum for an article in *The Charlotte Observer* about my history-teaching mission in 2017.

In 1992, Charlotte added a cultural notch to its belt with the opening of the Blumenthal Arts complex, featuring numerous theaters and auditoriums for traveling musicians, plays, and musicals. Located uptown, it eventually took over administrative duties for several theater venues in the area, including Spirit Square, where I had classes as a middle schooler attending Northwest School of the Arts. It was a prestigious public-yet-lottery school that required protective students to audition. I can't remember the name of the Shakespeare monologue I read in the spring of 5th grade when auditioning, but I must have killed it to be enrolled. Northwest began in 1993 out of an old West Charlotte High building as a middle school, eventually expanding through 12th grade in 1996. By the time I attended from 2006 to 2009, I felt so cool taking theater and art classes. I felt like I was getting a taste of adventure riding a bus for five minutes three times a week to Spirit Square during school hours.

It was the type of excitement I craved in a city where everything closed by 9 or 10 PM. Charlotte's reputation as "boring" had existed for a while, despite its best attempt to present itself as a cosmopolitan destination in a state regularly conflated with it's further-south brother. Said architect Ron Morgan, "The shame of it is that the city looks absolutely gorgeous. It's swept clean and polished. But nobody's there. We've created the most beautiful downtown of any new city in the United States, but in many ways it's empty and antiseptic."

A few critics mocked Charlotte when it hosted the 1994 National Collegiate Athletic Association Final Four Championship. Said *The Washington Post*,

"[Charlotte has] the vacant calm of a place where it's always 10:30 in the morning." This is certainly how I felt as a pre-teen and teenager in the 2000s, so I know people in the nineties were suffering. They craved fun— and the basketball tournament was an enthralling break from the norm. Hotels raised their prices, retailers expanded their inventory, and city planners erected temporary restaurants and clubs in vacant Tryon Street properties, christening it the 'Street of Champions'. Over 380,000 people visited the four-block "entertainment zone." Reported Peter Applebome for *The New York Times*,

> "Usually, there's no one here," said Brian Murphy of nearby Denver, N.C., as he sampled the wares today at Fat Tuesday's, which for five days will be dispensing frozen daiquiris, "jungle juice" and something ominously called "190 octane" from an other-times vacant savings and loan building. "Downtown is empty after 5 P.M. There's nothing to do."

The Charlotte Observer remarked: "Who are we trying to fool? ... Using the Street of Champions logic, we should put cardboard cutouts of cops on street corners to deter crime [and] pull the plug on the ailing Charlotte Symphony and fill the concert hall by playing classical favorites with the CD player turned up really loud." Despite the criticism, the Final Four brought tremendous tourism dollars and flight traffic to Charlotte. Because the Arkansas Razorbacks beat the Duke Daredevils, President Bill Clinton was in attendance, drawing even more attendees.

But, noted Bernie Kohn, "they enjoyed Charlotte while they were here. But out of town visitors didn't find much reason to stick around once the Final Four was over." Locals, however, wanted more. They desired a "New Orleans Mardi Gras atmosphere [with] activities on a closed-off street filled with vendors, musicians, TV screens, and celebrities." Business owners who had erected temporary tents wanted something permanent for locals and tourists. City officials envisioned livening up downtown with a new football stadium and convention center, not a strip of bars or clubs. A failed downtown club owner told the *Times*, "They've taken a lot of vacant buildings and built a temporary circus, but when the circus leaves, there's nothing left behind. Charlotte is nothing more than one large suburban community. People in Charlotte are scared to death of the center city."

The same year of the Final Four, Charlotte was the third biggest banking center behind New York and San Francisco. Banking brought companies, jobs, and new luxuries, so unemployment was below 4%. Lots of locals were into sports, and there were plenty of ways to indulge. In 1992, night racing began at Charlotte Motor Speedway, making it the first track of its size in the world and drawing crowds to watch thrilling competitions under the blaze of expensive specialty lights. Lowe's, the second-largest home improvement store (and founded in North Carolina in 1909), began sponsoring the speedway in 1999.

The decision to establish an NBA franchise in Charlotte back in 1988 also paid off. The Hornets had top fan attendance and engagement from 1991 to 1997, selling out 362 consecutive games. The team's iconic purple starter jackets became a staple of nineties streetwear fashion. The arrival of the NFL's Carolina Panthers in 1995 was also celebrated, and the Ericsson Stadium stadium was completed the next year. If there had been no Panthers, would former wide receiver Steve Smith have stumbled across a newspaper feature about me in high school and decided to bankroll my education?

Charlotte's growing sports scene eventually helped nightlife flourish. Athletes and their orbit of entourages, WAGs, groupies, and stray celebrities wanted places to mingle, and they couldn't exactly party at Charlotte's most historic offerings. Growing up, I'd often hear radio ads for the historic Black-owned Excelsior Club, which had first been established in a two-story house in 1944 by Jimmie McKee. The club was important to the Black community and also played a key role in the rise of the city's first Black mayor, who helped Charlotte flourish as a banking capital.

In 1983, Harvey Bernard Gantt, a Charleston, South Carolina native who had integrated Clemson University, was elected mayor of Charlotte on a platform of rehabbing Charlotte's urban areas. While past leaders focused on the city's growing suburbs, Gantt aimed to capitalize on banking investments and corporate relocations. He was elected twice and served until 1987. Gantt would later credit part of his political success to his connections at the Excelsior Club and to Jimmie McKee, saying, "It was a huge mistake if you didn't drop in. That was the place to be if you wanted to meet the movers and shakers in politics in Charlotte…"

But the Excelsior's sway would not help Harvey Gantt in his 1990 bid to unseat three-term North Carolina Senator Jesse Helms. To this day, only twelve U.S. senators out of over 2,000 have been Black, so in 1990s North Carolina, Gantt faced a slim chance of victory. Less than two weeks before the election, Gantt was ahead in the polls. But Helms launched an infamous ad campaign featuring white hands crumpling a job rejection letter, while a narrator condemned affirmative action. There were multiple commercials like this.

Described Robin Toner in 1990: "The new Helms commercials accuse Mr. Gantt of running a 'secret campaign' in homosexual communities and of being committed to 'mandatory gay rights laws,' including 'requiring local schools to hire gay teachers.'" Gantt was also accused of running a "secret campaign" just for Black voters and was berated for being pro-choice. Helms took 53% of the vote, but it was the closest he had ever come to being unseated. He defeated Gantt again three years later. Gantt remained a prominent fixture of my childhood, and the Harvey B. Gantt Center for African-American Arts + Culture was later named in his honor.

Helms' success at the polls was a stark reminder of Charlotte's conundrum. It was a somewhat-progressive city in a hostile and homophobic red state. Every attempt to be innovative, or just a little weird, was therefore newsworthy. In December 1993, club Mythos was opened by entrepreneur Andy Kastanas. Described by Dennis Romero for *The Charlotte Observer*,

> "Ten skylights let in a radiant view pierced by skyscrapers. Hipsters in platform shoes collide in the unisex washroom. Glamorous people dressed in black groove to a dance beat so thick you can taste it. This is not some event out of '70s New York. This is Charlotte, today. Clubs like uptown's Mythos - which opened Wednesday under the glare of the uptown skyline - are popping up in Charlotte to meet a growing need for urban nightlife. In the past six months, spots including Clarence Foster's, Club 2000 and The Underground have appeared, to the delight of young club-goers and some civic boosters."

It took a while for these clubs to attract a consistent clientele. Wrote Pam Moore, "[Kastanas's] idea, stoked with some other people's money, was that Mythos would be very cutting edge, very *Not Charlotte*. It would have a distinct club ethos: Dress up, don't expect top-40 dance tunes, and don't come if you can't handle gay people, straight people, Black people, white people, and very loud, progressive dance music." People grooved to house, Euro-disco, and trance music in an inclusive space. Said a Charlottean to *The Charlotte Observer* in 1993, "Uptown closes at 5, as you know. So it's exciting to have some more entertainment outside of the performing arts."

As the decade continued, more clubs popped up. Popular nightlife venues included Bar Charlotte and Cosmos, and for Black people there was the Savoy Nightclub and CJ's at the Adams Mark Hotel. Wrote Tonya Jameson about her first trip in 1996, "The line to get inside CJ's snaked from the lounge's door to the lobby. The crowd was a mix of button-down young professionals and people old enough to be my parents. I had a good time, and over the next decade, CJ's became my Plan B nightclub, the place to go on the weekends when nothing else was happening." Charlotte's nightlife scene had grown so much that Tonya's column, *Paid to Party*, ran from 1993 to the mid-2000s. She wrote in 2006, reminiscing on nineties nightlife, "I can't recall the number of times I sang *Sweet Caroline* as the *Paid to Party* columnist."

In the mid to late nineties, city events could be attended at the brand-new Charlotte Convention Center, which opened in 1995. The Plaza Midwood and North Davidson, or NoDa, neighborhoods were infused with cultural events and cash. There were other new communities to explore, like the upscale Ballantyne, which was annexed by Charlotte (like so many enclaves in Mecklenburg County) in 1997. The massive mall Concord Mills opened two years later.

Charlotte's queer community was experiencing an evolution as well. My mother regaled me with her own tales of attending CJ's and The Savoy in the nineties, but as a bisexual woman, her main club was the LGBTQ venue The Scorpio Lounge (simply called "Scorpio's" by locals). It opened in 1968 on South Blvd before eventually relocating to Freedom Drive. Scorpio's was my first club experience at age 18. I watched my first voguing competition there. Scorpio's was a necessary safe space in the Queen City.

As evident by the success of Jesse Helms' smear campaign of Harvey Gantt, I really cannot understate the religiosity and accompanying homophobia of my hometown. For example, local reverend Joseph Chambers made headline news for his views on my favorite childhood character. Reported the *Cox News Service* in 1993, "Barney, adored by millions of toddlers and preschoolers, is yet another sign that "America is under siege from the powers of darkness," [said] the politically active Chambers. And for a donation to his 25-year-old Paw Creek Ministries in Charlotte, Chambers will send you a booklet explaining it all: "Barney the New Age Demon," recently retitled "Barney the Purple Messiah.""

The following year, the 14th annual North Carolina Pride parade was held in Charlotte. According to Matt Comer and Kayla Schultz, the success of the event led to a yearly pride celebration called *Out Charlotte*. In 1996, when the state's youngest and longest-serving mayor, Pat McCrory, was first elected at age 39, the queer play *Angels in America* was set to debut at the Charlotte Repertory Theatre. At the time, *The New York Times* noted, "the telephone book lists 713 churches in a county of 580,000 people." The controversial, nearly seven-hour production, which depicted gay life in the 1980s and the fallout of HIV/AIDS, featured a nude scene that led to protests and condemnation. The actors and crew were warned they could be arrested for indecent exposure and there were rumors of a bomb threat.

During a planned protest, *The Charlotte Observer* reported two types of protest signs on display outside the theater: "Homosexuality is not art" and "World class? Try backwater." *Creative Loafing* editor Perry Tannenbaum told Slate, "It turns out that the Concerned Charlotteans showing up en masse to protest the opening numbered 15 or thereabouts. And the number of people picketing in favor of Angels numbered between 150 and 200!" *Angels in America* was ultimately staged, thanks to the last-minute intervention of a judge. But a year later, Mecklenburg County commissioners, republicans known as "Gang of Five" voted to revoke $2 million from the Arts and Science Council budget, which affected a variety of programs popular for families. Four out of the five commissioners who supported the measure were voted out in 1998, and the funding was restored the following year.

The scandal was covered extensively by the alternative free weekly paper *Creative Loafing*. When I began working at Food Lion at 15 and was able to travel uptown by myself, I devoured issues of *Creative Loafing* every week, picking up my copy from the Epicentre next to the bus station. It was the one paper I could count on for nightlife news, queer news, and features on minorities. Later, in 2017, *Creative Loafing* would do a feature on me. It was truly a full-circle moment and a fond memory, because I was benefitting from the newspaper's shift toward hyper-local reporting and inclusive coverage, overseen by editors Mark Kemp and Ryan Pitkin.

In October 1997, Charlotte made national headlines due to the Loomis bank robbery, in which eight people stole $17.3 million in cash, and even more friends and family helped launder it. Two of the thieves made the FBI's job easy when they moved from a trailer park to a mansion. By the end of the decade Charlotte was the nation's second-largest banking capital after New York, thanks to the NationsBank Corporate Center merger that became Bank of America.

The same year as the heist, bank executive Joe Martin advocated for "Race Day," encouraging people to have lunch every Thursday with someone of a different race. He argued that the city needed to be more intentional about breaking down racial barriers and was often seen dining with Black community leaders at the historic McDonald's Cafeteria. Two years later, the chairman of Bank of America publicly stated that Charlotte wasn't reaching its full financial potential because of the ongoing racial divide.

Growing up, I always knew white, Latino, and Asian people, especially because my mother tried to immerse me in as many cultures and activities as possible on a budget, and I attended magnet schools. Still, the racial divide, as I explore in my memoir *Angry Black Girl*, became increasingly evident as I got older. My city was drenched in subtle racism that was evident in the nineties. Outside of the sparkling allure of uptown and fancy suburbs, black neighborhoods had been sacrificed for business and tax interests. In 1996, a 93-year-old former black church was burned down just 100 yards away from the congregations' new building. That same year, Observer columnist Doug McCurry reported in *Closet Racism: White America's Dirty Little Secret*:

> "Last week, I used the pool at a south Charlotte apartment complex where several friends of mine live. While I was reading by the pool, a half-dozen black children arrived and began swimming and playing water volleyball. About an hour later, a police officer showed up and forced the kids, who were not residents of the apartment complex, to leave the pool. Minutes later, the apartment manager came up to me and, thinking I was a tenant, abashedly apologized for the children being there. She then said something that would only be said to another white person: "I didn't want you to think you were living in Harlem." I did not respond to her comment, but it haunted me for days."

No wonder the city's carefully cultivated school integration protocol was also at risk. In Autumn 1999, the same year a judge ruled in favor of a local white parent who challenged the city's busing policy as discriminatory (in an effort to overturn *Swann v. Charlotte-Mecklenburg Board of Education*) I began kindergarten at Barringer Academic Center, one of the jewels of Charlotte's magnet program. It was my home school, meaning I lived in the neighborhood and could enroll without going through the competitive lottery system, but others had to apply for a spot. I was very fortunate to have attended Barringer.

The school was nestled along West Boulevard, just a one minute drive from my grandfather's tire shop. My grandfather, who I call 'Papa', never graduated from the sixth grade but he knew how to run a business and crunch numbers. Knowing he was down the street from my school was both a comfort and a terror, because all the teachers who had ever blown a tire on their way to or from work knew Mr. Clay. If I acted up in class, he'd know about it. Papa often picked me up from school sometimes in a rumbling teal Chevy. I'd spend a lot of time at his shop, initially as a nosy child watching oldies on the TNT channel on a small TV in his office, and eventually as a 12-year-old worker in the hot dog shop he added to the building.

Both my Papa's shop and Barringer were located in what was considered "the hood," yet white parents from across Charlotte actively sought to send their children to the elementary school. Many of my classmates lived in fancy homes in South or North Charlotte; their parents fetched them in luxury cars. They came back from Summer break tanned and ruddy from vacations at Disney World. One of my classmates lived on a fucking horse farm near Latta Plantation! Going to a sleepover revealed she lived in a massive house and her own horse. What was she doing all the way over on West Boulevard?

Barringer offered a range of benefits: access to a Talent Development Program, a Greater Enrichment Program, a newly funded science initiative for girls, a computer lab filled with Macintosh machines, a science lab with small animals, a morning chess club, a fabulous library, and more. The same year I started, award-winning principal Linda Morris launched the Horizons Program for twelve exceptionally gifted students, those who could handle high school geometry and excel in niche humanities. The program would later expand to include more students.

The public school, which was just two years away from being designated a prestigious Blue Ribbon School by the Department of Education, was built on a former gold mine and named for white supremacist Osmond L. Barringer. An investigation by Dr. Willie Griffin found over 30 streets, schools, and other locations in Charlotte named after Confederates and white supremacists, from Ardrey Kell to Zebulon B. Vance. In 2021, Barringer was renamed in honor of Charles H. Parker, a formerly enslaved man who became a community leader and developer of the West Boulevard neighborhood.

Despite micro-aggressions and white superiority complexes, I have fond memories of Barringer and the city that raised me. I remember gallivanting around Eastway near Eastland Mall, which was established in 1975 and peaked in the nineties, when my mom would take me ice skating. I loved visiting South Charlotte, home to historic residences, luxury shopping centers, and better walkways and parks. I adored uptown, where I could walk along the Overstreet Mall sky bridges, feeling like I was in a mini New York City. I'd visit the Charlotte Mecklenburg Library main branch in search of chunky books and new friends.

A lot of my youth was spent at local libraries, using up the internet in sixty-minute increments. It makes perfect sense to me that Charlotte Public Libraries were voted Library of the Year by *Library Journal* in 1995. Two years later, Charlotte's Public Library collaborated with the Children's Theater of Charlotte to begin dreaming up the amazing ImaginOn center. Voters approved it in 1999, with the Charlotte Observer listing it among other "high glamour" proposals meant to bring the city into the new millennium with a bang. The 113,000 square foot complex, which opened in 2005, featured fresh performances in a brand new theater, the teen loft, and computers outfitted for multimedia and animation. I attended the Children's Theater of Charlotte for one short and amazing week in 2002. For six days, kids from all over Charlotte prepared a bite-sized production of *Little Shop of Horrors* for our parents. I was cast as Ronnette, Crystal, or Chiffon— can't remember who— but I can still remember belting out the lyrics to the titular song!

In addition to its libraries, Charlotte also has a reputation for good food. The foodie scene has exploded in recent years, especially in uptown— but this wasn't always the case. One of my favorite eateries, Mert's Heart and Soul, was opened in 1998 by James Brazelle and was a pioneer of uptown dining. Brazelle said of his beginnings, "Weren't no arena, weren't no buildings, weren't no restaurants around us, nothing. Just a hotel." The restaurant became a hit for its low country dishes, thick and amazing cornbread, and slices of red velvet cake. It's still open to this day, and I need to return the next time I go home.

Final Thoughts

During the first week of kindergarten at Barringer Academic Center we had a school shooting drill. We were led to the corner of our darkened classroom, far from the locked door, and silenced by our teacher for ten minutes, as classrooms across the campus participated in the same activity. As five-year-olds, we giggled and didn't take anything seriously, just like when they had us crouch in the hallways for tornado drills. My teacher told us something along the lines of, "This is in case anybody dangerous ever shows up."

At five years old, I didn't know who Osmond Barringer was. I didn't know my school was in "the hood." I didn't know that some white parents desperately wanted their children to attend my prestigious school and I didn't know that being surrounded by such a diverse mix of faces in a classroom was becoming increasingly uncommon. I didn't know that my mother was viewed with contempt by homophobes or that she boosted clothes and scrounged together coins to send me to pricey enrichment programs. I certainly didn't know that just a few months earlier, a pair of teenage boys had gone on a shooting spree at their high school in Littleton,

Colorado. I was unaware that my city, bursting with diversity and opportunity, was on the precipice of change— and that I would benefit in so many ways. I was just a baby, ready to soak up the world like a sponge.

On The Spice Girls

When I was five-years-old, there was nothing I loved more than the Spice Girls, more specifically, their 1997 film *Spice World*. It made me want to be British, to live in London, and to own a Union Jack wardrobe. Not only did I wear the movie out on VHS, but I also begged my mother to give me bantu knots after seeing Mel B rocking hers in the movie. It was high cinema. It was art. It was… critically panned.

Unbeknownst to me, the Spice Girls, along with their movie, while extremely popular, were dragged for being manufactured and ultimately "bad." Wrote Chris Heath for *Rolling Stone*, "To so many people, the Spice Girls are nothing but bad. They are the new pop devil, threatening musical seriousness and polluting the pure well water of rock's higher meaning."

People derided their "girl power" motto as contrived and hollow, accusing them of invading feminism and rendering it useless. After all, 'Girl Power' had originally been the rallying cry of the Riot Grrrl movement and music genre before it was co-opted by mainstream pop. Among British music snobs, the Spice Girls were lowbrow fluff, intruding into a space traditionally dominated by male talent. Explained *Hot Press* magazine, "You could almost compare it to Beatlemania, except it's girls screaming at other girls." Thom Yorke of Radiohead called them "the antichrist." One critic even asked, "Why do parents support cultural rape of their girls by acts like the Spice Girls?"

Despite America's dominance on the global music charts, the British girl group had invaded pop culture and the music business, reaching me all the way in North Carolina. There was Spice Girls branding on over 100 products, from mirrors to cameras to dolls to a PlayStation video game, even pizza in the shape of "Spice." This level of mass product endorsement among celebrities would soon become the norm. By 1998, they had generated between $500 and $800 million. How did the Spice Girls invade and dominate the world? And how does their rise, success, and fall reflect the United Kingdom at the End of History?

Creating The Spice Girls

In the nineties, the type of music available in the United Kingdom was changing and becoming more diverse. For instance, in 1990, Choice 96.9 FM began broadcasting. It was the first 24-hour Black music station for South London and expanded to Birmingham in 1995. At the time, approximately 1.6% of the U.K. (including Northern Ireland) was Black, or roughly 890,727 people. In addition to Black hip hop and R&B imported from overseas, there was a thriving local Black music scene to enjoy.

A key inspiration for the Spice Girls, at least for Melanie Brown, according to one interview, was the mixed Neneh Cherry. Cherry is a Swedish-born singer and rapper who was living in London when she released 1988's hit *Buffalo Stance*. The song appeared on her 1989 album *Raw Like Sushi*, which remains a banger of an album title. She went on to have a long music career, including her 1992 track *Buddy X*, which featured a then relatively unknown Biggie Smalls. While she didn't become a massive mainstream success after *Buffalo Stance*, Neneh's popularity demonstrated that there was a desire for eclectic women of color in the U.K. music scene. In her trail came girl-group acts like Eternal (*I Wanna Be the Only One*), Cleopatra (*Cleopatra's Theme*), and Mis-Teeq (*Why*). But the biggest Black singer from the U.K. in the nineties— since Sade was on hiatus— was Mel B of the Spice Girls.

Mel B was 19 years old when she and Melanie Chisholm, Geri Halliwell, and Victoria Adams showed up to audition for a girl group, competing against 400 other women. Father-and-son management team Bob and Chris Herbert were looking to create a female version of the popular boy band Take That. They signed the four, added a fifth member who was later replaced by Emma Bunton, and placed them in a house in Maidenhead, where they were trained for pop stardom under the name Touch.

The original plan was to have a lead singer with backup vocalists all wearing identical outfits. The girls rejected this format, fired the Herberts, and sought new management. By 1995, they were working with future *American Idol* creator Simon Fuller and had signed a record deal with Virgin Records under their new name: The Spice Girls. Their debut single, *Wannabe*, took the world by storm in June, topping the charts in 35 countries. Their debut album, *Spice*, sold 2 million copies in its first week and went on to sell over 23 million worldwide, placing it among the bestselling albums of all time. At the peak of their fame, the group was being compared to another iconic British cultural export, Beatlemania.

The girls were on an extremely tight and busy schedule, operating like well-oiled machines. "The stories you hear from those who have worked with the Spice Girls corroborate easily. They worked incredibly hard, they were polite and professional and never ran late. There were no diva antics. But they would run circles around those in whom they could smell fear with their jokes, provocations and overzealous hands," recalled *The Telegraph* in 2019.

Their strong personalities never went unnoticed. Their unique image, combining femininity, sexuality, and friendship, lured people in. Their personalities were distinctly different and vivacious. As one newspaper article described at the time: "Chisholm is a keep-fit fanatic rarely seen without her Adidas sportswear, Adams is a fan of expensive labels, Halliwell has Seventies style with a Nineties edge, Brown likes rap, hip hop and jungle and dresses accordingly, while Emma Bunton favours chart pop and garage and hot-pink High Street fashion."

Melanie C was the working-class, athletic Sporty Spice. Victoria Adams was the upper-class, aloof Posh Spice. Emma Bunton was the blonde and bubbly Baby Spice. Geri Halliwell was the outspoken and sexy Ginger Spice. Melanie Brown was the wild and outrageous Scary Spice. Their nicknames were bestowed upon them by *Top of the Pops* magazine, which makes the choice of "Scary Spice" for the sole Black and mixed-race member especially noteworthy.

Scary Spice

Over the years, the Spice Girls racked up nine more number-one hits. My favorite songs included *Say You'll Be There*, *Too Much*, and *Spice Up Your Life*. They ultimately sold 105 million albums worldwide, making them the bestselling girl group of all time. It's hard to say if they would have achieved such success had any one girl been missing.

Like my ignorance of the group's reputation as a child, I had no idea that my favorite member was the least popular Spice Girl. According to a 2013 poll, reported *The Independent*, "Baby Spice is apparently the most popular Spice Girl, the poll of more than 31,000 Brits found, with more than 37 per cent of the vote. She was followed by Sporty Spice, at 23 per cent, then Ginger, at 19 per cent, and Posh on 12 per cent. Scary Spice was reportedly the least popular of the group, with just 9 percent naming her the best member."

In my opinion, Posh had the least singing responsibility and couldn't really dance, but she was Posh Spice. She gave what she could, and we ate it up just fine. The future fashion designer would later remark, "While singing and dancing was fun for [me], it wasn't [my] passion." Baby was nauseatingly cutesy, but she could sing and went on to have a successful solo career. Geri Halliwell, a former glamour girl in *The Sun* when she was 19, had endless charisma and adequate vocals. She claimed to be 21 when joining the group but was actually 25, which caused minor controversy later. Melanie C was the best singer, and it's no wonder she went on to release the highest-selling solo album of all the girls, 1999's *Northern Star*.

Though I loved them all, my favorite Spice Girl, for obvious reasons, was Melanie. In addition to being able to carry a tune and dance, she was beautiful and seemed so carefree. Her tongue piercing, and my mother's, made me want one when I eventually got older. I adored how frequently Mel. B wore leopard prints, and I was obsessed with her hair. She refused to straighten her tresses for the *Wannabe* music video, setting an important precedent for her image in the band. Mel B. would later remark that she received "really emotional letters from girls, and their mums, saying how incredible it was that they had someone to 'be' when they did dances in the playground at school and they were actually daring to wear their hair out and proud rather than scraped back or straightened. That was a big deal to me."

To be clear, there are no complaints from Mel B that she disliked or objected to the name Scary Spice. She, whose mother is white and father is Black, was proud of both her boisterous personality and her mixed-race heritage. Growing up, she said, "I was called all these names I didn't understand like 'Paki,' 'redskin,' and obviously the N-word." During her time with the Spice Girls, she reflected, "[The most offensive thing said about me was] ...being called half-caste. I got called that in one interview, and that's degrading, like a mongrel. I'm not half of anything; I'm mixed race."

Unfortunately, Mel B had become somewhat used to being treated differently than her bandmates. The power of the Spice Girls was so immense that in 1997, they were invited to meet South African leader Nelson Mandela, who said, "These are my heroes. This is one of the greatest moments in my life." But even in that historic moment, racism lingered. When shopping for the event in South Africa, recalled Melanie, "I was asked to leave a designer clothes shop...when I was with all the other girls. Of course, all the girls had a go at the assistant because they were so shocked."

During a 1997 interview on the show *Laat de Leeuw* in Holland, the group was collectively shocked again when a troop of *zwarte pieten*, or "Black Petes," hit the stage. These offensive hallmarks of Dutch Christmas tradition feature blackface, red lipstick, and curly wigs. Said Melanie, still media-trained but honest, "I think they shouldn't paint their face. You should get proper Black people to do it. You shouldn't paint their faces. I don't think it's very good... You shouldn't have their faces painted. This is the nineties." Melanie C and Geri agreed. The host, clearly befuddled, insisted, "No, no, no, but that's tradition. That's culture, that's tradition," before joking that one of the people in blackface was named Mandela. Mel B wasn't swayed: "Update your culture. You should get proper ones, proper Black people."

Like other Black people in Europe, Melanie experienced both overt and covert racism. She often expressed frustration with "walking into meeting after meeting with the Spice Girls and never seeing another Brown face." While the U.K. was steeped in the Cool Britannia aesthetic and Tony Blair's progressive branding, racial tension simmered beneath the surface. For instance, the parents of Stephen Lawrence, a Black 18-year-old who was murdered by a gang of white teenagers, were fighting for justice and being stonewalled by police. It was a major moment in 1997 when *The Daily Mail* publicly called out the perpetrators on its front page, and Home Secretary Jack Straw launched an official inquiry into the case.

To help her bandmate understand her experiences as a black person, Melanie took Geri to her hometown of Leeds. Mel described,"We went to one of these really old-school underground blues and bass clubs that all the Black kids in the area went to. It was tiny and really packed, and when we were standing there, I said to Geri, 'Look around and tell me what you see.' And she looked around and said, 'Everyone else in here is Black except me.' And I said, 'That's what it's like for me nearly every day. I'm always the only Brown girl in the room.'"

Spice World: The Movie

The press quickly made the Spice Girls a key part of their strategy, so they dominated newspapers, tabloids, magazines, and television. All of the Spice Girls' British sensibilities, mannerisms, and motifs, including Ginger Spice's iconic Union Jack outfit at the 1997 Brit Awards, were great for British soft power and media appeal. Said Prime Minister John Major in 1996, "Our fashion, music and culture are the envy of our European neighbors. This abundance of talent, together with our rich heritage, makes 'Cool Britannia' an obvious choice for visitors from all over the world."

At the time, the notion of *Cool Britannia*, a motto describing British cultural revitalization, was gaining momentum thanks to the success of zeitgeist-defining works like *Four Weddings and a Funeral*, *Bridget Jones's Diary*, and *Harry Potter*. Designers such as Stella McCartney, Ozwald Boateng, and Alexander McQueen were rising to international acclaim. British natives Naomi Campbell and Kate Moss walked the hottest runways. Suddenly, the UK had crossover appeal. On the smash-hit American sitcom *Friends*, the gang spent a few episodes in London to watch Ross Geller call his betrothed by the wrong name during a wedding ceremony. The episode featured not only Virgin billionaire Richard Branson and actor Hugh Laurie, but also actual royalty, with an appearance by Sarah Ferguson, The Duchess of York.

Speaking of television, in March 1998 the British Broadcasting Channel launched its services in America to showcase its programming. That's how my mother became addicted to the nineties sitcom *Keeping Up Appearances*, featuring the snobby, wannabe-socialite Hyacinth Bucket (pronounced "Bouquet," if you please). "London Swings Again," declared *Vanity Fair* in 1997. Britain, which had been under stuffy Conservative Tory leadership for decades, elected Labour Party leader Tony Blair that same year, further cementing London's image as modern, young, and cool. Capitalizing on the global thirst for British culture, a movie was, of course, next on the Spice Girls' agenda. Directed by Bob Spiers and written by Kim Fuller, the film was shot in the summer of 1997 while the girls simultaneously wrote and recorded their sophomore album, *Spiceworld*.

Spice World, the movie, debuted on January 25, 1998, raking in massive box office returns worldwide, including nearly $11 million in the U.S. In the film, similar to The Beatles' 1964 movie *A Hard Day's Night*, the girls poked fun at themselves, the music business, and tabloid culture. Few people saw its brilliance. "Critics get downright zesty with their *Spice World* reviews," proclaimed *The Kansas City Star*. Said the *Los Angeles Times*, "What you'll want, what you'll really really want, is your money and your 90 minutes back." Roger Ebert was especially unimpressed, awarding the film half a star.

"The Spice Girls have no personalities; their bodies are carriers for inane chatter," he wrote. "The Beatles film had such great music that every song in it is beloved all over the world. The Spice Girls' music is so bad that even

On The Spice Girls

Spice World avoids using any more of it than absolutely necessary." Mind you, each of the girls' personalities was drastically different, and the movie featured 16 of the group's songs. Ebert added, scathingly, "The Beatles were talented, while, let's face it, the Spice Girls could be duplicated by any given woman under the age of 30 standing in line at Dunkin' Donuts." Says the guy who wrote about movies for a living, an occupation now highly threatened by *Rotten Tomatoes* because, technically, anyone can do his job too. Sorry, Roger. The Spice Girls have never been duplicated.

They ran the U.K., the last years of the nineties, and the press, a fact that was parodied in the film by a vengeful newspaper editor. He becomes so enraged while ranting about the girls in his office that a storm cloud gathers and it begins to rain indoors. That entire storyline cracked me up as a child, even though I didn't understand it. I also didn't understand what anyone was saying half the time because the accents flew over my head. When the film was being reviewed by Sony, they reportedly added a note: "Can we subtitle Mel C's voice? Nobody can understand it. Can we subtitle all of her stuff?"

When re-watching the movie as an adult, I found it extremely funny, surreal, and nostalgic, and very clearly satire. There's a scene where movie execs pitch a film making the girls orphans, based on a real-life Disney pitch about "a young single mother of one of the girls, fighting hardship to form the band." Thank goodness the girls rejected Disney to do something more risqué— though I can't believe the movie got away with a PG rating, especially since there's a whole scene featuring men's butt cheeks in thongs.

One of my favorite scenes shows the girls express being tired of getting stereotyped, so they decide to shake things up at a photoshoot. They dress up in a variety of costumes, with Scary Spice portraying Whitney Houston and something stereotypically tribal. Then they all dress in each other's signature outfits. Their clothing was a recurring topic and point of criticism during the peak of their fame, especially among some feminists. Being sexy and into beauty was assailed as performing for the male gaze and being poor role model material for young girls. Said a female critic named Lee Hill Kavanaugh, who insisted the movie "exploited gender": "Little girls should have higher expectations than trying to seduce others. If you saw Ginger Spice on the street, she would look like a hooker, or at least like a lingerie model. Do the Spice Girls do one brainy thing in this movie?"

Kavanaugh had clearly ignored the scenes in which Ginger Spice acts as a human encyclopedia. The critics just didn't get it. I mean, neither did I, but to be fair, I was five. In addition to the jokes flying over my head, I certainly didn't recognize any of the many cameos, like the bus driver being the singer Meat Loaf, who referenced his famous song *I'd Do Anything for Love (But I Won't Do That)*. Other cameos included Elton John, Stephen Fry, Roger Moore, and Hugh Laurie. A cameo by performer Gary Glitter, who was charged with possession of child sexual abuse media shortly before the film premiered, was cut.

At the movie's premiere, the Spice Girls were joined by Prince Charles, who reportedly fawned over Ginger. According to Mel B, when she pointed out that he seemed to be enjoying the film, he replied, "I'm a good actor." Mel B. felt his response was quite rude. A reviewer named Randy Myers was more astute than Roger Ebert (and the Prince), writing: "Years from now, *Spice World* will either be utterly forgotten or elevated to cult status, being shown in midnight screenings much like *The Rocky Horror Picture Show*. It's a movie that's good at being bad, and therefore is fun. Got that? Some, chief among them young female fans, did."

I need a midnight screening of *Spice World*, by the way.

In May 1998, Geri "Ginger" Halliwell left the band, citing creative differences, exhaustion, and depression that was triggering a return of her eating disorder. Rumors swirled about behind-the-scenes fights, Mel B bullying Geri out, and irreparable damage to their relationship. Years later, gossip circulated about a romantic relationship gone sour between Geri and Mel B, rumors both parties denied, though the latter did confirm a one-time sexual encounter.

The group of five became four. They continued their sold-out world tour in 1998 (even stopping in Charlotte, North Carolina) and released their final album in 2000, featuring the well-received *Goodbye* as a tribute to Geri. Along the way, each member released solo projects, though none would ever reach the level of dominance achieved by the Spice Girls.

Posh and The New Royals

Between March 7 and March 13, 1997, there were at least 141 newspaper stories featuring the Spice Girls, just a typical week of publicity. That's how big Spice Mania was. Naturally, this level of fame spilled over into their personal relationships.

When Victoria "Posh" Adams and David "Becks" Beckham got married in 1999, it was a massive event, meant to be exclusively covered by *OK!*

Magazine for millions of dollars. But *The Sun* snuck cameras into the wedding and beat them to the punch. The world's biggest football player, who would later greet Prince Charles while wearing a durag, had locked down Posh Spice. Their fashion choices and relationship became constant media fodder, and the nickname "Posh and Becks" was coined by the press. "Many argue that celebrities are the new royalty, and everyone wants to catch a glimpse of the couple," reported *BBC News*.

The tabloid press was an unstoppable, hungry beast with daily circulation numbers in the millions. At the start of the decade, the royal family was already facing an invasion of privacy and a breakdown of its perceived strength that only worsened from endless tabloid coverage. As Ginger Spice once quipped, "...the royals... [are] the best soap opera in the world." This was significant because the monarchy, having survived Oliver Cromwell and multiple revolutions, was a symbolic relic of British culture that boosted national morale and generated billions in tourism revenue.

So, naughty tabloid stories began to spark widespread criticism that the royals were no longer esteemed, or even necessary. In 1992, Duchess Sarah Ferguson, wife of Prince Andrew, was photographed topless having her feet kissed by her financial advisor while on holiday. The couple, who had been married for six years at the time, were separated, but the press pounced on the story. Ferguson later denied allegations of "toe-sucking," though the damage was already done.

Sarah and Andrew divorced in 1996. One week after the foot scandal emerged, Princess Diana's phone call with former companion James Gilbey was leaked to the press and became known as 'Squidgygate', named after the affectionate nickname Gilbey used for the princess. The following year, a December 17, 1989 phone call between Charles and Camilla became public knowledge. In it, the prince famously said he wanted to "live in [her] trousers," and that if he were reincarnated, he'd want to come back as a tampon so he could live inside her. 'Tampongate', as it came to be called, revealed that the affair was not only long-term, but that many people within the royal circle had known about it and helped facilitate it. The man who recorded the call came forward to sell it only after Squidgygate had already exploded. He was paid £30,000 by *The Daily Mirror*.

A poll taken at the time showed that 58% of respondents believed Charles had tarnished both his own reputation and that of the crown. Princess Diana and Prince Charles officially finalized their divorce in 1996, creating a media vacuum and fueling editorial desire for a new celebrity power couple. When

Diana, the most photographed woman and royal in the country, died in August 1997 after being hounded by the press in a tunnel, a new royal couple emerged: Posh and Becks.

Spice Girl Politics

In December 1996, the Spice Girls sat for an hour-long interview backstage with a reporter from the right-wing *The Spectator* magazine. It was assumed they'd be liberal, but their views were more complex.

"The old-fashioned Victorian family of 2.4 kids is dead forever, but every child needs one decent parent. They must learn honesty, openness about sex, and tolerance," said Geri Halliwell, summing up the group's liberal views on child-rearing and sex education. The progressiveness stopped there. Geri and Victoria were the conservatives of the group and considered Labour Party prime minister candidate Tony Blair to be dangerous for the economy. Ginger said, "We Spice Girls are true Thatcherites. Thatcher was the first Spice Girl, the pioneer of our ideology, Girl Power. But for now we're desperately worried about the slide to a single currency." Added Victoria, "We are patriotic. The single currency is an outrage. We want the Queen's head, or the King's head if we have a king, on our own coins."

Meanwhile, Melanie C, who grew up working class, was pro-Labour. Melanie B considered herself an anarchist, and Emma didn't care about politics. But Geri, who was the loudest and oldest, was the de facto leader of the group. She incorrectly attributed the Girl Power ideology to Margaret Thatcher, who was socially and economically conservative. The phrase Girl Power had first come into use by feminist musicians and activists in the Pacific Northwest who made up the Riot Grrrl movement and music genre, formed in the early nineties in response to sexism in the punk scene.

Halliwell was the one most associated with the phrase "Girl Power," but she clearly didn't care to extend this ideology to poor British women. She commented, "Labour does things for everyone, which might create laziness." In 2007, she would say, "For me, feminism is bra-burning lesbianism. It's very unglamorous. I'd like to see it rebranded. We need to see a celebration of our femininity and softness." This has been a common misconception about feminism from the start, but it demonstrates the hollow feminism that people criticized the Spice Girls for. Said Mel B, "I like [Thatcher]. Even if her policies were hard-headed, socialism is bad, you work for your living and you deserve to keep what you've earned."

Despite this belief, Scary's existence as the lone Black girl drummed up allegations of radical politics. Said *The Spectator*, "There is even a militant tendency in the frizzy-haired, bare-bellied Black figure (with a stud in her tongue) of Mel B, who is, if you like, the Clare Short of the Spice Girls." Clare Short was a leftist Labour Party member of the British Parliament who had been unfavorably called "Crazy Clare" and "Killjoy Clare" for her 1986 proposal to ban topless models from British tabloids. The *Spectator* interview caused endless discourse, as the two most dominant members (Ginger and Posh) seemed to be supporting John Major and the Tories in the upcoming general election.

"They were talking about us in the House of Commons... It was ridiculous," said Mel C.
"What is the state of the government if...?" Geri asked.
"...they're talking about us?" said Mel B.
"Exactly... If we can have an influence, that's terrible," agreed Ginger.

Perhaps the women underestimated their own star power and the rise of celebrity influence on politics. In the end, none of them voted, and Tony Blair won. Mentioned *Hot Press* magazine, "Tony Blair listed *Wannabe* in his Desert Island Discs and, when tested, successfully named three Spices. When John Major was asked the same question he could only manage two. So now you know the real reason why the Conservatives lost the election."

Melanie C, years later, voiced her regret that Geri's support of Thatcher was applied equally to all the Spice Girls. She said, adamantly refusing that Margaret was the first Spice Girl, "I'm from Liverpool. It was a name that was not celebrated in that region."

The Spice Girls were involved not just with politics, but royalty too. Described *Rolling Stone* in July 1997, "Geri pinched Prince Charles' royal bottom." Geri, the one who insisted on sex education in British schools, wasn't fazed. "I pinch everyone's bottom. Why am I going to stop at the Prince?" she said. She's lucky that not only did Prince Charles like having his bottom pinched, being kissed with red lipstick, and getting called sexy, but the dynamics of consent were radically different in the nineties.

The night before the Spice Girls' first concert in Istanbul, Turkey in 1997, Melanie C was sexually assaulted while receiving a massage at the band's hotel. She didn't reveal this for nearly two decades, until penning her memoir. She wrote, "I didn't want to make a fuss but also I didn't have time to deal with it." While the girls were money-making machines whose brand spouted *Girl Power*, in this instance, they didn't have the power to challenge rape culture. As Mel C put it, they were too busy. And knowing what we know, would she have been believed if she had spoken up?

After all, the girls had a negative reputation among hardened feminists, with *Bitch* magazine co-founder Andi Zeisler explaining, "the Spice Girls felt like a step back." The group's sexy and playful image might have played against them. While they could chant *Girl Power* all they liked, they were still treated as exploitable products. In addition to being told she should lose weight, Posh Spice was weighed live on television for an amused audience. Ginger Spice, the eldest of the group, was also criticized for her age and weight. She recalled, "In the newspaper, it said Podge Spice. That's really fucking negative and dangerous for little girls. Can you imagine a big girl who looks at herself and looks at me and thinks, 'Shit, if she's getting called Podge Spice, what does that make me?'" In her 2018 memoir, Melanie B wrote,

> "I barely saw [Geri] eat, but I didn't think about it. Apart from me and Emma [Bunton] (my partner in crime in midnight snacks and fried breakfasts), all the girls were quite quirky eaters... Melanie [C] ate mushed-up vegetables, and Vic only ever ate breadsticks and dips. I didn't think twice about it, and it was only years later, after Mel C and Geri started to speak out about their eating disorders and the pain they went through, that I really began to think deeply about it."

In addition to being criticized for their weight, the Spice Girls' sex lives were forced into the public conversation. Emma, who was characterized as the sweet and innocent Spice Girl, was betrayed by the man she lost her virginity to. The creep, who was 20 when he met her at 15, spilled all of their alleged sexual business to tabloids in 1997. Two of her other boyfriends followed suit, and other Spice flings and exes spilled the beans. Said Mel B, "I'm going to get them to sign a secrecy form from now on." Recalled Victoria, "My dad opened the paper one day to find that one of my ex-boyfriends had sold a story about me having sex with him on a train, and as rock & roll as it sounded, and as much as I'd have loved for it to be true, it was actually very untrue." Additionally, the tabloids constantly re-released topless glamour model photos of Geri.

While tabloids hunted down former lovers and online forums discussed their deaths, there was also a website game called Slap A Spice Girl, based on Whack-a-Mole. It was the dawn of internet trolling and misogyny gone digital. Said the site, "The rules are Spice Girl simple. Every time you hear one of those awful voices and spot a spicy airhead popping up, give it a resounding virtual slap." When the site faced backlash, the authors added a disclaimer: "This game does not in any way condone hitting women. It makes a joke out of delivering a cartoon slap to the manufactured, Tory-loving, plastic, cartoon phenomenon that is the Spice Girls. The game delivers a pretend slap to pretend people making pretend music in a pretend showbiz world. We do not advocate violence against women in any shape or form."

The dehumanization of celebrities had reached new heights. At the center of mega fame is the bargain every celebrity makes, the dual deification and dehumanization that is both lucrative and alienating. Said Melanie C in 1998, "I do feel like I can't meet anybody at the moment, or, maybe, ever again, that's not going to think, 'It's a Spice Girl.' It's a horrible feeling. It's just human nature, when people see me, they don't see me, they see a Spice Girl."

Final Thoughts

While it's important to note the imperfections of the Spice Girls, or any artist, really, it's also important to remember that women are not perfect or pure. Our choices are not made in a perfect world that protects us, and we are the sum of our experiences. Our choices are not inherently feminist. For the time period, the Spice Girls were groundbreaking. The women both monetized Girl Power and empowered girls. They were the original Girl Bosses, in every good and bad way.

They succeeded in a pivotal period of British history, though, like Tony Blair, their peak popularity would not transition into the new millennium. "At least former Prime Minister Margaret Thatcher was honest about her 'systematic destruction' of the trade union movement and working class," said musician Bobby Gillespie in 1998, before ripping Tony Blair a new one. More anti-Blair sentiment was on the way. At the turn of the century, Cool Britannia was going out of style, the Labour Party was under fire for its centrist policies, and the Spice Girls were still popular, but would never again reach their 1995–1998 peak fame. Still, their legacy is immense.

From their massive endorsement deals, à la carte feminism, empowerment brand, and extreme commercialization in a world in the throes of hyper-capitalism, the Spice Girls paved the way for future girl groups and musical acts. They inspired countless artists, like the singer Adele. While they were initially manufactured to be a star singer with four flunkies, the girls managed to take agency and create themselves. Each went on to have her own entertainment career, with varying degrees of success.

When the Spice Girls went on a reunion tour in 2007 that racked up $170 million, they were once again showing their commercial power, banking on nostalgia and branding. It was less Girl Power than it was capitalist power. They reunited again briefly for the last time as a quintet for a performance at the 2012 Summer Olympics closing ceremony, which became a huge trending Twitter topic. A 2019 reunion tour followed without Victoria. It was massive, despite only touring in the UK and Ireland for 13 sold-out dates. They managed to make money comparable to trendy k-pop bands. Reported *The New York Times* in *The Rise of the Spice Girls Generation*, "South Korean boy band phenom BTS out-grossed the Spice Girls by less than 1 percent, earning $78.9 million to their $78.2 million."

The Spice Girls were good celebrities, and despite the hating of Roger Ebert, they couldn't be duplicated. But they would be emulated. Girl groups would rise, feminist pandering would eventually become the norm, and sexy fun would continue to sell. Good celebrities continued to be strong extensions of a nation's cultural power. Through the Spice Girls, a five-year-old girl in North Carolina encountered globalization for the first time and became enamored with British culture, accents, and history. She learned not to apologize for being outspoken and to never dim her light, even while the women she admired would later open up about exploitation, unhappiness, and abuse in their own personal lives.

90s Food

The Hershey's Cookies N Creme bar was born the same year I was. It was my favorite candy as a child, providing a delectable experience of white chocolate and chocolate cookie bits that I begged for whenever I was in the vicinity of a box at the grocery or corner store. In a just world, I could drive to a QuikTrip today and buy a piece of my childhood for whatever ridiculous price candy bars go for now. I could unwrap that white and silver packaging and lick the grooves of the twelve rectangles until I felt satisfied enough to bite and savor. It would taste exactly the same— like pleasure, like being free from the responsibility of bills, like youth. But I can't. Hershey's changed the recipe in 2008, removing the premium white chocolate and destroying the integrity of a once amazing candy.

At least, that's what I tell myself. Was the confection really ever as good as I believed it to be? Or was I just a silly child who didn't yet know the allure of real chocolate? Was I misremembering? I'll never know. That's the drug of nostalgia. On a related note, looking back on the delicious nineties food scene is ripe with opportunities for understanding America and the world.

1990

Food Premieres: Dunkaroos, Teddy Graham Breakfast Cereal, KFC Hot Wings

In 1990, a little under two years before the fall of the Soviet Union, the doors of the first Moscow Pizza Hut and McDonald's opened to throngs of hungry Russians. That same year, Frito-Lay debuted a commercial of the Soviet Union's leadership, flanked by portraits of Karl Marx and Vladimir Lenin, being "munched" from the screen, revealing Doritos Light, Ruffles Light, and Cheetos Light underneath. "Something revolutionary is happening," said the narrator. "Soon they'll be taking over parties everywhere."

Peanut allergies were taken more seriously than ever in the nineties. "Peanut allergy nothing to sneeze at," declared Dr. Jean Mayer in just one of hundreds of articles this year explaining the threat. The next year, a peanut allergy test was developed, and as the years went on, peanut foods would be phased out of diets, menus, and classrooms. Some experts theorized that peanut allergies grew because before this period, doctors had recommended introducing peanut foods to babies under one so they would gain a tolerance. After they stopped recommending this in the nineties, peanut allergies spiked—but there could be other scientific factors at play too.

Convenience increasingly ruled the world of food. Fast food wars were raging and restaurants were always looking for a new edge. For instance, Burger King, wanting to experiment outside of Whoppers, began exclusively using Newman's Own Salad Dressing for its line of salads. Kentucky Fried Chicken added Hot Wings to the menu, and within two weeks of running the first ad, KFC sold 9 million pounds—three million more than its expectations. The company had to pull the ads while it restocked it's supplies. Fast food restaurants were also invading school cafeterias. Said one 1990 news report, "A financially ailing private school is becoming the first high school in the nation to scrap its standard school food fare for a McDonald's fast-food restaurant on the cafeteria premises."

That was just one Texas Catholic school, but reported the Tampa Bay Times the same year, "Orange County students gobble up about 2,000 Domino's pizzas a day in middle and high school cafeterias. Now Pizza Hut wants to get in on the act." The addition of fast food to schools would become more popular as the decade went on, especially in school districts where money was tight. Additionally, many schools ended the practice of allowing students to leave for lunch, as was the case in a southeast school district in Los Angeles. Students were given the options they craved from off-campus. Reported Psyche Pascual in 1993: "Taco Bell started supplying burritos this month to three of the district's four high schools. Now school officials are considering bringing in Pizza Hut and Kentucky Fried Chicken. And many students are all for it."

At home, semi-homemade meals were getting a little razzle dazzle, like Ragu Chicken Tonight, which came in Sweet and Sour, Creamy Curry, Country French Chicken, and Spanish Chicken. At the center of many American kitchens for latchkey kids and adults alike was the microwave. Three in four American homes had one, and they were a two billion dollar industry. There was a bustling market of frozen meals for adults, and kids meals had been done in the past, but companies really wanted to clench the market with new products like Tyson Looney Tunes Meals and Kid Cuisine.

Companies copiously studied the top kids meals, and found that pizza, nuggets, hot dogs, burgers, mac and cheese, spaghetti, fried chicken, tacos, and grilled cheese were their most popular meals. They then set out to make cost-effective and somewhat tasty meals from that list—so stuff like tacos and grilled cheese were dropped. The food was dripping with sodium and fat, which bugged nutritionists. One of my earliest disappointments in life was the hardened brown rock that Kid Cuisine called a brownie, nestled between neon yellow macaroni and cheese and half frozen chicken nuggets.

I probably saw commercials for the meals on TV, which featured bright colors, cartoon characters, and the promise of fun. Children were using microwaves at younger ages, sometimes leading to injuries. 62% of American children under thirteen used the microwave one or more times a week. More than ever before, kids were direct targets of grocery consumer marketing. During this decade, they would see 10,000 food commercials a year, many directed at them—featuring fun new products like the famous Dunkaroos.

This year legislation passed requiring nutrition labels, and the final regulations for this rule were published in 1993. The law went into effect on May 8, 1994. The battle over American waistlines would rage this decade, especially after it was found that between 1980 and 1990, the percentage of overweight Americans rose from 15 to 23%. Many companies tried to get ahead of the curve, especially with new data about fast food contributing to heart disease.

McDonald's, Burger King, and Wendy's announced that they would no longer fry their French fries in beef tallow, replacing it with trans-fat-heavy vegetable oil. McDonald's stock fell by 8.3% after the announcement. Also, Burger King introduced the BK Broiler this year, a chicken sandwich presented as a healthy alternative that customers went nuts for. Wendy's had its own Grilled Chicken Sandwich.

While Bush waged war against Iraq in 1990, he also waged a war against broccoli. "I'm President of the United States, and I'm not going to eat any more broccoli!" he declared. Bush mentioned broccoli 70 times while in office, each time with malice in his heart. Mused one columnist named Joan Beck, "Bush finally finds something safe to hate." Although his comments pissed off broccoli producers (with one even presenting Barbara Bush with a bouquet of broccoli and ten tons of the veggie for an upcoming White House dinner), sales were boosted by approximately 10%. The ten tons of broccoli were donated to a local food bank.

Women's Day magazine hosted a $7,500 *How To Get George Bush To Eat Broccoli* recipe contest in 1990. An accountant named Priscilla Yee was announced as the winner, thanks to her "broccoli lemon" sauce—a combination of cream of broccoli soup, mayonnaise, green onion, and lemon juice—poured over potatoes. Hillary Clinton and Tipper Gore playfully campaigned to put broccoli back in the White House. Broccoli wasn't the only area of food that Bush influenced. Remarked Maureen Dowd, "when Mr. Bush expressed a taste for pork rinds, sales jumped 11 percent and he was ordained 'Skin Man of the Year' by pork-rind makers."

1991

Food Premieres: Sunchips, Brisk Iced Tea, Fruit Gushers, Honey Crisp Apple, Wendy's Chicken Cordon Bleu

In 1991, the same year that General Mills expanded to its 500th Red Lobster location, salsa beat ketchup sales to become the most popular condiment. According to the *New York Times*, industry analysts were quick to confirm that salsa's ascension was not the work of fringe or elitist groups with aberrant appetites. "The taste for salsa is as mainstream as apple pie these days." Ketchup manufacturer Heinz, who faced competition from smaller labels and salsa, obviously needed to diversify. They bought the popular Bagel Bites company for $500 million, and it became a popular after-school snack.

In September 1991, Clif Bars were introduced at a bike show by Gary Erickson in three flavors: double chocolate, apricot, and date oatmeal. They went to market the following year and thrived during the growing natural foods movement. Energy bars were huge by 1997, when Constance L. Hays reported, "What began as a blip on the health-food screen has become a $200 million business that is fast spreading east and north." Erickson split ownership of the company with his friend Lisa Thompson 50/50, and later in 2000 she sold her shares back to him for $72 million because he refused to sell the company to Quaker Oats for $120 million. The company was later worth billions.

This year McDonald's introduced the first of its deluxe product line, the

McLean Deluxe (made with 90% lean beef and 10% seaweed), for sophisticated adults who wanted premium healthy ingredients with the same flavors they were used to. McDonald's spent a hefty $100-150 million on advertisements but the product could't find its footing and was abandoned in 1996. The company also rolled out the Catfish Sandwich in 1991, made with a catfish patty, lettuce, and tangy sauce, slapped on a McRib-style bun. It was sold at 214 McDonald's locations in Kentucky, Tennessee, Alabama, Arkansas, and Mississippi for a brief period in March 1991, but never debuted nationally. The next year, McDonald's tried another seafood product with Southern Catfish Platters.

If you wanted to dine like an A-lister, allegedly, the place to be was Planet Hollywood, which opened in New York on October 22 1991 with prominent promotion by stakeholders Arnold Schwarzenegger, Sylvester Stallone, Bruce Willis, and other celebrities. The company was founded by former Hard Rock Cafe CEO Robert Earl. Every restaurant opening was huge and expensive, with celebrities brought out to schmooze and peacock on the red carpet for cameras and rabid fans. Hollywood props and memorabilia adorned the wall of each eatery, which served everything from cheeseburgers to Captain Crunch coated chicken.

Customers streamed in daily to catch a glimpse of stars. A multitude of celebrities from Donald Trump to Nelson Mandela to Johnny Depp visited a Planet Hollywood at least once. Many owned stakes in the restaurants, and by appearing at openings or randomly popping up at locations when they were in town, they earned the company more money. In our celebrity obsessed culture, Planet Hollywood capitalized on parasocial relationships long before social media. Wrote Kate Storey for *Esquire*,

> There once was a time, before Instagram stories and reality TV, when the only place we regular folks saw famous people was in character onscreen, on *Letterman*, or in *People* magazine. They seemed impossibly far away and glamorous. But at Planet Hollywood, they were right there, in person: a supermarket-checkout experience come to life. Instead of reading about celebrities in *Us Weekly* while buying rubbery frozen pizza bread, you could eat that pizza bread and see the stars in real life one table over. It was a living, lowbrow mecca. Stars: They're just like us.

Planet Hollywood influenced the opening of the Fashion Cafe chain in 1995. The company's spokesmodels were Naomi Campbell, Christy Turlington, Elle MacPhereson, and Claudia Schiffer. Serving "fashion cobb salad, fashion crab cakes, fashion tarte, and turkey meatloaf" according to Elise Taylor for Vogue, the restaurant opened right across the street from Planet Hollywood. It didn't last past 1998. Planet Hollywood went public in 1996 (the same year that profits plummeted) and there were over twenty locations by the end of the decade— when celebrities were abandoning ship and the food was known to be overpriced and bad. It declared bankruptcy in 1999, but survived in a limited capacity in the new millennium.

1992

Food Premieres: Trix Yogurt, Fruit By The Foot, Red Lobster Cheddar Bay Biscuits , Butterfingers BBs, KFC Popcorn Chicken, Wendy's To Go Salads, Wendy's Spicy Chicken Sandwich

This year at a spelling bee in a Trenton, New Jersey school, Vice President Dan Quayle was seen on camera correcting a student's spelling of "potato" by telling him it should have an "e" at the end. Everybody in the room just agreed and clapped.

On the campaign trail, Hillary Clinton had been accused of being too ambitious, to which she replied, "I suppose I could have stayed home and baked cookies and had teas, but what I decided to do was to fulfill my profession, which I entered before my husband was in public life." This comment ticked off housewives, including one angry June Connerton of New Jersey, who said, "If I ever entertained the idea of voting for Bill Clinton, the smug bitchiness of his wife's comment has nipped that notion in the bud."

Family Circle magazine, who saw a PR opportunity, hosted a cookie recipe contest pitting Hillary Clinton and Barbara Bush's cookie recipes against each other while their husbands battled for the presidency. Described Marian Burros, "The contest pits Mrs. Clinton's version, made with oatmeal and shortening, against Mrs. Bush's, made without oatmeal but with butter." Ross Perot's wife, Margot, had been invited to participate but declined. Hillary took the contest seriously, and her cookie recipe beat Barbara's in a poll, and again in 1996 when facing Elizabeth Dole's pecan cookies.

As for Bill Clinton, who hated chocolate, his eating habits were up for discussion this year. Detailed a 1992 exposé,

> "[The] President-elect... prefers the stuff with fat in it: jalapeño cheeseburgers, chicken enchiladas, barbecue, cinnamon rolls and pies." Clinton's weight was also tracked, with observers noting that he had gained over 30 pounds on the road to the primary, during numerous stops at local eateries. Here's Clinton at The Varsity in Atlanta. At Sims BBQ in Little Rock, reporters noted he gorged on "sliced pork bbq, baked beans and slaw, sliced beef, potato salad, and sweet potato pie."

Joked Marian Burros, "Hillary probably has more influence on cabinet appointments than on her husband's eating habits." Added Bill's senior campaign strategist James Carville, "He's a seafood man. He sees food, he eats it." Bill Clinton's eating habits reflected the diet of many baby boomers: "heavy on the meat, dessert at every meal, and tiny amounts of vegetables." The Silent Generation diet of George H.W. Bush may have been even worse, with his regular chows including "beef jerky, nachos, tacos, guacamole, chili, refried beans, hamburgers, hot dogs, barbecued ribs, candy, popcorn, ice cream and cake." And again, he hated broccoli as if his life depended on it.

The ways Americans viewed food was changing. The United States Department of Agriculture issued the 1992 Food Pyramid, which incorrectly placed red meat on the same nutritional level as poultry and fish. Fats and oils were restricted, and no nuanced information was included about saturated fat (found in red meat and dairy) versus the good polyunsaturated fat found in vegetables and fish. As a result, "fat is bad and carbs are good" became the prevailing sentiment of the decade. Atkins Nutritionals products, which were low-carb, had hit the market in 1989—but became much more popular in the nineties, along with products like SnackWells. These ubiquitous fat-free chocolate cookies debuted in 1992 and were packed with carbohydrates. People tended to overeat these, mistakenly believing they were healthy, leading to the term "Snackwell Effect."

The rise of clear beverages coincided with the blossoming health consciousness in American food. Clear symbolized purity and wellness. Pepsi and Coke released Crystal Pepsi and Tab Clear, respectively. Crystal Pepsi was the pioneer, and it was billed as healthy (it wasn't) and tasting like Pepsi (it didn't, allegedly). It was discontinued by 1993. Even as waistlines expanded due to the proliferation of non-fat fattening foods, restaurants wanted in on the new health consciousness. McDonald's replaced fried apple pies with baked pies. They also dropped their cinnamon rolls from the breakfast menu. Still, people wanted to indulge in rich food and beverages.

The Starbucks coffee chain went public on June 26, 1992. Reported Lawrence M. Fisher on the company's appeal, "Its stores stand out as bright and inviting and are typically clustered in high-traffic urban and suburban areas. Many serve as informal neighborhood gathering places where regular customers linger over caffe latte and muffins. And even though coffee beans at $7 a pound or a cup of fresh coffee at $1 are luxuries, they are affordable luxuries at a time when many people are shying away from big-ticket items." At the time of the company's Initial Public Offering, there were approximately 165 stores. In 1993, there were 272.

"Can't afford a new pair of $80 designer jeans at Nordstrom? Stop at the store's shiny espresso bar on the way out and splurge on a $3 coffee drink. Nordstrom, also based in Seattle, uses only Starbucks coffee," reported the *Los Angeles Times* in 1993. Six years later, there were 2,498 locations. Clearly, the pricey coffee was becoming a status symbol. Vanilla, caramel, and hazelnut syrups became regular additions to premium drinks. Another iconic beverage of the decade was Arizona Iced Tea, which launched from New York this year.

1992 also brought the nation Popcorn Chicken at KFC and an accompanying MC Hammer commercial. For $4.69 (or $10.26) in today's money, you were served a small popcorn chicken, small fries, drink, and a pack of gum. Their new Honey BBQ Wings were appealing, too. The Columbus, Ohio based Wendy's had a hit on its hands this year with it's Spicy Chicken Sandwich, which didn't hit locations nationwide until 1996.

Two cookbooks from the seventies by Marcella Hazan were re-issued in 1992 as *The Essentials of Classic Italian Cooking*, kicking off an Italian-American food craze. Suddenly, American consumers were requesting risotto and polenta, not just spaghetti and pizza. Italian gourmet cookbooks grew in popularity, with one bookstore owner in Baltimore saying, "All of a sudden this year we were bombarded." Cooking pasta and other popular Italian dishes at home was much easier and cheaper than making French food, which was suddenly passé. Buca di Beppo was founded the next year, with non-Italian owner Phil Roberts wanting to capitalize on the craze with highly stereotypical Italian family restaurants. The first one was originally called Buca Little Italy and opened in Minneapolis.

The last meal of Ricky Ray Rector, a mentally handicapped man sentenced to die in Arkansas on January 4, made headlines. In 1981, after a friend was denied entry at a restaurant in Conway, Arkansas because he couldn't pay a $3 fee, 31-year old Ricky Ray shot three people, one of whom died. He spent three days on the run until his sister and mother convinced him to turn himself in. He agreed to surrender to Officer Robert Martin, a friend of the family. When Martin came to arrest him, Rector reneged and shot and killed the officer as he chatted with his mother. Rector then went outside and shot himself in the head, obliterating his frontal lobe. His lawyers argued that he was incompetent to stand trial from the damage of the gunshot, which amounted to a lobotomy. The trial continued anyway and he was found guilty and sentenced to death by electrocution. He was to be put to death on

January 24 1992.

Clinton, then on the campaign trail and still serving as governor of Arkansas, refused to grant a pardon. Reported *The Guardian*, "Some of Clinton's staunchest admirers, aware of his compassion and warmth, confidently expected him to intervene. 'Nobody could believe that he would go through with it,' says one. 'You might as well execute a child.'" He had steak, fried chicken, red Kool-Aid, and pecan pie, and requested that the guards save his pie "for later," indicating he didn't understand he was a condemned man. Bill Clinton infamously flew home while on the campaign trail to watch the execution and signal to voters that he wasn't the typical liberal Democrat who was soft on crime.

1993

Food Premieres: Craisins, Zima, Sprinkle Spangles, Fingos, Doritos Taco Supreme

The entrance of Clinton into the White House generated stories on Arkansas food culture permeating Washington, D.C.'s stuffy bubble. "Washington caterers think a Clinton White House will mean the South rising again in terms of what they will be serving during Inaugural festivities and for the next four years," said one reporter for the *South Florida Sun Sentinel*. Arkansas Wedding Cake, aka cornbread, was in— along with and lemon chess pie.

The TV Food Network was launched from New York City on a shoestring budget. The channel elevated the tradition of celebrity chefs and "kicked it up a notch," to borrow the parlance of Emeril Lagasse. Lagasse, a Portuguese-French-American chef with a restaurant in New Orleans, hosted *How To Boil Water*, which was very popular among the 6.8 million homes reached by the Food Network in 1993. In these early days, chefs had to be trained to know how to cook and talk on camera at the same time—and due to a super tight budget, there was no money or time for re-shoots so mistakes were always aired. According to Allen Salkin in *From Scratch: The Uncensored History of the Food Network*, the company was receiving 10,000 written requests a week from viewers for recipes.

The channel became simply Food Network in 1996. The following year, it was the fastest growing cable channel, coincidentally when an overnight engineer accidentally put porn on the air for two minutes. This mistake showed advertisers that the channel had a bunch of viewers when they called in to complain. The channel quickly expanded, and Emeril got his own shows, *Essence of Emeril* and *Emeril Live*. I was an Emeril stan in my youth so I just had to give him his flowers.

Steve Ells was a graduate of the NY Culinary Institute of America when he opened the first Chipotle restaurant in Denver, Colorado, near the University of Colorado campus with an $85,000 loan from his father. They calculated they would need to sell 107 burritos a day to be profitable—and within a month the humble location was moving 1,000 burritos a day. The store eventually expanded to other locations in 1995. Not everything that launched in 1993 would be as successful.

Burger King unveiled Dinner Baskets this year in an attempt to entice people looking for a bit of luxury. The meal included fries or a baked potato and coleslaw or side salad with a meatloaf sandwich, steak sandwich, or chicken dinner. Asked a franchisee, "Where else can you get a dinner of eight fried shrimp, choice of potato, green salad or cole slaw, and a roll for only $4.59?" If that wasn't enough, you got popcorn brought to your table while you waited for your basket, which was also brought out by a "server". Burger King emphasized that tipping wasn't required. This campaign didn't last long.

Ad executives for Coke completely missed the mark when trying to sell Generation X on OK Soda in 1993. Said a Coke employee, "It underpromises. It doesn't say, 'This is the next great thing.' It's the flip side of overclaiming." For seven months, the "unique fruity soda" cans featuring art by alternative cartoonists were supposed to appeal to "teenagers, primarily boys" who liked Mountain Dew and Dr. Pepper but were wary of advertising in select testing locations across the country. It allegedly tasted like "Coke, root beer, Dr. Pepper and some orange." Asked one can motto: "What's the point of OK? Well, what's the point of anything?" Said another, "OK Soda does not subscribe to any religion, or endorse any political party, or do anything other than feel OK." It was a tremendous failure and was pulled by Coke.

A fresh formula of spices was created for Slim Jims by Len Adams, and the 64-year-old company needed bold marketing. Wrestling star Macho Man Randy Savage was introduced as spokesman in a series of funny commercials, making the company alluring to teen boys. Another popular ad was the *Got Milk* Aaron Burr commercial for the California Milk Processor Board. When a librarian attempts to answer a trivia question in a radio contest after taking a bite of a peanut butter sandwich, he fails to deliver because he doesn't have any ice cold milk to wash it down.

That commercial was directed by Michael Bay, who went on to direct *Bad Boys* the next year. Despite the popularity and familiarity of the *Got Milk* campaign, which would be regularly parodied and mentioned in pop culture, milk consumption declined overall. Speaking of milk, this year the Bovine Growth Hormone, or rBGH, was approved for Monsanto by the Food and Drug Administration—and experts warned that the controversial drug for cows hadn't been sufficiently tested on humans. In the following years, arguments would occur over whether or not cow milk containing the hormone should be labeled.

Lastly for 1993, a Pittsburgh man named Carl R. Grady sued the Frito-Lay company, claiming that the sharp edges of Doritos caused damage to his throat. This lawsuit dragged on until 2003, when the judge pointed out "the common sense notion that it is necessary to properly chew hard foodstuffs prior to swallowing."

1994

Food Premieres: French Toast Crunch, Danimals Drinkable Yogurt, Hersheys Cookies N Cream, Cookies n Mint, Poptart Crunch, Reeses Puff, Wingstop, RapSnacks

In 1994, the actor Robert De Niro helped Nobu Matsuhisa launch a Peruvian-Japanese fusion restaurant named Nobu, featuring a famous black cod with miso. Frito-Lay spent $50 million redesigning Doritos to be "larger and more strongly seasoned," with rounder edges. Chips also evolved into the world of hip-hop when entrepreneur James Lindsay used $40,000 raised from friends and family to start Rap Snacks, using the flavors *Bar-B-Quin' With My Honey* and *Back At The Ranch*. One of the first rappers to become involved was Master P. The line eventually carried snacks with Lil Romeo, Bell Biv Devoe, and Warren G on the packaging.

A sugary treat to become popular nationwide in 1994 was the Breyers Viennetta ice cream, a British import that originated in the eighties. The confection was short-lived in the states and wouldn't stay on shelves for long. 1994 is also the year the Quentin Tarantino's *Pulp Fiction* showcased the perfect $5 milkshake and the Big Kahuna Burger. Speaking of burgers, if you wanted to lean into the no-fat trend, you'd probably slide your burger on a George Foreman Lean Mean Fat-Reducing Grilling Machine, which hit the market this year.

The politics of food and fat came to a head in when Kelly Brownell, a psychologist who proposed the nation "get slim with higher taxes," wrote in *The New York Times*:

> "Congress and state legislatures could shift the focus to the environment by taxing foods with little nutritional value. Fatty foods would be judged on their nutritive value per calorie or gram of fat; the least healthy would be given the highest tax rate. Consumption of high-fat food would drop, and the revenue could be used for public exercise facilities—bike paths and running tracks—or nutrition education in schools."

The idea of promoting healthier food and providing healthy programs for everyone, including the poor, was noble. However, it missed the fact that poorer people have limited food budgets so there would need to be an overhaul in the quality of food available at the base level as well as an eradication of poverty—but this was not the focus of most of the people who pounced on the idea and ripped it to shreds. The purported "Twinkie Tax" turned into a battle of 'Merican rights. "The high-fat Gestapo is trying to follow in the footsteps of the smoking Gestapo, in an effort to force the American people to act in the 'proper' way," said Rush Limbaugh. By the way, Rush, who would die from advanced lung cancer in the future, said in 1994, "There is no conclusive proof that nicotine's addictive... And the same thing with cigarettes causing emphysema, lung cancer, heart disease." This was the man advising Americans to stand up for their rights to eat without nutrition information.

After all, there was money to be made. Back in 1991, California placed an 8.25% tax on numerous snack foods to close its $14.3 billion deficit. While snack sales dropped by 10%, the California Grocers Association and the Don't Tax Food Coalition lobbied against the tax, pressing 60% of California voters to reverse it in 1992—and legislators looked towards replacing the snack tax with a higher tobacco tax. A similar tax on soda in Ohio had been targeted and ultimately repealed after soda companies spent eight million dollars to fight it.

The Guest Choice Network, a lobby made up of fast food restaurateurs, meat barons, and the tobacco industry, was formed in 1995 to push the idea that Americans should have access to all the unhealthy slop and sugary swill they liked. It later became the Center for Consumer Freedom, and $600,000-900,000 in startup cash was provided by the Philip Morris tobacco company. In the years to come, their main targets would be environmental groups, medical whistleblowers, and people who demanded the government address obesity, lung disease, and alcoholism.

In 1994 more Americans than ever before drank non-carbonated pre-prepared juices and teas, creating a $5.3 billion market. Snapple spent the previous year enduring false rumors that it donated money to the Ku Klux Klan and Operation Rescue, the anti-abortion organization. People claimed that the small K on the label, meant to signify that the drink was kosher, stood for the KKK. Also, reported *The Los Angeles Times*, "Another story says an illustration on the label of Snapple iced tea portrays ships bringing black slaves to America. But the illustration...is a drawing of the Boston Tea Party." Snapple took out an advertisement in newspapers saying, "We are not involved in any way whatsoever with the KKK, Operation Rescue or any other type of pressure group or organization, period." They did, however, advertise on *The Rush Limbaugh Show*, and by 1994 they had cornered a quarter of the iced tea and fruit juice trade.

Pepsi-Cola wanted the iced tea market, and Coke wanted the fruit juice market, though both tried everything. The latter's contribution would be the famous Fruitopia through its Minute Maid brand, which launched in March. Coke poured millions into the campaign for its six flavors, touting them as "for the mind, body, and planet." The cute bottles featured 17% juice and "mystical" sayings and names like *Pink Lemonade Euphoria, The Grape Beyond*, and *Strawberry Passion Awareness*. Fruitopia machines were unveiled in workplaces and schools around the country, but struggling profits saw the brand die by the early 2000s. More beverage innovation abounded. Two baristas named George Howell and Andrew Frank created the Frappucino at The Coffee Connection in Boston, and the next year it was purchased by Starbucks, where it became popular.

The alcoholic beverage Zima went nationwide in 1994. Coors put $38 million into promoting it as "zomething different" in marketing materials. The advertisements were ambiguous about what the beverage was, tempting new drinkers into buying a six-pack to take a sip. Coors guessed that 70 percent of America's regular drinkers tried Zima. The thing is, the 10% proof lightly carbonated malt beverage attracted women, which Coors hadn't been anticipating. The drink became a punchline in ongoing jokes as being effeminate, and the fragile masculinity resounded everywhere from *Late Show with David Letterman* to *Friends* to *The Simpsons*. Coors' attempted to court men with Zima Gold in 1995 and failed. While Zima went in and out of the U.S. market for the next two decades, it was a hit in Japan, where it was not attached to gender.

More beverage controversy occurred this year when 79-year-old Stella

Liebeck was awarded $2.7 million by a jury after she sued McDonald's. Why? In February 1992 in Albuquerque, New Mexico, she had been served a cup of coffee so hot that when it spilled on her in the passenger seat of her son's car. She suffered second- and third-degree burns on 16% of her body. McDonald's, who offered the woman $800 for her $10,000 medical bills, required its franchises to "brew its coffee at 195 to 205 degrees and sell it at 180 to 190 degrees"—meaning it was much hotter than other fast-food chains. The company had received over 700 complaints in the previous decade about burns from coffee—so it was aware that this was an issue.

When Liebeck's settlement was announced, much of this information was missing from media retellings—making people complain that Americans were becoming too litigious and drumming up calls for tort reform, which was linked to racial discrimination and sexual harassment lawsuits. Said an Ohio representative, "If a lady goes to a fast-food restaurant, puts coffee in her lap, burns her legs, and sues and gets a big settlement, that in and of itself is enough to tell you why we need tort reform." In a December 1994 op-ed that was reprinted nationwide, Liebeck was listed alongside killers and hate crime perpetrators as a symptom of America's so-called lack of responsibility. Stella's compensation was reduced to approximately $500,000 after numerous appeals, and she later took a private settlement. Said Liebeck, "I was not in it for the money. I was in it because I want them to bring the temperature down so that other people wouldn't go through the same thing I did."

McDonald's also started a new doomed venture this year, the Hearth Express restaurant. Reported the *South Florida Sun Sentinel*, "It has neither golden arches nor Big Macs. It does have a counter full of steaming pans of mashed potatoes, creamed spinach, rotisserie chicken, apple turnovers, baked ham and, of course, meatloaf. Lunch costs $4.99 to $5.99, which includes a main dish, two side orders and bread." The sole Darien, Illinois location was closed by the following summer. Rotisserie chickens and homestyle meals were really big this decade, like with the growth of Boston Market, a 1985 creation that expanded too rapidly in the early nineties and ended up filing for bankruptcy in 1998. Even KFC had introduced Colonel's Rotisserie Gold back in 1993, which lasted for three years.

The emergence of the Flavr Savr tomato, the first genetically engineered creation approved for consumption in the US, was controversial in 1994. The tomato, which had been tinkered with to stay fresh longer when picked at ripeness, opened up wider concern that genetically modified foods were not required to be labeled. They were discontinued in 1997. GMOs would be criticized frequently in the future, especially after a Hungarian scientist named Arpad Pustazi published claims in 1998 that genetically modified potatoes fed to rats stunted their growth and immune systems.

The beginning of the North American Free Trade Agreement in 1994 meant that avocados, once scarce in the US outside of the southwest, were easily and cheaply shipped in from Mexico. Guacamole grew popular, especially as a Super Bowl party menu item, and many restaurants began offering it as a table side service.

1995

Food Premieres: Pizza Hut Stuffed Crust Pizza, Taco Bell Volcano Menu, Digorno Rising Crust Pizza, Qdoba, Blue M&Ms, KFC Crispy Strips, KFC Chicken Pot Pie

The color blue beat out pink and purple with 55% of the vote to become the new M&M color. Ten million votes were cast, and there was a grand rollout, including a commercial starring blues singer B.B. King.

The National Black Farmers Association was established this year by John Boyd, leading to a class-action lawsuit, *Pigford v. Glickman*, in 1997, alleging systemic discrimination by the USDA. Reported Sam Fulwood III, "Blacks represent less than 1% of all farmers, a steep drop from the 1920s when 925,000 African Americans owned about 14%, or nearly 50 million acres, of the nation's agricultural landscape. Census data show that there now are about 18,000 black farmers (about 250 in California), and, if current trends continue, few will be tilling the soil in the next century." In 1999, courts ruled in favor of black farmers, and approximately two billion dollars was ordered to be issued in a settlement to 22,363 people— though 70,000 weren't eligible. The petitions for compensation would be dragged out for the next decade.

Chef and pioneer of the Farm-to-Table movement, Alice Waters, penned a letter to Bill Clinton and Al Gore asking for more and sustainable food in December 1995. As a California restaurateur and food activist, she promoted sustainable food production in American schools, demonstrated most clearly when she established the Edible Schoolyard Program at Martin Luther King Jr. Middle School in Berkeley. Because of her efforts, the students grew and cooked food from a community garden.

The role of chefs and food activists in politics and media was growing even larger, thanks in part to the internet. Online food media began to really take root with the 1995 creation of Epicurious, which culled recipes from Condé Nast print publications *Bon Appétit* and *Gourmet*. Other sites like Allrecipes and small food blogs followed, along with a new generation of food magazines like *Saveur*, which included indulgent recipes and writing about cuisine.

While shopping for ingredients needed for fancy new recipes, shoppers may have noticed some changes at the grocery stores. The square footage of the average grocery store was climbing and the choices were seemingly endless —if you didn't read too much into nutritional labels. Reported Julie Creswell in *Fortune* magazine, "Since 1995, the market share of the five largest grocery chains has climbed from 25% to 40%. Manufacturers who once could push their products onto the shelves of regional stores with ease now face national chains with more buying power. And in the mid-1990s, retailers began to grow their own private-label businesses."

Kiwi Strawberry, which Snapple unveiled three years previously, was announced as the company's most popular flavor this year. Kiwi had been grown in notable quantities on American soil since 1970, but faltered in appeal through the late eighties. The Snapple flavor inspired numerous drink companies to seek more exotic flavors than the routine grape, apple, or orange. This expanded to other products as well. Explained Jaya Saxena, "In the '90s, there was strawberry-kiwi-flavored Gatorade, applesauce... wine coolers, Jell-O, Airheads, Kool-Aid, lip balm, yogurt, and Mad Dog 20/20." Snapple was the originator however, and it was reported that New York–based spokesperson Wendy Kaufman was receiving over 2,000 fan letters a week. She claimed that people said the Kiwi Strawberry flavor was improving their sex lives.

In the seventh season episode of The Simpsons, *Lisa the Vegetarian*, Lisa gives up meat. Paul McCartney guest starred in the episode, after showrunners agreed to keep Lisa a vegetarian for the remainder of the show. 1994 also birthed *The Soup Nazi* episode of Seinfeld. It was inspired by a real Iranian soup vendor named Ali Yeganeh, who ran the Original Soup Kitchen, and later the Soup Kitchen International in New York City. It's worth noting that this popular character, played by Larry Thomas, would star in a commercial for the Center for Consumer Freedom in 2004, denying food to people he thought to be too fat. The video has since been scrubbed from the internet.

1996

Food Premiere: Waffle Crisp

Binge eating was called a serious problem in the *Journal of the American Dietetic Association,* affecting 20 to 50 percent of the US population that was overweight. Nutritional fat continued to be targeted as the main enemy, and the additive olestra was approved as a fat substitute, especially in WOW! chips. It was hyped up because it didn't add calories, but in the years to come, side effects like cramping and explosive, grease filled diarrhea would lead to it being phased out of American food.

On April 1st, using seven full page advertisements in major newspapers, Taco Bell announced that it had purchased the Liberty Bell and would be renaming it, you guessed it, Taco Bell. They wrote, "In an effort to help the national debt, Taco Bell is pleased to announce that we have agreed to purchase the Liberty Bell, one of our country's most historic treasures... While some may find this controversial, we hope our move will prompt other corporations to take similar action to do their part to reduce the country's debt."

According to the *Philly Voice*, the National Park Service "received hundreds of phone calls from furious Americans." Journalists also inquired with federal agencies to find out if the announcement was true. Said a park ranger, "The one I remember the best was (that) NBC News in New York called me and asked if it was true. I remember saying to those guys, 'Have you looked at the calendar today?'" Taco Bell, soaking up the publicity, announced it was a hoax and extended $50,000 to Philadelphia for upkeep of the bell.

With the passage of The Personal Responsibility and Work Opportunity Reconciliation Act this year, the rest of the decade would see SNAP benefits slashed for hungry families and individuals without dependents because states could allocate block grants without federal requirements. In 1996, a company partnered with Paramount to cook up a Bubba Gump Shrimp Co. restaurant chain based off the 1994 Tom Hanks film *Forrest Gump*. The menu included shrimp of course, but also a bunch of smoothies, things like "All American Nachos" — homemade Idaho potato chips covered in "smoked Wisconsin cheddar sauce— and 75 cent pieces of chocolates from "Forrest's Own Collection Box of Chocolates."

McDonald's spent 200 to 300 million dollars rolling out the Arch Deluxe, a burger made with a potato sesame bun, peppered hickory bacon, leaf lettuce, tomato, cheese, onions, ketchup, and a combination dijon mayo. It retailed for $2.08 to $2.49, and like other deluxe products, didn't last long. The same year of this doomed burger, Oprah held a segment about Mad Cow Disease on her show. In April 1996, it was a rare yet incurable and fatal disease that spread from infected cows to humans and was a growing problem in the United Kingdom. Oprah, who had an average of 13 million viewers a day at this point, spoke with Howard Lyman, a rancher turned vegetarian. She said, after learning that cows were being fed other cows, "You said this disease could make AIDS look like the common cold?" "Absolutely," Lyman replied, leading her to declare, "It has just stopped me cold from eating another burger!"

This segment infuriated Texas beef barons, who later initiated a lawsuit for libel, even though pro beef spokespeople, including a USDA expert, had appeared on the show. They claimed they had lost 10 billion dollars in business. The lawsuit was eligible under a 1995 law that resulted from the 1989 *60 Minutes* controversy about the chemical Alar being sprayed on apples. Environmental activists said that Alar caused cancer. As a result, millions of people stopped buying apples and the apple industry voluntarily decided to stop using the chemical.

The government, meanwhile, bought $15 million worth of apples to reduce the surplus. The apples largely went to schools, prisons, and food aid programs. Critics called the Alar scandal overblown, but the Environmental Protection Agency did ban Alar because it was a potent carcinogen. Food producers, terrified that unwanted public criticism could cost them money, lobbied for favorable legislation. Thirteen states, particularly those with major agricultural and meat industries like Alabama, Florida, Georgia, Idaho, and Texas, had passed laws since 1989 making it illegal to falsely disparage products. Troublingly, if you didn't have Oprah money, this could make speaking up about food and other products a costly mistake.

1997

Food Premieres: McChicken, McDouble, McFlurry, Cookie Dough Bites, Wendy's Fresh Stuffed Pitas, Gogurt, Oreo Os

Being able to speak up about food and food safety was important. 1997 was the year of the largest food recall in US history at the time. Hudson Foods closed its Nebraska plant and recalled 25 million pounds of ground beef that was potentially contaminated with E. coli. This, along with Oprah's statements the previous year, cast a spotlight on food illness and safety. It was reported that up to 9,000 people died a year from foodborne bacteria, with millions more becoming sick. For instance, E. coli had also killed three children in 1993 thanks to undercooked Jack in the Box hamburgers. In 1994, Schwan's Ice Cream was contaminated with salmonella, infecting a little under a quarter of a million people. After this massive 1997 recall, it makes sense that journalist Eric Schlosser began a three-year investigation into American food that begat one of my favorite non-fiction reads of all time, 2001's *Fast Food Nation*.

Foodborne illnesses became a pertinent issue during the so-called Burger Wars, which flared up this year when Burger King (who had beef supplied from the Nebraska Hudson Food Plant) and McDonald's introduced the Big King and Big N Tasty, respectively, to encroach on each other's bestsellers: The Whoppers and the Big Macs. But the American palate was diversifying—just having burgers and fries wasn't enough. Wrote Glenn Collins, "it becomes increasingly obvious that the only way for McDonald's or Burger King to sell more food is to steal the other guy's customers."

Burger King spent a whopping 70 million dollars to promote its new crispier French fries as "the taste that beat McDonald's," by giving away a free small serving of French fries to every customer on January 2nd, and utilizing Hasbro's Mr. Potato Head in its ads. Reported the *New York Times*, "Among the television commercials Burger King will begin broadcasting next week is one intended to appeal to blacks...The spot shows the singer Isaac Hayes and Mr. Potato Head at a piano." Some diners weren't impressed, and claimed the fries weren't real. Said one reviewer at *Deseret News*, "The secret is a potato-based batter that is sprayed on the freshly sliced potatoes before they are frozen...Burger King fries are a fried potato product, like a potato tempura or a fritter."

After the Liberty Bell prank, Taco Bell invested in the Chihuahua *Yo Quiero Taco Bell* advertising campaign. The Chihuahua was played by a Deerhead Chihuahua named Gidget. Taco Bell released toys featuring the dog. However, some Latino Americans, including civil rights activist Mario G. Obledo, objected to the dog as a negative cultural stereotype. Cuban Americans in Florida, ever the anti-communists, were pissed when Gidget wore a beret that they believed to be a reference to Che Guevara. By 2000, after many complaints, the commercials ended—and from 1997 to 1999, the company had lost 6 percent of its yearly revenue—and would later be sued for stealing the Chihuahua concept.

1997 was the year that the Center for Consumer Freedom published, "We know too well what happens when government gets an open invitation to go into its 'I'm from the government and I'm here to help' role—more regulations. Can you imagine government regulation of menu selections or mandatory calorie contents by each menu item?" This was in response to an op-ed in the *Wall Street Journal* demanding that the government spend more money fighting obesity.

If you were a kid, especially a kid at the movies, a highly coveted candy in 1997 was the Nestle Magic Ball, a chocolate sphere containing a tiny toy. These got discontinued because it was considered a choking hazard, and the toys were replaced with tiny tangy candies. It was actually a litigation showdown between two giant companies. Nestle hired lobbyists and lawyers to write new regulations that allowed their chocolate-encased toy and Mars, their fierce competitors, paid lobbyists to make a 1930s law that banned toy-candy combinations stick.

In New York, luxury dining was all the rage. As the economy appeared stronger than ever, and the city's revitalization projects took hold, the restaurants got pricier, offering exotic menus and after dinner cigars. Reported *Vanity Fair*, "Near Balthazar in SoHo and Tribeca are a half dozen other new places that fill every night with diners eager to pay upwards of 250 dollars for two with wine and tip." Political food continued this year in an op-ed by a mystery writer named Elaine Viets, who was pissed off by a Food Network declaration that "more ethnic food is ahead." As the country's population diversified, white American anxieties about American culture being "spiced up" became more prominent.

Elaine was so pissed at the suggestion to spice up macaroni and cheese that she said, "chipotle peppers are smoked dried jalapeños... those suckers are hot enough to burn the enamel off your teeth... no Whitebread mom would let her children eat chipotle peppers." Another anonymous writer for Newsweek complained about all the ethnic fusions available, writing, "In the last few weeks alone, I've been confronted by Thai barbecue pizza, moo shu duck burritos, blueberry soup with lemongrass, french fries topped with melted Gorgonzola... Bakeries are turning out bagels made with blueberries that belong in a muffin or pancake. On one Santa Fe menu, I found tortilla soup with Chinese pot sticker... Maybe it's time for some ethnic cleansing in the new American pantry."

Statements like these didn't exist in a vacuum. At the time, along with actual genocides happening, there was increased anti-immigration sentiment while America's illegal and legal immigration numbers were swelling—and many of the newcomers were from Mexico. They opened up a number of grocery stores, butcheries, and restaurants featuring authentic ingredients that were now easily shipped in thanks to NAFTA. While the trade agreement made it easier to have Mexican ingredients and cheaper goods, the exploitation of Mexican farmers and workers meant millions of them eventually left home and resettled in America. Lastly this year in Denver, Colorado, Chipotle was known to offer free burritos to journalists covering the trial of Timothy McVeigh, who committed the Oklahoma City bombing in 1995.

1998

Food Premieres: Baby Bottle Pop, Belvita breakfast biscuits, Doritos 3D, Taco Bell Gordita, Dinosaur Egg Oatmeal, Burger King Cinni Minis

The trial for the lawsuit brought against Oprah and Howard Lyman by Texas cattle ranchers began in Amarillo, Texas in 1998. Oprah merrily moved her TV show down to Amarillo for the six-week trial, where local townsfolk were given free tickets. According to the *New York Times*, "The president of the local Chamber of Commerce initially forbade chamber employees to attend, explaining that Amarillo stood by its beef producers and adding that 'we are not going to have any red-carpet rollouts, key to the city, flowers' for Ms. Winfrey. But he quickly rescinded his order," when the local NAACP got involved. The wife of Amarillo's mayor, Nancy, reached out to Oprah and played nice, disrupting the power structure of the town, whose money came from the cattle ranchers.

There were pro-Oprah bumper stickers and t-shirts, but some critics too, and during the trial a beef expert called her audience a "lynch mob." According to *Texas Monthly*, most of the locals were on Oprah's side. Reported Skip Hollandsworth and Pamela Colloff, "Every morning, just for her benefit, one local television station reported the temperature in Chicago, while another offered a daily sightseeing tip just for her. One television reporter gave a sincere look at the camera and said, 'Oprah, if you're watching, please come down to the station, and we'll talk about anything you wish!'"

In the end, the all-white jury acquitted Oprah and Lyman of any wrongdoing, and her profile only rose in the national media. Oprah had the money and time to take on the wealthy cattle barons and protect her right to free speech, but the average critic of big meat (or big tobacco, big sugar, big anything really) did not, and defamation lawsuits could end a person. So the Oprah trial served as an intimidation tactic.

This year, McDonald's bought shares of Chipotle, and invested roughly 360 million dollars to expand the company. Americans were ready. Donna Gabaccia wrote in 1998's *We Are What We Eat: Ethnic Food and the Making of Americans*,

> "Italian, Mexican and Chinese (Cantonese) cuisines have joined the mainstream. These three cuisines have become so ingrained in the American culture that they are no longer foreign to the American palate. According to [a] National Restaurant Association study, more than nine out of ten consumers are familiar with and have tried these foods, and about half report eating them frequently. That same report found that since 1994, the number of respondents who had tried "German, Soul Food, French and Scandinavian dishes has declined."

Lastly, *Sex and the City* debuted on HBO, putting the sexy Cosmopolitan cocktail on the map. The popular show would also regularly feature New York City eateries that became trendy crazes for tourists, like Magnolia Bakery and Cafeteria. The latter, a 24/7 restaurant that opened in Chelsea in 1998, was extremely popular among the late night party crowd with a diner menu of everything from breakfast to tacos to meatloaf.

1999

Food Premieres: Sierra Mist, Little Debbie Cosmic Brownies, Splenda, Reptar Crunch

This year, home chef, hobbyist, mogul, and former stockbroker Martha Stewart took her company Martha Stewart Living Omnimedia public. Launched in 1997, the company handled all of Martha's lucrative ventures in print (*Martha Stewart Living Magazine*), merchandise (Martha Stewart Everyday at K-Mart), and television (*Martha Stewart Living*, the show). The IPO made her the country's first female billionaire. According to CNN, she "celebrated by serving fresh-squeezed orange juice and brioche to the money-thirsty traders on the floor of the New York Stock Exchange."

The US Chamber of Commerce named 1999 The Year of the Restaurant, which was fitting because it was reported that over 50 percent of the average American's food dollar was being spent outside of the home. Americans wanted interesting new food and increasingly, drinks. In New York, Florence Fabricant reported on the new trend of "sexy colorful fruit filled drinks... vacation style drinks." Divulged a restaurant owner, "In the mid-80's you had mostly big frozen drinks or liquor on the rocks, but for about the past three years, all our restaurants have had drink menus with special cocktails." This new trend of restaurants fusing with bars inspired the Zagat Restaurant Guide to publish a New York Nightlife guide. This same year, Anthony Bourdain's essay, *Don't Read Before Eating This*, was published in *The New Yorker*.

Bourdain wasn't yet a celebrity chef or world traveler. He was just a zesty, charismatic, and jaded executive chef at French eatery Brasserie Les Halles. In the piece, he dragged people who ate well-done red meat. "People who order their meat well-done perform a valuable service for those of us in the business who are cost-conscious: they pay for the privilege of eating our garbage. In many kitchens, there's a time-honored practice called 'save for well-done.'" In addition to critiquing customers, he revealed restaurant secrets about the reality of kitchen life. He wrote, "If you are one of those people who cringe at the thought of strangers fondling your food, you shouldn't go out to eat. By the time a three-star crew has finished [your meal], it's had dozens of sweaty fingers all over it."

Thanks a lot for that mental image, Bourdain.

Bourdain's essay made such a splash that he signed a book deal for *Kitchen Confidential*, which would premiere the following year and become a bestseller. Bourdain also voiced his dislike for vegetarians, who were growing in number. Throughout the decade, approximately 1 to 6 percent of Americans claimed to be vegetarian. Even more people regularly went meatless, even if they weren't fully vegetarian. A bunch of studies were published this decade showing the link between plant-based diets and improved health, with one 1991 study finding that plant-based oil-free diets reversed heart disease.

According to the *Vegetarian Journal*, by 1994, "over half of all American households ate two or more meatless dinners each week and 20 percent of US households ate four or more meatless dinners per week." This resulted in a new market for them. A man named Eric Brent launched HappyCow.com, which listed vegan and vegetarian friendly restaurants. At grocery stores, "soy-based frankfurters, veggie burgers, frozen tofu desserts and vegetable burritos" became more common. Americans were moving on from Snackwells though, and the company's market share dropped this year. Low-fat was going out of style, and low sugar was the new wave, which explained the immediate popularity of the newbie Splenda.

Kroger, Walmart, Safeway, and Albertsons were expanded, and had disproportionate power over the cost of groceries, outpricing small stores and forcing them to close. During this decade, there were over 380 grocery mergers. According to the American Economic Liberties Project, "Prior to this wave of consolidation, only 17 percent of shoppers went to the top four supermarkets. Now, that number has risen to roughly 60 percent." Food Lion bought Hannaford Brothers Inc for 3.3 billion.

Kroger purchased Fred Meyer for 13 billion dollars, further consolidating grocery stores, meaning small retailers in rural areas often closed down. This would shape the future of food— and food prices— in America. The *Greensboro News and Record* reported that "The average household will have to work 40 days to buy its food for the year and will spend 11 percent of household income on the annual food bill."

On King of The Hill

In the early 2000s, when my mother would do my hair on Sundays for the upcoming week of school, there were times when this dry-looking cartoon would come on, and I knew it was past my bedtime. It wasn't really on my radar, until the episode with the murder. I remember begging my mom to let me stay up to finish the episode.

Years later, I grew to appreciate that *King of the Hill* was good at weaving current events and trends, and the people who embodied them, into a realistic yet fictional city called Arlen, Texas. Focusing on the lives of propane salesman Hank Hill, his wife Peggy, and their 11-year-old son Bobby, the show was a funny and grounded satire of American life in the nineties, while still being outrageous and surreal.

Texas

Before discussing *King of the Hill*, what did Texas look like at the top of the decade? Because of its size, diversity, border location, and resources, the Lone Star State has always been a mighty political arena that both influences and reflects national politics. In 1990 there was a change in the political establishment. Described *Texas Monthly* that year, "Now that Texas has almost as many Republicans as Democrats, Democratic candidates must choose between appealing to the party's traditional base or broadening it. The person who opts for stirring up his own troops runs the risk of appearing too partisan, and the person who reaches out to conservatives unleashes charges of selling out."

The governor was Ann Richards, the second woman to serve in the position in Texas history. She was born in 1933 in Lakeview and grew up in Waco. She graduated from Baylor University and was a housewife to a liberal lawyer named Dave by the age of 19. A budding socialite interested in civil rights and left-leaning politics, she helped work on political campaigns for Texas Democrats in the 1960s. She and other women founded the North Dallas Democratic Women's group, performing political satire skits in the mid to late 1960s. She was known for hosting parties and being able to knock back multiple martinis with the big boys.

In the early seventies, her family moved from conservative Dallas to liberal Austin, where her husband started a civil rights practice. Ann successfully ran for County Commissioner in 1975, but by the end of the decade, her drinking problem, along with her budding neoliberal ideology and fancy outfits, was destroying her marriage. She went to rehab in 1980, became Texas State Treasurer in 1982, divorced her husband in 1984, and was re-elected without opposition in 1986. At the 1988 Democratic National Convention, she made a splash with her charm and humor by criticizing Reagan and Bush. She said, "I'm delighted to be here with you this evening, because after listening to George Bush all these years, I figured you needed to know what a real Texas accent sounds like."

In 1990, Ann sought and won the Democratic nomination for Texas governor, igniting the fury of opponent State Attorney General Jim Mattox. He accused her of having a drug habit and courting a lesbian following, but Richards' charm, openness about her sobriety, and liberalism appealed to the 49% of voters who pushed her into the governor's office. This included 60% of the female vote and a majority of minorities, some of them suburban Republicans. As governor, she oversaw the creation of the Texas Lottery to boost education budgets, and she bought the first ticket six months before it went live. She pushed for growth in Texas's film and music industries, keenly wanting to integrate the state into America's emerging information and entertainment economy.

Texas was becoming the "Third Coast" of American film, with the 1990 cult hit *Slacker*, filmed around Austin on a shoestring budget, kicking off the decade. The 1993 ensemble movie *Dazed and Confused* was also shot in Austin. There was 1994's *Reality Bites*, shot mostly in Houston. *Walker, Texas Ranger*, starring Chuck Norris, became an iconic symbol of Texas in 1993, and a source of myths about policing.

As for Ann, she installed the first Black person on the board of regents of the University of Texas, Zan Wesley Holmes Jr., and appointed Black men and women to the Texas Rangers police force. She orchestrated surprise raids on nursing homes to check for inadequate care, led insurance reform, served cornbread and coffee to lobbyists, and attracted pro-abortion Republicans. Observers briefly wondered in 1992 if Ann's uncanny knack for drawing both Democrats and Republicans would lead to a presidential campaign for the grandmother of eight. Whereas fellow Democrat Hillary Clinton repelled housewives and conservative women, Ann appealed to them, and days after Hillary's jab about being too busy to sit around baking cookies, Ann served cookies and coffee from her office and posed for a picture.

In addition to her grandmotherly image, Ann was both a reformed addict and tough on crime. While she introduced substance abuse programs to prisons, providing 14,000 beds, she also earmarked money for new prisons and cracked down on violent parolees. The Texas prison industry was booming, and she was one of its architects. She spent valuable time providing tax breaks and infrastructure deals to major companies to help fix the failing economy, which didn't impress many of the constituents who had voted for her.

Richards was touted as a supporter of minorities and queer people, but her loyalty to the latter group was called into question when she signed a 1993 criminal code that kept Texas's sodomy law on the books. While she openly called for repealing the sodomy law, her veto would have still allowed it to stand, so she signed the legislation in order to push through other liberal measures. Texas famously doesn't have a state income tax, and Ann refused to support a Democratic push to introduce one. She was a Democrat operating within a historically conservative state, and the next election would show how precarious that position really was.

Because she lost support from more left-leaning constituents and repelled conservatives with decisions like vetoing a right-to-carry law, the 1994 election spelled trouble. George H. W. Bush, a Texas transplant by way of Connecticut, was at the helm of the country, leading from a position of "compassionate conservatism." His son, George Walker Bush, had similarly made a fortune in oil before becoming a majority owner of the Texas Rangers baseball team. He made quite the splash around Dallas, a city licking its wounds in the aftermath of a recession and a damaged oil industry. Bush, encouraged by consultant and lobbyist Karl Rove, wanted to differentiate himself from his father by playing the Texan.

Reported *D Magazine* in a 1992 feature, *George Bush Too*:

> "The welcoming committee from the Chamber of Commerce, which has invited him to town to speak, has been thoughtful enough to arrange for a black stretch limousine, on loan from the funeral parlor, to drive us from the airstrip into town.

Bush is crestfallen. He doesn't like to ride in limos in small Texas towns-for the same reasons that he doesn't want to wear his tuxedo to meet local reporters at a press conference scheduled in about half an hour. Bush is constantly fighting the patrician image he inherited from a father who sport-fishes in Florida and summers in Maine. If George Jr. is to carve out a political niche of his own, it will be as a Texan-and not one who flies in four or five times a year to glad-hand millionaires and shoot quail."

Back in 1978, when Bush Jr. ran for a Midland, Texas congressional seat, he lost, partly because his opponent emphasized his prep-school background. That loss guided his future campaign strategy. When he faced off against Ann Richards in 1994, she vastly underestimated Bush, calling out his youth and inexperience, qualities he reframed as signs of fresh ideas. Like his brother Jeb, who was also running for governor over in Florida, he targeted cultural and religious voters among white communities, while pushing for tort reform, welfare reform, and "juvenile justice." Despite Richards' expansion of prisons, it wasn't enough for Bush, who called her "soft on crime." Wrote Fox Butterfield, "[Bush ran] a series of grainy black-and-white commercials depicting a man abducting a woman at gunpoint in a parking garage and, a moment later, a police officer draping a blanket over the woman's body."

Though the Richards campaign anticipated Bush going off-script and doing something damaging, he didn't. Instead, Richards drew ire when she referred to him as "some jerk" and a "boy." When the votes were tallied, Bush won with 54% of the vote. Richards secured 83% of the Black vote and 75% of the Latino vote. Bush received 63% of the white vote. This marked the last Texas gubernatorial election in which a Democrat won more than 45% of the vote. Bush was one of many candidates benefitting from the nationwide Republican Revolution of 1994, but not his brother. Jeb lost Florida by less than 2% of the vote, but would come back and win in 1998. Together, Ann Richards and ousted New York Governor Mario Cuomo starred in a Doritos commercial during the 1995 Super Bowl.

Ann Richards would go on to become a lobbyist, including for tobacco companies. She also guest starred in a season five episode of *King of the Hill*, in which she was mooned by Hank Hill and began dating Bill Dauterive. As for George W. Bush, he never guest starred on the show, but he was integrated into the universe. During the same season as Ann's guest role, Hank became disenchanted with the Republican presidential candidate because of his weak handshake.

Making The King

In the late mid-nineties, Mike Judge was enjoying the success of his MTV creation *Beavis and Butt-Head*. He was a physics and math graduate who could also draw and write fiction. *Beavis and Butt-Head* had been picked up based on Judge's premise that it would be a "reaction to the whole fringe aspect of the political correctness movement." It was perfect for MTV, inappropriate and tuned into pop culture, with an acid trip appeal for teen boys, making it the channel's highest-rated show. It even led to a 1997 spin-off, *Daria*. Judge's next idea, however, was a little harder to pitch.

When Judge, who had once lived in Garland, Texas, pitched *King of the Hill* to Fox, the network was skeptical of a cartoon set in the Lone Star State. So they paired Judge with *The Simpsons* writer Greg Daniels. Daniels was responsible for turning Judge's incomplete concept into a full show by adding Hank Hill's abusive World War II veteran father, Cotton, and his ditzy niece Luanne. Daniels also created Dale Gribble's conspiracy theorist persona. His contributions earned him a co-creator credit.

When *King of the Hill* premiered on January 12, 1997, it was an immediate hit, benefiting from airing right after the wildly popular *The Simpsons*. Wrote Diane Holloway, "*Walker, Texas Ranger* notwithstanding, *King of the Hill* is the most Texan television series since *Dallas*. It's set deep in the heart of Texas and focuses on characters who are Texan through and through." This was deliberate. Daniels sent the show's writers to Texas to interact with locals, observe, and take notes, generating real situations. That's why Arlen felt so lifelike. Daniels would later use the same immersive research approach for other shows he co-created that I love, namely *Parks and Recreation* and *The Office*.

Arlen is a fictional town of approximately 145,300 in one episode and 1,454 in another. It's a place filled with contradictions, just like its characters. If Arlen were real, it's hard to say exactly where it would be located. One episode places it about 96 miles outside of Dallas, while another suggests it's three hours from Houston. In actuality, according to Mike Judge, the show was loosely based on an amalgamation of places: Humble, Texas; Arlington; and a suburb of Dallas called Richardson.

Arlen, like much of Texas and the South, is steeped in football culture. Tom Landry Middle School was named after the legendary Dallas Cowboys head coach, and Roger Staubach Elementary honors a famed Cowboys quarterback. At the time the series was being conceptualized, the Dallas

Cowboys had won three Super Bowls, in 1992, 1993, and 1995. During that era of football glory, numerous Cowboys players were rumored to be partying with sex workers and using drugs at a private residence nicknamed "The White House." Meanwhile, Dallas maintained a reputation for snobby socialites and oil magnates.

In the season one episode *Peggy the Boggle Champ*, Hank tells Peggy that he doesn't want her going to Dallas because "it's crawling with crackheads and debutantes. And half of them play for the Cowboys." For Hank, that kind of riffraff existed outside of family-friendly, simple Arlen, even if he did love the Cowboys. A later episode from 2005 humorously rewrote Arlen's history to trace back to a booming brothel town called Harlottown. It eventually became Harlen, and then Arlen, because, according to Peggy Hill, "People were in such a hurry to get to Harlottown that they didn't have enough time to call it such."

But who is the king of this setting and the show's guiding protagonist, expertly voiced by Mike Judge? Describing Hank Hill, Judge joked in 1997, "Andy Griffith is back and he's pissed." When fleshing out Hank's background and mindset, Greg Daniels had the writers read *The Death of Common Sense: How Law Is Suffocating America* to get inside the propane salesman's head. Written by Philip K. Howard and published in 1995, the book was essentially a libertarian treatise criticizing government regulation and bureaucracy.

It fit perfectly for someone like Hank, who would never have read such a book but would be damned if you tried to get him to pay state income taxes or expand welfare. Judge, who insisted that Hank was "someone who'd be voting for Ross Perot," also claimed, "It's not a political show. It's more a populist, common sense point of view. . . . It started out as very autobiographical. I identify with Hank quite a bit. He gets kind of irritated at everyday, annoying things. I've known about 20 guys like this."

Howard's writings emphasized that entitlement rights, like providing accessibility measures for the disabled or safety nets for the poor, did nothing but cause division, adding that "we have deluded ourselves into thinking that the right decisions will be ensured if we build enough procedural protection." This strand of libertarianism had been encroaching on traditional conservatism since at least the 1960s, but the political splintering of the 1990s, driven by the culture wars, made these issues far more pertinent.

King of the Hill, on the surface, depending on your own political beliefs, can appear to be a show that affirms conservatism. After all, during its prime years, the show had a predominantly male viewership between the ages of 18 and 49, with nearly a quarter of them owning pickup trucks. In many ways, it did affirm conservatism: Hank often falls back on stereotypical beliefs about masculinity, he hates communism, and he despises laziness. In a 1998 episode, he even rebukes the Americans with Disabilities Act when a spoiled white drug-addicted slacker takes advantage of its provisions.

When Hank's son, Bobby (Pamela Adlon), wants to do things that are non-masculine coded or not patriotic enough, Hank is often aghast, though he sometimes comes around to support Bobby. Hank also balks at sexual liberation and lewd behavior. For instance, when the ill-fated Debbie Grund flirts with him on the phone in *Hanky Panky*, Hank becomes disturbed because he believes he just "had phone sex." As rigid as Hank can be, his conservatism isn't fundamentalist. In the 1997 season two episode *Hilloween*, for example, Hank, who is a practicing Methodist, encourages the celebration of Halloween in Arlen, despite a local busybody's campaign to liken it to devil worship.

Hank is also surprisingly elastic, such as when he and Peggy (Kathy Najimy) visit a nude beach after he has sex dreams featuring Dale's wife, Nancy. The show liberally made fun of conservatism and satirized it by showing how conservative values often come second to human nature, or how they're hypocritical, or ripe for bias, blind allegiance, and exploitation. In another episode, the defeatist school principal, Carl Moss, complains that the school used up its budget fighting the installation of accessibility ramps for wheelchair-bound students, leaving no money for shop classes. This angers Hank enough that he volunteers to teach the class himself. It's not the first or last time that stubborn conservatism negatively impacts Hank's life or disrupts the balance of Arlen.

A frequent running gag, running parallel to his political beliefs, is Hank's devotion and submission to his near-thankless job as a propane salesman. Raised by an abusive and hateful war veteran who loved to brag about killing "fitty men," Hank also had a fragile, submissive mother. Still, he shows near-unshakeable respect for his father, Cotton, and continues to endure much of his abuse throughout the show. This dynamic ripples into other areas of Hank's life.

As an adult, Hank is committed to the chain of command and reveres high-ranking officials in propane, but on numerous occasions, it's shown that he is underpaid and taken advantage of. His boss, Buck Strickland, is an amoral addict, womanizer, and gambler, values completely at odds with Hank's, but ones he chooses to ignore because Buck is his boss, the man who introduced him to sweet lady propane. When Buck conspires with other propane dealers to price-gouge customers, whom Hank treats with the utmost respect, Hank doesn't snitch or quit. Instead, he helps Buck and the other men avoid jail. His naivety and blind loyalty run so deep that, in a 2008 episode, it's revealed he paid sticker price on cars for twenty-five years.

Hank's loyalty is ironclad. Despite the moral shortcomings of his best friends, Dale, Bill, and Boomhauer, the fact that they played football together in high school is enough to seal a lifelong bond. Hank is also endlessly committed to his wife, Peggy, a transplant from Montana whom he met in high school. Peggy is a somewhat arrogant and very naive substitute teacher who has size 16.5 feet and loves Boggle. She brags about her Apple Brown Betty, Frito pie, and Spah-Peggy and Meatballs while pretending to be an adept Spanish speaker despite all evidence to the contrary.

While Peggy and Hank have traditional aspects to their relationship (he mows the lawn and does repairs, she cooks and cleans, though the food isn't very good), Peggy is far from a stereotypical housewife. As Hank tells Bobby in a season one episode, "Women were not put on earth to serve [men]." Hank's misogynistic father, Cotton, often berates both Peggy and Hank for their nontraditional relationship. He never once refers to Peggy by name, simply calling her "Hank's Wife." Yet in a typical display of the show's layered storytelling, Cotton is the one who helps Peggy learn to walk again after she injures herself while skydiving.

The golden years of *King of the Hill* were a humorous study of 1990s and early 2000s center-right conservatives making sense of a globalizing and increasingly partisan world. The show highlighted their weaknesses and humanized them. Key themes included parenting, authority, and discipline, with storylines exploring issues like explicit music, dating, smoking, and co-ed sleepovers.

In *To Spank, With Love*, Peggy is disrespected by her students and snaps and spanks one of them. When she is fired, parents and teachers rally around her and get her reinstated. The new prestige and authority, of course, send the overconfident yet insecure Peggy on a predictable power trip. Spanking in schools, as well as in the home, was a hot-button issue in the nineties, and by 1994, a total of 26 states had banned the practice.

Political tribalism was skyrocketing, and Democrats, seen as the natural enemies of Republicans, were offering up neoliberal hypocrites like Bill Clinton. Hank's own party, in an era of Pat Buchanan, Ross Perot, Clinton, and George Bush, was splintering. Some Republicans latched on to Buchanan's extremism, others to Perot's populism, Clinton's triangulation, or the Reagan legacy upheld by Bush and candidates like Phil Gramm. Hank was certainly the latter kind of Republican, saying more than once that he missed voting for Reagan.

What about Dale Gribble (Johnny Hardwick), the conspiracy theorist, who once said Perot was "the one man who knew about the lizard people"? He grew up in the shadow of Watergate and The Pentagon Papers, and his conspiratorial tendencies represent the disillusioned boomers whose mistrust was mired in conservative bias. It makes perfect sense that Dale, or Rusty Shackleford as he likes to be called, the one with cameras in his home and a mixed-race child, is in complete denial about his wife's infidelity. He's deeply mistrustful of government, so he doesn't vote or pay taxes, but he does accept welfare under Rusty Shackleford's name. In *Dale To The Chief*, when he rereads the Warren Report and comes to agree that there was no conspiracy to kill JFK, he flips from conspiracy theorist to super-patriot, humorously revealing two sides of a very dystopian coin.

Despite Fox's general dislike of animated shows that allowed characters to grow and have continuous storylines, *King of the Hill's* characters, and Arlen itself, evolved over time. When presented with new information, scenarios, and people, Hank and company could be swayed to go against their static characteristics, or it was revealed they didn't hold the prejudices audiences may have assumed. In the 2002 episode *My Own Private Rodeo*, Dale Gribble's father comes out as gay. When Nancy asks Dale if he's okay with it, he says he is, because he's been cool with John Redcorn this whole time.

In season two, a corporation called Mega Lo Mart (modeled on Wal-Mart) comes to Arlen, swallowing up small businesses and altering the lives of its residents. Hank's own job is absorbed by Mega Lo Mart, and in a series of comedic events, the store is eventually blown up in the season finale. A recurring character is killed, which not only changes Arlen's landscape once again but also affects everyone's mental health in the episodes that follow. Similarly, when Peggy Hill nearly dies in a skydiving accident in the season three finale, her mental health and relationships are visibly impacted throughout the first half of season four.

King of the Hill definitely dealt with mental health in a way that other cartoons from the era did not. In the show's first Christmas episode, *Pretty Pretty Dresses*, Hank's best friend and neighbor, Bill Dauterive (Stephen Root), whose abusive wife Lenore left him before the show began, has a mental breakdown during the holiday season. After numerous suicide attempts that Hank clumsily mishandles, Bill begins dressing as Lenore and pretending to be her.

When Bill shows up at the Hills' Christmas party, guests become hostile, with one saying, "Go back to Hollywood," and another adding, "This isn't the Democratic National Convention." At that moment, Hank, whose conservatism could have splintered into either hateful dismissal or quiet compassion, chooses the latter. Realizing that his friend truly needs him, Hank eschews traditional gender norms, dresses as Lenore, and helps Bill find closure through roleplay. Though Bill remains depressed and is often written as the sad "loser" character throughout the series, Hank sticks by him despite his breakdowns, bizarre behavior, and body odor.

Hank's commitment to his friends, and his boomer-era understanding of mental health, is consistent throughout the series. Country legend Tammy Wynette voiced Hank's mother, Tilly, from 1997 to 1998 until her untimely death. In the 1999 episode *Escape from Party Island*, Hank is forced to confront the emotional abuse his mother endured at the hands of his father. While he initially mocks Tilly's obsession with collecting glass miniatures, he eventually comes to understand that they were a vital outlet for her survival and emotional stability. Of course, because this is *King of the Hill*, the episode also features Hank being caught up on San Padre Island during a wild MTV-style spring break full of raucous college students, proving that even deep emotional arcs can unfold in the most hilariously absurd situations.

With so much humor and empathy bursting from its seams, who exactly did *King of The Hill* appeal to? In 2005, Matt Bai discussed the phenomenon of *"King of the Hill Democrats,"* writing,

> "If *South Park* is libertarian, then *King of the Hill* might best be described as populist. It makes no bones about its heroes' failings: Hank Hill is naive and repressed, his family is eccentric, and his best friends are a loser, a womanizer, and a raving paranoid. But their world exists in a kind of balance, where everyone's good qualities make up for everyone else's flaws; you get the impression that their Texas suburb can take care of itself. Real trouble comes when outsiders try to interfere: regulators, managers with MBAs, Ritalin-dispensing doctors, left-wing or right-wing ideologues."

Two-time governor of North Carolina, Mike Easley, who served from 2001 to

2009, loved the show so much that, according to Bai, "he instructs his pollster to separate the state's voters into those who watch *King of the Hill* and those who don't so he can find out whether his arguments on social and economic issues are making sense to the sitcom's fans." To be a Democrat in a heavily red and centrist state like North Carolina calls for conservative compromise, or losing your seat. Like Clinton, Easley was a supporter of the death penalty and oversaw 27 executions.

Women and Race in King Of The Hill

The dynamics of Hank and Peggy's relationship were examined in the stellar season one episode *Joust Like a Woman*. Excellent guest star choice Alan Rickman played the king of a Renaissance fair whom Hank hopes to entice into a propane business deal. Peggy's know-it-all attitude and egalitarian ways offend the king, who seeks to tame the shrew by forcing her to serve as a wench. While Hank initially goes along with it to seal the deal, King Phillip eventually goes too far, angering Hank enough to challenge him to a fight. Hank loses the joust, but Peggy comes to the rescue in a fun reversal of expected gender roles.

In addition to its interesting gender dynamics, the show's depiction of the white lower class fit squarely into the larger cultural conversations of the nineties. Hank, who sips beer in the alley behind his house and drives a pickup, hates being called a redneck and has even used the term derogatorily toward others, such as Luanne's eventual husband, Lucky, who lives off a lawsuit settlement. Rather than relying on racist tropes about Black people abusing welfare, being lazy, or being criminals, the most nefarious, greedy, and lazy characters on the show are white. When Hank naively buys crack in *Jumping' Crack Bass*, thinking it's fishing bait, he gets it from a white man. When he lets a white woman stay with his family and later finds out she's a sex worker in *Ho Yeah!*, her pimp Alabaster (Snoop Dogg), is also white.

The pretty blonde Nancy Gribble was cuckolding her husband Dale with the Native man John Redcorn, and when asked about her obviously mixed-race child, she claimed that Dale's grandmother had Jamaican ancestry. The lie is accepted by everyone in Arlen without question. The news of the affair shocks Peggy, who is the last person in the neighborhood to find out.

While the Hills represented lower- to middle-class Texans, their niece, Luanne, embodied the "white trash," redneck, and "trailer trash" culture that was becoming increasingly visible in nineties media, particularly through shows like *Judge Judy, Roseanne,* and *Jerry Springer.* Luanne was expertly voiced by Brittany Murphy, fresh from her breakout role in *Clueless.* In the episode *Leanne's Saga,* we meet Luanne's mother, Leanne, who was married to Peggy's fraternal brother and was abusive. She ended up in jail for stabbing him with a fork, which is why Luanne lives with the Hills. When Leanne is released from prison, she proves she's still not a good mom, shamelessly flirting with Luanne's boyfriend and starting a fight at the neighborhood cookout. In this episode, Luanne makes peace with the reality that her mother is not a good person.

One of my favorite Luanne episodes is *Fun With Jane and Jane,* which sees Luanne and Peggy get absorbed into a cult on a college campus, believing it to be a sorority. Cults were a major part of the 1990s cultural landscape, but the show's decision to frame this one as an all-female cult, sustained by the elitism of sorority culture, eating disorders, and the ultra-feminine act of making jam, is especially funny. It's even funnier when the cult's spell is broken by Hank Hill grilling up steaks.

In contrast to what viewers might expect of Luanne, who begins the series somewhat promiscuous and naive about boys, she becomes a born-again Christian and a self-declared virgin at Hank's insistence. That same episode also reveals that Peggy had sex with one other person before Hank, which upsets the foundation of their relationship. Hank had always believed they were both virgins at the altar. Peggy lost her virginity to a gay friend, just to help him confirm that he was gay, yet another example of Peggy defying conservative ideals of womanhood.

Unlike Hank's mother, Peggy does not tolerate emotional or verbal abuse. And while Hank is often oblivious to the little things, he is generally respectful of Peggy's needs. When she wants to go back to work after being convinced to become a stay-at-home-mom, Hank eventually realizes it's for the best. One of my favorite episodes dealing with womanhood is the one in which Peggy, arrogant about both her looks and intelligence, enters a beauty pageant against legitimately accomplished and conventionally attractive women, only to get embarrassed when she realizes she's not all that.

There are multiple main characters on *King of The Hill* who aren't white, and one of the funniest aspects of the show is how Hank and other Arlen residents interact with people of different races, often resulting in cringe-worthy moments that feel like obvious winks to a racially aware audience. When Arlen's resident Native, John Redcorn, speaks to Bobby's class in *Spin The Choice* and tells them about the genocide of his people, Bobby replies,

"Are you sure it's the white man who did all that stuff? Because I come from white people and this is the first I'm hearing of it." Redcorn responds simply, "Yes, I am sure."

John Redcorn is one of my favorite characters. He's the lead singer of Big Mountain Fudgecake, an expert and advocate of his Indigenous culture, and a masseuse. He's also the father of Nancy Gribble's son, Joseph, which her husband, Dale, is oblivious to. It's so great that the conspiracy theorist is a cuckold. Redcorn was originally voiced by Victor Aaron Ramirez for two episodes, but he died in a 1996 car crash before the season aired. He was then replaced by Comanche and White Mountain Apache member Jonathan Joss.

There were over 65,000 Native people living in Texas at the dawn of the nineties, and most belonged to three federally recognized tribes: Alabama–Coushatta, Kickapoo, and Ysleta del Sur Pueblo. They lived on three reservations in Polk County, Maverick County, and El Paso. Though the state of Texas makes no attempt to officially recognize tribes, a 1988 federal act gave legal status to gambling operations on Native lands. Each of the three Texas tribes opened gambling halls that were challenged by the state in the nineties. In the episode *Nancy's Boys*, Dale Gribble helped John Redcorn research how to get his land back by maneuvering through federal and tribal laws, eventually winning him 12 acres on the side of a loud highway, out of a desired 130,000.

Hank's Laotian neighbors, the Souphanousinphones, were a major part of the series. Bobby's first and main love interest, Connie, and Peggy's frenemy, Min, were voiced by Chinese-American Lauren Tom, who incidentally voices Amy on *Futurama* and Dana on my second favorite *Batman* series, *Batman Beyond*. Tom also played Ross Geller's girlfriend Julie on the sitcom *Friends*. There's a great episode that tests Hank's comfort level when Connie gets her period while staying at the Hills'.

Problematically, Kahn, Hank's least favorite neighbor and an uptight yuppie, was voiced by Iowa-born Toby Huss, who also voiced Cotton. But it was the nineties, and nobody cared about voice actors playing characters of different races. The show utilizing an Asian character at all was an interesting choice, and likely served as an introduction to Laotian people for many American viewers. When the Souphanousinphones meet the Hills, while Hank and his neighbors grumble that Kahn is either Chinese or Japanese, the only person to correctly identify them as Laotian is Cotton, who ironically harbors deep hatred toward Japanese people. Other than him, nobody on Rainey Street even knew Laos was a country. Neil Huff noted that,

> "While [Peggy] undoubtedly deserves credit for kindly extending a dinner invitation to the Soupanousinphones, she cooks them Chinese food—the food of the oppressors of Laos—she welcomes them to the United States (again, despite the fact that they've been Americans living in California for the past 20 years) and, from afar, she muses: 'It's like we get to travel to the Orient without having to worry about diarrhea or being jailed for our pro-democracy beliefs.'"

Laotians arrived in America in large numbers after the Vietnam War (along with Vietnamese refugees), fleeing the communist dictatorship that emerged in 1975. During the war, the U.S. had covertly conducted operations against Laotian communists, who were allied with North Vietnam. The U.S. dropped hundreds of millions of bombs on Laos, 30% of which failed to explode on impact and would cause injuries and deaths for decades after the "secret war" ended. Minh, the daughter of a general, and Kahn, the son of peasants, apparently fled Laos during this time. In building their American lives, the Souphanousinphones deeply embraced the capitalist American dream.

The Souphanousinphones constantly compare themselves to another Laotian family, the extremely wealthy Wassanasongs, who are members of the exclusive Nine Rivers Country Club. Minh's competitive nature and extreme expectations of Kahn Jr. are emblematic of the "Tiger Mom" stereotype often attributed to Asian women, but it's unfair to say that everything about these characters was stereotypical. Connie, who had a brief infatuation with bluegrass music, genuinely loves school regardless of her parents' pressure, and she has a cousin named Tid Pao who was in a gang, made meth, and conned Bobby Hill. Kahn and Minh had the healthiest sexual relationship and marriage on Rainey Street.

A really good late-series episode is *The Redneck on Rainey Street*. The Souphanousinphones give up their buppie lifestyle after the loss of affirmative action and become rednecks. Minh, happy to be done with reading Toni Morrison books for her book club and pretending to care about current events (read: being the "smart Asian"), relishes the chance to have some fun before the financial hardships take their toll.

Asians are also weaved into the storyline because of Cotton Hill's racism against Japanese people. In the season six two-part episode *Returning Japanese*, it is revealed that during Cotton's time overseas, he impregnated a woman who has a son named Junichiro. Hank then travels to Japan to meet his half-brother. After the dual episodes, Junichiro is seen five seasons later in the audience when Luanne gets married.

Another group of people included in the show were Latinos. Hank's full first name is Henry, and the Spanish version of that is Enrique, the name given to Hank's Mexican co-worker at Strickland Propane. In *Lady and Gentrification*, Hank is chosen to speak at Enrique's daughter's *quinceañera*, a task he treats with great respect and honor. In the world of Arlen, Texas, Latinos and immigration are rarely contentious subjects, except for one early shining example.

During the 1998 episode *Junkie Business*, Hank is shaken and uncomfortable when a Latina named Maria Montalvo applies to be a propane salesman. She's knowledgeable and professional (even though she doesn't know who Troy Aikman is). Hank speaks with Peggy about whether or not he should hire Maria. Peggy asks if he's hesitant because he's attracted to her. Hank hilariously describes Maria as "handsome," but Peggy says he shouldn't feel threatened by a beautiful Chicana and that he should hire her. They then flirt and have sex. Hank, freaked out that a similar scenario could happen at work, passes over Maria and instead chooses an unqualified white male drug addict. Peggy then feels threatened, playing into stereotypes about the exotic Latina being every man's fantasy. In the end, the junkie is fired, Maria is hired, she squeezes Hank's butt, and is only heard from once again, seamlessly relegated to the background of Strickland Propane.

Peggy Hill's obnoxious ass was a self-proclaimed Spanish expert whose interactions with Latino culture always go hilariously wrong, because she cannot, in fact, speak the language. Peggy's most egregious mistake was in the season six episode *Lupe's Revenge*. While an uncomfortable Hank deals with sexual harassment and assault by a female police officer, Peggy kidnaps a child from Mexico during a field trip because she can't effectively communicate.

In the 1990s, the Texas Latino, or Tejano, community was surging. Tejano culture has its own distinct music, food, and history that adds to the fabric of Texas. Selena Quintanilla took the male-dominated Tejano genre by storm in the late 1980s and brought it into the national spotlight in the early 1990s, selling out stadiums and becoming a Grammy winner. On March 31, 1995, she was murdered by her friend and former business associate Yolanda Saldívar. Selena's fame was so immense that Governor George W. Bush declared April 16 as Selena Day. In July, her posthumous album *Dreaming of You* shot to the top of the *Billboard* 200.

The album was primarily bought by Latinos and demonstrated their purchasing power within the U.S. Her popularity also contributed to the growth of Latin pop. Additionally, Selena became one of the top 100 most popular names for girls in 1995. Selena's father, Abraham, began working on a movie within weeks of her death, seeking to immortalize her in history and stamp out negative rumors. Mexican actress Salma Hayek turned down the role, and Puerto Rican Jennifer Lopez was cast, initially angering fans until her performance wowed critics and skeptics. Selena's stamp on Texas history was even joked about in *King of the Hill*, when Hank discovers that Bobby's textbook has a section on the singer but not on the Alamo.

Black women are not distinctly represented in *King of the Hill*, save for a mean classmate of Luanne's in cosmetology school and a guest appearance by George Foreman's daughter, Freeda, as herself. The absence of Black women characters in a mainstream 1990s-2000s television show sadly isn't surprising. However, Black men have been featured in several storylines. There's the Black Texas Ranger who correctly solves the murder behind Sugarfoot's in the episode *High Anxiety*.

In the season two episode *Traffic Jam*, Chris Rock plays a driver's ed instructor whose jokes make Hank uncomfortable and lead to Bobby Hill telling white supremacist jokes in front of a crowd of Black people. The season seven episode *The Son Also Roses* features Michael Clarke Duncan as an intense rose-growing aficionado named Morgan, who berates Hank for bringing Bobby into such a competitive "sport." That same episode showcases Hank's flexibility with Bobby's interests, and his naivety, as he fails to realize that the store sponsoring their rose in the competition is actually a head shop for weed. Morgan wins first prize thanks to his rose *Ruby My Dear*.

In a 2003 episode, Bernie Mac guest-starred as a repairman who thinks Hank's dog, Ladybird, is racist. The word gets around that the Hills are raising a racist canine, and they get treated like lepers in the conservative town. In fact, Ladybird is prejudiced against repairmen because Hank has never needed to use one. Speaking of Ladybird, in a season one episode, Hank proudly revealed that she, named after Lyndon B. Johnson's wife, was born to a bloodhound who helped chase down James Earl Ray, the convicted assassin of Martin Luther King Jr.

What was the reality for Black Texans in the nineties? There were a lot of new transplants. Hundreds of thousands of Black people left California,

Chicago, Philadelphia, and New York for the South during this decade, and many settled in Texas. They noted that the South of the nineties was not the same politically disenfranchised, overtly racist South of generations past. While there were still sundown towns, KKK rallies, and police brutality, the "new South" had more to offer Black people at the End of History than it had their ancestors just three decades earlier. For those moving to Texas, suburbs like Arlington were an attractive option. In 1991, the area celebrated the opening of its first Black hair care salon, showing how white the community had been up until that time.

Other expats moved to Dallas and Houston, where they joined or created new high-powered social and political networks that invigorated middle-class enclaves. The historically Black area of Houston's Third Ward lost a significant portion of its Black population, many of whom relocated to the suburbs. At the same time, the Third Ward grew in Latino residents by between five and ten percent. The city's preservationists worked to protect historic blocks of Third Ward property.

In 1995, Ron Kirk became the first Black mayor of Dallas. He had previously served as Secretary of State of Texas under Ann Richards, the first woman elected governor of Texas. The key to Kirk's success was his support of Dallas business interests. While some thought Kirk would generate strong Black voter turnout, consultant Rufus Shaw remarked, "This is not a Black campaign. This is a Black in a white campaign. This is a guy white folks have chosen." Indeed, Kirk's primary supporters were Dallas business titans, and he racked up endorsements from Roger Staubach and prominent real estate developers. Kirk won 62% of the vote. Said an unimpressed political scientist, Joseph Stewart, on Kirk's bipartisan appeal: "The white power structure decided it was time to have a Black mayor and move Dallas into the 1970s." Kirk was re-elected in 1999 with 74% of the vote, having impressed citizens and the business elite.

In 1998, Lee Patrick Brown was elected as the first Black mayor of Houston. He had gained support after previously serving as the city's first Black police chief back in 1982. In the early nineties, Brown served as New York City's police commissioner under the city's first Black mayor, David Dinkins, and faced criticism from Rudolph Giuliani for not being tough enough during the Crown Heights riots. Said Giuliani upon Brown's election: "I hope he does a better job as mayor of Houston than he did as police commissioner in New York City." Brown captured not just the Black vote, but also a healthy share of the white and Latino vote, ultimately beating out a wealthy white real estate developer. During his first term as mayor of Houston, Brown invested significantly in infrastructure and expanded affirmative action programs.

Death, Taxes, and Texas

In the 1999 episode *Death and Texas*, Peggy becomes acquainted with a man she believes to be a former student who is awaiting execution on death row. As a recurring character flaw and gag, Peggy's overinflated sense of intelligence leads her to commit to becoming the man's teacher, only to end up being conned into smuggling cocaine into the prison. This is one of my favorite episodes, and it's worth mentioning because, during the governorship of George Bush, Texas executed 154 prisoners, more than any other governor in American or Texas history at the time. By comparison, Ann Richards approved fifty executions during her four-year term. For some reason, Bush only granted clemency to one person: Henry Lee Lucas, who, while falsely confessing to dozens of crimes, was actually convicted of eleven murders.

In the nineties, the death penalty had heavy public support. One national July 1999 poll showed 71 percent in favor and only 21 percent opposed. Everything's bigger in Texas, where crime and punishment sustained the economy. New jails and prisons served a local purpose: bringing jobs and industries to small, dusty towns being left behind in the information age. Texas became a breeding ground for private prisons and mass incarceration. Andy Collins, then-executive director of the Texas Department of Criminal Justice, who awarded a $33.7 million contract to a company supplying meat substitutes originally intended for dogs to human prisoners, summed it up:

> "The public was absolutely hoodwinked into thinking that the only way the crime problem could ever be solved was prosecution and incarceration. We should've been interceding at an earlier age, dealing with these kids before they ever became crooks. But instead, we're just taking juveniles and feeding them directly into the system. I mean, look who was behind it all. Prosecutors, cops, politicians, all of them with a self-serving agenda."

In 1993, the state created a jail felony system which, according to *The Washington Post*, "diverted nonviolent, low-level offenders away from costly and overcrowded state prisons to low-security facilities for up to two years." But instead of helping these offenders transition back into society with adequate resources, the program exploited their free labor and increased recidivism rates.

The state's prison population tripled between 1990 and 2000. In the late eighties, Texas counties issued municipal bonds to build more jails, but by the mid-nineties, they were scrambling to pay them off, as the state prison system had added numerous new facilities under Ann Richards. Reported *Prison Legal News* in 1996: "Counties stuck with the empty jails and facing payments on their bonds looked to Dominion Management, Inc. of Oklahoma, a private brokerage firm dealing in state-to-state prisoner transfers, to help them fill their empty cells. So far, nearly 8,000 prisoners from 11 states have been exiled to shoddily built county jails in Texas."

In 1997, video footage of a 1996 Brazoria County Detention Center training session showed prison guards "kicking inmates [from Missouri] in the groin, siccing dogs on them, and shocking them with stun guns." One of the inmates filed a lawsuit, prompting George Bush to comment, "The conditions in Brazoria County, from what I hear, were appalling. The law will rule. Let's get the facts on the table." Meanwhile, the jail's chief deputy, Charles Wagner, said, "I grant you, that film depicts a lot of unprofessional actions. [But[there's not any real brutality."

The Brazoria incident sparked discourse about the treatment of inmates in Texas prisons, especially because inmates were being shipped in from as far away as Hawaii and Montana. Texas prisons were paid approximately $80 per inmate per day, amounting to millions in annual revenue. After the incident, Missouri terminated a $6 million agreement to send its prisoners to Texas, and 2,100 Missouri inmates won a $2.2 million settlement, with 40 percent going to the lawyers. Bush and other officials disavowed the video in an effort to protect Texas's booming prison industry, which would continue to commit human rights abuses and influence prison systems nationwide.

Bush also slashed the alcohol rehabilitation program from 14,000 beds to 3,000. Because prisons were prioritized, other things predictably suffered. According to one budget analyst, "Spending for public schools was 36.4 percent of the budget in 1999, compared with 41.3 percent in 1989, while spending for prisons was 7.8 percent, up from 5.2 percent." Alongside this shift in spending, punishment became the preferred treatment for juvenile offenders, especially those of color. A 1999 report stated that 75% of the inmates held by the Texas Youth Commission (TYC) were Black or Latino, kids who grew up in poverty and cycles of oppression. As *The New York Times* described in 1999, "Among his changes was lowering the age at which juveniles can be sent to adult court for serious crimes to 14, increasing the maximum sentence for a juvenile to 40 years and requiring a one-year minimum sentence for anyone sentenced to the juvenile prisons."

The TYC was also given the power to hold juvenile offenders, no matter how short their minimum sentences or how minor their offenses, until their 21st birthday. Bush defended his new policies by saying, "Our juvenile justice laws . . . say to our children, 'We love you, but you are responsible for your actions.' I want our kids to understand that if they choose a life of crime, we will hold them accountable for their behavior." A piece of nineties media that incorporated this brutal Texas system is Louis Sachar's 1998 classic, *Holes*. The 2003 movie adaptation is a favorite of mine, but the book was much more explicit about race.

While Bush's father had been promoting "compassionate conservatism," Bush Jr. went out of his way to be an uncompromising conservative. In 1995, he signed the concealed-weapons bill into law, making Texas one of 31 states where people could carry concealed guns, something that would become a hot-button issue in 1999 after the Columbine shooting. He vetoed the Patient Protection Act that same year, which would have mandated that insurance companies cover cancer treatment from certain facilities and would have given patients more choices in their state-regulated healthcare plans. He even called out Bob Dole during the 1996 election cycle for trying to attract pro-choice conservatives into the party. Bush broke with conservatives on just one thing: he increased the amount of wind power produced in Texas.

In 1998, Bush was re-elected. He won 69% of the vote, carrying 49% of Latino voters and 27% of the Black vote. Bursting with confidence, he knew he had a good shot at entering the White House. So, in 1999, the same year Mike Judge released *Office Space* (filmed in and around Dallas and Austin), just six months after being inaugurated for a second term, George Bush announced his candidacy for the 2000 presidential election. He had shed his prep school snob reputation and now embodied Texas law and order, as well as populism. At that time, more than one in every 100 Texans was behind bars, and one-quarter of Texas's Black men were either incarcerated or on parole, ranking Texas just behind Louisiana in total prison population.

Final Thoughts

When Ann Richards momentarily dominated Texas politics in the early nineties and generated speculation that she would be a powerful presidential candidate, it was because she attracted both Republican and Democratic votes during a tornado of culture wars, and for a while, she nimbly played with the boys without being a radical threat to patriarchy or capitalism. But that same centrism, incremental progressive change that also preserved old traditions, repulsed a significant portion of her voter base into abstaining or seeking alternatives and inspired new Republican voters.

With Texas's ability to foreshadow and reflect national politics, her defeat at the hands of Bush signaled what lay ahead for America once Clinton's time was up. Despite George Bush's handshake being too limp for Hank Hill's tastes, he still rushes to vote at the last minute during the 2000 elections. To him, the only other option is to let a Democrat, aka a harbinger of government regulations, crime, bureaucracy, and other unmentionables, waltz into office off the strength of his wasted vote. He doesn't dig deeper into Bush's policies, doesn't consider alternatives, and doesn't think about cycles. As such, his options are to abstain or pick the lesser evil. That sums up not just Hank's politics, or *King of the Hill*'s politics, but the very nature of partisanship in the U.S., especially in the nineties.

King of the Hill was my introduction to Texas culture as a youth. The show's diversity and humor wouldn't have been possible in the eighties, and certain jokes that were funny during its peak would not land today. At the end of the day, it was, and still is, entertainment, but it was developed and written for an audience navigating the culture wars of the nineties and, later, the early 2000s. The politics of the era bled into Arlen and made it rich. "I think people who analyze shows like this probably tend to put too much of politics on it," said Mike Judge in 2009. Too bad no art is devoid of politics.

90s True Crime

My mother could never resist *Forensic Files*, the 1996 investigative true crime series that chilled my bones every time I heard Peter Thomas's haunting voice. For my mother, the show was a catalog of tidy police work and crime solving, a mental exercise where she could deduce the culprit by the first commercial break. For me, it was my introduction to the seediness of human nature.

From the Menendez Brothers and O.J. Simpson trials dominating CourtTV (launched in 1991) to shows like *Forensic Files* and the indulgent documentaries on cable networks, true crime was sensationalized and consumed at unprecedented levels in the 1990s. The ways these crimes were covered, interpreted, and responded to also spoke volumes about American culture, anxieties, and politics.

1990: The Isabella Gardner Art Museum Heist

In Boston, Massachusetts, the St. Patrick's Day celebrations were still in full swing in the early hours of March 18. Two guards, 23-year-old Ricky Abath and 25-year-old Randy Hestand, were clocked in for $6.85 an hour at the Isabella Stewart Gardner Museum of Art. It was Hestand's first day on the job, and aside from a few fire and smoke detectors going off for no apparent reason earlier in the evening, the night had gone pretty smoothly.

The museum had opened in 1903 to showcase the art collection of millionaire Isabella Stewart Gardner and her late husband. There were approximately 16,000 pieces sourced from around the world during their travels, including 3,000 rare books and 7,500 paintings, such as *The Story of Lucretia* by Botticelli. Gardner died in 1924. In her will, she specified that the museum's holdings couldn't be rearranged, sold, or significantly added to, otherwise, the property would transfer to Harvard.

By the eighties, endowment funds were running low, so the museum was not only strapped for cash but also suffering from severely outdated security infrastructure. There were no cameras inside. Guards could only summon police by pressing a lone button at the front desk, and unlike at other museums, there were no required hourly check-ins with law enforcement. Instead, guards were only required to make solo rounds each hour, as infrared motion sensors recorded their movements. As one guard walked, the second guard remained at the desk with his walkie-talkie, ready to press the emergency button if need be.

Amid St. Patrick's Day revelry, a few partygoers later reported seeing two police officers outside the building at 12:30 AM. Inside the museum, sometime after midnight, Abath briefly opened a side entrance and quickly shut it. He then switched duties with Hestand at 1:00 a.m. Shortly before 1:24 a.m., two men dressed as police officers sought entry into the building through a side entrance monitored by a surveillance camera, claiming they were investigating a disturbance. Abath, a former student at Berklee College of Music, who would later admit he sometimes came to work drunk or high (though not on this night, he insisted), buzzed them in.

According to Abath, the fake officers asked him to provide identification. When he stepped out from behind the desk to hand it over, one of them said, "This is a robbery," and handcuffed him. When Hestand returned to the desk, he too was handcuffed. Now, neither guard had access to the emergency button. The intruders blinded both guards with duct tape and led them to the basement, navigating there without hesitation, suggesting they already knew the layout.

Approximately 24 to 26 minutes after entering, the thieves ascended the main staircase into the museum and began carefully stealing 12 works of art from the Dutch Room and the Short Gallery, trimming several paintings directly from their frames. Among the stolen pieces were Rembrandt's only known seascape, *The Storm on the Sea of Galilee*; his painting *A Lady and Gentleman in Black*; and *The Concert*, one of only 34 known paintings by Johannes Vermeer. *The Storm on the Sea of Galilee* had been hung on a false wall that doubled as a door, but the thieves simply opened it, furthering police suspicions that this was an inside job. They also took a few lesser-valued items and unsuccessfully tried to remove a Napoleonic flag, ultimately taking the gilded eagle statue attached to it instead.

Their total haul was estimated to be worth between $200 million and $600 million at the time. Meanwhile, far more valuable works, such as *The Rape of Europa*, a 16th-century painting by Titian, were left untouched. While most art robberies, and robberies in general, are brief, the Isabella Stewart Gardner Museum heist was a puzzling 81 minutes. The thieves could have stolen more, and better-valued, art, but they didn't. Remember how I mentioned they stole 12 pieces from two rooms? A thirteenth piece, a small Manet called *Chez Tortoni*, was taken from the Blue Room, which the museum's infrared sensors never recorded anyone entering, except Abath, earlier in the night. Like the others, it had been cut from its frame, but its empty frame had been left at the front desk.

That's suspicious. That's weird.

The thieves took the video tapes from the surveillance camera at the entrance and finally left at 2:45 a.m. The guards were found tied up in the basement later that morning. Police developed two overlapping theories: that Ricky Abath was involved, and/or the Irish Mafia had orchestrated the heist. For starters, the faux cops reportedly called the guards "mates" when putting them in the basement, an Irish slang term. Secondly, the fire detector alarms going off earlier in the evening resembled a tactic commonly used by the Irish Provisional Army overseas. Mob boss Whitey Bulger, who had connections within law enforcement and access to police uniforms, also had ties to the IRA. Multiple Boston Mafia leads were pursued.

But no suspects were arrested. The empty frames where the stolen paintings once hung remain on display, a silent reminder of the most infamous unsolved art theft in U.S. history. In 1994, the museum's director received a letter from someone claiming to be a third-party mediator, offering to attempt to return the stolen art. The writer claimed the pieces were being kept safe in a "non-common law country" and advised the museum to print a coded message in *The Boston Globe* if they wanted to proceed. The museum director contacted the Federal Bureau of Investigation, who determined that the writer knew pertinent details only someone close to the case would know. So, *The Boston Globe* printed a coded message on May 1, 1994.

Within days, a second letter arrived at the museum. This time, the writer seemed nervous and backed out of the proposed arrangement. No further letters came. A $10 million reward issued by the museum didn't lead to any results. Fast forward to 2013, long after the statute of limitations had expired. The FBI announced that it believed "the art was transported to Connecticut and the Philadelphia region, and some of the art was taken to Philadelphia, where it was offered for sale..."

In August 2015, the FBI released surveillance footage of a car matching the description of the thieves' vehicle parked outside the museum exactly 24 hours before the robbery. And guess who the driver was speaking to? You guessed it, Ricky Abath. He claimed not to remember the interaction. It was later revealed that the man in the footage was the museum's deputy director of security. Abath died in 2024. Shortly after the footage was released, the FBI announced they believed they knew who the thieves were: two low-level mob associates, both deceased. Their identities weren't revealed, likely in an attempt to preserve leads or negotiations to recover the lost artwork, which has still never resurfaced.

1990: Happy Land Arson

In the early morning hours of March 25 in the Bronx, New York, Happy Land was filled with people. The unlicensed social club had been operating for four years and was a popular spot for the local immigrant community from Honduras and St. Vincent and the Grenadines. In 1988, the club had been ordered to shut down by the fire department for lacking proper exits, sprinklers, and alarms, but that order was never enforced. Meanwhile, by 1990, the leaseholders of the building were planning to evict the club's owner.

On that March morning, a club employee named Lydia Feliciano had an argument with her ex-boyfriend, Julio Gonzalez. A refugee from the Cuban Mariel Boatlift, Gonzalez wanted Lydia to quit her job and leave with him. When she refused, he threatened her and was kicked out by the bouncer around 3AM. As he left, he declared that he'd be back. Lydia tried to warn her co-workers, but no one listened. So, she decided to leave, fearing he might come back and do something violent.

Conflicting reports say she left before Gonzalez returned, while others claim she left just as he arrived. Either way, he went to a nearby gas station, filled plastic bottles with fuel, and returned. He poured the gasoline through the club's only entrance, set it on fire, and walked away. Gonzalez's cruelty, combined with the negligence of the building owner and the city, led to the deaths of 87 people, most from trampling or asphyxiation, on the 79th anniversary of the Triangle Shirtwaist Fire. That 1911 blaze destroyed the top three floors of the building at 23–29 Washington Place, killing 146 workers, mostly immigrant women, who couldn't escape through the locked or burning exits.

At Happy Land, the club's owner was killed alongside 86 employees and patrons, 61% of them men, 26% women. A firefighter later described the scene: "Some looked like they were sleeping. Some looked horrified. Some looked like they were in shock. There were some people holding hands. There were some people who looked like they were trying to commiserate and hug each other. Some people had torn their clothes off in their panic to get out."

This was a massive blow to the local community because it impacted everyone. Nearly everybody in the area knew someone who was directly affected, many of them Black and Brown. In the neighborhood, 90 children were left orphaned, and 40 parents lost sons and daughters. The club owner's wife and four others, including the DJ, managed to survive, though with severe injuries. Gonzalez went home and fell asleep before being arrested in his apartment the next day. He was quickly found guilty of 87 counts of murder and arson, earning a 25-years-to-life sentence, which he served until his death in 2016.

Lydia Feliciano was "confronted" by some of the victims' families, who were angered that she survived. The building owner and landlord, meanwhile, pleaded guilty to building code violations. They paid a fine and completed community service. They were also taken to court by the families, with Robert Lueck reporting in 1995 that "they agreed to a $15.8 million settlement... which provided an average of $163,000 for each family or injured victim... far less than the total of $5 billion that they had originally sought..."

Just as the Triangle Shirtwaist Fire tragedy led to workplace reforms, the Happy Land arson prompted the creation of a task force to regulate social clubs. In the following year, 1,500 venues were inspected, and 320 were shut down permanently for failing to meet code requirements. While the event inspired a 1991 episode of *Law & Order* and was referenced in lyrics by Duran Duran and Jay-Z, this mass casualty event, one involving mostly Black and Brown victims, has largely been overlooked in national retrospectives.

1991: Father's Day Bank Massacre

A little over two weeks before CourtTV hit the airwaves, on Father's Day 1991 in Denver, Colorado, a man claiming to be "Robert Bardwell," attempted to gain entry through a side door of the United Bank Tower at

9:14AM. The problem? Robert Bardwell, the bank's vice president, was on vacation with his family. Puzzlingly, at 4:00 AM earlier that morning, an alarm had gone off in a basement storage room. The on-duty control center guard disabled it and moved on, treating it as a minor disturbance. Until the fake Robert Bardwell appeared at the side door, it had been the only unusual activity of the day.

A guard named William McCullum Jr. met with the impersonator using a service elevator. The man forced McCullum at gunpoint to return to the lower levels of the bank. Due to a policy change the previous year, United Bank Tower guards were no longer authorized to carry firearms. McCullum complied without resistance and was murdered once the gunman made it inside. The shooter then killed three more unarmed guards, using 18 bullets sourced from a variety of manufacturers. He eventually reached a vault, where six employees were counting and storing a deposit. Described as being between 50 and 60 years old, with a bandage on his left cheek, the gunman ordered the vault manager to fill his satchel with cash, approximately $200,000. Although he had access to well over a million dollars, he chose not to take more.

While the four unarmed guards were killed, the six vault employees were spared. One had hidden from view, while the other five were secured in a man trap door as the gunman fled. Investigators theorized that the shooter had run low on ammunition. They believed after eighteen shots that only two bullets remained in the chamber, and he didn't want this to become obvious in front of potential hostages.

After the initial investigation, police focused on 55-year-old James King, a former police officer and bank security guard who had worked at United Bank Tower between 1989 and 1990. Not only was he $25,000 in debt and facing bankruptcy, but the real Robert Bardwell had reported his access card missing the day after King resigned as a bank guard. Additionally, during his time as a Denver police officer, King had been issued a .38 caliber revolver, which held a maximum of 20 bullets. At the police shooting range, there were buckets of mixed-manufacturer rounds, which officers were known to pilfer, further strengthening the connection.

When police asked James King for an alibi, he claimed to have been at a chess match that didn't exist, in a building where no one recalled seeing him. Contradicting this, a neighbor stated she wished him a Happy Father's Day around 9:00 a.m. as he mowed his lawn. All of this raised serious suspicion. During a search of King's home, police found a map of the bank's interior inside a folder labeled "Plans," along with five fake IDs featuring King's face, though the latter would later be suppressed at trial. King told authorities he had disposed of his .38 caliber revolver.

None of the bank employees were able to identify King as the shooter, until a second photo lineup was conducted using altered images. However, these identifications were deemed inadmissible in court. The robbery and murder trial aired nationally on Court TV during the summer of 1992. Despite the suspicious evidence, conflicting statements, and a nonexistent alibi, King was acquitted. The FBI monitored him for years, hoping to trace any of the roughly $200,000 in stolen cash. But King died in 2013, and was never re-charged. The case remains unsolved.

1992: Shanda Sharer

12-year-old Shanda Sharer was born in Kentucky. A child of divorce, her mom Jacqueline Vaught had remarried and moved twice before they settled down in New Albany, Indiana in 1991. At Hazelwood Middle School, she met 15-year-old Amanda Hearvin during a fight, but the two quickly became romantic. Amanda had an ex-girlfriend named Melinda Loveless, who was fifteen when the pair dated two years before. Melinda was furious and jealous.

Melinda's last name was truly apt, as she grew up in a loveless, physically and sexually abusive household under parents Larry and Marjorie. Larry was a Vietnam war veteran who allegedly wore his wife and daughters' underwear and makeup, raped Marjorie, molested his daughters and nieces on several occasions, and forced Marjorie into swinging with other couples. He also had Marjorie gang raped. Marjorie tried killing herself twice. Larry eventually filed for divorce and moved to Florida.

This was the home life of 16-year-old Melinda Loveless, who began hanging out with a 17-year-old lesbian named Laurie Tackett, who grew up in an abusive Pentecostalist household and was rumored to be a devil worshipper. Melinda confronted Shanda in October 1991 and began making public threats to kill her. That same month, Jacqueline found sexual letters from 15-year-old Amanda to her 12-year-old daughter. She transferred Shanda to the private parochial school Our Lady of Perpetual Help. Shanda was banned from seeing Amanda. She got acclimated to her new school, even joining the basketball team. Later witnesses would claim that despite this, Shanda had already begun drinking, smoking "pot", and "having lesbian sex."

On January 10th, 1992, Tackett invited her two friends, 15-year-olds Hope Rippey and Toni Lawerence, to accompany her and Loveless to go 'scare' Shanda. The girls agreed, and were soon told by Tackett and Loveless that they planned to murder Shanda. They piled into Laurie's Chevy and drove to Shanda's father Stephen's house. Hope and Toni tried to lure her outside, saying her forbidden love Amanda wanted to see her. Shanda told them to come back after midnight when her father was asleep, so the girls left, went to a concert, and came back. When Shanda went out to the car, she was surprised by Melinda Loveless, who subdued her. They transported the 12-year-old to a nearby stone structure ruin called The Witches Castle and tied up Shanda with rope before questioning her about her relationship with Amanda and taunting her.

With Shanda in the trunk, they drove around to multiple locations before taking her to an abandoned area to strip her naked, beat her, and kill her, but their attempts to strangle and stab her only left her unconscious. They threw her back in the trunk. When they went to Tackett's house to clean off, they heard her screaming in the car, so Tackett grabbed a kitchen knife, went outside, and stabbed her again. Tackett and Loveless then left the other girls behind to drive around with Shanda, who was still clinging to life. Hearing her struggle to breathe, they pulled over so Laurie could beat her with a tire iron. She also sexually assaulted the girl, who was unbelievably still alive. Later that morning, they burned Shanda alive in a field in Madison and then went out for breakfast at McDonald's, while Shanda's father realized she was missing and informed the police.

All four of the perpetrators told people what they had done, including friends and the aforementioned Amanda Hearvin. Lawrence and Rippey confessed to police by 8 p.m. that evening, and Laurie and Melinda were arrested the next day. In the process of untangling how such a horrific crime came to be perpetrated by four teenage girls, their backgrounds became pertinent. All of them had engaged in self-harm and/or had been sexually abused. Said Jacqueline Vaught later, "These girls were not born murderers. Something made them capable of this."

Locals were disturbed. Reported Bob Lewis for *The Los Angeles Times*, "The case... has unsettled Madison, a picturesque town of antique shops, cozy bed-and-breakfasts and 19th-Century houses nestled along the Ohio River." Richard Grant blamed small town boredom, describing Madison thusly:

> The problem with Madison is the problem with any small town. There is nothing to do. Life is a constant battle against boredom, in which alcohol and cannabis are the

most dependable allies. Otherwise, one can have sex in cars, drive at high speed along the winding country back roads, or, for an added thrill, drive drunk at high speed... The girls make frequent trips to the Louisville shopping malls, for a blissful afternoon of air-conditioned stores and free make-up samples at the beauty counter. Almost without exception, the girls wear heavy make-up, and have permed, teased and frosted hairstyles. Eighty per cent of them are fiercely blonde. They marry young and divorce young. They dream about escaping from Madison, but seldom make it past Louisville...Their horizons extend 80 kilometers south to Louisville, 160 kilometers north to Indianapolis, and 80 kilometers east to Cincinnati, Ohio. Beyond that, the world is televised.

The boring, slow, and traditional pace of Madison made residents indignant about lesbians and rumors of Laurie Tackett being a devil worshipper. That was big city stuff. Said an elderly resident to Richard Grant, "If that poor young girl had been killed in New York, instead of Madison, Indiana, none of you fellows would have batted an eyelid. We've got a nice little town here, and I think it's a shame that it takes something like this to get us noticed."

All four of Shanda's murderers were charged as adults and accepted plea deals. Toni Lawrence got twenty years and was released in 2000. Hope Rippey got thirty-five years and was released in 2006. Laurie got sixty years and was released in 2018. Melinda Loveless was given sixty years too. They were also sued by Shanda's parents to stop them from receiving potential profits from film executives who sniffed around for rights to the story.

When Larry Loveless was exposed during Melinda's trial for his crimes against his wife and daughters, he spent two years awaiting trial for one charge of sexual battery that wasn't protected by the statute of limitations. He was found guilty but released for time served. In 2012 Jacqueline Vaught donated a dog to the imprisoned Melinda Loveless to train for the Indiana program that gives service pets to people with disabilities, saying Shanda would have supported it. Loveless was released from prison in 2019.

1993: Lorena Bobbit

Twenty-three-year-old Marine John Wayne Bobbitt and twenty-year-old Lorena Gallo married in June 1989, after gentle and romantic courting in Manassas, Virginia. Lorena was an Ecuadorian immigrant who had long wanted to move to America and achieve her version of the American dream: marriage. After they tied the knot, the couple moved into a big house, and Lorena alleged the physical, emotional, and financial abuse started. Police responded to multiple domestic violence complaints, and by 1993, John, now working as a bouncer after cycling through roughly a dozen jobs, was taking his wife's earnings as a manicurist. This was especially tough for Lorena, as she depended on him for her citizenship status. On June 23, he came home, raped Lorena, and fell asleep.

Lorena claimed that she had a psychotic break when she went into the kitchen to get a glass of water after the rape. Snatching up an 8-inch carving knife, she went back into the bedroom and sliced off Bobbitt's penis. She fled in her car with no shoes, tossing the penis into a field adjacent to a 7-Eleven. She called police and told them what she had done and where to find the penis. Police were dispatched to locate it so it could be reattached in time. When they found it, no joke, they put it in a hot dog box from 7-Eleven. The surgery to reattach the penis was successful and took nine and a half hours. Lorena was charged with assault, facing twenty years, and John Wayne was charged with marital sexual assault in a case that became a major story.

In 1996, Linda Pershing explored the folklore and commentary that emerged in the months and years following the Bobbitt case making headlines. She documented women dressing as Lorena for Halloween, a short sandwich at a local restaurant christened the Bobbitt, and vendors selling buttons outside of the Manassas courthouse that read "Lorena Bobbitt for Surgeon General." In some Miami coffee shops, patrons asked for "Lorenas," or black coffee with a little milk. Novelty stores offered Bobbitt Penis Protectors for sleeping men. Chain emails joked to recipients: "What did John Bobbitt say when he was propositioned by a hooker? Answer: Sorry, I'm a little short this week."

From the name John Wayne Bobbitt, to the hot dog box, to the fact that Lorena's maiden name was Gallo, which means cock in Spanish, the jokes seemed to write themselves. The fact that witnesses for both John and Lorena affirmed he was physically and financially abusive diminished some of the public sympathy previously given to him.

According to Pershing's analysis, approximately 1,300,000 column inches had been devoted to the Bobbitts. Underneath the torrent of near-constant CourtTV coverage, TV show jokes, stand-up routines, columns, and email jokes were anxieties about the so-called gender wars, feminism, abuse, and marital rape. Women who supported Lorena emphasized that they understood why she did it, citing their own rapes, abuse, and trauma. Interestingly, most of Lorena's strongest supporters were fellow Latinas and, more often than not, working class.

Feminists argued over whether or not Lorena was worthy of support, with middle- and upper-class white women leading the attack on what they considered to be "victim feminism." Argued Susan Estrich, "Lorena Bobbitt is a criminal, not a feminist heroine. Those feminists who have flocked to her defense have done a disservice not only to the cause of feminism, but more important, to the real victims of battered wives' syndrome, the millions of women who are beaten by their husbands and do not respond by assaults on their organs."

The penis had also become a public spectacle, a word in everyday conversation and news broadcasts. The tale was an uneasy revenge story that some men, laden with guilt for whatever reasons, had to contend with. When Lorena Bobbitt was found not guilty of assault by reason of insanity, the verdict pissed off more than a few men. "In the battle of the sexes, this was like stealing the other team's mascot. This is the result of feminists teaching women that men are natural oppressors," said the director of a Brooklyn men's rights group. At the time, marital rape was nearly impossible to prove in Virginia. Crowed shock jock Howard Stern, who held a fundraiser to help pay John Bobbitt's mounting legal bills, "I don't even buy that he was raping her. She's not that great looking."

John, who essentially became a sympathetic hero and joke for men who may have raped or abused before, was acquitted of marital rape. The couple's divorce was finalized in 1995. Lorena reverted to her maiden name of Gallo and continued to live in Manassas, Virginia, despite being a local celebrity and, to some, a boogeyman. She turned down $1 million to pose for *Playboy* and infamously visited Ecuador to a hero's welcome, where she met with President Abdalá Bucaram in October 1996. Together, they baptized a child as someone's godparents. She was later arrested for assaulting her mother in 1997, before being acquitted.

John, meanwhile, went on to make appearances at hot dog eating contests and starred in *John Wayne Bobbitt: Uncut*, which became the best-selling porn release of 1995. He said he wanted to show people his penis still worked. At one hot dog eating contest at The Abbet Road Grill in 1993, reported *The Palm Beach Post*,

> "[Said the announcer]: Ladies and gentlemen, let's have a warm welcome for John Wayne Bobbitt!" The warm welcome is tepid at best. Most diners don't even bother to put down their burgers and look up, and those who do squint wincingly into the blazing TV lights, none with a more pained and awkward expression than John Wayne Bobbitt himself."

Bobbitt's surreal career continued with *Frankenpenis*, and a trail of domestic violence, battery, and theft arrests followed him through the decade and beyond.

1994: The Taco Bell Strangler

This story hits close to home for me. One of the victims attended my high school, my mom knew the murderer, and I've been to nearly every place mentioned at least once growing up.

On April 1, 1990, in Barnwell, South Carolina, the body of Tashanda Bethea, an eighteen-year-old high schooler, was found in a pond. An honorably discharged Navy veteran and crack user named Henry Louis Wallace was questioned and released. Unbeknownst to investigators, who had no immediate access to interstate files, Wallace had already committed robberies and assaults while in the Navy. After being released, he moved to Charlotte, North Carolina in November 1991, where he became the manager of a Taco Bell at 3612 Sharon Amity Rd, near Central Avenue.

In May 1992, a sex worker named Sharon Nance, who was a mother of one and liked to draw and write poetry, was murdered by Wallace near Rozzelles Ferry Road after asking to be paid for her services. The murder slipped under the radar. The next month, at the Darby Terrace Apartments on Central Avenue, Wallace raped and killed his girlfriend's roommate, a twenty-year-old Garinger High School alum and Bojangles employee named Caroline Love. Wallace had tried to kiss Caroline while his girlfriend wasn't home. When she told him she'd keep it a secret if he never did it again, he attacked. He took Caroline's body to his car and dumped it in a wooded area. When his girlfriend went to the police station to file a missing persons report, he went with her and feigned concern. Police had no idea that Caroline had made it home after work, with newspapers noting she walked the six blocks from Bojangles to her apartment shortly after midnight before going missing.

For months, Wallace lay dormant, continuing to run the Taco Bell and also attend kickbacks near Central Avenue, where my own mother and her circle of friends socialized with him over Spades tables, food, and alcohol. People around him didn't know that he was a murderer and rapist, or that he had a crack habit. On February 19 1993, he raped and killed one of his part-time weekend employees, twenty-year-old Central Park Community College student Shawna Hawk, who had just seen her mother earlier that day after attending classes. Their last exchange? "Who loves you, baby?" To which Shawna replied, "You do, Mommy." Shawna was found in the bathtub of their family home, and Wallace later went to her funeral. He hugged her mother, Dee, and told her he was sorry her daughter had been killed.

Wallace waited four months before striking again in June 1993, this time visiting the Glen Hollow Apartments and killing twenty-four-year-old Audrey Spain, another one of his employees at Taco Bell. To put things in perspective, consider that in 1993 there were 132 reported murders and 350 reported rapes in the city of Charlotte alone, making it one of the worst years on record, and the following year it would be christened the eighteenth most violent city in the country. There were just seven investigators tasked with handling all homicides. So they were thin on manpower, money, and time, and they barely interviewed families, not to mention their potential racial bias.

The Charlotte-Mecklenburg Police Department (CMPD) asked the FBI for advice, and the bureau reported back in early 1994 that the killings weren't serial, leaning on the belief that Black people aren't smart enough to be serial killers and noting the lack of a clear "signature" in the murders. But if they had pursued the case diligently, the cops would have noticed the glaring similarities between the murders of Audrey and Shawna. Both crime scenes showed no forced entry, meaning they knew their killer. They were both Black, both robbed of small sums of money, both washed off, and both worked at the same Taco Bell. Even more damning, both were killed by strangulation. Strangulation was rare in Charlotte, with only six such cases in Mecklenburg County in 1993.

Still, Wallace threw curveballs at the investigation. In August 1993, at the Greenbryre Apartments on Sharon Amity Road, he killed Valencia Jumper, a twenty-one-year-old college student who was friends with his sister. She worked at Food Lion and a department store while attending Johnson C. Smith University. Wallace soaked her body in rum and started a fire to throw off police, with the medical examiner erroneously ruling that she died of "thermal burn."

In September 1993, twenty-year-old Michelle Stinson, a regular at Taco Bell and a graphic arts student at Central Piedmont Community College, was his next victim. Her three-year-old son Ernee witnessed the crime. A $1,000 reward was offered by Crime Stoppers USA for information. After mounting public outrage from Central Avenue residents, police increased patrols of the area. Compounded by Wallace becoming a father in December of that year, the murders came to a stop, until February, when Wallace was again in need of cash for his worsening crack habit. He was arrested on February 4 1994 for shoplifting a $48 sweater from Eastland Mall and released the next day.

By this time, Wallace was no longer employed at Taco Bell and had bounced around at various restaurants, including Captain D's. Sixteen days after being released for shoplifting, Wallace went to Wilkinson Road in West Charlotte, outside of his usual zone, raping and killing his former girlfriend's sister, Vanessa Mack. The twenty-four-year-old's four-month-old daughter was in the other room. Vanessa had previously worked with Wallace at Taco Bell. He took her ATM card and demanded her PIN number before killing her. She gave him the incorrect code, which he didn't discover until trying to withdraw cash from it hours later. The day before, Shawna Hawk's mother, Dee Sumpter, had begged the public to pay attention.

On March 8, at The Lake Apartments, Wallace went to his best friend Berness Woods' house with the intention of murdering and robbing his girlfriend, Brandi Henderson. He believed Berness was at work. When Berness opened the door, Wallace made an excuse and left, before deciding to visit the home of Betty Jean Baucom, who lived in the same complex. She worked with his ex-girlfriend at Bojangles, and he demanded that she give him the code to the Bojangles safe, which she insisted she didn't know. He raped her, killed her, and stole a bunch of items from her house, along with her car. He later pawned everything but the vehicle, which would eventually be recovered with his palm print on the trunk.

Nobody knew Betty Jean was dead yet. He returned later that day to the Lake Apartments, after Berness had finally gone to work, and knocked on Brandi's door. He was let inside, where he raped her with her infant son pressed to her chest, and killed her. As the baby wouldn't stop crying, Wallace attempted to strangle him, but he survived. Police did not inform the public that a serial killer was targeting Black women in the Charlotte area until the week of March 9, when the bodies of Betty and Brandi were found. They still had no idea who the murderer was. Police presence was increased in the area, but on March 12, Wallace made his final kill in the same region, at the Glen Hollow Apartments—where Audrey Spain had been murdered—just half a mile from the Lake Apartments.

His last victim was the oldest: Debra Ann Slaughter, a 35-year-old employee at Harris Teeter and another of his ex-girlfriend's co-workers at Bojangles. When Wallace tried to force her to perform oral sex, she told him, "I don't do that. You might as well go ahead and kill me." After a struggle that yielded him $40, he stabbed Debra 38 times and left to buy crack, before returning to smoke it in her bathroom. The next day, Wallace was arrested on an outstanding shoplifting warrant. During interrogation, he confessed to ten murders, including one in South Carolina. Police were shocked. Wallace's friends were shocked. Like my mother, they all looked back on how normal he had seemed.

Reported *The Charlotte Observer*, "To them, Wallace was a well-spoken man who enjoyed playing cards, drinking beer, and listening to rap music. He especially liked rap star Snoop Doggy Dogg." Seven children were left motherless, while Wallace was put on trial and found guilty of the nine Charlotte murders in 1997. He claimed he had been beaten by his mother growing up and had witnessed the gang rape of a teenage girl during adolescence, events that sparked his violent fantasies. He was sentenced to death row, where he remains as of 2025. Said Wallace's mother at the time of his arrest, "You try to raise somebody, do your best, and then something like this happens."

Shawna Hawk's mother, Dee, founded Mothers of Murdered Offspring, which has supported over 3,000 families in grieving the aftermath of murder, including help with funeral planning. In the wake of the murders, the group asked the Charlotte City Council to investigate the police. The council requested an official report on the murder investigation from CMPD, but it was never followed up on. "The victims weren't prominent people with socio-economic status. They weren't special. And they were Black," Dee told *The Charlotte Observer*.

In March 1994, a photo of a whiteboard behind investigators showed that they had categorized Sharon Nance, a sex worker who was beaten, not strangled, as a domestic violence case. Shawna Hawk, who was strangled and found by her boyfriend, Darryl, was also viewed as a potential domestic violence victim. Police had little to go on regarding Caroline Love, who remained missing until Wallace revealed her location. Valencia Jumper's death was ruled accidental due to the fire, and Michelle Stinson's white boyfriend, along with the survival and presence of her children at the crime scene, complicated the investigation.

Vanessa Mack's ex-boyfriend, whose fingerprints were found at the scene, also became a suspect. He failed two polygraphs, which further intensified suspicion. The lack of a consistent modus operandi across cases ultimately derailed the investigation. While former CMPD homicide detective Garry McFadden acknowledged that race played a role in the investigation, other officers denied it, citing the city's high murder rate, the ongoing crack epidemic, and limited resources, factors that, they argued, drove support for

1994's Crime Bill, not only among Charlotte's voters but nationwide.

Analyses of CMPD data showed that between 1992 and 1994, there were 237 Black homicide victims and 60 white victims. The clearance rates were nearly identical, 84.8% for Black victims and 84% for white victims, suggesting that Black murder cases were being solved. However, this was CMPD's first investigation involving a Black serial killer, an idea that, at the time, was considered novel.

The FBI later stated that Wallace didn't fit the "right" profile of a serial killer because he targeted friends and co-workers rather than strangers. The lack of research and awareness around Black serial killers continued to cost lives. For example, by 1993, the prolific and sadistic Samuel Little was already dozens of murders into his killing spree and would remain at large for nearly two more decades. Since his imprisonment, Henry Louis Wallace has confessed to additional murders of Black women that have yet to be confirmed.

1994: The Assault of Nancy Kerrigan

Tonya Harding grew up poor near Portland, Oregon. In addition to hunting and other outdoor activities, she trained as an ice skater throughout her youth while managing asthma. Her mother, who was abusive, spent most of her wages on the competitive skating circuit, which was dominated by the predominantly middle-to-upper class. After years of disappointing scores, Harding had a breakthrough in February 1991 at age twenty during the U.S. Championships, when she landed the near-impossible triple axel. The move was so difficult that she became the first American woman, and only the second woman in the world, to land it in competition.

At the World Championships the following month, she landed another triple axel and won silver, finishing second to Kristi Yamaguchi. Twenty-one-year-old Nancy Kerrigan, from Massachusetts, placed third, making it a full American sweep. Though Kerrigan came from a similarly working-class background, she embodied the refined, WASP-y image favored by the figure skating world. While this would be Tonya's last successful triple axel in Olympics competition, and she would never again match those scores, she was, for the time being, shaking up the sport with her rough edges and homemade costumes. She attracted a fan base.

In her personal life, Tonya was married to an abusive man named Jeff Gillooly, whom she had been dating since 1986 and living with on and off since 1988. He helped pay for her skating expenses. Tonya's career was lackluster in 1992, the same year she was involved in a road rage incident, during which she allegedly threatened someone with a bat. According to police and media, it was a baseball bat; according to Tonya, it was a wiffle bat. Commentators noted that she was out of shape and no longer performing the triple axel. Her coach explained to the *Chicago Tribune,* "A lot of the behavior she had and statements she made were because she thought her privacy was invaded." The writer added, "That may no longer be a problem... the way she is skating..."

In 1993, Tonya began to train more seriously. She still had support. Tonya Fever had swept Oregon, and a fan club was established in her honor. Susan Orlean described the group as "suggesting additional opportunities to support Tonya... fundraising... giving her cosmetics, hair care, and nail care... making calls about her to sports talk programs, or... mailing her encouraging cards." Tonya's main rival for the upcoming January 1994 nationals was Nancy Kerrigan, the reigning 1993 champion. Tonya hoped to channel her energy into unseating Nancy, but her personal life continued to unravel.

She and Jeff planned to divorce a second time, though they'd be back together by October. That same month, it was reported that Tonya allegedly fired a gun during a domestic dispute. In November, Tonya received a threatening phone call that caused her to withdraw from a competition. Jeff Gillooly's friend, Shawn Eckardt, a braggadocios compulsive liar, became her bodyguard and would later claim that Tonya hired him to make the threat herself.

On January 6, 1994, Nancy Kerrigan was practicing at the Detroit Cobo Arena when an assailant named Shane Stant, who had followed her from Cape Cod to Detroit, struck her leg with a 21-inch baton. A cameraman filmed Nancy crying out in pain, sobbing "Why?" Stant fled toward a set of locked doors, threw himself headfirst through a sheet of plexiglass, and jumped into a getaway car driven by his uncle, Derrick Smith. Nancy's leg was bruised, forcing her to withdraw from the upcoming competition. Immediate suspicion fell on Tonya Harding, who won the U.S. Championship title on January 8, securing her spot on the 1994 Olympic team. On January 10, when asked if someone she knew had planned the attack, Tonya replied, "I have definitely thought about it."

The incident became an immediate media sensation, with figure skating thrust into the national spotlight. Reporters descended on sleepy Portland,

and thousands came to watch Tonya practice at her usual ice rink in Clackamas Town Center. Reported *The Washington Post*, "This quaint, mellow city of parks, coffee houses and microbreweries sitting in the shadow of Mt. Hood has largely been divided between Harding supporters and detractors. But a new, bigger group has emerged: those who are sick and tired of this sensational soap opera."

Some locals welcomed the economic boost. Added *The New York Times*, "One eatery... hung a 28-square-foot sign outside its doors that reads 'Lila's Tonya Special: A Club Sandwich and Chicken Soup.'" Many were inspired to join the Tonya Harding Fan Club and support the working-class Harding for $10. One member told Susan Orlean after the scandal, "Scum. That's what they call us. It's a class difference, that's what all this mess is about, Tonya. She's just a regular Clackamas County girl. In my opinion, she's a modern gal, what we would call a tomboy. She can hunt, she can fix a car. She calls herself the Charles Barkley of figure skating, and she's right. She's a stud."

Orlean wrote, "The Tonya Harding Fan Club, which was started a year ago, has seen its ranks almost double to around 800 members from 32 states and seven countries, including Australia and South Africa." While Tonya publicly denied knowing anything, Shawn Eckardt bragged to nearly everyone that he had orchestrated the attack on Nancy, and even his own father joined in the boasting. Eckardt, Shane Stant, and Derrick Smith were arrested by January 13, thanks to their lack of discretion and a series of foolish mistakes. The men implicated Tonya, claiming she had been involved in the plan.

Tonya again denied any prior knowledge through her lawyer three days later. On January 18, she told the FBI in a ten-and-a-half-hour interview that she only learned of the plan after January 11. Jeff Gillooly began cooperating with the FBI on January 26, telling agents that he and Tonya discussed mailing threatening letters to Kerrigan. He also claimed she seemed interested in a plan to physically harm Nancy.

The next day, Tonya announced at a press conference that she had learned Jeff plotted to harm Nancy. On February 1, the day after Nike pledged $25,000 to sponsor Harding in the Olympics, the owner of a Portland restaurant called the Dockside Saloon discovered discarded garbage in her private trash cans. Searching through it out of spite so she could send the garbage back to the owner, she found a check stub made out to Tonya and a piece of paper in Tonya's handwriting detailing Nancy Kerrigan's practice venue in Detroit and her training schedule. The handwriting was later matched to Tonya's after the restaurant owner, Peterson, contacted the FBI.

Jeff Gillooly secured a plea deal to serve two years in exchange for testifying against the others. Shawn Eckardt pleaded guilty to racketeering and received 18 months but was released 109 days early. Shane Stant and Derrick Smith pleaded guilty to conspiracy to commit assault and each received 18-month sentences, Stant served only 14.

On February 5, the U.S. Figure Skating Association gave Tonya 30 days to respond to allegations of misconduct, while the U.S. Olympic Committee prepared to remove her from the team and replace her with Michelle Kwan for the 1994 Winter Olympics in Norway later that month. Tonya filed a lawsuit on February 10, but two days later, she was officially allowed to skate. Michelle Kwan was sidelined, for now, but she would bounce back by the end of the decade to become one of the most iconic names in figure skating, if not the most iconic. The Olympics leaned into the Harding vs. Kerrigan drama, and the world watched eagerly to see them face off. The event's ratings surpassed the Super Bowl, becoming the third most-watched televised event in history at the time.

On February 25, Kerrigan earned the silver medal. Tonya, after breaking a bootlace and pleading to restart her lackluster performance, ultimately finished in eighth place. The next month, Tonya pled guilty to conspiracy to hinder prosecution, admitting that she had learned about the attack after it was committed and helped Shawn and Jeff come up with a cover story on January 10. She received three years of probation, a $100,000 fine, fifty hours of community service, and a lifetime ban from the U.S. Figure Skating Association. She was also stripped of the U.S. Championship title she had won that January. Jeff Gillooly, whose name, and mustache, had become a national punchline, leaked photos from their wedding night sex tape to *Penthouse* Magazine and *Hard Copy* in August. Tonya received a cut of the profits when *Penthouse* sold the tape. By October, the remaining loyalists in her fan club disbanded.

The case became a defining piece of cultural lore in the 1990s, touching on class, gender, and media spectacle. Tonya came to represent the "white trash" stereotype that the national media increasingly obsessed over, and if not for her ability to land the triple axel, she likely would have remained shut out from the skating world altogether. Mused Jill Smolowe for *Time*,

> "Tonya Harding is not, nor has she ever been, like most skaters. She is neither politic nor polished, sociable nor sophisticated. Instead, she is the bead of raw sweat in a field of dainty perspirers; the asthmatic who heaves uncontrollably while others pant

prettily; the pool-playing, drag-racing, trash-talking bad girl of a sport that thrives on illusion and Nationalism, Whiteness and Tonya Harding politesse. When rivals fairly float through their programs, she's the skater who best bullies gravity. She fights it off like a mugger; stroking the ice hard, pushing it away the same way she brushes off fans who pester her for autographs."

Tonya's anger issues and involvement in the attack swept her into a pop culture category alongside other infamous women of the decade. One 1994 chain email joked: "I dreamt that I went to bed with Hillary Clinton, Lorena Bobbitt, and Tonya Harding. When I woke up this morning, my knee was killing me, my manhood was gone, and I didn't have any health insurance." As the nonstop coverage and punchlines faded, Tonya sporadically popped up to capitalize on her celebrity by taking on odd jobs, including being hired as a skater at hockey games, where she was often booed. She performed well in the ESPN Professional Skating Championships in 1999, but her skating career never rebounded. Eventually, she transitioned into boxing, even fighting Paula Jones in 2002. Tonya won by technical knockout when Paula quit.

Nancy Kerrigan briefly continued her skating career. While she received widespread sympathy from the public and media leading up to and during the Winter Olympics, the tone shifted afterward. When Nancy was overheard saying, "This is so dumb. I hate this," during a visit to Disney World, a comment taken out of context, she was labeled as ungrateful and bitchy. Remarked Ira Berkow for *The New York Times*, "So now you hear how people have gotten nauseous from Kerrigan's smile, 'too many teeth', and her girlish voice, which they perceive as masking something darker within her heart."

1995: Freddy's Fashion Mart

In 1995, the United House of Prayer owned a building in Harlem on West 125th Street. The church asked one of its tenants, an Orthodox Jewish man named Fred Harari, who owned Freddy's Fashion Mart, to evict his subtenant, a record store owned by a South African man named Sikhulu Shenge. Neither Shenge nor local Black residents responded well to the eviction, and Al Sharpton led protests outside of Freddy's Fashion Mart for weeks. The core issue was the growing presence of non-Black businesses in predominantly Black Harlem, along with continued chafing between the Black and Jewish community.

Protesters were joined by the 125th Street Vendors Association, which was actively boycotting white and Asian businesses after being banned from selling merchandise on street tabletops. One of the protesting street vendors was a 49-year-old Black nationalist and separatist named Roland James Smith. Back in 1967, Smith had rebuffed the Vietnam draft, declaring he had no obligation to serve in "the armed forces of the enslavers of my forebears." He served two years for draft evasion and later made a living in Florida, where he published a newsletter and led a small political circle in Tampa. After being sentenced to community service for allegedly assaulting police officers, he moved to Harlem in 1991. There, he and his sister sold Afrocentric jewelry and books on 125th Street. After the city restricted and shut down street vendors under Giuliani, Smith became increasingly paranoid and conspiratorial.

By December 7, Fred Harari was ready to close his store under the pressure of the boycott. Signs in the store read: "That's It. We've Had It. Freddy's 125th Street Location Only. Wall To Wall Liquidation." On December 8, Roland entered Freddy's Fashion Mart and ordered the Black shoppers to leave before setting the store on fire. He shot four hostages who tried to escape and then killed himself. Including Roland, nine people died in the incident, most of them Latino. The store's sprinkler system, in violation of safety codes, had been turned off. Eight days after the tragedy, Mayor Rudolph Giuliani arrived in Harlem with a camera crew, urging residents to shop for the holiday season. This under-remembered event underscored the ongoing racial tensions in New York, fueled by inequality, economic displacement, and untreated mental illness.

1995: Tracie McBride

On February 16, 1995, Louis Jones Jr., a Grenada and Gulf War Army veteran, wasn't feeling well. That day, he kidnapped and sexually assaulted his ex-wife. She later told police that since returning from the Gulf, he had "lost his humor, suffered daily headaches, and drank too much." He had also begun hitting her. Counseling services on the Army base hadn't helped, and the two had divorced prior to the February assault. She said he seemed to be spinning out of control. Two days later, Jones drove onto Goodfellow Air Force Base in San Angelo, Texas, again looking for his ex-wife. Instead, he encountered 19-year-old Private Tracie McBride, an aspiring music teacher who had left Minnesota to join the Army and pay for college. Jones kidnapped her from the base, took her to his home, raped her, and took forensic precautions to conceal the assault. He then drove her to a remote location and beat her to death.

For two weeks, authorities searched for signs of her. On March 1, Jones's ex-wife reported his assault to the police, and he was arrested. During interrogation, he confessed to killing McBride, though he initially denied raping her, only admitting to it after the autopsy confirmed the assault. Because McBride had been kidnapped from a military base, Jones was charged federally and faced the death penalty. His attorneys argued that he suffered from Gulf War Syndrome, a mysterious illness affecting a significant number of Gulf War veterans. Symptoms included "severe fatigue, chronic headaches, spasms, convulsions, and nausea."

Prosecutors and critics rejected the Gulf War Syndrome defense, pointing to Jones's calculated efforts to conceal his crime, such as making Tracie McBride wash herself and walk on towels when leaving, to avoid picking up fibers from his home. If he were truly out of his mind, they argued, why would he go to such lengths to hide evidence? Jones was found guilty in October 1995 and sentenced to death. The very next year, the Pentagon acknowledged that sarin gas had been released when the U.S. destroyed Iraqi weapons stockpiles. Initial estimates suggested that 5,000 soldiers had been exposed, but the number continued to grow, with Jones among them. As *The Washington Post* reported, "The Pentagon twice informed [Jones], while he already was in prison, that he was among about 130,000 soldiers who apparently were exposed to low levels of nerve gas from a weapons depot destroyed during the war."

Sarin became a global topic of concern due to the Aum Shinrikyo subway attack in Japan in 1995. Jones's attorneys filed multiple appeals to stop his execution up until 2001, citing the new evidence. They also ordered a blood test, which revealed that Jones lacked a common enzyme that would have helped his body metabolize nerve gas. But Jones was never likely to receive clemency, especially considering that the president in 2001 was George W. Bush, who had overseen more executions than any other Texas governor. At the time, public support for the death penalty hovered around 80%, and debate around its use was ongoing. On March 18 2003, Jones became the third person executed by the federal government since the reinstatement of the federal death penalty in 1988.

1996: Maria Farmer and Jeffrey Epstein

In 1991, Jeffrey Epstein was granted full power of attorney over billionaire Leslie Wexner's affairs. Wexner, CEO of L Brands, which included The Limited and Victoria's Secret, was also a major donor to The Ohio State University. By 1995, Epstein was directing multiple Wexner businesses and regularly attending Victoria's Secret fashion shows. He was in the orbit of many prominent celebrities, business leaders, and politicians. That same year, a 24-year-old artist named Maria Farmer was introduced to Epstein and his companion, Ghislaine Maxwell, by Eileen Guggenheim, Dean of the New York Academy of Art.

Ghislaine was the wealthy daughter of British-Israeli media publisher and fraudster Robert Maxwell. When her father turned up dead (possibly murdered) in 1991, his funeral in Jerusalem was attended by top Israeli figures, including the Prime Minister and President. Ghislaine received a hefty yearly pension from his estate and embarked on a socialite existence in New York with Epstein. By 1992, she was his main confidante and responsible for managing his staff.

Maria Farmer, who painted nudes and figurative pieces exploring girlhood and body acceptance, didn't think much of the encounter at the time, but Epstein expressed interest in buying her work. It marked the beginning of a series of encounters with the multi-millionaire. Epstein invited her and three other artists to a post-graduate, all-expenses-paid workshop in Santa Fe, New Mexico, for a commission job that ultimately did not exist. He later hired her as an "art advisor" and something akin to a secretary, during which time she witnessed young girls coming and going from his properties at all hours.

By 1996, Epstein had slashed his federal income taxes by 90% by basing his firm in the tax shelters of the U.S. Virgin Islands. That year, Maria was commissioned to paint two pieces for the film *As Good As It Gets*. To complete the work, Epstein invited her to use Wexner's guest home in New Albany, Ohio. When Maria arrived in May, she encountered armed security and was informed that she could not leave the property without permission from Abigail Wexner, Leslie's wife.

While confined to the home for twelve hours, Maria was sexually assaulted by Maxwell and Epstein. Unbeknownst to her, her younger sister Annie, also an artist, had been assaulted by the same pair in a similar setup the previous month in New Mexico. Maria managed to call her art teacher and her father, the latter of whom drove from Kentucky to retrieve her. On August 26, 1996, Maria reported Epstein, Maxwell, and others to the New York Police Department, but neither they nor the FBI acted. The only notation made concerned "artwork theft" by Maxwell and Epstein.

In 2003, while journalist Vicky Ward wrote a profile of Epstein for *Vanity Fair*, she made some troubling discoveries. Not only did numerous sources reference underage girls, but Maria and Annie Farmer came forward to share their experiences. Ward, who was pregnant at the time, later claimed that Epstein threatened her. Editor-in-Chief Graydon Carter killed the allegations from the final story, which included Epstein calling Ghislaine his "best friend." Epstein and Maxwell's tangled web of abuse and privilege only continued to grow more brazen and unchecked.

1996: Jon Benet Ramsey

JonBenét Ramsey was born in 1990 in Atlanta to businessman John Ramsey and his wife Patsy, a former West Virginia pageant queen. The family, including their son Burke, moved to Boulder, Colorado in 1991, where JonBenét began competing in beauty pageants. The Ramseys were experiencing personal hardships: John's daughter from a previous marriage died in 1992, and Patsy was diagnosed with ovarian cancer the following year.

On Christmas Day, 1996, the family hosted their annual Christmas party. Apart from a brief 911 call made at 6:48 p.m., which was later dismissed as accidental, nothing appeared out of the ordinary. The next morning, shortly after 5 a.m., only the immediate family was in the house: John, Patsy, JonBenét, and 9-year-old Burke. According to Patsy, she discovered a long, handwritten ransom note on the stairs, stating that JonBenét had been kidnapped and demanding $118,000, the exact amount of John's Christmas bonus from work. Despite the note's instructions not to contact authorities, Patsy called police at 5:52 a.m.

Officers arrived within 3 to 7 minutes and began searching the house for signs of forced entry or possible escape routes. The only room that was sealed off as a potential crime scene was JonBenét's bedroom, where her bed showed signs that she had urinated. One of the responding officers did not open the wine cellar in the basement, believing it irrelevant because the door locked from the outside and he was focused on identifying potential exit routes.

For hours, the Ramseys and police didn't check the wine cellar— but to be fair, the home was massive. It was a 7,571-square-foot Tudor-style five-bedroom house built in 1927. Multiple friends and family members had entered the residence to comfort the Ramseys, contaminating everything they touched. At 1 PM, John and his friend Fleet White searched the home for inconsistencies. They opened the door to the wine cellar and found JonBenét's corpse. Duct tape was on her mouth, and a broken paintbrush from Patsy's art supplies and a nylon cord had been used as a garrote. John picked up her body and took it upstairs, where she was then moved again, meaning her body was contaminated twice and the crime scene disturbed. Fleet White would come to be suspicious of his friend after they found JonBenét in the basement.

An autopsy found pineapple in JonBenét's stomach, and a bowl had been photographed by forensic investigators in the kitchen, but neither parent remembered feeding her pineapple. Burke's fingerprints were found on the bowl, but the Ramseys insisted Burke was asleep throughout the night and wasn't woken up until after police arrived. Investigators and the American public wondered if there was an intruder, thanks to evidence like an unidentified boot mark in the basement and unidentified DNA found on JonBenét's underwear and stockings. Plus, two windows had been left slightly open for Christmas lights to pass through, there was a broken basement window, and an unlocked door. Police said there were undisrupted cobwebs on potential entryways, but it only takes 30–60 minutes for a spider to spin a web.

Within a two-mile radius of the Ramsey home, there were 88 registered sex offenders, and there had been 100 burglaries in the neighborhood in the previous months. Because JonBenét competed in kiddie pageants, *People* magazine accused her parents of dressing her like a "French courtesan." *People* also zeroed in on the men who engaged in the pageant circuit, like a 46-year-old photographer named Randy Simmons, who blurted, "I didn't kill JonBenét," when approached by police. Police gathered a list of suspects and people of interest that totaled over 1,600 by 1997. The local cops weren't used to too many murders, let alone complicated ones. JonBenét's murder was the sole homicide in Boulder in 1996.

Most of the public seemed to believe the Ramseys, either Patsy or Burke, killed JonBenét accidentally or on purpose and then covered it up. JonBenét had been to the doctor 27 times for urinary tract infections in the last three years of her life, with her pediatrician citing bubble bath as the culprit. Whoever wrote the really long ransom letter had used multiple movie references and the family's own office supplies, even writing a second version while on the scene.

There were eventually over 2,000 webpages dedicated to the case, with uninvolved, self-styled experts like Susan Bennett given unprecedented media coverage to discuss the case. These internet sleuths posed all kinds of theories, and it's unsurprising that the Ramseys closed ranks and refused to talk to the police without their defense team present. Their wealth and privilege allowed them a gigantic buffer that the average parent doesn't have. The Ramseys moved back to Atlanta and offered a $100,000 reward on April 27, 1997. Said Patsy as cameras snapped away, "We feel like there are at least two people on the face of this earth that know who did this. And that is the killer and someone that that person may have confided in." Knowing the rumors being whispered about them, Patsy added, "...Let me assure you that I did not kill JonBenét. I did not have anything to do with it. I loved that child with the whole of my heart and soul."

The appearance didn't do the couple any favors, with observers noting the pointed language of "I did not have anything to do with it" and "that child." Wrote James Brookes, "The Ramseys have consistently maintained their innocence. But for four months after the murder, they declined to talk to the police. Instead, they mounted a defense team that sounds like a defense lawyer's Christmas carol: eight lawyers, four publicists, three private investigators, two handwriting analysts and one retired F.B.I. profiler." The Ramseys were torpedoed by the press, even though six handwriting experts couldn't find a match between the Ramseys and the note.

The story was pure media fodder. In October 1999, Governor Bill Owens told the Ramseys to "quit hiding" and move back to Colorado to help find their daughter's killer. Police announced the Ramseys were under an umbrella of suspicion, but the Ramseys maintained their innocence. The Ramseys faced a possible grand jury indictment for putting JonBenét at risk and obstructing a crime scene. Ultimately, they were never charged. Nobody ever faced justice for JonBenét's murder, despite 30,000 pieces of evidence introduced to a grand jury to support both the intruder or parent theory. The jury was dismissed in 1999.

Patsy Ramsey died in 2006. Other suspects would arouse interest and be dropped, like the notorious John Mark Carr, a pedophile and former teacher who falsely confessed and later became Alexis Reich. The false confession brought renewed attention to the case in 2006.

1997: Sherrice Iverson

On May 25 1997 in Primm, Nevada, 7-year-old Sherrice Iverson was left in the care of her 14-year-old brother while their father drank and gambled at Primadonna Resort & Casino. At approximately 3AM, while her brother played video games in an arcade, she was spotted in the casino alone by 18-year-old Jeremy Strohmeyer, who was on vacation with his 17-year-old best friend David Cash and his father.

Strohmeyer followed Sherrice into the women's restroom, where Cash witnessed Strohmeyer dragging Sherrice into a stall. He exited. In the twenty minutes that Cash could have went to flag down help, Strohmeyer sexually assaulted Sherrice and strangled her. He told Cash, who did nothing. The teenagers went out to other casinos for the next few hours before going home to California. Three days after the murder, Strohmeyer was arrested because he had been caught on the casino cameras.

Strohmeyer immediately confessed and was sentenced to life in prison the following year after pleading guilty to avoid a trial. Reported *The Washington Post*, "The prosecution contended Strohmeyer is a killer who hoarded pornography and admitted fantasizing about sex with young girls. Strohmeyer's defense, on the other hand, had portrayed the former high school honor student as a troubled youth whose father is in prison and whose biological mother is in a mental hospital..."

The public, and Sherrice's mother Yolonda Manuel (who lived in California), were outraged to find out that David Cash witnessed the crime and did nothing. Because Nevada did not have a law requiring people witnessing a crime to do something or call law enforcement, he got off without punishment. People demanded a new law. Reported Don Terry, "The uphill campaign has attracted a coalition of supporters rare in this era of polarization: blacks, whites, Jews, Christians, Muslims, radio talk-show hosts, conservatives and liberals." Said Yolanda, "This ain't a race issue. This ain't a political issue. It's a human being issue. It's a justice issue for a little girl who will never be able to reach for her goals. My baby won't ever get to go to college."

In 1998, when Strohmeyer was about to go on trial and Cash was a sophomore at University of California Berkeley studying nuclear engineering, several students protested in an effort to get him expelled. Two former friends came forward alleging that Cash witnessed the sexual assault, not just the kidnapping. Cash was brutally cold in interviews, saying to the *Long Beach Press-Telegram*, "I'm no idiot. I'll get my money out of this." When asked if he felt empathy for Sherrice, he said to *The Los Angeles Times*, "I'm not going to get upset over somebody else's life. I just worry about myself first. I'm not going to lose sleep over somebody else's problems." A year before the Columbine massacre, he represented the apathetic, dangerous, and privileged white sociopath. Described Stephanie Salter,

"He says he feels sorrier for Strohmeyer than for the murdered child - after all, he didn't know her. He once said his newfound notoriety makes it easier to "score with women." He says he just wants to get on with his life, majoring in, of all things, nuclear engineering. He says if he had it to do over again, he'd make the same choices. Each time Cash turns his pale, unexceptional face to the world and does not say, "I'm sorry, I did a horrible thing," the easier he is to hate, the more we want to wash our hands of him. Clearly, this boy-man is not lying or in denial; he does not believe he did wrong."

A writer and spokesman for the Sherrice Iverson Memorial Bill in California named Earl Ofari Hutchison said, "We can't deny that race has a role in this case. But the mother doesn't want to bring it in. And that makes sense. After O. J., as soon as you mention race, you've polarized, you've drawn a line in the sand." In the end, everyone failed Sherrice, including her father, the casino, and Cash. Both California and Nevada passed Good Samaritan legislation making it a crime to not report crimes to the police.

1997: Mary Kay Letourneau

Mary Schmitz was born in 1962 to a strict Republican and Catholic family in California. Her father John G, Schmitz was a U.S. House Representative and ardent racist. Mary was the fourth of seven children, and her childhood was rather unhappy. Her three-year-old brother drowned in the family pool when she was 11. Her father's political reputation was destroyed when it became public knowledge that he had two secret children with a former student. He refused to give the mother any money and never had anything to do with the children.

These troubled beginnings were what people pointed to years later when she began sexually assaulting her 12-year-old student, a Samoan-American boy named Vili Fualaau in the summer of nineties. She met him when he was 7-years-old. At the time, Mary Kay was married with four children to Steve Letourneau. On June 18 1996, she was found by police in a parked car with Vili. She was seen getting into the front seat, and lied to police about his age. The two were brought to the police station where Vili's mom was phoned. Without mentioning that Mary Kay lied about Vili's age, police asked his mom what they should do. She told them to release her son into Mary Kay's custody, which they did.

The sexual assaults continued, and Mary Kay ended up pregnant. A relative of Mary Kay's husband alerted the police in early 1997. She was arrested on March 4th and after being charged, pled guilty to second degree child rape. She gave birth on May 29th to a daughter while waiting to be sentenced. She faced six years but only received a three month suspended sentence and three years of sex offender treatment. She was ordered to not contact any children, including hers or the victim. She was released from jail in January 1998, and two weeks later was found by police with Vili in her car, along with $6,200 in cash, baby clothes, and Letourneau's passport. Her plea agreement was violated and she received 7 1/2 years in prison.

Unfortunately, sexual encounters with Vili from February led to another pregnancy, and Mary Kay gave birth to another daughter in October 1998. Vili and his mother took care of the girls while Mary Kay served her prison sentence, and was profiled and softened by the media. Her supporters chalked up her behavior to manic depression, and her psychiatrist said she returned to her senses when on meds. I wonder if she was on her meds when she co-wrote a book with Fualaau called *Once Crime, Love*, which was only published in France. Her supporters were noted by her lawyer as lobbying political figures on her behalf and encouraging her to move to a country where she could legally marry Vili.

In mainstream press her repeated rapes of the adolescent were turned into "trysts" and "forbidden romance," indulging the woman's absurd justifications for her actions. People referred to her victim as her "young lover." Vili became addicted to alcohol and struggled in school to the point of dropping out. He also attempted to kill himself. Letourneau was released from prison in 2004, prompting Vili to petition the court to remove a restraining order placed on her as part of her punishment. The two got married the next year, and it was covered relentlessly by *Entertainment Tonight* and other tabloids. The couple legally separated in 2019, and Vili was at Mary Kay's bedside when she died in 2020.

1998: Thurston High School

On May 20 1998, nearly a year before the Columbine tragedy, 15-year-old Kipland Kinkel was suspended from Thurston High School in Springfield, Oregon, for being in possession of a stolen gun. He was then arrested and released that same day into the custody of his father. His father, William, had indulged his early fascination with guns, gifting Kipland his first one at 12, the same age he first started hearing voices in his head. William later bought Kipland a semi-automatic gun when they realized bullets were cheaper.

In addition to his obsession with guns and the 1996 film *Romeo + Juliet*, the contemporary and beautiful version of the Shakespeare classic, featuring guns and starring Leonardo DiCaprio, Claire Danes, and Harold Perrineau in one of his best performances, Kipland had been struggling with his mental health. Kipland claimed the therapist his parents took him to had suggested his interest in guns be nurtured with father-son target practice.

Kipland murdered his father three hours after being picked up from the police station, shooting him in the back of the head. He then waited for his mother to come home 3½ hours later. He murdered her too, then listened to an aria from *Romeo + Juliet* on repeat until the next morning. Kipland then drove his mother's car to Thurston High School, carrying three guns and two knives under a trench coat. He shot two students before entering the cafeteria and unloading a total of 51 rounds from his semi-automatic at the 300 people assembled inside.

One of the people he hit was 17-year-old Jacob Ryker, who pushed his girlfriend to safety and absorbed a bullet. When Kipland ran out of ammo and started to reload, Jacob, a member of the wrestling team, tackled him with several other boys. In the process, Jacob was shot again as other members of the crowd helped subdue Kinkel, who begged anyone to kill him. Kipland tried to attack an approaching school safety officer with one of his knives in anticipation of being shot, but was pepper-sprayed.

When the attack was over, two students, Mikael Nickolason and Benjamin Walker, were dead. Dozens were injured, including Jacob and future astrophysicist Anthony Case, who later helped develop a space probe that traveled close to the sun. Anthony had expected to go to college and play baseball, but the shooting weakened his athleticism, so he turned to science.

The violent school shooting stunned pre-Columbine America. There had been three school shootings between 1997 and 1998, but this case resulted in multiple murders and involved semi-automatic weapons. Unlike many future school shooters, Kinkel did not kill himself. Later, while stable on medication, he admitted he was too afraid to die after killing his parents and wanted others to do it for him. Though the shooting occurred on a Thursday and shocked the country, the school reopened by Tuesday.

In Oregon, a 1994 measure imposed mandatory sentences for certain crimes and removed a judge's ability to consider mitigating circumstances that might prevent a minor from being sent to adult court. Regardless of a child's history, Oregon pursued harsh sentences for sixteen specific crimes committed by youth. Wrote Merritt, Fain, and Turner: "Sentences range from 70 months for second-degree assault, kidnapping, robbery, and certain sex offenses, to 300 months for murder." Kipland had been diagnosed with schizophrenia but had been on and off his medication in the months leading up to his trial so that the defense could pursue an insanity plea. However, Kipland chose to avoid trial and pled guilty to murder and attempted murder charges.

In the end, Kipland was sentenced to 112 years, a decision that was controversial for some. Begged one of Kip's lawyers, Mark Sabitt, "I would submit to you that in a civilized society, we don't lock away our 15-year-old offenders without hope. Children are and should be judged by different standards from those imposed upon adults. To say that a 15-year-old offender should spend 200 years in prison is draconian." Kinkel is still serving his sentence and is a certified yoga instructor and mental health advocate. Jacob Ryker, meanwhile, was championed as a hero. He married the girlfriend he saved and became a Marine.

1999: Barry Winchell

Twenty-one-year-old Barry Winchell was a Missouri man serving in the Army at Fort Campbell, Kentucky. Sometime in 1999, he was invited by his colleagues, including a 25-year-old named Justin Fisher, to The Connection in nearby Nashville, billed as "the largest gay bar in America." Fisher was particularly fascinated by the trans performers and urged Winchell to come along. While there, Winchell met a 29-year-old trans performer named Calpernia Addams. Like Winchell, she had also served in the military as a member of the Navy. They began dating and fell in love.

For months, as their relationship grew, Winchell was harassed by his fellow soldiers for being "gay", particularly by 18-year-old Calvin Neal Glover and the same guy who had invited him to the club, Justin Fisher. It was rumored that Fisher had a crush on Calpernia and was jealous of Barry. Fisher even went to his superiors and claimed he knew a gay private in the military, in flagrant disregard of Don't Ask, Don't Tell, but wouldn't give a name. The harassment continued, with the *Associated Press* reporting that for the last few months of his life, Winchell was called a slur daily.

On Fourth of July weekend 1999, the harassment reached a boiling point. Winchell fought Glover, the main instigator, and won. Fisher then accused Glover of being a slur as Winchell left to get some sleep. In the early hours of July 5, Glover beat Winchell nearly to death with a baseball bat as he slept. Winchell was taken to a hospital but succumbed to his fatal injuries the next day. When arrested, Glover, who had been drunk at the time of the murder, claimed he was provoked by Fisher and expressed remorse. The murder sent a ripple of fear through people in the military secretly hiding their sexualities and gender identities. Said one friend of Winchell's who asked to be discharged, "I honestly think that if the Army didn't promote this hatred of gays, this wouldn't have happened."

Glover was given a life sentence for murder and paroled in 2020. Fisher was charged with obstruction of justice and other lesser felonies and received 12.5 years. He was paroled in 2006. In the aftermath of the murder, Secretary of Defense William Cohen ordered a review of Don't Ask, Don't Tell, which LGBTQ activists, Winchell's parents, and Calpernia Addams all pushed for. She said in 1999, acknowledging the transphobia that tainted the case: "The reason he was killed was because he was dating me. That makes it even more devastating, to think that I had played some role in it." The report on Don't Ask, Don't Tell and homophobia in the military found that "Of 71,570 soldiers surveyed, 80 percent said they have witnessed derogatory remarks being made against gays."

1999: Rae Carruth

Sacramento-born first-round draft pick Rae Carruth joined the shiny new Carolina Panthers NFL franchise in Charlotte, North Carolina in 1997. At the time, he had a son born during his sophomore year at the University of Colorado Boulder. Carruth had to be dragged to court to pay child support. His baby mother, Michelle, accepted a reduced payment on the promise that he would spend time with his son, a promise he refused to keep.

Charlotte, and that sweet four-year, $3.7 million deal (with a $1.3 million signing bonus), was calling Carruth's name. The 23-year-old sent his 17-year-old girlfriend, Amber Turner, ahead of him to get their house ready, which her mother sanctioned. While Rae had a good rookie season and toured his way through Charlotte's strip clubs and nightlife, Amber would be gone by 1998 because of all the other women. After a post-breakup hook-up, Amber got pregnant and told him. Carruth "joked" that he'd send somebody to Colorado to take care of her if she didn't abort it. Amber's blood ran cold, remembering the time he had made a similar death-threat "joke" to his first baby mother. She decided to have an abortion and cut off contact.

After a great rookie season with the Carolina Panthers, Rae's luck changed the following year. Wrote Peter Richmond in *GQ*, "Frequently injured, no longer a starter, Rae had by now become that singularly sorry football phenomenon: a first-round draft pick gone bust. Taxes and agents had taken half the bonus. He'd invested in a car-title-loan scam that had promised the trappings of easy money, and lost his money... He'd signed a contract on a new house, but he'd had to pull out when he couldn't get the financing, and the owners had sued him."

While Rae had been out partying, he met a 24-year-old real estate agent and stripper named Cherica Adams at The Diamond Club. They had a casual sexual relationship, and she ended up pregnant. According to Carruth, he was not excited about becoming a father but ultimately looked forward to the responsibility and began helping Cherica prepare for the baby. He claimed he first learned her last name during a Lamaze class.

On the evening of November 15, 1999, Rae and the eight-month-pregnant Cherica went to a 9:15 showing of *The Bone Collector* at a movie theater. Earlier that night, while at Carruth's home, Cherica had talked to her mother, Saundra, on the phone. Saundra later told *The Charlotte Observer* that Cherica said, "Mom, I don't even know why I'm here. I don't know what this is about. Because he's got all these people in the house." The people in the house weren't friendly. According to Carruth, before they left for the movies he had gotten into an argument over a drug deal with two associates, Michael Kennedy and a career criminal and nightclub manager named Vann Brett Watkins Jr., aka "New York."

When leaving the movie, Rae drove ahead of Cherica in his car. According to phone records, he made two phone calls at 11:51 PM and 12:19 AM. Along Rea Road, Rae came to a sudden stop as a gold Nissan Maxima pulled up beside Cherica's car. She was shot four times by an assailant in the Maxima. Carruth fled when the Maxima did. Cherica managed to steer into the front yard of a nearby home and called police at 12:31 AM as she lay inside the car, bleeding out. She told them that the father of her child, Rae Carruth, had been in front of her when she was shot.

Cherica was rushed to the hospital and went into a coma, but before she did, she scribbled out notes further implicating Carruth in the crime. According to reports, Rae drove to his friend and teammate Hannibal Navies' house and played video games while Cherica's mother called him repeatedly from the hospital. Doctors delivered Cherica's baby via C-section. When Carruth finally arrived at the hospital, he showed up with another dancer and girlfriend, Candace Smith. After collecting evidence, Rae Carruth was arrested for murder on Thanksgiving Day, making him the first active NFL player charged with murder. Prosecutors alleged that he had hired the assailant, who turned out to be Watkins.

Carruth was released on bond for $3 million, agreeing to return to custody if Cherica or the baby, christened Chancellor Lee, died. For over two weeks, the Panthers scrambled to decide whether they should defend or release such a problematic player. Meanwhile, Cherica was taken off life support by her family on December 14. Rae Carruth fled in the trunk of a car. The woman who drove him was a hair salon owner named Wendy Cole. She called his mother, Theodry, and told her where they were. Theodry then informed authorities. Rae was found in the trunk of the car in Tennessee on December 15, with money, snacks, and bottles of urine.

The Panthers officially released Carruth on December 16. The driver, Michael Kennedy, and Watkins, both pled guilty to second-degree murder, stating that Carruth paid them $6,000 for the deed. The phone calls Carruth made the night of the murder? They were to Michael Kennedy. A third man in the car, Stanley Abraham, served 90 days for accessory after the fact. He didn't know about the plan but had been accompanying his best friend, Kennedy.

Watkins detailed his actions during the murder trial, saying: "The window didn't go down all the way… And there's no light. And… a black BMW with black tinted windows. So that's an almost impossible shot. But I was lucky… Rae was looking in the mirror. And he smiles… Rae pulled off once the last shot was done." That scumbag wiped himself down with gasoline after shooting Cherica and went to Waffle House.

Carruth's guilt seemed obvious. It turned out the plan had been months in the making. Carruth had tried to have Cherica harmed on other occasions. Wrote Michael Bramberger,

> "New York later testified… Carruth told him to meet them after [a] class and beat up Cherica and make her lose the baby. But New York didn't show. He was nothing if not a con man, so he strung Carruth along. One time New York agreed to find Cherica at her apartment and kill the kid there. Another time he was going to ambush her behind a restaurant. He took cash payments of $300 and $2,000 and kept delaying. Finally, they settled on a plan to murder Cherica."

The Charlotte Observer reported that Watkins claimed he had been hesitant to kill a woman and procrastinated the murder. Carruth, through his defense, since he didn't take the stand, denied either version of events, arguing that Cherica had been killed in retaliation for drugs and money. His team insisted that he had been excited to be a father and that the multiple phone calls to Michael Kennedy were made because Carruth feared bringing

Cherica back to his home while Watkins was there.

The story, arrest, and murder became a major scandal for the still-new Panthers franchise, especially because this was a capital crime in a religious, pro-life red state. The case was aired on CourtTV and got more than a little messy. For instance, married Hornets basketball player Charles Shackleford was called to testify because he had a relationship with Candace Smith, the dancer who accompanied Carruth to the hospital and worked with Cherica. She informed Shackleford that Rae had practically confessed to her, and she also testified against him in court. Carruth's legal team painted Candace as a scorned lover.

ESPN explored the relationship between pro-sports, strip clubs, and the groupies who chased pro-ballers. Various women were brought in during Carruth's trial to provide character testimony. He even sent a four-page letter to his ex-girlfriend Amber, instructing her to testify that he loved and missed his first son and didn't mind paying child support. She refused and told the truth on the stand. Her own mother Barbara, who testified in Carruth's defense, mouthed "I love you" to him when she finished providing her statement. She had practically instructed her 17-year-old daughter to hook Carruth, and now took his side.

Also in 1999, the owner of the Charlotte Hornets, Charles Shinn, was acquitted of kidnapping and sexually assaulting a woman, and in the process admitted to having affairs with women on the Hornets' cheerleading team. The resulting public relations fallout contributed to the Hornets' relocation to New Orleans. On a larger level, the case of O.J. Simpson, Carruth's trial, and smaller scandals like Shinn's generated broader discourse about toxic masculinity in professional sports. Wrote Richmond,

> "If Rae Carruth loved women so much, why did he keep threatening to have them killed... And how could such a man wind up finding a home, even flourishing, in the National Football League? Well, because he really didn't like women at all. (He liked to fuck them, and he liked their attention, and he liked the idea of them, but he didn't like them.) And because he was accustomed to violence. And because he was making a living in a league in which a man and his basest instincts are encouraged to run wild."

Ultimately, Carruth was found guilty of conspiracy to commit murder and other lesser charges. He was sentenced to 18–24 years, escaping the death penalty. Watkins, the gunman, was given 40–50 years and died in 2023, with Cherica's mother, Saundra forgiveness. Chancellor Lee, despite being born 10 weeks premature with slim odds of survival, is still alive, and he graduated from Vance High School. He rides horses and dances. He was raised by Saundra, whom Carruth had tried to undermine with a smear campaign and custody filings aimed at transferring guardianship to his own mother. In 2001, a judge, despite Saundra's protests, allowed Carruth's mother to take baby Chancellor to visit him in prison once.

Carruth was released in 2018 after serving 18 years. He spent most of that time working as a prison barber and had the audacity to write a public letter stating that he would seek custody when Saundra died, writing, "I mean, come on Ms. Adams, the reality is you aren't going to be around forever." That earned him widespread backlash, and he retracted the idea. He now lives in Pennsylvania.

90s Serial Killers

There had been heightened interest in the 1970s, but the 90s sensationalized and glamorized the serial killer like no decade before. "It's like stopping and gawking at a car accident. It's literally rubbernecking and you think, thank God that's not me," said John Waters, director of the 1994 black comedy *Serial Mom*. It was a post-Soviet period of fear about alleged 'superpredators', feminism, gay culture, and alternative lifestyles. There was a looming cloud of drug and crime problems plus a neglected mental health crisis. No wonder the serial killer dominated.

"Serial killers have become what vampires were to Victorian audiences and giant lizards and bugs were to audiences during the height of the cold war," wrote Frank Bruini in 1994. In the same article, one professor named Harold Schechter was quoted as saying, "Every particular era embodies its deepest fears in some archetype of a monster… inventing new clothing for the archetype, the serial killer is our mythic monster."

Except serial killers exist.

The decade opened with a flurry of real and fictional violence. In 1990 the eerie mystery show *Twin Peaks* began airing, featuring a serial killer character and changing the course of serial television dramas thanks to the ingenuity of show runners Mark Frost and David Lynch. *Henry: Portrait of A Serial Killer*, starring Michael Rooker, was filmed in 1986 and struggled to find distribution because of its violence and nihilism but eventually released in limited theaters in 1990. It was loosely based on the lives of Henry Lee Lucas and Ottis Toole. Filmmaker John McNaughton had a sparse budget of $110,000 to make a horror film— and knowing that monsters would be too expensive, McNaughton culled his story from real life. The film's tagline was, "He's not Freddy, He's Not Jason… He's Real."

Ottis Toole was convicted of killing six people, though he confessed to other murders that he later recanted. Henry Louis was a drifter who was confirmed to have killed three people and convicted for the murder of eleven, including his abusive mother. While interred in prison in the eighties, he falsely confessed to killing over 600 people for clout, which was facilitated by Texas detectives wishing to clear cold cases. McNaughton wasn't aware that the confessions were fake when he directed *Henry: Portrait of A Serial Killer*.

Another polarizing piece of media was Brett Easton Ellis's 1990 book, *American Psycho*, which is a million times darker than the 2000 film adaptation. Ellis, who first gained national attention for 1985's *Less Than Zero*, was bouncing back from his poorly received sophomore entry *The Rules of Attraction*. The novel *American Psycho* centered on the unreliable viewpoint of an attractive and wealthy Wall Street yuppie serial killer with sick misogynistic impulses and an appreciation for music and designer goods. When portions of the book were leaked, the publishing world was thrown into chaos.

The world of Patrick Bateman was a ghastly one. *The New York Times* reviewer Roger Rosenblatt found the lack of plot and excessive dismemberments reviling, but also hated the obsession with product placement. He wrote in *Snuff This Book! Will Bret Easton Ellis Get Away With Murder*:

> *American Psycho* is the journal Dorian Gray would have written had he been a high school sophomore. But that is unfair to sophomores. So pointless, so themeless, so everythingless is this novel, except in stupefying details about expensive clothing, food and bath products, that were it not the most loathsome offering of the season, it certainly would be the funniest."

When living in New York in 2015, I made the mistake of purchasing the book for my ex-boyfriend, because we both loved the movie. He never read it, but I did. Well, I tried to. I still remember taking infuriatingly long rides to the Bronx, flipping through the pages, waiting for a plot to materialize between the rape, torture, explicit words, and unending luxury. Eventually I gave up and chucked it somewhere in my ex's closet. I can't imagine a black or female author being paid six figures to write a 112,000 word experiment on the limits of gratuity.

Back in the nineties, the distaste for *American Psycho* was so widespread that, wrote Elizabeth Vavant, "The original publisher, Simon & Schuster, abruptly canceled the book in mid-November, just a month before its scheduled release, and Ellis kept his $300,000 advance. The novel was then picked up by Vintage Books, a trade paperback division of Random House." The Los Angeles Chapter of the National Organization of Women, led by Tammy Bruce, started a nationwide protest of Vintage and Knopf books not written by feminist authors starting on November 19th.

Still, 60,000 copies of *American Psycho* were shipped to bookstores in February 1992. Major distributors carried the novel, but a few small bookstores refused. Judith Walker of The Corner Bookstore in Albuquerque New Mexico, for instance, told *Entertainment Weekly*, "My job is to provide my customers with the best cross section of literature I can find, and Mr. Ellis is a terrible writer, always has been. As a bookseller, good writing is my agenda, not violence against women." Roger Straus Jr., a respected publishing executive, said, "[it is] the most revolting book I have ever read. To say that it has any redeeming social value, or that mainstream film and television contain equally offensive material, is bullshit. The horrors perpetrated on women in that book go far beyond anything that has either been written or depicted. I'm sorry. I just don't see the thing as being defendable."

Simultaneously, there was a backlash to what some referred to as a culture of censorship in publishing. Wrote a pissed off reader to *The New York Times*, "I doubt that "American Psycho" could move me to greater revulsion than Roger Rosenblatt's pious, reactionary pre-review of it. This vicious hatchet job, rife with the putrescent stink of prejudice and sour grapes, represents the worst of the self-righteous claptrap that is currently circling this book like vultures over carrion."

Despite the controversy, *American Psycho* went on to became a literary darling in certain circles. Patrick Bateman, the unreliable narrator and serial killer (if you believe his version of events, that is), was just one of many characters on the serial killer scene of the nineties.

One of my favorite movies, 1991's *Silence of The Lambs*, starring Anthony Hopkins and Jodie Foster, dropped the same year that the Justice Department estimated there were approximately 100 serial killers nationwide. The film was based on the 1988 novel by Thomas Harris, who took classes at the FBI and consulted with former FBI agents Robert Ressler and John Douglas when creating his infamous character Hannibal Lecter for his 1981 book *Red Dragon*.

While forming the FBI's Behavioral Analysis Unit in the 1970s, Ressler and Douglas first coined serial killer to mean offenders who killed three or more people with periods of cooldowns in between. Their first subject was Edmund Kemper, a necrophiliac who was released after serving six years for murdering his grandparents at the age of fifteen. He went on to kill at least eight women before 1973. He came to be the archetype of the helpful and intelligent serial killer, who became a model prisoner and told the FBI agents about his past to contribute to catching other killers. He recorded at least 5,000 hours of audiobooks for the blind from prison by 1987.

One of John Douglas's most popular lectures was *The Silence of The Lambs: Myth and Reality*. Directed by Jonathan Damme, the film follows FBI academy student Clarice Starling, who is recruited to interview imprisoned serial killer and former psychiatrist Hannibal Lecter. After a series of events, Starling eventually tracks down Jame "Buffalo Bill" Gumb, who kidnaps women and skins them to make a suit for himself. Buffalo Bill was inspired in part by Ed Gein, who robbed graves and murdered at least two women, fashioning their skin into corsets, leggings, and other clothing items. Gumb isn't the star serial killer though—Dr. Hannibal Lecter, a cultured and intelligent cannibal is the true star. He fancies wine, fine art and music, and good conversation. He can also clock a good bag and cheap shoes.

The *Silence of The Lambs* made 272 million dollars and became the fifth highest grossing movie worldwide. It was the first and only horror film to win the Oscar for Best Picture. In addition to the plot and performances, Hannibal Lecter's classy characterization attracted people. Wrote Roger Ebert when reviewing the film, "One key to the film's appeal is that audiences like Hannibal Lecter... He may be a cannibal, but as a dinner party guest he would give value for money (if he didn't eat you). He does not bore, he likes to amuse, he has his standards, and he is the smartest person in the movie... He bears comparison, indeed, with such other movie monsters as Nosferatu, Frankenstein... King Kong and Norman Bates." Anthony Hopkins' performance was so marvelous that his then-girlfriend Martha Stewart broke up with him after seeing the movie because she couldn't separate him from the character.

In the film, Clarice Starling represented a new and soon to be popular blend of the hardboiled yet sensitive female investigator, and the common archetype in crime fiction: the ruthless cop who had the power of profiling to catch bad guys. Cops were the focal point of most serial killer media in the 90s. Explained David Schmid, "If audiences were inclined to feel guilty about their interest in serial murder, the mass media reassured them that being fascinated by serial killers was acceptable because in the process of consuming serial killer pop culture they learned about psychology and law enforcement procedure while also participating vicariously in the apprehension and conviction of these criminals." This implied that the evil of mass murderers could be prevented, predicted, and controlled—except, what about when it couldn't? What about when the justice system lets the most dangerous people slip through the cracks?

1991 was marked by a real cannibalistic serial killer that hit the headlines. Between 1978 and 1991, Jeffrey Dahmer killed 17 boys and men, 16 of them in Milwaukee and 1 in Ohio. Most of them were minorities, and nine of them were black. It didn't have to be this way. In 1989, he Ohio State University dropout pleaded guilty to sexually assaulting a 13-year-old boy in Ohio. At the time he had already killed four people. Ludicrously, he was released until sentencing and murdered his fifth victim, a 24-year-old named Anthony Sears. Nobody knew this when he was being sentenced for the sexual assault of a child. His father Lionel begged the court to give his son a maximum sentence and treatment. Instead, Dahmer got five years probation and one year of jail with work release.

Dahmer went on to kill twelve more people, removing their body parts for consumption and display, and dissolving other body parts in a 57-gallon drum filled with acid. Attempting to make his own zombies, Dahmer drilled holes in several of his victims skulls to deposit hydrochloric acid. One of his victims, 31-year old Tony Anthony Hughes, was deaf. They communicated with notes before Dahmer attacked. His next victim, Konerak Sinthasomphone, was the 14-year-old brother of the boy he had molested in 1988. After being drugged and left alone on May 27th, 1991, a naked Konerak managed to escape, where he was found wandering the streets by a black woman named Glenda Cleveland, and her daughter and niece.

Dahmer, coming back from the store when police arrived, told them that the 14-year-old Laotian-American child was his drunk boyfriend. Ignoring the black women insisting the boy was bleeding and hurt, police did a quick glance in Dahmer's stinky apartment and left the child in his care. Konerak was murdered the same night. Glenda Cleveland recognized Konerak's photo in a missing persons report a few days later and she called the FBI. Nothing happened, and Dahmer killed another four people after Konerak.

Police indifference and bias was indicative of a larger problem nationwide, but especially in Milwaukee, which was plagued by racism and economic hardship for black residents. They were desperate for economic relief and changes. At the time, reported Don Terry for *The New York Times*, the city's police force was 80 percent white— and the twenty percent of minorities on the force was thanks to a 1975 court order forcing the city to hire them. The revelations about Jeffrey Dahmer, and the lack of police investigation into missing black and brown boys and men, shook the city of Milwaukee. Like in other cities, white residents continued to be prioritized, which Terry catalogued in a series of interviews.

Explained a reverend named LeHarve Buck, "It's a great city by a great lake, but it depends on what color you are. If you're not an Anglo-Saxon white male, you're treated differently by the police in this city. The police have a picture of what a good citizen looks like. If you don't fit that description, you're not a good citizen and you're not worth serving." The city's gay community was also outraged by the crimes. Dahmer had hunted for victims in gay bookstores and clubs. Said an 18-year police veteran named Sgt. Leonard Wells, "If you're poor, black, Hispanic, gay or lesbian then in the eyes of many on the Milwaukee Police Department you are engaging in deviant behavior." Added newspaper editor Terry Boughner, "...somebody will call the cops for help and they don't come for 30, 45 minutes. A couple of weeks ago, two cops watched while five men beat up two gay people. They did absolutely nothing."

Dahmer's last attempted victim, 32-year-old Tracy Edwards, agreed to go back to his apartment on July 21 1992 to pose in nude pictures for a fee. When Tracy's guard was down, Dahmer placed a handcuff on one of his wrists, threatened him with a knife, and told him he was going to eat his heart. Tracy stayed calm and placated Dahmer to the point that he could eventually escape, running through the unlocked front door. He flagged down cops, who initially treated him with homophobic disdain and suspicion, eyeing his handcuff and asking "Which one of us did you escape from?" When Tracy explained the situation, they took him back up to Dahmer's apartment.

The police eventually arrested Dahmer after looking around and finding photos of body parts and the severed head of a black man, Oliver Joseph Lacy, in the refrigerator. How long would Jeffrey Dahmer have been permitted to operate had Tracy Edwards not been able to fool him and escape? Tracy appeared on *Geraldo* before the year was over to recount his experiences, telling a story that differed greatly from his court testimony. This was likely to avoid the time period's violent homophobia.

Dahmer immediately confessed after being arrested, and a competency trial found him sane when he was committing the acts of murder, rape, necrophilia, and cannibalism. The apartment building where Dahmer committed his crimes was destroyed on November 17, 1992, and supporters of his victims held protests against the police. Despite the perversity of his offenses, Dahmer quickly racked up fans and adulation. Dahmer received fan mail and at least 12,000 dollars, including coins from a 74-year-old nun, and an anonymous London woman who sent nearly 6,000 dollars.

Dahmer's privilege as a white man netted empathy from people who thought, "that could be my son, my brother, my father." While serving out his sixteen life sentences, he became a born-again Christian, demonstrating that evils may lurk behind any average person's piousness. He told Stone Phillips on *Dateline NBC*, "If a person doesn't think that there is a God to be accountable to, then what's the point of trying to modify your behavior to keep it within acceptable ranges? That's how I thought anyway."

In 1992, the popular TV movie *To Catch A Killer* debuted, featuring a dramatization of the life of John Wayne Gacy, who killed 31 teen boys and men near Chicago, Illinois between 1972 and 1978. Two years after the TV movie, Gacy was executed, and his collection of art, which he had made in prison, was auctioned off by his lawyer, with the money being given to his victims and charities. One 50-year-old man named Joseph Roth bought 21 of the items for 20,000 dollars and torched them. When Jeffrey Dahmer was murdered in prison by a man named Christopher Scarver in 1994, his entire estate was left to eleven of the families of his victims, who decided to auction them off. Items included "a hypodermic needle, pornographic movies and letters he received while in prison in Portage, Wis." Not all victims' families were in favor of this auction, nor were many locals.

A Milwaukee real estate developer named Joseph Zilber asked how much it would cost to stop the auction—and was told one million dollars. A civic group organized 407,225 dollars, with 100,000 donated by Zilber, to buy the stuff and destroy it. Said the relative of one victim, "We're just supposed to sit back and let everybody make money off of Jeffrey Dahmer, and what do we get? We get nothing. I don't care what I have to do, if we don't do it, down the line, someone else is going to be making money off this."

In a country that historically sent lynching postcards, in the nineties there were people making money off of Dahmer, with trading cards, comic books, apparel, and eBay listings of crime scene items. America wasn't the only country with a cannibal making headlines—in Japan, a man named Issei Sagawa, who killed and ate a classmate in Paris in the 80s and managed to be free within five years, wrote books, was celebritized, and treated as an avant-garde intellectual in the nineties.

Humans have long celebrated killers. From Genghis Kahn to King Henry VIII to Jack The Ripper, conquerers and murderers have always held prestige. This prestige and public fascination was satirized in *Serial Mom*, starring Kathleen Turner and Matthew Lillard. In the movie, Kathleen plays Beverly, who after committing a slew of murders for trivial reasons, becomes a nationwide sensation and gets acquitted.

In 1994, Oliver Stone's *Natural Born Killers* also satirized the American media response to mass murderers and spree killers, who typically kill a large amount of people over a short period of time. In the movie, Mickey (Woody Harrelson) and Mallory (Juliette Lewis) are a pair of violent lovers pursued by detective Jack Scagnetti (Tom Sizemore), who is secretly a serial killer himself. As the death toll rises, they become media sensations thanks to journalist Wayne Gale (Robert Downey Jr.). The polarizing film, which was a rewritten version of a Quentin Tarantino script, would be the alleged inspiration for multiple copycat crimes in the years to come, and teen-killers and terrorists Dylan Klebold and Eric Harris referred to their 1999 plans for Columbine High School as "going NBK."

The next film to evolve the serial killer genre was the extremely gritty *Se7en*, another one of my favorites, starring Brad Pitt, Morgan Freeman, and Gwenyth Paltrow. To modern audiences, nothing in the movie is truly outrageous, because many of us are desensitized and we've become accustomed to more gore. But in 1995, the David Fincher-directed film was considered to be too macabre, sinister, and evil. Denzel Washington turned down the role played by Brad Pitt because he thought the script was too evil, a decision he came to regret. Multiple other actors and crew refused to participate. Screenwriter Andrew Kevin Walker was inspired to write the film while living in New York.

Said Walker, "There's lots of evil out there, and you're not always going to get the satisfaction of having any sort of understanding of why that is. That's one of the things that scares people the most about serial killers." The year that *Se7en* debuted, John Douglas published *Mindhunter: Inside the FBI's Elite Serial Crime Unit*—and it makes perfect sense that David Fincher, also director of 2007's *Zodiac*, based on the crimes of the Zodiac Killer, would be an executive producer on the 2017 series adaptation of Douglas's book for Netflix.

In *Se7en*, the killer, John Doe, chooses his victims based on the seven deadly sins. A lawyer is forced to carve a pound of flesh from himself. A sex worker is raped with a bladed dildo. A fat man is made to eat until he bursts open. Explained John Doe, "We see a deadly sin on every street corner, in every home, and we tolerate it. We tolerate it because it's common, it's trivial. We tolerate it morning, noon, and night. Well, not anymore. I'm setting the example." The movie's plot-twist climax, in which one of the detectives pursuing Doe finds his wife's head in a box, almost didn't get made, with executives believing it would piss off audiences.

Se7en collected $320 million worldwide and changed the trajectory of crime thrillers by encouraging darker topics, more gore, and faith-based horror. Similar films would follow, including *Kiss The Girls* and the regretful Denzel Washington in *Fallen* and *The Bone Collector*. Andrew Kevin Walker would also be a writer on *Sleepy Hollow*, the 1999 Tim Burton-directed film starring Johnny Depp and Christina Ricci featuring the investigation of a paranormal serial killer in 1799.

Another hallmark of nineties serial killer culture was inspired by real life.

In 1994, screenwriter Kevin Williamson learned about the serial killer Danny Rolling, who murdered five Florida college students in August 1990, and three others in Shreveport, Louisiana. Rolling claimed to want Ted Bundy-style fame, invoking the name of the murderer with over 30 victims, who had met the electric chair in January 1989. Rolling collaborated on a book with serial killer groupie Sondra London, and they were engaged for a short period of time. London's 1997 AOL website, Serial Killers Talk To Sondra London, was briefly removed by the company when people complained.

Kevin Williamson went on to create 1996's *Scream* using Rolling as inspiration. The film, directed by Wes Craven, depicted the role of the media in killer culture, represented by Courtney Cox as the ruthless Gale Weathers. It was also a satire of slasher flicks, which had gone critically stale in the 1980s and first half of the 90s. *Scream* was well received, especially the surprise ending revealing that horror movie obsessives Billy Loomis (Skeet Ulrich) and Stu Macher (Matthew Lillard) were both the masked killer.

Mused Billy Loomis (who I knew was guilty from his first moment on screen),"Movies don't create psychos. They make psychos more creative." According to Williamson, the Motion Pictures Association of America pressured the crew to drop the line from the film, but it wasn't. Added Stu, "Watch a few movies, take a few notes. It was fun!" Though *Scream* released at Christmastime in 1996 with low expectation of box office success, the film eventually earned 173 million dollars worldwide. Kevin Williamson went on to write other teen horror flicks like *The Faculty* and *I Know What You Did Last Summer*, which similarly explored themes of mortality, innocence, and suburbia.

Wrote Amy Taubin, "Unlike urban action pictures, which imply, with rare exceptions, that the threat to America is ghettoised, that it can be policed and locked away (as long as the invading third world hordes are kept at bay), serial killer films are set in white neighborhoods—suburbia, the farm belt, the backwoods. The serial killer is a marauder: he might turn up anywhere. And in fact, almost all serial killers are white males who kill within their own racial group. Bred in the heartlands, he's the deformed version of the American dream of the individual."

While serial killer fictional media continued to evolve, so did the real ones. Hybristophilia, or an attraction to criminals and most often killers, was elevated into the spotlight. In 1996, it was reported that Doreen Lioy, an editor for *Tiger Beat* magazine who helped actor John Stamos become famous, was just one of several women who had tried to win over Richard Ramirez, aka the Nightstalker—a man who had killed over fifteen people in the early eighties. With over 75 letters and multiple phone calls and visits, Doreen won her prize and married Richard in a prison ceremony. She said, "I just believe in [Ramirez] completely. In my opinion, there was far more evidence to convict O.J. Simpson, and we all know how that turned out." Lioy was just one of many serial killer groupies.

Because serial killer culture thrived in the 1990s, preconceptions about them and their victims meant more danger for non-white people. The flaws of serial killer profiling meant that non-white men were committing repeated murders with little interference. In the last chapter, we discussed the serial murders of Henry Louis Wallace, who terrorized my hometown between 1992 and 1994. Charlotte police were told by the FBI that the killings weren't serial, and that serial killers didn't kill people they knew. The murders of seven white women by Derrick Todd Lee from 1993 until 2000 were profiled to be done by a white man— because FBI profiling guidelines said serial killers typically kill within their own race.

Jerome Denis raped and killed five women and girls in New Jersey between 1991 and 1992. Benjamin Atkins murdered 11 women, mostly sex workers and homeless women, around Detroit from 1991 to 1992. James Swann killed four people and injured five others in a series of random drive-by shootings between February and April 1993. Andre Crawford, a necrophile, killed 11 women between 1993 and 1999 in Chicago, before finally being caught in 2000. There was also Samuel Little, who killed approximately 100 women between 1970 and 2005.

There were Latino serial killers like Altemio Sanchez, Ramon Torres Hernandez, and Francisco del Junco. Asian serial killers included Sebastian Shaw, Harnoko Dewantono, and Andrew Cunanan, whose final victim was the designer Gianni Versace. In 1997, Giovanni 'Gianni' Versace was on top of the world, leading the supermodel wave by championing Naomi Campbell, Linda Evangelista, and the other top names. Versace was a $807 million fashion house with 130 stores around the world.

On July 15th, 1997, Gianni walked from his Miami mansion to a local shop to buy magazines and coffee, which he did daily. When he returned home, he was shot and murdered by Andrew Cunanan, an Italian-Filipino American con artist who had killed four people in the months before. He previously lived in San Francisco as a sex worker, doing drugs and dating wealthy older men. According to friends, he had a flair for lying. After killing Versace, Andrew fled to a nearby houseboat and killed himself. His body was found on July 23rd, the day after Versace's funeral was held at the 14th century Duomo cathedral in Milan. It was attended by 2000 people, including Princess Diana.

Another type of serial killer who had long been under the radar until the 90s was the female serial killer—best embodied by Aileen Wuornos—but overwhelmingly, the cunning and elusive serial killer was mostly characterized as an intelligent and charming white man.

Additionally, the occupations and races of victims played a role in police, media, and public reactions. In Louisiana, the white so-called Storyville Slayer killed 24 mostly black women and girls between 1991 and 1996. A white man, Russell Ellwood, who bragged in a previous prison stint about committing the killings, was convicted of killing one, but not the others. The murders stopped when he went to prison.

On August 13 1997, an anonymous caller to the *Howard Stern Show* referred to himself as 'Clay' and gave details on twelve of the murders. Hoax or not, the show's tapes were confiscated by the FBI. It appears little effort has been made ever since to get justice for the remaining 23 women, or ascertain if Ellwood was the perpetrator. Another interracial crime serial killer that showcased the poor attention paid to black victims was Ronald Joseph

Dominique, who killed 23 men and boys in Louisiana between 1997 and 2006. He was named "The Bayou Strangler." Dominique had previously been arrested for rape and attempted murder, dressed like Patti LaBelle while attending gay bars, and once punched a woman in the face. 15 of his 23 victims were black men.

By the time of the Bayou Strangler's arrest in 2006, the attention paid to real-life serial killers had diminished. They were no longer the big bad boogeyman in a post-9/11 society. A few still aroused interest but they didn't garner 1990s levels of attention. While serial killers are regularly depicted in police procedurals like *Criminal Minds*, most neatly captured by the end of the hour thanks to handy profiles and law enforcement competence, there have been fewer of them in real life, where competence isn't guaranteed.

In addition to more cameras and tracking technology, better profiling, and more mental health services, there's less lead exposure, which has been linked to violent crime. Stephen J. Dubner and Steven Levitt, the authors of *Freakonomics: A Rogue Economist Explores the Hidden Side of Everything*, proposed that the availability of birth control and abortion from the 1970s onward, along with other factors, led to fewer killers. Still, serial killers exist.

Summed up Phillip Martin, Virginia's Radford University found "72 murders were attributed to serial killers in the 1950s; this number practically tripled in the 60s (217), and nearly tripled again in the 70s (605). In the 80s, 768 murders were attributed to serial killers; in the 90s, 669. That declined to 371 in the years 2000 to 2009 and to 117 since 2010." Those numbers are still high as hell if you ask me, and a little less than half of America's murders are solved every year.

Considering half a million people are missing at any time in this country, and the existence of undocumented immigrants and marginalized people, plus what we know about police incompetency—will retrospectives in the future reveal new truths about modern serial killings? As it stands, approximately 1% of all U.S. murders are serial. As abortion rights and birth control access are on the decline, and mental health services become more expensive or deprioritized in our conservative country, will there be more neglected and/or abused children growing up into unhappy and vengeful adults? Only time will tell.

90s Halloween

I can still remember hearing *Monster Mash* for the very first time as a kindergartener in art class. Our teacher cranked up the 1962 classic by Bobby 'Boris' Pickett while we crafted pumpkins with construction paper. As a millennial whose spooky seasons were filled with nineties reruns and films, I was destined to be obsessed with Halloween.

1990

Flicks: *Night of The Living Dead, Jacobs Ladder, Graveyard Shift, It, Misery*

Trunk or Treat events emerged in the late eighties but came into greater prominence in the nineties, when newspapers began reporting that they were becoming a popular trick-or-treat alternative for some parents. Instead of taking kids out into neighborhoods where it was dark and filled with careless drivers, parents could head to a sanctioned parking lot with their costumed children. Said one mother of five to *The Sacramento Bee*: "We know where [the candy's] coming from, so we know it's safe, and they're not out on the streets."

Tragedy struck twice this Halloween when two accidental hangings occurred during venue attractions. In Toms River, New Jersey, attendees of a haunted hayride witnessed 17-year-old Brian Jewel, an employee, hanging from a tree. It was part of his usual stunt, but something went wrong, and he asphyxiated himself. Callously, before Jewel was even buried in the ground, the haunted hayride re-incorporated a gallows scene featuring a new hangman. His family privately settled a lawsuit with the owners of the company in 1994. One week after Brian's death, in York, South Carolina, 15-year-old named William Odom from Charlotte, North Carolina, accidentally ended his own life while wearing a pirate costume at a Halloween party in his aunt's basement.

Lastly, *The Simpsons* aired its first Halloween Special during its second season. These anthology episodes would all eventually be entitled *Treehouse of Horror*. They featured three different stories and often parodied horror literature and films, while being more graphic than usual. Some people were a little disturbed. Complained Tim Chavez in *The Daily Oklahoman*, "Humor is subjective, but this rule must be modified when little kids are watching. On the *The Simpsons* Halloween special, an evil force took over the family, and the kids woke up grabbing knives saying "kill Mom and Dad." I love Bart and the bunch, but that's too much, dudes."

The first episode played with haunted house tropes, a Twilight Zone episode, and a comedic rendition of Edgar Allen Poe's *The Raven*, narrated by James Earl Jones. *The Simpsons* in general were a quickly growing phenomenon, and it was reported that Bart masks and Marge costumes were particularly popular. Marge wigs could be found for approximately $36. A Florida supermarket assistant manager was featured in the *Sentinel Tribune* for painting faces of The Simpsons family on pumpkins. The *Treehouse of Horror* installments came to be some of the most popular features of the long-running series. A comic book series based on the episodes launched in 1995.

1991

Flicks: *Childs Play 3, The Addams Family, Cape Fear, The Silence of The Lambs*

On October 27 of this year, meteorologists warned that a "dangerous storm" with unusual features would form in the Northeast from Massachusetts to Maine. The next day, the short-lived category two Hurricane Grace contributed to the formation of what was called *The Perfect Storm*. Thousands of people evacuated coastal areas before record-breaking waves flooded homes and businesses, even reaching as far as North Carolina. The storm didn't dissipate until November 2 and killed thirteen people.

Six of the victims were the crew of the *Andrea Gail*, a commercial fishing boat from Massachusetts captained by Frank William "Billy" Tyne Jr. Despite being warned of poor conditions, Captain Billy, desperate to get their catch back to port before it spoiled due to a broken ice machine, headed back inland. His final words, heard over radio, were: "She's comin' on, boys, and she's comin' on strong." The event inspired both a book and a movie, *The Perfect Storm*.

Hoping to capitalize on the American public's growing obsession with Halloween, the Universal Studios amusement park launched Fright Nights as a three-night event on October 25, 26, and 31. It cost $8 to attend. In 1992, the event was rebranded at California's Universal Studios park as Halloween Horror Nights, in an effort to steal business from Knott's Scary Farm, which had been operating for nearly twenty years at the Knott's Berry Farm theme park. Reported Chris Woodyard in 1992: "One interesting, publicity-driven twist is a promise to have a team of psychologists standing by to counsel overwrought guests."

1992

Flicks: *Alien3, Bram Stoker's Dracula, Twin Peaks Fire Walk With Me, Buffy The Vampire Slayer, Candyman*

On October 17 1992, Japanese exchange student Yoshihiro "Yoshi" Hattori and his host-family "brother" Webb Haymaker set out for a Halloween party in East Baton Rouge, Louisiana. The 16-year-old Yoshi wore a *Saturday Night Fever* costume. While looking for the party, they got lost trying to find house #10131. Instead, they approached a home with the number 10311, owned by Rodney and Bonnie Peairs. Yoshi knocked on the door. Bonnie opened it.

"We're here for the party," Yoshi said, smiling with his camera before Bonnie shut the door in his face. She ran to tell her husband that she was scared of someone at the door and told him to get his gun. As Yoshi and Webb prepared to leave, Rodney Peairs opened the door, aimed his gun, and told Yoshi to freeze. Yoshi didn't understand. As he took a step forward, still smiling, Peairs shot and killed him. In his police statement, Peairs said: "I pointed the gun and hollered, 'Freeze!' The person kept coming toward me, moving very erratically. At that time, I hollered for him to stop. He didn't; he kept moving forward. I remember him laughing. I was scared to death. This person was not gonna stop, he was gonna do harm to me."

Baton Rouge prosecutors initially refused to press charges until immense pressure came from Governor Edwin Edwards and the Japanese consul. The incident sparked national and international debate, was it a tragic accident, or deliberate racism and murder? When Rodney went on trial for manslaughter and Bonnie was put on the stand, she said, "I guess [Yoshi] appeared Oriental. He could have been Mexican or whatever. He was taller than me, and his skin was darker colored."

"It is widely believed that Hattori would be alive had he understood what his assailant meant when he pointed a handgun and ordered Hattori to 'freeze,'" said a 1993 report discussing how the Japanese travel industry planned to distribute pamphlets to it's citizens explaining what "freeze" meant, and how to navigate a society where millions of people own guns. Said Japanese correspondent Yoshitio Okubo, "We Japanese don't understand the gun society of America. And we don't understand why this man had so much fear that he would shoot a boy." At the time, 1,200 people a year died in handgun accidents in America, with even more lost to deliberate shootings. There were 200 million guns in the country.

Correspondent Shinsuke Tanaka explained the culture shock for Japanese people: "In America, when the police pull you over, you keep your hands on the wheel [so they won't shoot you. In Japan,] even a policeman firing his gun at a criminal is top news, even if he doesn't hit him." After a seven-day trial in 1993, Peairs was found not guilty of manslaughter. In a civil suit, Yoshi's parents were awarded $650,000, to be paid by Rodney. His insurance company paid out $100,000, but the rest was never sent. Yoshi's parents become gun reform activists, rallying 1.7 million Japanese citizens to sign a petition to Clinton advocating for tighter gun control in supporting the Brady Bill.Not only did Yoshi die 366 days after the Luby's Massacre in Texas, but another tragedy followed just a few weeks after his death, on Halloween night.

After 17-year-old named Adam Provencal watched friends toilet-paper a house in Grand Haven, Michigan, he went to the home to make sure he was not mistaken for one of the culprits. The 25-year-old homeowner, Todd Vriesenga, shot him in the face with a shotgun. Adam, who had just won a soccer game earlier, died the next day. Vriesenga claimed he believed the gun was unloaded when he squeezed the trigger, hoping to scare off what he thought was an intruder. He was acquitted of manslaughter the following year, but convicted of using a firearm. He served 19 months. Remarked Adam's father, "I feel awful for our family and I feel awful for Adam. What about all the teenagers who approach a door innocently or all the other people who answer doors with guns?"

The October 16 1992 release of *Candyman* was a major moment in horror history. In the film, a graduate student at the University of Illinois Chicago named Helen (Virginia Madsen) researches urban legends. She decides to pursue details on the story of Candyman (Tony Todd), and finds trouble. Eddie Murphy was originally considered for the role of Candyman but was deemed too expensive to cast. Thank goodness. Tony Todd not only delivered a haunting performance, but earned a $1,000 fee for each of the 23 bee stings he endured during filming.

Candyman stirred minor controversy in the wake of the Rodney King verdict and the Los Angeles riots. Some studio executives worried that portraying an evil Black supernatural entity might provoke backlash. Director and screenwriter Bernard Rose adapted the plot from a Clive Barker short story entitled *The Forbidden*. The original narrative was set in Britain with white characters. He said about making the film,

> "I had to go and have a whole set of meetings with the NAACP because the producers were so worried... and what they said to me when they read the script was, why are we even having this meeting? This is just good fun. Their argument was, why shouldn't a Black actor be a ghost? Why shouldn't a Black actor play Freddy Krueger or Hannibal Lecter? If you're saying that they can't be, it's really perverse. This is a horror movie."

Candyman was frightening because, as *The Chicago Tribune* noted that year, though the villain was a formerly enslaved man tortured and killed by a white mob, "Candyman preys mostly on Black women and children whom he guts and mutilates with his hook." While white people had turned Candyman into a monster for falling in love with a white woman, he haunted the mostly Black neighborhood of Cabrini Green, a real-life housing project in Chicago. The Cabrini Green projects were built in 1942 and were originally 75% white, but would become riddled with crime, neglect, and drugs as the city increasingly segregated its Black population.

Conditions deteriorated so badly that Mayor Jane Byrne, the first female mayor of a major American city, moved into the neighborhood in March 1981 to generate publicity around the high crime and murder rate and to rally support for her proposed handgun ban. Byrne would later write, "How could I put Cabrini on a bigger map? Suddenly, I knew I could move in there!" This certainly made headlines. While Byrne stayed at Cabrini, the elevators were fixed, trash was picked up, and the violence stopped, for a few weeks.

Complained resident Jackie Grimshaw, "All of a sudden you've discovered paint for Jane Byrne. All of a sudden you discovered rodent control. Where's all that been all this time?" The problems at Cabrini continued once Byrne left. She vacated the building after just three weeks when her Easter egg hunt and move-in were assailed by protestors as a publicity stunt for her next campaign. A minor riot was filmed as people chanted, "Jane Byrne is Ku Klux Klan" and "We need jobs, not eggs."

In *Candyman,* Helen willingly entering Cabrini Green mirrored Mayor Byrne, except in the end, she was corrupted and consumed by the violence lurking in the projects. Black directors Reginald Hudlin and Carl Franklin criticized the movie's tropes as irresponsible and racist. They also objected to Candyman's obsession with the white main character. "Be my victim," Candyman tells a catatonic Helen in a silky smooth voice that still gives me goosebumps.

In response to accusations of the film being racist, Virginia Madsen said, "What's wrong with Candyman craving a white woman? That's not a stereotype, that's real." She also added, "I don't think Spike Lee will like this film." *Candyman* was ultimately well received and made a modest $25 million on a budget of eight to nine million. A sequel, according to Madsen, in which Candyman and Helen doppelgängers fall in love, was scrapped due to studio anxieties around interracial romance. Still, the franchise continued with three sequels.

1993

Flicks: *Hocus Pocus, Nightmare Before Christmas, The Addams Family Values, Leprechaun*

The Halloween classic *Hocus Pocus* starring Bette Middler, Sarah Jessica Parker, and Kathy Najimy as evil Salem witches, was widely panned when it debuted this year. Roger Ebert gave the movie one star, writing "Of the film's many problems, the greatest may be that all three witches are thoroughly unpleasant. They don't have personalities; they have behavior patterns and decibel levels. A good movie inspires the audience to subconsciously ask, "Give me more!" The witches in this one inspired my silent cry, "Get me out of here!" *Hocus Pocus* went on to become a cult Halloween staple.

In the early hours of Halloween 1993, 23-year-old actor River Phoenix overdosed on a mix of cocaine and heroin outside popular hot spot The Viper Room in West Hollywood. The club was partly owned by Johnny Depp. Phoenix was there with his brother Joaquin and due to perform with friends, including Flea and John Frusciante from the Red Hot Chili Peppers.

At Yosemite High School in Oakhurst, California, nestled, no joke, between "Hangtree Lane," "Spook Lane," and "Black Road", it was reported on the 31st that: "Two teenagers wore Ku Klux Klan costumes and pretended to lynch another boy wearing blackface at a high school Halloween party... They won prizes for their costumes, but the school's principal now says he regrets letting them attend." One 17-year-old told the news, "They walked in and a lot of people were like, 'That's not nice.' But a lot of people said, 'That's cool,' like original."

In Isla Vista, California, a weekend-long Halloween celebration that had begun in the late 1970s had grown so popular and rowdy that by 1992, law enforcement could barely keep up. Reported Lexi Pandell:

> "People from Washington, Oregon, New Mexico, Colorado, Wisconsin, Arizona, Nevada and all over California flocked to the area for the weekend-long celebration. Over 70 out-of-town schools were represented among the arrested and cited students... 1,090 out of 40,000 attendees, 95 percent of which were for alcohol violations... Two people fell off the cliffs, including a teenager who fell 65 feet from the 6600 block of Del Playa."

In 1993, local leaders launched the Five Year Plan to crack down on Halloween in Isla Vista. This included banning outdoor music after 6 PM, confiscating costume props that could be used as weapons, and restricting access to the neighborhood. Attendance dropped from 40,000 to 25,000 in just one year. By 1995, the number had fallen to 1,750 and didn't recover until the 2000s.

1994

Flicks: *Interview With The Vampire, The Crow*

In 1994, Halloween was reported to be a $1.5 billion-a-year holiday, not including candy sales. Explained *The New York Times*, "No longer just a day, Halloween is a season that begins early in October, when many families lavish their homes, both inside and out, with decorative Halloween displays that rival those for Christmas...Eighty-seven percent of children between ages 7 and 12 go trick-or-treating with an adult or with friends, as do 75 percent of children under 7." With the boom in Halloween celebrations came greater spending on costumes. *Mighty Morphin Power Rangers* topped the list of most popular costumes, followed by *Teenage Mutant Ninja Turtles, The Lion King,* and Belle from *Beauty and the Beast*. Prior to the late eighties and early nineties, most Halloween costumes didn't come from pop culture but were generic things like witches and ghosts.

On October 25 in Union, South Carolina, 23-year-old mother of two Susan Smith alerted police that she had been carjacked by a Black man who drove off with her sons. For the remainder of the Halloween season, law enforcement combed the area as Smith pleaded on national media for her sons' safe return. However, her story fell apart, and on November 3 she admitted to rolling her car into John D. Lake with the boys locked inside. After being quickly found guilty of murder, her lawyers worked to keep her from receiving the death penalty.

Smith was eligible for the electric chair thanks to a provision included in the 1994 crime bill that expanded the federal death penalty. Prosecutor Tommy Pope was adamant that Susan be sentenced to death, while the public debated whether she should be executed. Prosecutors insisted she killed her sons to win back the affections of a man named Tom Findlay, whose father she had also slept with. Ultimately, jurors declined to put her to death and instead sentenced her to life in prison.

Two days after Susan invoked the stereotype of a scary Black man in her initial statement to police, on October 27 the Department of Justice announced that the U.S. prison population had surpassed 1 million people making the country second only to Russia in terms of incarceration. The imprisoned were disproportionately Black, just like death row, where in 1994, 42% of the 2,890 people awaiting execution were Black. Susan Smith, who had been molested by her Republican stepfather up until a few months before the murder, narrowly avoided the death penalty so staunchly supported by conservatives. As Robert Scheer mused in *The Los Angeles Times*, "What would have happened if the authorities had caught someone fitting the description of the Black man whom she initially accused of kidnapping her babies?"

Lastly, there was the American Eagle Flight 4184 crash on Halloween day. Sixty-eight people died on a flight from Indianapolis, Indiana, to Chicago, Illinois, during an accident caused by icy weather. Two other fatal plane crashes would occur on Halloween during the nineties: one in Brazil in 1996, killing 99 people, and another near Nantucket in 1999, killing 217. That latter flight, EgyptAir Flight 990, reportedly inspired Osama bin Laden to devise an event that would change the course of American history.

1995

Flicks: *Tales From The Hood, Halloween: The Curse of Michael Myers*

On this year's Halloween, Cleveland Indians baseball player Albert Belle's Euclid, Ohio, home was egged by teenagers. Why? They were mad there was no candy. "We hear a bombardment of egg shells on my door... So I come outside and chase them," Belle told *The Los Angeles Times*. Belle hopped into his Ford Explorer after telling a police dispatcher, "You better get somebody over here, because if I find one of them, I'll kill them."

Belle chased and struck one of the trick-or-treaters with his SUV. He was charged with Reckless Operation of a Vehicle and fined $100. "Don't Ring Albert's Belle," reported newspapers. While the four boys were charged with delinquency, a guardian of the boy hit by the vehicle sued Belle for $850,000. The case was settled privately the next year, with neither side allowed to speak publicly about the terms. The four teenagers were sentenced to five hours of community service.

1996

Flicks: *Scream, From Dusk Til Dawn, The Craft*

During the spooky season of 1996, one of my favorite comics, *Batman: The Long Halloween*, was first published. It was written by Nick Loeb and influenced the next wave of *Batman* TV adaptations. On Halloween day, the Wisconsin Daily Pick 3 lottery numbers came up 666, which freaked out locals. "This is frightening, to say the least," said State Revenue Secretary Mark Bugher, who oversaw the lottery.

"HALLOWEEN IS NEARING. TIME TO DRESS UP AS YOUR FAVORITE SERIAL KILLER," announced the *Chicago Tribune* sarcastically, before detailing how one area costumer was selling Unabomber-themed accessories, orange jumpsuits, fake beards, and plastic dynamite packs. Ted Kaczynski, who had been mailing bombs for nearly 20 years, killing three people and injuring dozens more, was finally caught in 1996. Halloween costumes had evolved from generic ideas like witches and goblins to include more pop culture and current events, for better or worse. Lastly, it was reported that a 7-year-old in San Francisco was hospitalized after supposedly eating cocaine-laced candy, when in reality, he simply couldn't breathe through his costume's mask. A blood test revealed no cocaine or drugs whatsoever.

1997

Flicks: *Tower of Terror, I Know What You Did Last Summer, Scream 2*

The *Scream* mask was a popular Halloween costume thanks to the runaway success of the groundbreaking slasher film, released the previous Christmas. Halloween was also on the rise in France. Wrote Roger Cohen, "It seems clear that French Halloween is merely another sign of the growing power of American culture in France, where fast-food restaurants, American movies, reversed baseball caps, and American basketball stars play an ever larger part in national life. Attempts to defend French language and culture have proved increasingly vulnerable to this onslaught." French candy makers and companies eagerly latched on to the lucrative new holiday, especially after the orange Ola Phone campaign by France Telecom, which promoted the delights of *Aloween*.

On October 24 in East Granby, Connecticut, a woman suffering injuries from a hit-and-run accident was mistaken for part of a haunted house attraction. Thousands of visitors walked or drove by while she bled out and died on the sidewalk. Reported *The Hartford Courant*, "One passerby, Gale Fulton, later told police he thought he saw the woman, identified as Kimberley Kitrinos, reaching up from her position prone on the ground. He kept on walking." The danger of nighttime travel during Halloween season felt especially urgent that year.

The Centers for Disease Control and Prevention (CDC) reported that "findings indicate that the number of childhood pedestrian deaths increased fourfold among children on Halloween evenings when compared with all other evenings." During 1975–1996, from 4 PM. through 10 PM. on October 31, a total of 89 deaths occurred among pedestrians aged 5–14 years, compared with 8,846 on all other evenings. On average, four deaths occurred on Halloween during those hours each year, compared with one death per day on every other evening. The CDC issued a series of safety recommendations that parents and children should follow to make trick-or-treating safer.

In New York City, rumors swirled around public schools that new prospective members of the Bloods gang would carry out their initiations on Halloween by slashing people at school or while they were out trick-or-treating. A wave of fear allegedly swept through the city, and many parents kept their children home. Half of the city's 300,000 high school students didn't show up on Halloween. Though no violence occurred, reported Jacques Steinberg,

> "While attendance at the city's public schools is traditionally lower on Halloween than almost any other day in the school year, principals and teachers described yesterday as among the most sparsely attended school days in recent memory. At the city's elementary and middle schools, only 63 percent of students were in class

yesterday, 16 percentage points fewer than last Halloween, and 26 percentage points fewer than most other days."

Shortly before October 8, 1997, someone placed a pumpkin, estimated to weigh sixty pounds, on the lightning rod atop the 173-foot McGraw Tower at Cornell University in Ithaca, New York. It was unclear how anyone could have done so without being seriously harmed or injured. Reported *The New York Times*: "While there is a staircase leading to the tower's chimes, open to the public at specified times, and a small service hatch above the bells that opens to the bottom of the slanted roof, the prankster would have had to scale an additional 20 feet of the very steep roof to reach the bottom of the lightning rod."

Joking about the average wealth of the student body, librarian Ellen Ingersoll suggested, "One of the students got a helicopter from their father and borrowed it overnight." In true nineties fashion, the pumpkin earned its own dedicated webcam and website, along with a flurry of media coverage speculating whether it was even real. It quickly became part of Cornell campus lore. Students placed fresh pumpkins at the base of the tower while administrators waited for the one on top to fall naturally. An orange fence was installed around the bell tower with a sign reading "Beware of Falling Pumpkin." It stayed up for five months. When a crane finally knocked the pumpkin down in front of a cheering crowd on March 13, 1998, it was freeze-dried and put on display, until it fully decayed. According to the most ardent pumpkin truthers, three students pulled off the prank, but they were never officially identified.

Lastly, Halloween day marked the end of a 39 day standoff between a mentally ill woman named Shirley Ann Allen and authorities in Roby, Illinois. The incident was compared to Ruby Ridge, in which the son and wife of white separatist Randy Weaver were killed by the federal government in Boundary County, Idaho. Shirley had lost her husband to cancer in 1989 and her mental health reportedly deteriorated to the point that in 1997 family members thought she would harm herself. She wielded a shotgun when police turned up for a wellness check on September 22 and then barricaded herself in the house. She refused to negotiate with anyone, not even her children. For thirty nine days, local police attempted to remove her from the home in a variety of methods while libertarians, militiamen, and conservatives cheered her on, nicknaming the standoff 'Roby Ridge.' Reported Julie Grace for *Time*,

> "At first the sheriff's deputies lobbed a tear-gas canister into the house. But Allen was prepared. The former nurse had apparently covered herself with petroleum jelly and a

wet towel to prevent the skin irritation that comes with the gas. Then they tried to stun Allen by firing some beanbag-like projectiles at her, but she was ready for that too, having armored herself in several layers of clothing. The gathering crowd of militiamen stand in awe and see her expertise as proof of a survivalist sensibility. Says Glad Hall, president of the Southern Illinois Patriots League: "She is good."... The police have blared classical music and Barry Manilow tunes to soothe her. They have also cut off the electricity and the water supply–all to little effect. Neighbors have told police that Allen frequently canned food and stored bottled water because the well on her property had run dry."

When Shirley was finally removed from her property on Halloween thanks to well-aimed rubber bullets, the tab for the operation was $650,000. Some people criticized the police for not storming her property after she fired her shotgun (twice) and allowing the siege to last for so long. But in the shadow of Waco and Ruby Ridge, the Roby police force moved with extreme caution.

1998

Flicks: Scooby-Doo on Zombie Island, The Faculty, Halloweentown, I Still Know What You Did Last Summer, Bride of Chucky

This year, *American History X* was released on Halloween weekend, hopefully stopping a suburban white teenager or two from wearing a Nazi or KKK costume. In this film, which explores the lives of two Nazi brothers, William Russ took a break from playing Cory Matthews' father on *Boy Meets World* to spew racism at a very different dinner table. Speaking of the teen comedy, the masterpiece *Boy Meets World* episode *And Then There Was Shawn* premiered this year— though not at Halloween. While it has since been featured in annual Halloween marathons, it originally aired in February. The plot involved most of the main cast being killed off in classic slasher fashion, parodying the teen horror movie craze that dominated the late nineties. Jennifer Love Hewitt, star of *I Know What You Did Last Summer* and its sequel, guest starred in the episode, likely because she was dating cast member Will Friedle at the time.

The episode also included references to the new and wildly popular Comedy Central animated show *South Park*. Concerning the episode's gore and humor, director Jeff McCracken said, "There was concern from the network. They said to us, 'Nothing can be graphic.'" One standout moment came when the character Kenny is killed with a pencil through the skull. As he sinks to the ground, he leaves behind a trail of pencil. *"OH MY GOSH! THEY KILLED KENNY!"* Eric yells, delivering one of the most iconic crossover lines of the decade.

Another Halloween staple to drop this year was *Scooby Doo on Zombie Island*, which Time Warner had commissioned after noticing Scooby was getting popular again thanks to Cartoon Network syndication. Screenwriter Glenn Leopold worked with producer Davis Doe to craft a spooky story set in New Orleans— featuring real supernatural zombies hunted down by the gang, reimagined as a television show crew with Daphne as host. Leopold had been given relatively free rein to experiment with the story, as Time Warner just wanted to capitalize on the direct to VHS format. Said a representative of Warner Home Entertainment, "We have a library of franchises we know people love. Entertain the family without going to the theater and spending, say, 8 bucks times four."

Warner spent $50 million advertising the movie. *Scooby Doo on Zombie Island* dropped for $19.95 on tape in September, but debuted for the first time on Cartoon Network on Halloween day. On my fifth Christmas, I received this movie on tape with a spanking new VHS player. It scared the shit out of me. No wonder the *Los Angeles Times* warned in its review, "Some of the cartoon gruesomeness is too intense for very young viewers." While kids, tweens, and teens were getting their fill of Halloween media this year, on Halloween day, President Clinton signed the Iraq Liberation Act to begin disarming Iraq and removing Saddam Hussein from power. Iraq announced it would no longer cooperate with United Nations disarmament inspectors.

In the Bronx, there was a tragic shooting over egg throwing. Reported *The New York Times*: "A 21-year-old computer programmer [named Karl Jackson] from the Bronx... was driving his girlfriend and her son home from a Halloween party on Saturday night when a group of young men threw an egg at his car and then shot him to death after he confronted them." The paper elaborated that two people had also been killed over egg throwing in 1994 in Brooklyn, and another in the Bronx in 1995. While the threat of Halloween pranks gone wrong still lingered, the fear of tainted candy, which had grown in the 1970s, eased in the nineties.

In Orange County, California, hospitals and private practices announced in 1998 that they would no longer allow parents to have children's candy X-rayed for potential razors, a practice dating back to the 1960s. Explained a reporter for the *Los Angeles Times*: "The virtual elimination of the X-ray machine at Halloween comes in the wake of changes in how the holiday is celebrated. The growth of organized events, from school parties to church- and shopping mall-sponsored festivals, has been fueled in part by parents haunted by fears that children let loose on the neighborhood streets could come home with tainted candy." One chiropractor who had been X-raying candy for 18 years said, "When I first started, there was all sorts of homemade stuff, brownies and popcorn balls and cookies. Now it's all wrapped candy."

1999

Flicks: *The Blair Witch Project, House on Haunted Hill, Stigmata, The Sixth Sense*

1999 was the year Halloween sales were estimated to be five billion dollars, and it's no wonder that popular mall retailer Spencer's Gifts purchased Spirit Halloween. At the time, the seasonal chain, which had launched in 1983, had 69 locations. Spirit grew in popularity and became increasingly ubiquitous in the following decade, as Halloween celebrations became more elaborate. The rise of Halloween, both at home and abroad, sparked concern for some. A report by CNN noted that in Mexico, many people felt Halloween, yet another American import, was overshadowing *Día De Muertos*, or the Day of the Dead. Complained one author and environmentalist, "Day of the Dead is a family day. Halloween is a superficial and commercial holiday."

If you thought the Satanic Panic from the late eighties and early nineties had fully ended, think again. In 1999 there were reports about black cat sacrifices. Published the *New York Daily News*: "Black cats, beware. Long associated with witches, bad luck and the dark side, black felines are often used for pranks, party props and even satanic, sacrificial rituals around Halloween." Some people feared that the practice could spread. The director of animal placement at the ASPCA warned, "This is a time when blood rituals take place. Black cats are often sacrificed." As a result, some animal shelters refused to allow black cat adoptions during the month of October.

Said one Montgomery Animal Shelter Director to *The Washington Post*, "Personally, I am not aware of any kinds of problems with black cats specifically at Halloween. The nature of the ban is to have a better-safe-than-sorry policy. Due to the recommendations of the national organizations who may have seen problems in other areas, we observe the ban." Lastly, while Hell Houses were a common alternative to pagan Halloween fare for evangelical youth in the nineties, they were missing out on haunted houses, which were growing in number and becoming more elaborate. Hauntworld.com provided information about attractions across the country.

On Boy Meets World

In the fourth grade, my Italian-American best friend and I were obsessed with two things: grinding away in Neopets on her family's home computer and watching as many *Boy Meets World* reruns as we possibly could. I first stumbled upon the show at eight years old. Reruns would air on Disney Channel West after my bedtime, around 2AM, so I'd quietly sneak downstairs to watch in the living room with the volume turned all the way down so my mother wouldn't hear.

To be honest, I was mostly hoping for glimpses of all the kissing.

So obsessed were my friend and I with *Boy Meets World* that her father created a fan site for us on Geocities (founded in 1995). Years later, I still have a fondness for the show. *Boy Meets World* has remained in syndication since its original airing in 1993 and has aged about as well as can be expected for any "wholesome" show created at the end of history, thanks to the storylines of the best character. While Cory Matthews was the Boy in *Boy Meets World*, he wasn't the most interesting boy in the world.

Making The Boy

In 1990, The Walt Disney Company invested heavily into its TGIF lineup on ABC. Thank Goodness It's Funny, which aired for two hours starting at 8 p.m., was moderately successful thanks to shows like *Full House* (1987–1995) and *Family Matters* (1989–1998). But after a slew of duds the network needed something big. They approached *Dinosaurs* creator Michael Jacobs, seeking a show aimed at 12–14-year-olds. Developed by Jim Henson in the final phase of his life, *Dinosaurs* (1991–1994) had been an experimental and expensive comedy program, featuring an animatronic and anthropomorphic family of dinosaurs watching their world change.

The patriarch, Earl, works for an evil corporation named Wesayso. The show's finale, *Changing Nature*, was shocking yet poignant. Facing an environmental crisis, the dinosaurs destroy their civilization and initiate the Ice Age that leads to their extinction. When told that the world is essentially doomed, the show's ruthless business executive villain, a triceratops named B.P. Richfield (Sherman Hemsley), responds, "It's a fourth quarter problem… Right now my biggest problem is trying to figure out what to do with all this money!"

Explained Rafael Motamayor Aguiton, "*Changing Nature* was certainly shocking, but it wasn't the show's first foray into heavy imagery and serious subjects. From workplace sexual harassment to masturbation and sexual awakening to homosexuality and homophobia, Dinosaurs took aim at a lot of taboo subjects before it killed all its characters in that climate-change apocalypse." ABC wanted another show with a similar level of depth, but in a more conventional format with broader appeal and less sticky topics.

Michael Jacobs knew that television programming typically focused on adults or the oldest children and wanted to explore the experiences of a middle child named Cory Matthews (Ben Savage). Ben Savage had been acting since the age of nine, appearing in a variety of productions including the 1993 sci-fi miniseries *Wild Palms* as a cunning child actor turned killer and the 1989 film *Little Monsters* with his older brother, Fred Savage. Fred was the star of *The Wonder Years* (1988–1993). Already under contract with ABC, Ben easily impressed Michael during a meeting and signed on to be "the boy."

Cory lives in Philadelphia with his parents, Alan and Amy (William Russ and Betsy Randle). He has a goofy older brother named Eric (Will Friedle) and an unobtrusive, unremarkable little sister named Morgan (Lily Nicksay). Cory's best friend is "bad boy" Shawn Hunter (Rider Strong). Their classmate Topanga (Danielle Fishel), named after Topanga Canyon, is the environmentally minded and eccentric daughter of hippies. The Matthews family lives in a middle-class home next to George Feeny, Cory's history teacher, who serves as a wise mentor throughout the series. To portray Mr. Feeny, *St. Elsewhere* veteran William Daniels required that the teaching profession be treated with respect. Network executives initially cut references to Shakespeare from the pilot, fearing it would alienate viewers. The first table read was reportedly disastrous and had to be rewritten overnight.

Danielle Fishel, Will Friedle, and Rider Strong would later describe creator Michael Jacobs as manipulative and difficult to work with, particularly given their young ages. On Danielle's first day as Topanga, Jacobs said in front of the cast and crew: "If I made everyone sit here through all of the notes I have for you, we would all be here for hours and no one would ever get to go home." He later threatened to fire her if she didn't improve. Jacobs' manipulative ways would be confirmed by director and producer David Trainer and explored in the *Pod Meets World* podcast. Trainer revealed that sometimes, while driving to work, he "wanted to stop and throw up, because of how unpleasant it was to do... Don't get me started, that's all I have to say."

Boy Meets World premiered on September 24, 1993, nestled between *Family Matters* and *Step By Step* in the TGIF lineup. "Where *The Wonder Years* was a whimsical look at childhood through the eyes of a child during the '60s, *Boy Meets World* is a whimsical look at childhood through the eyes of a child circa 1990s," wrote Ken Parish Perkins in a review that ran nationally. With 16.5 million viewers for the pilot and 19.2 million tuning in for the following episode, it was clear the network had a hit on its hands.

The Bad Boy

The first season of *Boy Meets World* made it pretty clear that love and dating would be a central component of the show's narrative. Even while many of the storylines focused on the evolving relationship between Cory and his big brother Eric, dating remained central. Though Topanga was initially meant to appear in just one episode (*Cory's Alternative Friends*), her popularity led to more appearances, and ultimately to the series' main storyline. As someone who wasn't officially allowed to date until age 16, Cory and Topanga's lifelong romance always seemed fantastical to me. The 12-year-olds share their first kiss in Topanga's debut episode, and their first "date" in episode 21. Cory's parents are excited that he is already dating.

Shawn Hunter does not have a series soulmate. From the outset, Shawn's decisions, like putting a cherry bomb in his neighbor's mailbox and then running away on the lam, and his lifestyle (living in a trailer park with absentee parents) effectively make him the "white trash" of the show. There was a significant poverty problem in Philadelphia in the nineties. Brookings summarized U.S. Census data, writing that "Low- and moderate-income households increased in number in Philadelphia during the 1990s, but the number of middle- and upper-middle-income households (earning $34,000 to $81,000) declined. As a result, the city's median household income dropped over the decade..."

Shawn is characterized as a handsome slacker with good hair. While he pulls the girls and delivers endless witticisms, Shawn being "white trash" is a recurring theme that fuels both comedic and dramatic plotlines. For instance, he once excuses a dumb statement by saying, "My mom smoked while she was pregnant with me." It's a joke, but Shawn actually has a bevy of traumas that are teased out over the series. His experiences were what kept me coming back to the show, and they often took precedence over Cory and Topanga, the teflon couple.

In season two, the trio begin their freshman year at John Adams High. They have a humorous bully named Harley Keiner (Danny McNulty) and an exciting new teacher named Jonathan Turner (Anthony Tyler Quinn). Not only does he have long hair, wear leather jackets, and drive a motorcycle, but he makes English class interesting. Cory and Shawn call him "Feeny with an earring." Another change? Feeny is now the high school's principal.

My favorite episode of this season is *Wake Up, Little Cory*. My interest was always piqued when the topic of sexuality was on the table. After watching his class struggle through *Much Ado About Nothing*, Mr. Turner asks the students to conduct video interviews with classmates on the topic of love and sex. When the partnered Cory and Topanga fall asleep overnight in the school A/V lab to edit their project and are found the next morning by the janitors, rumors quickly circulate. They enter the school hallway to a smattering of applause, which is obviously for Cory. "You are the man!" Shawn tells a bewildered Cory. Coming from Shawn, the cool ladies' man, this is a big deal. Harley Keiner even treats Cory with a newfound sense of respect. When Cory attempts to deny anything happened, Keiner asks "Are you the man? Or are you just you?" A hurt Topanga watches in the distance as Cory falsely confirms he is 'the man'.

Cory lives in the same universe where the real-life Spur Posse of Lakewood, California competed for male approval by having sex with as many girls as possible from 1991–1993. It was the same universe of toxic masculinity described in Susan Faludi's *Stiffed: The Roots of Modern Male Rage*. Topanga angrily stalks off while two tall male classmates leer at her with a new sense of interest, implying that her reputation has taken a nosedive. Topanga confronts Cory at his house. He attempts to mollify her. "People are gonna talk. And that's all it is, just talk... in a few days it'll be like this never happened," he says, clearly not understanding the gravity of slut-shaming and misogyny in the nineties.

Topanga, still pissed off, replies, "You want me, Cory? You want me? Take me. Everyone thinks you did it already. So go ahead and do it." This obviously makes Cory uncomfortable, and he admits he only went along with the false narrative to be popular. "I want my good name back," Topanga demands. In the end, Cory does the right thing and informs his classmates that nothing happened between him and Topanga, restoring her reputation and their friendship. I didn't learn until middle school how much of a fantasy this was.

In *Wrong Side of the Tracks* (which features Nancy Kerrigan as a guest star), classism is explored when Shawn Hunter is dumped by a girl for being poor. Heartbroken and fully cognizant of the classism permeating his world, Shawn begins hanging out with Harley Keiner's crew, believing that Cory will eventually wise up to his poverty and abandon him. "Look at where you live, look at where I live. Look at your parents, look at my parents!" He attempts to sever his friendship with Cory, reasoning, "I know where I'm gonna end up. Just let me get there now." Cory's plea falls on deaf ears. "Just let me get there now!" Shawn roars, storming off.

Mr. Turner tries to convince Harley to stop hanging out with Shawn, which doesn't go well. He instructs Shawn to destroy Mr. Turner's bike with a baseball bat. Cory stumbles upon the felonious scene and steps in, saying "It looks fun," and offers to take the first swing. "This is not your place," says Shawn, desperate to ruin his own life and authenticate his most anxious nightmares. Cory doesn't back down, even threatening Harley when he tries to intervene, calling his goon Joey a "rat face thug." Mr. Turner bursts onto the scene before Cory can get his ass beat and sends the bullies packing. "When he said rat face, was that like, pejorative?" asks Joey.

Mr. Turner pours light into Shawn, telling him that he isn't a lowlife. Cory and the audience are reminded how fragile Shawn's life is, always a few steps away from making the wrong choice or being in the wrong place. In this episode, because Danny McNulty had an undiagnosed bipolar disorder and suffered an emotional breakdown, he was temporarily replaced by an actor named Kenny Johnston. When Keiner is later sent away to reform school, his lackeys Joey and Frankie gain more prominence. Future *American History X* star Ethan Suplee played the intimidating yet poetic Frankie Stacchino, and was one of my favorite side characters.

As the series progressed, Shawn Hunter's life deteriorated in a number of ways as he grappled with abandonment issues. Explained Rider Strong in

2017, "Shawn was always a reminder that not everything in *Boy Meets World* land is happy, healthy, perfect family, [where] everybody's great. Shawn was an important reminder that outside the Matthews family there's potential for kids to go wrong, some way or another. Obviously within the confines of a safe family sitcom, so it's not like Shawn was shooting up or killing people."

In *Career Day*, after Shawn's father Chet (Blake Clark) speaks to his class and brazenly lies about what he does for a living, Shawn's mother Virna abandons her family by taking off in their trailer home. While Virna's reasons for leaving aren't plumbed at the time, later episodes reveal that Shawn's father Chet was an abusive drunk. When Chet leaves to find her, Shawn starts staying with the Matthews. It isn't a good fit, and the homeless Shawn eventually lands with Mr. Turner in the series finale.

In season three, when Danielle Fishel finally got paid as much as her male cast members (after the threat of a table read boycott), the first major Black character arrives in the form of Eli Williams, a teacher played by Alex Désert. He seems to fill some sort of diversity quota as Jonathan Turner's sounding board. Mr. Turner becomes a more central character as his apartment is used as a setting. We learn that he grew up wealthy in Connecticut and skipped out on joining the family business (and receiving his inheritance) to become a teacher. "So he gave up all that money and the good life to be a school teacher and teach kids like me?" Shawn asks Mr. Williams, who has just spilled all the tea in *New Friends and Old*. The poor semi-orphan Shawn can't believe it. "That is one sad, twisted man!"

The school bully in season three is now Griff, played by Adam Scott. A hilarious episode sees him face off against escaped-reform-school bully Harley Kiener. In this season, Cory and Topanga begin dating, and the early stages see them met with temptation and plagued by petty breakups. Speaking of Topanga, she delivers a powerful blow to Shawn's ego in *The Heart Is a Lonely Hunter*. When he whines that he can't find a "nice girl," she tells him that he treats girls like objects and that "the faster we are, the more you want us. And until you can grow up and see beyond that, no matter how many girls you go out with, you will always be lonely." Aside from the antiquated thinking of "good girls" and "bad girls", the premium placed on romance for wholeness reveals the show's underlying social conservatism.

Shawn's issues are deeper than romance. It's clear that Chet has used locating Verna as an excuse to abandon his fatherly duties. In *The Pink Flamingo Kid*, the fabulist Chet informs him over the phone that he's going to the racetrack with President Clinton for his birthday. When Shawn asks when he's returning, his father is elusive. Mr. Turner convinces Shawn and Cory to film a video that they can send, including scenes with the Hunter family back at the trailer park. Shawn says it'll be like CourtTV "without court," reminding us that his family is not just poor, but criminals.

The duo head to the Pink Flamingo Trailer Park and interview stereotypically shady people before being harassed by a jealous thug named Eddie, who accuses Shawn of "slumming." He says Shawn left his home for "the suburbs where there are fancy houses built into the ground." This episode shows the extent of the class divide between the two friends when Cory realizes he caught film of Eddie with a computer they assume to be stolen.

Cory immediately wants to send the tape to a local news station for a cash prize. Shawn is uncomfortable and prevents Cory from leaving with the tape by destroying it. A furious Cory goes back to the trailer park, gets caught doing surveillance, and is about to get beat up before Shawn intervenes. He reveals that Eddie is his half-brother through Virna. The situation is diffused, and we never hear from Eddie again.

When Mr. Turner wants to become Shawn's legal guardian, Shawn is uncomfortable because he misses his father. Chet eventually returns and reunites with his son along with Virna by the fourth episode of the fourth season, and it hurts Mr. Turner. Class again becomes a topic of conversation in *I Ain't Gonna Spray Lettuce No More*. When Alan abruptly quits his position as a grocery store manager, he angers housewife Amy for not discussing it with her first. Sending Eric to college is no longer feasible (not that he's upset about it). Cory, ever the dramatic child, asks Shawn for advice on how to be poor. They immediately sign up to undergo a scientific experiment for $100. This is a brutal reminder of how precarious the finances of a "middle class" family are.

At the end of the episode, Amy uses the family finances to buy a camping store, with Alan and Eric set to run it. While Cory's father can quit his comfortable job and use the family's savings to acquire a business, Shawn is humiliated in *Janitor Dad* when his father Chet begins working at John Adams High. Of course, he's ruthlessly teased by his middle-class classmates. "My father's a doctor and your dad... cleans toilets," taunts a generic bully. On that very day, they're reading *The Time Machine* by H.G. Wells, an 1895 sci-fi novel that explores class differences.

In *Dangerous Secret*, Shawn lets a classmate named Claire stay at his house because her wealthy bank executive father has been abusing her. According to writer and producer Jeff Sherman, "Every year I'd say, 'We should do something about school vandalism' or 'We should do something about child abuse.' And everybody would look at me like, 'Come on, man. It's a comedy, we're not doing that.' But I just kept wanting to give a backbone to the show. I would always push that a little bit more." Sherman certainly got his wish to add more complex themes to the show, though with a light Disney touch. Claire refuses to go to the police, but at the end of the episode, Cory and Shawn help her escape to Vermont and tell the authorities about her father. Because Cory initially thought Shawn and Claire were sleeping together, he tried to seduce Topanga, which upsets her. They conclude that they will stick to kissing, a resolution they don't challenge until their senior year of high school.

In *Turkey Day*, one of the most tense episodes of the season, Cory and Shawn learn about Rwanda and Burundi in class. The genocide that erupted in 1994 is framed by Mr. Feeny as a "class war" between the poor Hutus and the rich Tutsi, which strips the event of the ethnic strife between the groups (which was created by colonialism). It's not the only time the show botched a history lesson. In season seven's *No Such Thing As a Sure Thing*, Rachel serves as tutor and asks Pennbrook University's quarterback, "What African nation abolished apartheid in 1986?"

Cory and Shawn are uninterested in the lesson on Rwanda and Burundi ("He's making these names up!"). Feeny instructs the class to complete a paper on "the haves and the have-nots" during their upcoming break. Cory and Shawn coerce their families into spending Thanksgiving together after winning a turkey, and it goes horribly wrong. Chet warns Shawn, "It is unnatural to mix the classes, son." He calls Virna a "social climber" when she enthuses over the idea of mixing with a "better class of people." The middle-class Matthews, who would be out of place at a gala or The Philadelphia Club, are equally out of place in Shawn Hunter's trailer park.

The two families argue about which wine to drink while the Pink Flamingo trailer park residents encourage Chet to force the Matthews to leave. When the kids of the two families gather without the adults, neighbor Frankie, the poetic bully, says the adults are like the Hutus and Tutsi, "living with hatred and prejudices passed on from parent to child." While the families eventually settle down into a nice meal, the show once again reinforces the blatant class divide between the best friends. Shawn, who eventually becomes a poet and writer in later seasons, receives an A+ for his assignment from Feeny and is instructed to read it in front of class. "I discovered that even in my very own civilized country, people can be just as undeveloped and just as cruel."

The show again clumsily incorporates Black diasporic history in the episode *Chick Like Me*, in which Feeny discusses *Black Like Me* by John Howard Griffin, detailing his experiences disguised as a Black man in the Jim Crow South. Cory decides to go undercover as a girl to write a story about gender differences but isn't "pretty enough." Instead, Shawn goes undercover as 'Veronica Wasboyski' and becomes a sensation with the school's boys. Even Cory tells 'Veronica,' "You're kind of a babe," before offering to carry his books. 'Veronica' is embarrassed by the attention.

Coincidentally, Rider Strong felt uncomfortable with his status as a teenage heartthrob. He said in 2019, "It's not like everyone is sitting around reading *Bop* going, 'That Rider, he's a really great actor. He's really bringing it.' No, it's more about what my hair looks like or what I look for in a girl or the clothing I'm wearing. So that made me really uncomfortable. I was never good at being a physical specimen put on display." These feelings of discomfort and objectification for the young actor would be exacerbated at the height of his fame.

Strong elaborated, "I did a *Sail With the Stars* charity cruise when I was 15, and that was the most crystal-clear moment where I had a breakdown because it was just so alienating. You're stuck on a boat with, like, 600 fans and their families who feel like they have access to you. They want a certain version of you, whether that's Shawn Hunter or this perfect teen idol boyfriend, and suddenly, you have to be that person 24 hours a day. It was just the worst." Rider almost quit the show, but with support from his parents, he stuck around.

Back to 'Veronica.' When on a date with a handsy boy, 'Veronica' learns about the perils of being objectified and the importance of consent (which makes Shawn a teeny bit more sensitive in his relationships with future women, at least for a while). While the writers of *Boy Meets World* obviously count on the audience to laugh at the notion of Shawn and Cory being drag queens or trans women, a bit of empathy is laced into the narrative. Spotting Shawn as 'Veronica,' Feeny says, "If there's anything you need to talk about, my door is always open. I'm not here to judge." Before Shawn can fully explain himself, Feeny cuts him off and says, "I am not here to judge!"

In the following two episodes, Cory and Topanga almost break up because her parents move the family to Pittsburgh. Cory is confident that their love will endure. "What the hell kind of TV show is this?" asks Shawn as they watch Topanga ride off to Pittsburgh at the end of the first episode. As a self-proclaimed expert of the medium, he's shocked that his middle-class best friend isn't getting his fantasy ending. But he does. Unsurprisingly, Topanga later runs away to be with Cory, and all is right again with the world. Topanga's parents allow her to live with her aunt for the rest of high school. While Cory and Topanga's relationship drama was mildly interesting, it didn't move me like Shawn's ongoing woes.

Throughout the season, it has been alluded to that things aren't going well at home for Shawn, as on numerous occasions he is left alone while his parents are "out of town." Because school janitors aren't given much vacation time, we can surmise that Chet Hunter is unemployed in addition to being "out of town." Whether or not that was the polite way to say "in jail," "having affairs," "committing crimes," or something else negative is debatable, but suffice it to say that Shawn was not happy.

In *Easy Street*, Shawn begins working for the mob at a local restaurant. While Shawn, who is fed up with being poor, initially goes along with being a drug mule, Cory convinces him to abandon his post. Shawn thinks of the Robert Frost poem *The Road Not Taken*, that Mr. Turner taught them about in class. The good choices don't last for long. Nine episodes later, in *Cult Fiction*, the directionless, depressed, and abandoned Shawn becomes a prime victim of a cult called The Centre. This episode aired on April 25, 1997, just thirty days after the suicides of the Heaven's Gate cult in Rancho Santa Fe, California, but with references to a tanning center in the Bahamas and a "celebrity room," it's a spoof of Scientology.

Recognizing that Shawn is in trouble, his friends, the Matthews, Mr. Feeny, and Mr. Turner try to reason with him. Where are his parents? Out of town. What's interesting is that when Cory goes down to The Centre to rescue him, Shawn tells him that The Centre isn't for people like Cory because he has something to believe in. "Me? I'm still looking." Shawn understood that The Centre was an intoxicating pyrite, not an actual source of self-esteem and purpose. This harkens back to Shawn's season two declaration: "I know where I'm gonna end up. Just let me get there now." Shawn rationalizes that "it's not like I'm doing drugs," which Cory refutes.

When Mr. Turner gets into a motorcycle accident and is hospitalized, Shawn rejects the cult in favor of God, whom he begs to save Mr. Turner's life. He says, looking up at 'God': "I've never asked you for anything and I never wanted to come to you like this. But don't take Turner away from me. He's not done yelling at me yet. God, you're not talking, but I know you're here. So, I'm going to talk and you can listen. God… I don't want to be empty inside anymore." Mr. Turner doesn't die (though he is neither seen nor mentioned by the main cast for the rest of the series).

Season five brought in massive ratings for the series and introduced two new permanent characters who would shape the course of Shawn's life. First, the audience learns that, through Chet, Shawn has a half-brother, Jack (Matthew Lawrence). Virna has again left her family, this time, permanently. Chet convinces Jack and Shawn to move in together (probably so he can keep taking trips "out of town"). Jack serves not only as Shawn's brother but as a straight man to the increasingly unhinged Eric Matthews, who transitioned from a goofy yet charming teenager to a dimwitted young man. According to Friedle, Eric was dumbed down to play to his comedic strengths.

Though the second episode of the fifth season marked the arrival of the black character Angela Moore (Trina McGee-Davis), she did not become Shawn Hunter's primary love interest until *I Love You, Donna Karan*. At the beginning of the episode, Shawn and Angela break up after two weeks of dating off-screen, sticking to his personal relationship rule of a two-week expiration. Thanks to his abandonment issues, he hates forming romantic attachments. She's extremely cool with it— maybe even a little too cool.

Later, Shawn finds a purse with a book of sonnets, a Vivaldi CD, kiwi-mango lip gloss, Snowcaps, and other trinkets that cause him to fall in love with the mysterious owner, which is, of course, Angela. In *Chasing Angela*, Shawn convinces Angela to date him again after being initially rebuffed. It turns out she has commitment and abandonment issues too. "We're both scared," he tells her. When Shawn tries to woo Angela with fancy Italian food on a date like Cory and Topanga, she rejects Pâté for burgers and they decide to be themselves. He later invites her along to the Matthews' Thanksgiving celebration, sealing their relationship.

When showrunners cast the 28-year-old Trina to be 18-year-old Rider's love interest, they later insisted it wasn't about trying to be groundbreaking. Said Michael Jacobs in 2018, "It was one of the early interracial relationships on television where we never mentioned that aspect of it. We just never thought anything of that. And to be called forward-thinking [by press] for doing that, it's terrible. So the opposite spectrum of that was, well, it was an interracial relationship. What is the responsibility of saying they did not end up together? That to me is an example of backwards thinking as well. Forget the color. They never meshed. Every episode was about why Shawn and Angela would not sustain."

But the relationship *was* groundbreaking. Mainstream television had rarely depicted an ongoing interracial relationship. Rider would say in an interview that some of his "random cousins" said they wouldn't watch anymore because of it. When the WB show *Ally McBeal* featured an interracial relationship between the titular lawyer and a Black doctor in 1999, showrunner David E. Kelley intentionally wanted to keep the relationship colorblind, which miffed some viewers and critics. In the midst of media attention to interracial relationships, Trina wrote an op-ed for *The Los Angeles Times*.

> "My character, Angela, has intimately kissed Shawn (Rider Strong) a number of times, and the show's creators have never made an issue of our race. As our executive producer, Michael Jacobs, explained to us at the start: it's obvious what color we are. *The Los Angeles Times* apparently didn't think our kisses were of any threat to society, since no editorial or reportorial comment was ever offered, and no viewer response letter was ever printed. I, for one, saw that silence as very golden. The demographics of *Boy Meets World* lean toward young people, so the absence of expressed concern is all the more significant.
>
> I get lots of positive reactions from both Black and white teenagers wanting to know when Shawn and I are getting back together. The Black kids are not asking, "Why are you with that white boy?" When I attended the NAACP Image Awards, a Black girl lamented to me that Shawn and Angela are a perfect couple and should be back together. The next day, a white girl in a mall begged to know if Shawn and Angela are still in love. One was nine, one preteen. They are the new face of tolerance. These kids are not looking at race; they're absorbing the love story... Someday, through our efforts, I hope the real world will become as colorblind as *Boy Meets World* and *Ally McBeal*."

While Trina had dreams of a positive, racially blind future, that was not her reality on set, which was filled with white crew, actors, and writers. Will Friedle referred to her as "Aunt Jemima" at least once behind the scenes. She added in a 2020 tweet, "Called a bitter bitch when I quietly waited for my scene to finish rehearsing that was being f'ed up over and over due to [an] episode featuring my character. Told 'it was nice of you to join us' like a stranger after 60 episodes..." Friedle was made to apologize for his comments, but Trina said it didn't feel genuine at the time. He reached out to apologize again in 2020. Trina posted, "The man responsible for AuntJemimagate apologized to me 22 years ago and again days ago in a three-page letter. We talked more on it and he acknowledged that he really wasn't educated enough in his early twenties to know he was truly offending me. This should and could be a teaching moment for all."

Trina, whose hair changed nearly every episode, had to do her own hair or pay to have it done because there wasn't an adequate stylist on set. "I didn't have a hairdresser. All those little micro braids you see, I stayed up all night doing them right before I went on national television for myself." When Trina reprised her role as Angela on *Girl Meets World* in a single episode, she experienced distant behavior from her former co-stars (except Rider). Danielle tweeted in response, "I owed [her] an apology for being rude, cold, & distant when she guest-starred on *GMW* (her tweet regarding warm hellos being met with cold blank stares was about me). Trina and I spoke over a month ago and she gracefully accepted my apology."

During Trina's time on the original show, writers reminded the audience that Angela was indeed Black in a few funny yet non-offensive ways. In season six, Shawn proudly exclaims that Angela did well on her essay *Maintaining Black Identity When You Have Three Very White Friends*. When Cory bursts into her dorm room and asks what she's studying, she sarcastically says, "White history. You know, you people contributed quite a bit to this country." When tasked with configuring her soap opera character name based on her middle name and the street she lived on in *Everybody Loves Stuart*, she says, "Shanaynay Martin Luther King Blvd," after Shawn says, "Patrick Trailer Park." When none of the group laughs at the Martin reference (but the audience does), Angela says, "Gosh, I gotta get some Black friends."

In the following season, when Eric stumbles upon a stack of books (*Native Son, I Know Why the Caged Bird Sings, The Autobiography of Malcolm "Tenth"*), the audience with any knowledge of Black literature and history understands whose books those are before he does. When Shawn complains that Cory is acting like an "entitled white boy," Angela asks him, "What's wrong, my brother?" Angela also has the privilege of telling the overbearing Cory that they were never really friends, which shocks him into trying harder to get to know her as a person.

Shawn's first test with Angela came in the season five episode *First Girlfriends' Club*, when a group of jealous ex-girlfriends kidnap Shawn so that he can't make his anticipated Valentine's date with Angela. They justify their interference as keeping Angela from getting hurt because Shawn was manipulative with them in the past. Season five was great. In addition to *The Witches of Penbrook* Halloween episode and the famously well-received slasher parody *And Then There Was Shawn* (featuring a clandestinely pregnant Trina McGee-Davis screaming her heart out as Angela), season five saw Cory and Topanga's relationship go through its most trying obstacle so far: infidelity.

While on the senior ski trip, Cory cheats on Topanga with an employee named Lauren (Linda Cardellini). The pair break up and eventually get back together (obviously), but something really interesting happens before their reunion: Cory has his first taste of alcohol. He is suddenly the life of a party thrown by classmates. With a slug of Alan's cabinet liquor, Cory convinces Shawn to get drunk too, and they get in trouble later that evening after pissing on a cop car.

The class tensions resurface. Alan is convinced that Shawn is the one who convinced Cory to drink, which Shawn allows him to believe so that Cory doesn't get into more trouble. While Cory is punished by his parents and scared away from liquor, Shawn (who lives with Jack without adult supervision because Chet is only God-knows-where) continues drinking, even getting belligerent in class with Mr. Feeny. Jack tells Shawn that Chet was a drunk who was abusive to his mother, which Shawn has trouble accepting. Shortly after, Shawn drunkenly shoves Angela. Realizing what he's done, Shawn swears off alcohol and allows Alan Matthews to chastise him and punish him the way he wishes his own father would.

The fact that Shawn assaulted Angela is glazed over (even though she should have broken up with him). But it's a nineties family sitcom, and intimate partner violence among teens wasn't the focus. In fact, Angela slaps him in season six without any repercussions. In the episode *Prom-ises, Prom-ises*, which was banned from Disney Channel syndication, Cory and Topanga decide to have sex on prom night. A series of mishaps leads to them deciding to wait until they get married, affirming an earlier declaration that "kissing is enough." At the same time, the show made no mention of safe sex in the episode, which Rider Strong would later call irresponsible.

"The fact that we would not bring up Cory and Topanga using condoms or having a discussion about birth control at all, and yet the entire episode was about will they or will they not," explained Rider. When he mentioned his concerns to Michael Jacobs, he was ignored. "...He completely blew me off and told me it was a ridiculous thing to worry about and that we don't even need to discuss it."

It's interesting that sexual purity was a key part of the *Boy Meets World* storyline while the teenage actors were frequently expected to kiss each other and guest stars from the first season onward. This was common in the nineties, but not today. Said Danielle Fishel, "Maybe it's that the people writing the content are now uncomfortable asking real 12-, 13-, 14-, 15-year-olds [to kiss]? [Back then] we were actors. It didn't matter whether or not we were uncomfortable or comfortable with it. Whatever the writer wrote is what you did, and you were made to feel that if something did make you uncomfortable, it was inappropriate for you to express that."

Despite Cory and Topanga's declaration of abstinence in *Prom-ises, Prom-ises*, the pair are so horny in the pants for each other that the remainder of the series is a bullet train hurling toward marital sex. At the end of this season, the gang graduates from John Adams High (and they're briefly reunited with former classmate Stuart Minkus). Topanga, who has been accepted to Yale, decides to propose to Cory in the middle of graduation. While they don't get married in this story arc (and break up once more before their actual marriage), their dramatic abstinence stood out in a landscape of *Dawson's Creek*-style shows marketed at teens.

Topanga's decision to skip the prestigious Yale for Pennbrook (which even Eric Matthews, of all people, can attend) pissed me off. In college, the gang retains a sense of wholesomeness, though there is a co-ed bathroom, more suggestive jokes ("UNDERPANTS!"), and continued make-out sessions. Shawn and Angela break up because he wants to "meet new people." Speaking of new people, the addition of the tall redhead Rachel McGuire (Maitland Ward) gives Jack and Eric a source of contentious comedy. She was also the resident sex kitten, tasked with using her toes to smear pasta sauce on Eric's face, dance around in lingerie, and serve as a prize to be won by Jack and Eric.

Shawn comes to regret breaking up with Angela, and his deep, aching love for her is explored in *Poetic License: An Ode to Holden Caulfield*, in which Cory reads his private poems at a showcase without realizing they are about Angela. In *Cutting the Cord*, Shawn tells Cory and Topanga that because he lost her, he fears he doesn't know how to love, and will never again have a meaningful relationship. In *The Truth About Honesty*, another episode banned from Disney Channel syndication, the friends play an honesty game. When Angela bets Shawn that he can't hook up with her without strings, he loses. In this episode, and in season five's *And Then There Was Shawn*, it was implied that other characters (Eric, Jack, Shawn, Angela) were sexually active, but not Cory and Topanga. Topanga allows Cory, who is exasperated with being abstinent, to see her butt. He calls it the "Promised Land."

In the episode *Everybody Loves Stuart*, Fred Savage guest stars as a popular professor on Pennbrook's campus who sexually harasses Topanga in her dorm room while, go figure, discussing morality and ethics. Cory confronts Stuart, who admits to "coming on" to Topanga, prompting Cory to assault him. "Do you believe as a college professor that it's okay to be alone in a dorm room with a young female student?" Feeny asks during a hearing that threatens Cory's enrollment at the university.

Sexual harassment was a pertinent issue in the nineties, so it's good that the show explored power dynamics in this episode. But the episode's existence is ironic, because in 1993, Fred and *The Wonder Years* co-star Jason Hervey were sued by a costume designer named Monique Long for sexual harassment. Alley Mills, who played the matriarch on *The Wonder Years*, would later claim that this was why the show was cancelled that year. Monique Long was discredited by the studio and in media reports, eventually settling with ABC out of court. More sexual harassment allegations would surface against the elder Savage in 2018 and 2022.

Season six also saw Shawn's absentee father in the hospital after suffering a heart attack from eating Rachel's "Killer Chocolate Cake" in *We'll Have a Good Time Then*. As Chet lies on life support, Shawn asks, "Why couldn't you just stick around? Was I not good enough for you?" Chet's death causes Shawn to briefly spiral in the midst of his separation from Angela. He leaves on a "road trip to nowhere," eventually returning when Amy Matthews gives birth to a baby she found out she was pregnant with in *Prom-ises, Prom-ises*.

The final season of the show begins with Topanga breaking up with Cory because she has lost faith in love after her parents' divorce. In *Angela's Men*, Angela's father, Army Sergeant Moore, comes to Pennbrook's campus to recruit for the ROTC program. Because Shawn feels he has no future (and partly to impress Angela), he again gives in to his temptation to do something drastic. Instead of drinking himself to death, joining a cult, running away, or considering felonious property damage, he decides to join the army. Angela and Shawn get back together when Angela's father intervenes. It turns out that Angela's mother left her as a child, and they reunite despite their abandonment anxiety.

This reunion partially inspires Topanga, who reunites with Cory for the final time. While ABC executives were initially against marrying Topanga and

Cory at the age of nineteen, a poll of 280,000 people on ABC's new website showed that viewers were demanding it. The pair finally wed on November 5 1999 in *It's About Time*, which had 11 million live viewers. During that same episode, Cory calls Shawn "trailer trash," prompting Eric to laugh and point at him in an extremely funny sequence, saying, "Ha ha, Shawn's poor!"

In *Picket Fences*, Shawn's deep emotional wounds are again dragged to the surface when he doesn't allow himself to be happy and content with living alone with Angela in a nice apartment. He can't believe his good fortune while his best friend Cory and his new wife rot away in dreary family housing. "We don't deserve this," he tells Angela, before convincing her that they should move out in to seperate homes. I yelled at my television screen. The show's conservative values (no shacking up!) melded with Shawn's inferiority complex. In this same episode, Shawn gives Cory a much-needed reality check because he won't stop whining about his crappy apartment. After all, Shawn grew up in a trailer. In *Family Ties*, Shawn learns that Virna was not his biological mother when she sends him a letter confessing to this fact. Shawn doesn't get to meet his real mother, which wounds him. "I don't have a dad, and I don't have a mom. I'm an orphan. I'm an old orphan."

Alan and Amy Matthews tell Shawn they want to adopt him, but this offends him. He storms away and visits his father's grave. A ghostly version of Chet tells him that his real mother was a stripper. "She wasn't really the mother type," he says, before assuring his son that "he didn't love her enough to keep her." Fanatic *Boy Meets World* viewers may remember Shawn saying in *I Love You, Donna Karan*, "I've seen the pain in my father's face every time a woman walks out because he's not 'good enough.'" Shawn needed to know that his father, though charming and funny, repulsed his wives by being perpetually unemployed, drunk, and abusive. Not to mention he told endless lies. Understanding that he is deserving of love and has a place to belong, Shawn returns to the Matthews home and accepts his role within their family (though he rejects being adopted).

In *The War* and *Seven the Hard Way*, a series of pranks and misunderstandings lead to hurt feelings, and the group fractures into the old heads versus the newbies. Topanga, Cory, and Shawn are on one side, while Rachel, Angela, and Jack are on the other. The fallout nearly becomes permanent when Cory and Shawn decide to blow up a nude photo of Rachel and put it in the student union. In the process, it's revealed that Shawn allowed Jack to see a private sexual photo of Angela. Topanga isn't really upset about the revenge porn, just pissed off that she wasn't included. Hey!

It's the nineties.

In an imagined future where the friends never reunite, Shawn is an unhappy world-traveling *Rolling Stone* writer. Angela reveals that she's also a freelance writer, which Shawn knows because he secretly reads her work. The group eventually reconciles with Eric's help, and nobody ever again mentions that Rachel's private photo was put on display for the entire campus. Because the showrunners couldn't give Shawn a break, Angela leaves him for Europe to be with her father in the series' penultimate episode, *Angela's Ashes*. When given the opportunity to propose to Angela and pursue a middle-class fantasy like Cory, Shawn resists the urge and watches Angela leave with her father. "It's see you later," she tells him. When she leaves, he declares a forlorn and final "Goodbye." Behind the scenes, Trina was falsely told by someone that none of the cast wanted her in the series finale, which is why she made her exit early. It's unclear who that someone was, but it was alleged to be Ben Savage or Michael Jacobs.

Season seven contained some okay episodes, but the rapid, somewhat rushed pace toward the show's ending (plus Eric Matthews' redundant stupidity) was painful. On May 5, 2000, the series finale of *Boy Meets World* aired to ten million viewers. When the series first began in 1993, viewership never dipped below 14.9 million. TGIF wasn't as popular as it used to be, thanks to more cable channels, the internet, and fresher sitcoms. ABC had picked the perfect time to wrap things up. With nothing left tying him to Philadelphia (Jack joins the Peace Corps with Rachel), Shawn packs up his bags to move to New York with Cory and Topanga, as the latter has accepted a prestigious law firm internship.

Final Thoughts

While entertaining, *Boy Meets World* was never going to change the world. Nor, like Michael Jacobs' previous series *Dinosaurs*, would it leave viewers with a gloomy sense of dread and hopelessness. While Cory was centered as the "Boy" in *Boy Meets World*, the true protagonist of the series for me was Shawn Hunter. From the early episodes, it was set in stone that Cory Matthews was destined to get married to Topanga and eventually have a comfortable and conventional lifestyle. While Cory Matthews' journey was clear, the path to adulthood was not paved with such careful intention for Shawn "Trailer Trash" Hunter, the abandoned son of a stripper and an abusive alcoholic.

When Jacobs conceived the show, Shawn's life wasn't the focus. But watching Shawn flounder, persevere, and grapple with unchecked mental health issues (the man was clearly depressed) was infinitely more interesting than white-bread Cory Matthews and his lifelong unrealistic romance. After the writers found their footing in the TGIF lineup, they found ways to hammer home a major question: what would have happened to Shawn if he didn't have the stability of Cory and the Matthews family? What if he hadn't known Mr. Feeny or Mr. Turner? Writers didn't tackle poverty as a systemic issue, but they emphasized the importance of community, role models, and second chances.

By doing this, the writers posed larger questions about what happens to any impoverished child of the nineties if they were set adrift with abandonment issues. According to the show, the consequences could be alcoholism, an inability to form meaningful relationships, reckless behavior, joining a cult, or becoming an underling for the mob. Had the show been even a modicum darker, we would have seen a bleary-eyed Shawn Hunter teetering on the edge of a building, ready to jump, before Cory or Mr. Feeny talked him down.

90s Christmas

If I close my eyes and picture it, I can see myself as a five-year-old child, surrounded by gift wrapping paper in my nana's living room, lording over my Dirt Devil vacuum toy, my Easy-Bake Oven, and *Scooby-Doo* tapes for my new VHS player. I was doomed to love Christmas. From movies to toys to music, the holiday was so delicious in the nineties.

1990

Top Toy: *Teenage Mutant Ninja Turtles*
Flicks: *Home Alone, Die Hard 2*

1990 was the year that the popular Christmas film *Home Alone* was released, grossing $467.7 million at the box office, making it the highest-grossing live-action comedy at the time. That record wouldn't be beaten for nearly two decades. *Home Alone* starred Macaulay Culkin as Kevin McCallister, an eight-year-old who gets left home alone in Chicago at Christmas while two burglars (including one played by Joe Pesci) attempt to break in. While the wealthy Uncle Rob of the McCallister clan could afford to fly a family of fifteen to Paris at Christmastime (four of them seated in first class), 1990 was a sour year for the average family.

For many Americans, it wasn't the best time for shopping, due to the 1990–1991 recession. Reported *The New York Times*, "As the number of shopping days left before Christmas dwindle, shoppers and vendors in New York and across the nation talk of spending less, hunting for bargains, cutting frills and holding back on the holidays. Retailers are projecting what salespeople, Salvation Army volunteers and shoppers already know: Money, this year, is tight." Perhaps this was one of the reasons that there were so many Scrooges.

Wrote James S. Henry in *Why I Hate Christmas: The Grinch Has It Right*,

> "(Almost a quarter of Christmas season sales are financed by credit cards or charge accounts, and January is the peak month for credit card delinquencies) and reduces our flagging savings rate (now below 5 percent of national income)... Christmas now accounts for 60 percent of the United States' annual $17 billion expenditure on toys and video games... this year we will consume $18 billion of alcohol, including 81 million gallons of hard liquor, 1.1 billion pounds of turkey, and a huge quantity of ham, cookies, pies, eggnog, stuffing, plum pudding, and other trimmings."

Other Christmas critics complained about "Christmas Creep," citing that stores began pulling out their holiday displays as early as October, though this wasn't a new phenomenon. "I think it's pretty depressing," said the assistant director of the Center for Retailing Studies at Texas A&M University. In Monrovia, California, one reporter counted yuletide merchandise being hung alongside Halloween decorations during the first week of October. "Christmas Creep" would happen more frequently as the decade unfolded. On a 1999 episode of the MTV show *Daria*, the ironic *Sick Sad World* segment joked about "the world's largest nativity scene in August."

Meanwhile, Jewish people and the non-religious would continue to question the dominance of Christmas in America throughout the rest of the decade. "*Should Christmas Be Abolished as a National Public Holiday?*" asked Richard Ganulin in *Deseret News* in 1998, before answering in the affirmative.

1991

Top Toys: Nintendo and Sega Genesis

One of the biggest events of the nineties occurred on Christmas Day 1991, when Mikhail Gorbachev resigned as President of the Soviet Union. Shortly after his televised speech, in which he declared the office extinct, the Soviet flag was lowered for the final time and replaced with the Russian flag.

For kids and teens who couldn't be bothered with foreign policy, the talk of Christmas that year was the highly coveted 8-bit Nintendo game system, which went for roughly $99.99 (about $236 today) at Toys"R"Us. Games were $49.99 each, and if your parents were really balling, you'd beg for the deluxe Super Nintendo system, which was $199.99 (about $473). Of course, if you were lusting after Sonic the Hedgehog, which was released that year, you'd need the Sega Genesis, which could be bundled together for $149.99

(about $355).

1992

Popular Toys: Super Soakers, Troll Dolls
Flicks: *The Muppets Christmas, Batman Returns, To Grandmother's House We Go*

Caspar Weinberger and five other Reagan aides involved in the highly illegal Iran-Contra scandal were given the gift of a pardon by outgoing President George H.W. Bush on Christmas Eve this year. Because people were still on a budget, traditional toys like Troll Dolls and board games were popular. Claimed the *Associated Press*, "Santa will show up this season with familiar classic toys that won't require mortgaging the family sleigh."

1992 was also the year that *Home Alone: Lost in New York* premiered. Child star Macaulay Culkin was paid $4.5 million plus 5 percent of the film's gross, compared to his $110,000 salary for the first movie. Donald Trump allowed the film to be shot in the Plaza Hotel, which he owned at the time, in exchange for a cameo. For kids who had seen *Home Alone 2*, a popular wishlist item was the Talkboy, a handheld voice recorder that altered Kevin McCallister's voice. A real version of the movie prop was created as a promotional tie-in and retailed for $24.99.

In Cincinnati, a chapter of the Ku Klux Klan erected a cross next to a menorah downtown. The Klan possessed a city permit to do so, based on religious freedom. Back in 1990, the city had banned Jewish people from erecting a menorah, citing it as a religious symbol (even though the city decorated with Christmas trees and lights). The Jewish congregation secured a federal court order to place a menorah, which they did in 1991 without incident. In 1992, the Klan placed their cross next to an 18-foot menorah. Two to three hundred people protested.

Said civil rights activist and Reverend Fred Shuttlesworth, "Somebody is bad off if they need the Klan to put Christ in Christmas. The Klan may have a legal right to put a cross here, but not a spiritual right." The cross was swiftly taken down by a 44-year-old named David Miller, who was arrested for disorderly conduct. He told the news, "I just decided there's too many kids in this community. There's hundreds of thousands of kids in this community. They don't need something like this."

The first SMS text message was sent on December 3rd, and it read "Merry Christmas." Lastly, Christmas in former Soviet Union territories was a major deal, with Russia celebrating the holiday for the first time in 70 years. "The Bolsheviks replaced crosses with hammers and sickle. Now they are being changed back," said the head of the Russian legislature's committee on religion.

1993

Popular Toys: Super Nintendo and Mighty Morphing Power Rangers
Flicks: *The Nightmare Before Christmas*

In 1993, the year that hip hop group TLC released *Sleigh Ride*, the average parent once again with money to splurge for the holidays, for the first time in a while. Parents fielded requests for Super Nintendos and the slightly more expensive Sega Genesis. There were op-eds and reports about violence in edgy games like *Street Fighter II* and *Mortal Kombat*. Having more money was also good news for parents of children who wanted other high-end toys like the American Girl Doll, which surged in popularity this year after positive media coverage. Wrote one happy columnist:

> "...more and more parents are looking at Barbie and seeing their little girls becoming Barbie, a cheap tart in neon spandex pants and high heels, driving around in a pink Corvette for the rest of her life with her dyed hair floating in the breeze, the neutered Ken at her side. They see girls on television looking and acting like prepubescent bimbos, and they read all the statistics about sexual activity, substance abuse and rebellion starting earlier and earlier. The American Girls dolls, on the other hand, appeal to daughters and parents who don't want to be pushed prematurely into adolescence..."

The $80-90 American Girl dolls and accompanying books explored girlhood from different historical perspectives, while hawking a bunch of pricey merchandise in the process. The first black doll, Addy Walker, was introduced this year. Addy's most popular accessories included school supplies, a Christmas outfit to match her Christmas book, and a sweet potato pudding kit. Some observers were annoyed that the first black doll was a former enslaved person. Wrote Megan Rosenfeld, "While the other dolls face such traumas as wild bears, sailing during a storm or even choosing between loyalty to the crown of England or the patriots of the new Colonies, none can really compare with watching your brother being whipped by a cruel overseer because he "done run off."

The quintessential office Christmas party was going through changes in the nineties thanks to new expectations for companies to root out sexual harassment in the workplace. Reported one columnist in 1993, "You might remember the way it used to be. Typically, they were held at a fancy hotel or restaurant and often during the workday. The spouses were discouraged from attending. No one would even think about bringing their kids. Alcohol was everywhere... there'd be the guy who dressed as Santa Claus and asked a female subordinate to sit on his knee..."

There were multiple reports of office Christmas parties being troublesome and potential human resource disasters, with well-meaning columnists offering advice on party etiquette that wouldn't end in a trip to human resources. Experts warned people not to overindulge at holiday parties and risk destroying their reputations, saying the nineties had ushered in a new conservatism. *The Chicago Tribune* reported that parties were "evolving" with less extravagance, increased family involvement, and non-alcoholic beverages on hand. It said, "They're not saying bah humbug, they're saying let's have a very respectful celebration."

1994

Popular Toy: Might Morphing Power Rangers
Flicks: *The Santa Clause, Miracle on 34th Street*

A Toys 'R' Us manager commented on the continued popularity of *Power Rangers*, saying, "At this point in time, there isn't a line that can give *Power Rangers* any real competition. Anything associated with *Power Rangers* this year, from pencils to stickers to toys, is going to move."

On October 28, Mariah Carey released her fourth studio album, *Merry Christmas*. The album's genre was unexpected, and it featured the smash mega-hit *All I Want for Christmas Is You*. It didn't actually chart at number one until 2019, but every Christmas since 1994, the song has been ubiquitous. It has earned Mariah Carey an estimated $80 million in royalties. *All I Want for Christmas Is You*'s timeless composition made it a worldwide hit, with a Scottish reviewer writing, "Bing Crosby may well be turning in his grave, but no child of the 1980s will be surprised to see Mariah Carey's sublime *All I Want for Christmas Is You* bounding up the charts after being named the nation's top festive song."

Lastly, my favorite Christmas movie, *The Santa Clause*, premiered. Bill Murray and Chevy Chase both turned down the role of Scott Calvin, aka Santa Claus, which went to Tim Allen of *Home Improvement* fame. There was a line in the original movie where Scott says "1-800-SPANK-ME," and after a kid in Washington called the number, which turned out to be an actual phone sex line, and racked up a $400 bill, the dialogue was removed from VHS tapes after 1999.

1995

Popular Toys: Playstation One and Buzz Lightyear Toys

The PlayStation launched in September 1995, and its super cool marketing campaign aimed at teenagers made it a highly coveted Christmas gift, although it was $299 (roughly $605 today). On December 21st, 1995, John Boehner, an Ohio Republican in the House of Representatives (and protégé of Newt Gingrich), dramatically announced he was giving President Clinton a box of coal during a press conference during the second government shutdown since November. The shutdown, which lasted from December 16 to January 6, made holiday budgets especially tight for the 284,000 people furloughed from their government jobs. Lastly, Trey Parker and Matt Stone collaborated on *The Spirit of Christmas*, a five-minute short film featuring Santa and Jesus battling each other. The movie, of course, became the basis for *South Park*, which debuted on Comedy Central two years later.

1996

Popular Toy: Tickle Me Elmo
Flicks: *The Preachers Wife, The Long Kiss Goodnight, Jingle All The Way*

Nobody really cared about $30 Tickle Me Elmo dolls until Rosie O'Donnell featured one on her show in early October 1996. Within two months, it became highly sought after, with scalpers re-selling them for as high as $1,500. Rumors of scarcity and chaos at Black Friday sales only fueled the demand. In Chicago in early December, two women were arrested for fighting over the last doll in a store. At a "Midnight Madness" sale at a Walmart in New Brunswick, Canada, there was a stampede of 300 people looking for the toys. One employee endured "a pulled hamstring, injuries to his back, jaw, and knee, a broken rib, and a concussion."

In Santa Barbara, a DJ named Hal Abrams held an Elmo doll "hostage" and invited people to come watch him shred it. Local news claimed the radio station received calls from concerned citizens begging them to stop. A Santa Claus impersonator eventually arrived and donated the toy to a local children's hospital. There were false rumors swirling that mob boss John Gotti Jr., son of the imprisoned mafioso John Gotti, had purchased a case of them during a shopping session at a Toys R Us in Queens, New York. One million Tickle Me Elmo dolls were sold by the end of the holiday season, and *Sesame Street* saw a major resurgence in popularity. Beanie Babies also became a fashionable collector's item this year. By 1997, counterfeit versions of the toys had begun to surface.

The Christmas toy craze was parodied in the 1996 film *Jingle All the Way*, starring Arnold Schwarzenegger and Sinbad as two dads on a competitive, romcom-style quest for a popular action figure. When Sinbad's character, a postal worker, threatens police with a pretend explosive device, he insists that he'll really do it, saying, "I work for the post office, so you know I'm not stable." It was an obvious dark joke for the parents in the audience, especially those familiar with the real-life reports of stressed-out employees "going postal" and killing their co-workers. While filming the movie in Minneapolis–St. Paul, Schwarzenegger made sure to plug the Planet Hollywood at the Mall of America location, offering a $200 fancy fête for people to meet him and receive his favorite cigars. *Jingle All the Way* was the last movie starring Phil Hartman, who would be killed by his wife in a murder-suicide two years later.

The most-watched episode of *The Oprah Winfrey Show* every year beginning in 1996 until 2010 was her *Favorite Things* segment. It all began when a senior member of her staff gifted her a pair of cozy pajamas. Explained her creative director, "She loved them so much, she bought them for the whole staff. And then she decided she wanted to gift them to her entire audience." As the years went by, Oprah's favorites catapulted small businesses into the stratosphere with mega sales. From Garrett's Popcorn to UGG boots to Spanx, Oprah promoted it. The best part was that lucky audience members left with every favorite item.

1997

Popular Toys: Teletubbies, Giga Pets, and Tamagotchi Virtual Pets
Flicks: *Jack Frost, Beauty and the Beast: The Enchanted Christmas, Home Alone 3*

Tamagotchi digital pets were huge this year, but if they went out of stock or were too expensive, there were the knockoff *Giga Pets*. Kids and teens loved the opportunity to look after their digital companions. Both were compared to the "pointless" Pet Rock of the 1970s, but the toys cleared a billion dollars in sales within their first year. TNT began its iconic 24-hour marathon of the 1983 film *A Christmas Story*, which switched over to TBS in 2004. Between 30 and 50 million people tune in to watch at some point every year. Lastly, Fidel Castro officially declared Christmas a national holiday for the first time since 1969. Ever since restrictions on religion had been lifted in 1991, more Cubans had been celebrating, but now they could officially do so. For the occasion, the prices of rum and pork were slashed. Pope John Paul II was due to visit the island the following month, marking a new era in relations between Cuba and the Catholic Church.

1998

Popular Toys: Furbies, Game Boy Color, Sock'em Boppers
Flicks: *I'll Be Home for Christmas, Jack Frost, Home Alone III*

The idea of teaching a toy bird to speak English was the appeal of *Furbies*, which ruled the holiday season in 1998. They retailed for $35 but could be found in newspapers and online for hundreds of dollars due to high demand and limited supply. On December 19th, conservatives got a major present when the House of Representatives voted to impeach President Bill Clinton for lying under oath about his sexual conduct.

1999

Popular Toys: *Pokémon* Everything, Bop It Extreme

Pokémon was massively huge in 1999, and all of the accompanying merchandise made for great Christmas gifts. For Americans who were scared shitless by the looming threat of Y2K, when computers were expected to crash and plunge the world into chaos at the stroke of midnight, Christmas '99 came with more anxiety than usual. While e-shopping had been growing since 1995, the end of the decade saw the most online shopping yet. This year, Amazon debuted its wishlist feature, with Jeff Bezos claiming, "I like to type in a random name, say 'Smith' in New York, and buy them a little thing off their list. It's more fun than feeding parking meters." That quote appeared in an article detailing the mountains of money Amazon was spending to outrank its competitors after sloppy Christmas shipping from 1996 to 1998. The article ended, "There's only this Christmas, and maybe a few more, to find out just how big Amazon.com can be."

Some companies couldn't keep up with the pressure of holiday demand. Toys 'R' Us mailed out 62 million catalogs in November offering free shipping for orders from its website. It was the fifth most visited store online in December, with 1.6 million visitors in one week, but the company couldn't fulfill 5 percent of its orders and sent customers $100 gift certificates to make up for it. Lastly, the final Christmas season of the decade was slightly impacted in Seattle by protests and riots against the World Trade Organization summit. Plenty of the nation's gifts were being made in sweatshops in the global south, in the process devastating local economies and changing migration patterns. "Ten million dollars of lost revenue, plus the $2 million they're saying there was in property damage, is a big chunk out of their holiday cheer," said one anarchist.

On Moesha

At my aunt's daycare in the early 2000s, the one thing us six- and seven-year-olds couldn't get enough of between games of Uno, passes at the Ms. PacMan machine, rounds of dodgeball, and made-up dance routines was the 1997 television film *Cinderella* starring Brandy Norwood. It was a regular re-watch for us because we delighted in the idea of a black princess— which was groundbreaking at the time. Some Disney executives weren't sure it was the right move. Thank goodness Brandy had proven not just her star power as a singer, but also her acting chops on a hit UPN series that was another recurring feature of my childhood.

Black Television at The End of History

Networks were branching into Black TV shows that weren't in the style of *The Cosby Show*, *Family Matters*, or *A Different World*. NBC found gold with 1990's *The Fresh Prince of Bel-Air*. Fox had *Martin* (1992–1997) and *In Living Color* (1990–1994). In 1993, Fox premiered the first series headed and created by a Black woman: *Living Single*. The show centered on Brooklyn-based magazine editor Khadijah James (Queen Latifah), her ditzy cousin Synclaire (Kim Coles), her quick-witted fellow Howard alum and lawyer friend Maxine Shaw (Erika Alexander), and the man-obsessed, gold-digging Regina (Kim Fields). Their friends and love interests Kyle (T.C. Carson) and Overton (John Henton) rounded out the cast.

Executive producer and writer Yvette Lee Bowser designed the four women after herself, saying, "I've been as ditsy as Synclaire, as superficial as Regine, as bitter as Max, and as focused and driven as Khadijah." The show achieved its goal of depicting more kinds of Black women—professional, single, sexy, hardworking—and was consistently in the top five in ratings among Black audiences for all five seasons. But it never cracked the top fifty shows overall, even with a revolving door of celebrity guest stars and Queen Latifah herself.

When UPN launched in 1995, it was the lowest-rated of six similar broadcast networks, and it was actively courting Black viewers, much like The WB, which also launched that year. While UPN's bread and butter was *Star Trek: Voyager*, it also aired *Malcolm & Eddie*, starring Malcolm-Jamal Warner of *The Cosby Show* fame and comedian Eddie Griffin. There was also *In the House*, starring LL Cool J, Debbie Allen, and later Alfonso Ribeiro. And who could forget *Homeboys in Outer Space*, starring Flex Alexander? Who am I kidding, most people *did* forget it, because it only lasted one season.

So UPN, whose viewership skewed mostly male, definitely wasn't touching The WB, which was churning out hits like *The Steve Harvey Show*, *The Wayans Bros.*, and *The Jamie Foxx Show*. They also took over *Sister, Sister* in 1995 after ABC dropped it. UPN needed a win. Enter the triple threat Brandy Norwood, the star of *Moesha*, a pilot CBS had passed on.

Teen Idol

Brandy was born in 1979 in McComb, Mississippi, but she relocated with her family to Carson, California, a city about 20 minutes from Leimert Park, in 1983. By this time, she was already performing in public, having made her gospel solo debut at the age of two. Her singing voice, which would eventually come to be referred to as "the vocal bible," came from her father, gospel singer and choir leader Willie Norwood. By age 11, she was a regular in talent shows and showcases, and she auditioned for Atlantic Records, who told her to come back when she was 14.

While 13, Brandy starred in the short-lived sitcom *Thea*. She signed with Atlantic Records at 14, dropped out of Hollywood High School in 1994, and released the quadruple platinum album *Brandy* that same year. The album was cited as being part of Erykah Badu's inspiration for 1997's *Baduizm*. My favorite songs include *Best Friend, I Wanna Be Down*, and the platinum-selling *Baby*. The 1995 video for *Baby* was shot in Times Square by Hype Williams, who was transforming hip-hop cinematography and becoming the go-to director for music videos.

Brandy was beautiful, unambiguously Black, and wore an endless array of braided hairstyles. Her creative direction was intentionally girl-next-door and appropriate for the youth. Brandy told an interviewer, "I've been offered a couple of songs I wouldn't sing at my age. I've heard songs I wouldn't dare sing." She described her image as being, "Nothing too loose or baggy, but nothing too tight. Nothing that shows my navel... I want to be young and positive... Gradually I'll take my clothes to a different direction. Gradually my face will change. I'll be a girl, then a young woman, then a woman."

1995 was an even bigger year for Brandy. She contributed *Sittin' Up in My Room* to the *Waiting to Exhale* soundtrack. She also went on tour with Boyz II Men in 1995. Brandy dated lead singer Wanya Morris, who is nearly six years older than her, from the age of 16, and they collaborated on her song *Brokenhearted*. Brandy later told VH1, "I was on a high. It was love. It was real love." There was an alleged love triangle with *Freak Like Me* singer Adina Howard.

In 1995, Brandy was nominated for a Grammy, the same year that Jennifer Weiner profiled the young songstress, writing:

> "Her days are spent on 'interviews, interviews, interviews,' endless recounting of how she got her first acting gig, on the short-lived show *Thea*, when she was 14. And how she cut her first album, simply titled *Brandy*, that same year. And how the album's gone platinum, and how she's spent the spring opening for her heroes, Boyz II Men. And how she's got a song, penned by Lenny Kravitz, on the *Batman Forever* soundtrack, and how she just cut a pilot for a new CBS sitcom, and how she nabbed spokesmodeling deals with *Seventeen* magazine and Sears, and how she's slated to be back in the studio for album number two in August, although that might have to wait, because she's got concert dates in Japan all summer long. 'Sometimes I get really tired,' she said, with an apologetic grin. 'I'd like to be asleep right now.'"

Jennifer Weiner ended the article by writing that Brandy needed to watch her back because a 14-year-old singer named Monica was on the come-up. Two years later, Monica and Brandy exploited the media's depiction of a rivalry between the two and released *The Boy Is Mine*, the best-selling song of the year. Rumors that the pair were feuding followed them for the rest of the decade. The Grammy-winning song appeared on Monica's album *The Boy Is Mine* as well as *Never Say Never*, Brandy's highest-selling album, which also included the hit *Top of the World*.

Brandy polished off 1997 by starring in the TV adaptation of *Cinderella*. She was handpicked by executive producer Whitney Houston, her idol. This film was significant because it was the second, yet most prominent, time *Cinderella* had been played by a Black actress on television. Said one producer, when pressed by a Disney executive to consider hiring the singer Jewel as Cinderella and keeping Whitney as the Fairy Godmother: "The whole point of this whole thing was to have a Black Cinderella. We didn't want to make it with a white Cinderella. We weren't interested in a white Cinderella."

The colorblind casting for the rest of the production was posed as a reflection of America's supposed post-racial society. This didn't go without comment. In a *Newsweek* article titled *The Myth of Cinderella*, one woman complained, "I'm genuinely bothered by the subliminal message that's sent when you don't have a Black Prince Charming. When my stepson, who's five, looks at that production, I want him to know he can be somebody's Prince Charming." The film, while critically chewed over, drew over 60 million viewers for its original airing. The following year, Brandy starred in the blockbuster hit *I Still Know What You Did Last Summer*. But before Brandy was being lauded as the perfect Cinderella and scream queen, she was the perfect Moesha.

Mo to The

After the 1992 LA riots, Leimert Park Village emerged as an important center for lower- to middle-class Black Los Angeles. The vibrancy and fun of Leimert Park stood in stark contrast to the gritty South Central LA depicted in gangsta rap. Described Jonathan Gold in a 1993 *Rolling Stone* feature on Dr. Dre and Snoop Dogg: "Leimert Park is the intellectual center of African American life in Los Angeles—jazz clubs, coffeehouses, bookstores, art galleries, a theater in a fine old movie palace, the restaurants that draw people from all over town. Neatly suited Muslims stand on the street corners, offering newsletters and bean pies for sale. Reggae blasts from the record shops." It was the perfect setting for *Moesha*.

Moesha debuted on January 23 1996. It was created by producer Ralph Farquhar and the writing team Vida Spears and Sara V. Finney. When asked about writing for *Moesha*, Vida Spears said, "There hadn't really been a show like that before, where the star was a young Black girl with brown skin and braids… [we] always talked about how we never had a role model like that on television when we were kids." Not only was *Moesha* groundbreaking because the series was told from the first-person point of view of a Black teenage girl, but it was also filled with compelling family dynamics, historical cultural references, fly fashion and hair, all the good guest stars, and seasoned professionals William Allen Young and Sheryl Lee Ralph anchoring the cast as Moesha's parents. It's no wonder it became UPN's most popular comedy show.

Farquhar's 1994 Fox comedy series *South Central* had failed for allegedly being too gritty. Commented a critic on the change in tone with *Moesha*, "Farquhar has moved his new show into the bright, solid middle class of Los Angeles, where Moesha's biggest trauma is receiving a shiny new Saturn when what she really wanted was a Jeep." That particular storyline, from episode six of season one, was wild to me growing up as a girl who was never promised a car just because she got her driver's license.

Moesha was middle class to the core. A recurring trope is Moesha asking her father for money as he chuckles the infamous Frank Mitchell laugh. Even if the family budget is tight, as frequently alluded to, Frank manages to provide a little coin. The Mitchells live in Leimert Park. Moesha's mother died three years before the show started, and season one mainly revolves around Moesha getting used to her stepmother Dee, who is also her high school principal. I enjoyed the unfolding of their relationship during my 2020 rewatch of the series because my stepmother was white, racist, and generally mean aside from her scant positive qualities.

Growing up, I envied Moesha's life in a lot of ways. Moesha and her friends hang out at The Den, where there are books, vegetarian offerings, poetry readings, talent showcases, and smoothies. A real-life parallel is Leimert Park's Project Blowed, an open-mic event that began in 1989 at a health food cafe called Good Life Cafe. There was no cussing allowed, and if someone was bad, the audience would chant, "Please pass the mic!" In the first season, while Moesha dates a poetry-reciting loverboy named Ohaji, played by the handsome Merlin Santana. Moesha was a deep-thinking intellectual who enjoyed Black literature.

Explained critic Ken Tucker, "*Moesha* proceeds from the assumption that viewers are hip to current slang, down with the latest pop-culture references, and also know who Zora Neale Hurston is (Moesha cites the late novelist as one of her role models)." This was amazing for a show that was specifically trying to reach a Black teen audience. Mo writing in her journal to the theme music is one of the most iconic parts of the series. As a fellow writer, whose world was the pages between her books and diaries growing up, Moesha being a scribe will always resonate with me. The nineties were a thriving period for Black writers on television, in film, and of course, in books.

There are multiple references to Terry McMillan and *Waiting to Exhale* within the series, and McMillan's star power in the culture at large was undeniable. She commanded $5,000 speaking engagement fees while holding tenure at the University of Arizona. Wrote Daniel Max in 1992,

[she] might just be as far as you can get from the traditional image of a tweedy novelist. She wears stylish clothes, lives in a plush Southwestern-style house in Danville, near Oakland, and rolls off the amounts of money made or owed to her with the ease of an agent, book advances, foreign publishing contracts, movie option money, book club money, reserves held against returns. She has a walk-in closet with rows of designer dresses and negligees."

McMillan's success inspired other Black writers to enter the world of publishing, which adds a dose of realism to Moesha's obsession with the written word. Speaking of realism, *Moesha* was in tune with real events, even if the conclusions were limited. In Episode 5 of Season 1, *Million Boy March*, Moesha and Kim join an all-boys organization called the Council of Concerned Youth. The boys don't want them involved. Moesha, who is headstrong and opinionated, makes a big splash, pissing off the leader, Whitlock. She ingratiates herself with the group's leadership by securing guest stars Jodeci. Because it's a nineties TV show and misogyny is softened by comedy, Whitlock says he'll open up an all-male scholarship if Moesha agrees to go on a date with him.

Later that season, Moesha attends a ditch party, which was a thriving South Central phenomenon at the time. She was dragged to the event by her troublesome friends. Moesha has a cycle of friends throughout the series, but in particular, she has three besties, who are typically depicted as getting her into trouble. Kim (Countess Vaughn) was my favorite. She was loud, funny, bubbly, and well-dressed. While Kim is confident, vivacious, and a great singer and dancer, even kicking Moesha's ass in cheerleading auditions, she was often the butt of jokes about her weight and characterized as unattractive and desperate for Hakeem (Lamont Bentley), Mo's other best friend and sometime love interest.

In the season three episode *Halloween Pt. 1: Kim's Revenge*, Kim overhears Moesha and Niecy talking and making jokes about her weight. Nobody got dragged like Niecy (Shar Jackson). Other characters were always saying she couldn't get a man, bringing up how many siblings she had, how her parents didn't care, and otherwise coming for her when she didn't send for them. The show somewhat redeemed her in Season 5 when it was revealed that she was not only smart and hardworking enough to enroll at the same college as Moesha, but had also earned a scholarship for her efforts.

A key theme in the series is family. Unlike on the classic formula on *The Cosby Show* and *Family Matters*, the original mom is dead. It's a source of conflict that Dee is a new addition to the family, but they eventually manage to overcome it. The Mitchells eat dinner together, do activities together, support each other, apologize to each other, and allow the neighbor from next door to eat their food and attend their events. Hakeem having a single mother is a major part of his characterization, leading him to start working early, "joking" about needing food from the Mitchells, and taking on multiple jobs. Because Hakeem can lean on the Mitchells, who are initially presented as an ideal family, the message is that families can blossom into communities, taking in those who need love, structure, and guidance when they aren't getting it at home.

Frank, as the ideal Black man, is a surrogate father. Hakeem is a major part of the Mitchell family dynamic. For instance, he takes Frank to a father-son seminar that breaks down the walls between Frank and Moesha's boyfriend Q in Season three. But most important to me is the relationship between Moesha and Frank, because I did not have a positive relationship with my father. Frank is, at times, overprotective, and eventually revealed to be a hypocrite, but you can never say he didn't take care of Moesha or fail to provide her with the tools for success.

Season Two was really juicy because Moesha falls in love with a boy named Q, a transplant from Queens who is rough around the edges. Frank Mitchell, the chuckling buppie republican that he is, immediately hates Q, who was brilliantly played by rapper Fredro Starr. To be fair, Q *is* a source of problems in Moesha's life. In *Credit Card (Big Trouble)*, Moesha is forbidden from letting anyone drive her car. Of course, Mo lets her new boyfriend Q drive the vehicle to a party, and they get stopped in Beverly Hills. While Q tells her and everyone else to chill out, because obviously he's encountered police before, Moesha begins her typical know-it-all and pompous behavior, when finesse is required when dealing with cops.

It's not fair, and it's no justification for police brutality, but it's the reality for Black people, something that Q understood. After all, the teenagers live in South Central Los Angeles, just a few years removed from the beating of Rodney King. When Moesha pushes the officer with tiny jabs instead of simply providing license and registration, Q says, "How we gonna do this? Rodney King or MLK?" The officer replies, "I was gonna let you go until homegirl here mouthed off." Q is arrested, and it turns out he has a warrant for jaywalking, showing he's had negative and overblown encounters with police before.

Moesha bails Q out of jail using her credit card and then enlists a scammer friend to remove the charge from Frank's bill. It was a recurring joke when I was growing up that Moesha was a hoe, and I mean this in the most non–

slut-shamey way possible. She was hilarious as hell for almost kissing Q's friend moments after he committed credit card fraud for her. Of course, Moesha got busted for the credit card scam. Q and Moesha continue to date, and she pressures Frank to accept him. As a hip-hop-loving wannabe rapper, Q represents everything that middle-class Frank is opposed to for his daughter. In *Guess Q's Coming to Dinner*, Frank expresses his displeasure that Q intends to skip college and chase a music career.

Season 2's boiling point occurs when Q is caught in Moesha's bedroom in *Cold Busted*. Her parents dramatically move her from Crenshaw High to the private Bridgewood Academy in season three, which seems absolutely nuts considering the fact that Dee is Crenshaw's principal and because the Mitchell pockets are tight. When Moesha suggests a family trip to Hawaii, send-my-daughter-to-private-school-on-a-whim Frank says they can't afford it. But Moesha was at Bridgewood for a year, and we were subjected to a few characters we never see or hear from again after this season.

As it turns out, larger minority audiences mean lower advertisement rates, and these television companies didn't care about representation as much as they wanted money. So if you ever look back on nineties shows and wonder why so many random non-Black characters were brought in, like *Moesha*'s string of white, Asian, and Latino recurring characters in Seasons 3 and 4, it's because executives wanted to woo non-Black viewers. Vida Spears and Sara V. Finney had been told by executives at the end of Season 2 that there weren't enough white characters, so that's why Moesha got sent to Bridgewood.

The stale character Hailey was trotted out for a few episodes before disappearing entirely. Her whole personality was being rich and thirsty for Black men and culture. I do love this season because Kim, Q, and Hakeem create CPQ, which gave us one of the best fictional songs ever: *Around*. Moesha manages the band because she can't sing. I love that the recurring joke that Moesha isn't a good singer. She is, however, a great writer, and in *The Play Scene* she is tasked with writing a scene for a class at Bridgewood. It is one of my favorite episodes because it incorporated Black 1940s history. It also highlighted the experiences and labor of love that Vida Spears and Sara V. Finney put into writing and revising Black-centered stories.

Season Three also features *Talk of the Town*, in which the Los Angeles Police Department raids an overcrowded teen club during a party Q is hosting and antagonizes patrons, leading to Andell (Yvette Wilson) being arrested. Moesha and her friends host a meeting with community members and local businessmen who want to close the club, including the Black man who called the cops. This episode highlighted the generational and class divide happening among Black boomers and Gen X, who often shared the same spaces but not the same opinions on music or policing. As the teenagers argued for the club to stay open to stay out of trouble, the importance of a third space was emphasized. It turns out that the Black business owner just wants to gentrify Leimert Park. "How come there are only white people in this picture?" Asks an elderly black woman, referring to the black business owner's presentation board. "It's only a picture," he says. "And worth a thousand words!" She replies angrily.

During all of these events, Frank and Moesha's relationship really begins to deteriorate. As a 17-year-old, Moesha's desire to spread her wings and try new things is a major source of conflict. I will fully admit, Moesha is annoying and does seriously stupid things, like taking her drunk friend's keys and giving them to a complete stranger in Tijuana, Mexico (*This Time You've Gone Too Far*). But Frank exacerbates issues. When Moesha gets a tattoo in *Body Language*, he yells at her for looking like a tramp.

In the next episode, *Pajama Jam*, while Moesha is attending a co-ed sleepover, Frank barges in and forces Moesha to go home. Yes, she lied about boys being present, but him arriving to drag her home makes her feel controlled. After all, she had been in the middle of establishing agency and rejecting a boy's request to get physical. The boy in question was Moesha's Bridgewood love interest, Jeremy (Usher Raymond). This, and other issues, prompt Moesha to move out in a show of independence. When she makes it back home in Season Four nearly six months later, there are a bunch of new problems, based on creative decisions that eventually lead to Vida Spears being fired. But more on that in a moment.

When Moesha moves out, the stress causes her little brother Myles to start smoking weed. The episode, *Hello, What's This*, was adorably framed with messages from the cast about drug problems. The family eventually goes to therapy (a sign of nineties psychoanalyzing culture), but the uneasy tension continues to strain Moesha and Frank's relationship as she prepares to graduate from high school. For her senior year in season four, Moesha returns to Crenshaw.

While viewers were encouraged to watch the weed episode with their families to talk about what they had seen, no such messages framed the episodes in which an older person takes advantage of a younger one. Consider the season four episode: *Teacher*. Moesha recites a poem at the beginning, saying, "I am a Child of God, but I am not a child. I am my mother and father's child, but I am not a child." Right away, we know Moesha is about to be pushing limits. In this episode, Moesha has a new photography teacher named Channing. Niecey asks in front of the entire class, "Can I call you daddy?," in one of the series' most cringeworthy moments.

Later, after abundant flirting and an inappropriate after-school hangout, Moesha kisses Channing in a darkroom, and he definitely reciprocates, then admits if she wasn't his student it would have gone further! Channing quits, and somehow nosy Dee and Frank never find out about it, and the teacher never faces consequences for habitually blurring the line between teacher and student. In a similar season three episode, *Age Ain't Nothin' But a Number*, tellingly a title based on the debut album written by R. Kelly for his underage victim Aaliyah, the 17-year-old Hakeem dates a 25-year-old woman. The relationship only ends because Hakeem doesn't want to hide the fact that they're dating, and the woman goes off to live in the sunset without consequences or reprimand.

It was a reflection of the times, when age gaps between older teenagers and young adults were viewed much more benignly. What other plot elements during the first five seasons reflected dating and sex in the nineties? Back in season one, interracial dating was highlighted when Moesha and her love interest Matt encounter a racist on a date (*Reunion*). In season two, when a list says Moesha had the biggest butt, she tries to cover it up because she takes it as an insult (*The List*). While it is objectifying, the notion that a big butt is bad is some nineties shit. Before the rise of big butts in the mainstream outside of Black culture, nineties media and celebrities pushed a super skinny aesthetic that would have a larger impact on a middle-class girl in California like Moesha.

In the season two episode *Labels*, Moesha spreads a rumor that Hakeem's cousin Omar is gay. When Omar comes out to Hakeem, he doesn't take it well, and Omar never reappears. The situation never gets brought up again, and small jokes throughout the rest of the series remind you that heterosexuality is the default "norm" in the ideal middle-class Black world of the nineties. In season four's *Birth Control*, Niecey reveals that she lost her virginity. This prompts a curious Moesha to go to a health clinic (which is totally nineties) to ask questions about sex. At the time, Moesha wants to have sex with her college-aged boyfriend Aaron, who randomly rescued her in the previous episode at a party from being date raped while she was visiting the campus. Frank Mitchell hated age-appropriate Q, but not Aaron, who he welcomes with open arms.

Moesha ultimately doesn't go through with the sex because she finds out that Aaron isn't a virgin, though she does take home contraceptive pills. The thing I appreciated about this episode was how Niecey said she didn't regret having sex. Keep in mind that while white teen shows like *Dawsons Creek* incorporated a bunch of sex and characters lost their virginities, sex was a much more taboo topic for Black teenagers. Within the context of HIV/AIDS in the nineties and abstinence rhetoric, it was refreshing for a Black teen girl on a Black show beholden to respectability politics to say she had sex and wasn't ashamed about it.

Frank doesn't find out about the birth control pills until season five, but sex also popped up again in season four's *The Rite Stuff*, when a pregnant debutante is kicked out of the prestigious Ladies of Eminence ball that Moesha's mother once participated in. During a period of teen pregnancy being under the microscope, this made for a juicy storyline. The debutante in question is the bourgeois and wealthy Candace Owens prototype Mary Ellen, the one Bridgewood character who survived season three. While the two girls have always been rivals, Moesha leads a boycott to allow the pregnant Mary Ellen to be in the ceremony. When Mary Ellen is not reinstated and the ball continues as scheduled, Moesha is the only one to stick to the boycott.

In season four's *Life Imitating Art*, Moesha and other Black students at Crenshaw get into it with Latino students when her friend Antonio paints a mural dedicated to Cesar Chavez during Black History Month. Moesha questions why Black heroes can't be celebrated during her news broadcast. "Since it is black history month and 85% of the student body is African-American, maybe the administration should have considered signing off on a mural that depicted us too," Moesha says. This leads to to the mural being defaced and the two racial groups clashing. The standoff between the two groups reflected Latino-Black divides in Los Angeles that remained after the LA Riots.

Latino youth attended disadvantaged schools and dealt with anti-immigration sentiment, poverty, and racism. They wanted representation in schools and media. Antonio and his peers wanted a slice of that by having that mural, which Moesha and the audience contend with. The ending of the episode was actually realistic and disheartening as hell. Instead of either group getting a dedicated mural, the wall is painted a sickening white and everything goes back to normal. "It's ironic that both groups with so much to offer would rather have nothing than see the other group get just a little bit of something," Moesha notes as the episode closes.

Moesha graduates and turns 18 at the end of season four, and her messy ass friends invite all her many boyfriends over for the celebration. While I was rooting for Q, Moesha ends up choosing her ex-teacher Channing. That relationship fizzles quickly, thankfully. Moesha decides to forgo college at Northwestern University to work at *Vibe* Magazine by the end of the season. *Vibe* Magazine was born in 1992 and was a significant gatekeeper of Black culture. While it wasn't completely Black owned or exclusively Black, it highlighted Black artists and hip hop at its core. Like other Black television shows of the era, hip hop was always laced into the plots.

For me, Moesha is divided between the BD period and the AD period. The D stands for Dorian, played by Brandy's younger brother Ray J, and he arrived in the season five premiere. Ray J guest starred twice before, including in the *Million Boy March* episode, but this time he was introduced as Moesha's cousin. Dorian was annoying and barely added anything to the show, apart from his existence leading to a revelation that totally re-writes the fabric of Frank Mitchell, the upstanding father. Dorian's existence turns Frank into a liar, adulterer, and deadbeat. He cheated on Moesha's mother, fathered a child (Dorian), and sent him to live with his sister.

This element of Frank's backstory, strangely, is alluded to in earlier seasons. Back in season two, when committing the credit card fraud, Q's friend shows Moesha's father's salary at the Leimert Saturn dealership, making Moesha say, "Woah, Daddy makes that much? He must have another family." In *Million Boy March*, Ray J's guest appearance as an annoying hype man for the misogynistic Whitlock leads to Moesha telling him something along the lines of, "Last time I checked, my father had one son and he isn't you."

But the actual plot element of Frank the Cheater was added after these characters had been developed, to boost ratings and drama, and it conflicted with earlier coverage of the show as a positive depiction of Black families. Reported *Jet Magazine* in 2000, "Moesha has transformed from a show about a very nice happy-go-lucky family to a program that tackles social issues as drug use and premarital sex." It was vastly different from how Brandy originally described it in 1996, saying, "[Moesha's] responsible and listens to her dad. Her friends are wild, but she isn't. Most of the Black shows on TV now are so unreal. There's no moral. There is a moral on Moesha."

This change to thrilling and gritty drama didn't automatically translate into higher ratings. Viewership dipped from 3.3 million in 1998 to 2.4 million for season five in 1999. It still had some good episodes, like when Niecey and Moesha stand up for each other in a racist professor's class. The arguments about what was "politically correct" and when Black people were being "too sensitive" were potent. Season five also featured guest appearances by Maya Angelou, Jenifer Lewis, and Mary J. Blige. Ratings went back up to 3.3 million for season six, but this was below the series high of season four, which carried an average of 4 million viewers an episode.

Meanwhile, amidst ongoing rumors that Countess Vaughn and Brandy didn't get along, Kim Parker was given her own spinoff show in 1999 with her mother Nikki, played by Mo'Nique. Yvette Wilson also left *Moesha* and appeared on *The Parkers* as her character Andell. Vida Spears, the primary opposition to the darker storylines on *Moesha*, was fired in 1999. Sources behind the scenes claimed that Brandy and her mother, Sonja, were among the main people lobbying for more serious plot lines, and Vida's departure gave them greater control. Also, Brandy was in and out of medical treatment for dehydration and exhaustion during this period of production. Vida became a producer on *The Parkers*, which became UPN's new highest-rated show, beating out *The Steve Harvey Show* over at The WB.

After Frank's big reveal on *Moesha*, the storylines became darker for the remainder of the season and the next. The show was abruptly canceled in 2001, ending on two cliffhangers in which Miles was kidnapped and a positive pregnancy test was found in Moesha's dorm. Where was Miles? Who was pregnant? We'll never know, and we'd never get any more appearances from Lil' Kim, who guest-starred at the end of the series. Various cast members have since died, including Lamont Bentley, Merlin Santana, Bernie Mac, and Yvette Wilson, plus guest cast members like Maya Angelou and Kobe Bryant, who appeared in season two. Relatedly, it made headline news when Kobe invited Brandy to his prom at Lower Merion High School in Pennsylvania in 1996. His classmates weren't pleased that the attention for their special day was on the young NBA draftee and the most famous Black teenager in the world.

Brandy went on hiatus when *Moesha* ended and was struggling with depression, the fallout of an emotionally abusive relationship, and an eating disorder. It turned out she had been extremely unhappy during her late-nineties era of superstardom. The fact that Wanya Morris broke up with her in 1997 was part of the stress. She'd recall, "I wanted to be so thin. That was my main thing, so I started not taking care of myself, not eating properly, not eating at all, diet pills, regurgitating, and all of these things that girls do."

The season two storyline about Moesha hating her "big butt" is more potent when you consider how Brandy felt about herself.

UPN began phasing out its Black shows in the early to mid 2000s.

Final Thoughts

In the mid-nineties, when Black Americans were navigating a post–Rodney King world, reveling in the success of the Million Man March, and riding a new wave of Black achievement, the emphasis on the Black family, fatherhood, and responsibility dominated rhetoric and advice from all the noteworthy politicians and experts. The very first Black teen comedy centered around a Black girl had the family values that people were calling for, and it's no wonder why it was initially a hit. It provided stability and comfort, with heavy doses of Black culture that wasn't watered down like on *Sister, Sister*. It also depicted a fun and positive view of South Central L.A. by immersing Moesha and her family in Leimert Park, which was a beacon of Black creativity. It's a beautiful and imperfect time capsule of Black girlhood in the nineties.

90s Style

My mother found infinite pleasure in dressing her baby girl in the latest fashions. I've seen countless pictures of myself in carefully crafted toddler couture, rocking everything from a sailor outfit with 24K gold bracelets to bright cotton jumpers with matching jelly shoes. In an increasingly globalized and connected world ripe with innovations, investments, and cheap sweatshop labor, there were endless possibilities. Goths, cholos, skater kids, and designer divas walked the same streets as streetwear lovers, minimalist enthusiasts, and grunge fans. Clothes weren't the only form of self-expression. Many people became much more precise when choosing technology, perfume, hair, and cosmetics in what Paul Smith called the "age of mass customization."

Apple, Abercrombie and Air Jordans

No computer was as stylish as the iMac G3, which saved Apple when the company teetered on the brink of collapse. Steve Jobs was tasked with creating an all-in-one computer for a relatively low $1,200 (about $2,400 today) in 1997. Jobs delivered the G3, which was curvy, colorful, translucent, and boldly featured no floppy disk port. Instead, there was something new: Universal Serial Buses, or USBs. When the iMac G3 hit the market in 1998, it sold 800,000 units in 20 weeks, nearly half to first-time computer owners. Apple ultimately sold over 6 million units, and the product's design would make tech more imaginative and stylish, plus, now the floppy disk had one foot in the grave. The company introduced the must-have clamshell iBook in 1999.

While Abercrombie & Fitch was established way back in 1892 and had a 456-page catalogue by 1909 featuring sporting goods, apparel, and the mysterious game of Mahjong imported from China, its target audience would change in the nineties after being bought by The Limited in 1988. At the time, the company was losing $25 million a year. Enter president Michael S. Jeffries in 1992. With a new focus on the American teenager, Abercrombie selected Bruce Weber as chief of photography, and his brand of "beefcake"/ homoerotic black-and-white photography served the brand well. Its high price points for tight T-shirts, jeans, hoodies, and more set it apart in the teen industry and made it highly coveted. The white advertising, centering the "All-American" look, only added to the Abercrombie mythos. Rumors abounded that the store mostly hired white employees and fired minorities without cause, which would haunt the company in the next decade.

Abercrombie started with modest sales of $85 million in 1992, which jumped to $111 million the following year, and $165 million in 1994. But Abercrombie's decision to introduce *A+F Quarterly*, a scintillating magazine criticized as soft porn, changed everything. While American Eagle, JCPenney, and Delia's had produced magazine-style catalogs earlier for a nineties audience, *A+F Quarterly* was the most popular and the most controversial. The company's executives insisted the magazine was intended for consumption by young adults, not the children or teens perusing the aisles of Abercrombie. It included racy topics, highly stylized non-frontal nudes, and interviews with celebrities and politicians in between a few clothing ads here and there.

Lil' Kim was in the second issue. There were features on Spike Lee, Bret Easton Ellis, Rudy Giuliani, and Clive Barker. The only person on the record to turn down a feature was Donald Trump. By 1998, when the brand apologized to Mothers Against Drunk Driving for seemingly promoting binge drinking and drunk driving, Abercrombie was second in sales for teenagers behind *American Eagle*, making approximately $805.2 million. "I like girls who wear Abercrombie and Fitch," sang the band LFO in their platinum hit *Summer Girls* in 1999.

In the *A+F Naughty or Nice* Christmas catalog of 1999, a feature with porn star Jenna Jameson ruffled more than a few feathers. Parent groups and the lieutenant Governor of Illinois, Corinne Wood, called for a boycott. Abercrombie decided to sell all future issues of *A+F Quarterly* in shrink-wrap and require identification for purchase. For $6 a copy, or $12 a year, you could browse the latest Abercrombie styles and be in possession of the most controversial "magalogue" on the market. Circulation would eventually peak at over one million. The brand's status with teenagers and young adults would only rise in the new millennium.

A is also for Air Jordans. Beginning in 1990, Air Jordans were featured frequently on *The Fresh Prince of Bel-Air*. On January 26, 1992 during the Super Bowl, a Bugs Bunny and Michael Jordan advertisement featuring the shoe of the decade lead to a pitch that eventually created *Space Jam*, and shoes were a big part of the movie. Sneaker collecting escalated as an abundance of colorways and limited edition drops hit the market, including in Japan, where a series of muggings in 1996 pushed shoe prices up to between $600 and $2,000 USD. That $2,000 price, in particular, was for the '95 Air Max Yellow. Said one young man, "I see a lot of people who look like they want my shoes. I get nervous if too many people surround me."

In 1997, the same year that thousands of Vietnamese and Indonesian laborers went on strike at Air Jordan factories for an extra one cent an hour, Jordan Brand was established. The workers earned eight cents a day to Michael Jordan's $56,000 a day— an ugly feature of globalization, the World Trade Organization, and trade at the so-called "end of history." In Cambodia, because the country was not a member of the WTO, there were no quota limits on exports, sparking a wave of foreign investment and child labor, including by Nike. But in May 1998, amidst reports that $9.1 billion in sales were being drowned out by falling stock prices, layoffs, and criticism, the company announced reforms that didn't impress striking factory workers.

Bandanas, BBW, and Bags

Not only were bandanas big this decade, in part because of hip-hop and gang culture, but so was Bath & Body Works, which launched in 1990 as part of Express. In 1991, "it had just 95 stores with sales of $20 million. By 1996, [there were] 750 stores as sales hit $753 million," leading *Business Week* to call the store the "McDonald's of Toiletries." Can you smell the Plumeria and Cucumber Melon?

Bags became distinguishable "it" items this decade, which was relatively new. Take the Fendi Baguette bag, which debuted in 1997 and became popularized by Carrie Bradshaw in *Sex and the City*, alongside another B, Blahnik shoewear. The Baguette, which stood out from the big totes of the era, was a hit. Fendi maximized the trend by expanding the bag into hundreds of colorways. "Since the fall of 1997, when the Baguette was introduced, there have been 500 variations, ranging from a $475 black nylon bag to a $12,000 hand-loomed version of which only a handful were made," wrote Elizabeth Hayt in 1999.

Fendi's popularity surged so rapidly that a majority stake in the company was acquired by Prada and Louis Vuitton in 1999 for approximately $900 million. Hayt reported on the phenomenon of bag collectors, saying, "The basic black leather bag, a staple of most every woman's wardrobe, looks tired by comparison to newer purses in unusual fabrics or embellished with embroidery, beading and fur. The accessories market, whether low- or high-end, is peaking in part because of widespread handbag fever." Hayt also discussed a rise in handbag sales at luxury stores like Barneys, for trendy picks like the Dior Saddle Bag, the Prada Bowling Bag, or Kate Spade bags. This was partly because bags cost a fraction of a designer outfit and could still signal luxury, plus, you could wear them more often. Maybe you couldn't afford a $3,000 Gucci outfit, but you could possibly afford a $900 Gucci Jackie bag.

Coogi, Calvin Klein and Chic Heroin

Notorious B.I.G. admitted to not being a heartthrob but bragged about being "Coogi down to the socks" in the 1994 song *Big Poppa*. In addition to rapping "Every cutie with a booty bought a Coogi" on the 1997 *Hypnotize*, the New York rapper was regularly shown in *Coogi* sweaters. The Australian brand, which had been around since 1969, became an iconic part of the nineties hip-hop fashion landscape.

In 1992, Calvin Klein was on the brink of bankruptcy when it introduced Mark Wahlberg and Kate Moss in boxing shorts. The sexy ads also featured Kate topless. In 1993, she was the face of Obsession, whose advertisements were ubiquitous. She also promoted the unisex CK One, which made the company over $5 million in just ten days when it launched in 1994. It was the first unisex fragrance to become that popular. Later advertisements featuring Moss would cause criticism of her body, with people accusing her of having an eating disorder and drug addiction. Though Moss never confirmed those rumors, she embodied the "heroin chic" trend. Snorting heroin had come into vogue in certain circles in the nineties while injection use declined due to HIV/AIDS. Heroin addiction was explored in various films like *Pulp Fiction*, *Gia*, and *The Basketball Diaries*, and was forefront in the American mind when images of thin women with dark eye shadow graced fashion advertisements.

Another model associated with the heroin chic trend was Jaime King, who began her career at 14, and did confirm that she started using the drug on her first job. King was featured in numerous magazines and catwalks. A prominent photographer she worked with was Davide Sorrenti, who died with heroin in his system at age 20 in 1997. Said his mother Francesca on the drug problem in the fashion industry: "Heroin chic isn't what we're projecting. It's what we are. Our business has become heroin chic. Someone taking pictures of that magnitude has to have experienced hard drugs."

President Bill Clinton said of the heroin chic trend in 1997, "You do not need to glamorize addiction to sell clothes. American fashion has been an enormous source of creativity and beauty and art and, frankly, economic prosperity for the United States... and we should all value and respect that. But the glorification of heroin is not creative, it's destructive. It's not beautiful; it's ugly. And this is not about art; it's about life and death. And glorifying death is not good for any society." Two years before that comment, the president also criticized Calvin Klein's 1995 campaign featuring purported "teenagers" flashing their underwear in a wood-paneled basement. Bill Clinton and parent groups lambasted the company for its use of "half-dressed adolescents," initiating a Department of Justice investigation regarding potential violations related to child sex abuse media. While all of the models were over the age of 18 and no charges were filed, Calvin Klein announced it was pulling the ads that same year.

Dennis Rodman and Dress Codes

Dennis Rodman was at the peak of his career in the late nineties as a member of the record-breaking Chicago Bulls, but his on-the-court achievements paled in comparison to the media fodder surrounding his affair with Madonna, his random Vegas quickie marriage to Carmen Electra, his sexual assault settlements, and his androgynous sartorial choices. The buzzcut he wore in a bevy of colors. The piercings. The tattoos. The silver cami top. The gold crop top with the black velvet jacket. You also can't forget his wedding dress moment at a book signing for his 1996 autobiography, *Bad As I Wanna Be*. Androgyny was in, and no basketball player challenged the gender binary and expectations of style quite like Rodman.

If you wanted to dress like Rodman at school in the nineties, good luck. More schools than ever before were implementing stricter dress codes and uniforms. In 1990, the *Chicago Tribune* reported that numerous D.C. schools were seeing students and parents voluntarily adopt uniforms, "the familiar badge of parochial and private schools." For many advocates, school uniforms took the pressure off students to be in style, helping them focus more on learning. So in 1990, approximately 3,000 of the 80,000 D.C. public school students were wearing uniforms, all of them elementary or middle schoolers. At one elementary school, the principal "recalled a great deal of competition among students over who had the best clothes" before the adoption of the dress code.

In 1995, George Judson for *The New York Times* documented the restrictions taking place on American middle and high school campuses in Connecticut at a time when teenagers had more options for shopping than ever before. "No hats, no bare midriffs, no see-through clothing, no underwear showing, no vulgar T-shirts, no sunglasses, no beepers, no cellular phones, no oversized jewelry that can be used as weapons: the more or less standard list of prohibitions that Stamford is considering for its high schools is a world away from dress codes in the 60s, when blue jeans were banned and skirts had to reach the knee."

Meanwhile, school districts across the country were banning baggy clothes, symbols, gang colors, and certain streetwear in areas where violence, gangs, hip-hop, and/or racial infiltration were a concern. But as documented by Rob Killen, school dress codes were nowhere near consistent, sparking frequent battles between administrators, students, and even parents. Here's a list of what Killen found to be banned across the country:

> "Doc Marten shoes, baggy pants, a backward 'R'... the colors red, black, white, green, and blue, 'Old English'-style writing, peace symbols, crowns... dollar signs, Playboy bunnies, pitchforks, the color combinations black/gold and blue/black, Converse shoes, winged hearts, collegiate logos, backward swastikas, the word 'vegan,' the Cuban flag, Star of David, pentagrams, rosaries, and crosses."

Killen quoted a police officer as saying, "The list is endless." This list of prohibited items obviously expanded to include trench coats in the aftermath of Columbine. Of course, these rules didn't always please parents, some of whom noted that most of the controversy was over what girls chose to wear, making their bodies prime areas of sexualization and debate. Added Judson, "Outside Fort Worth, teachers in the Birdville School District began the year measuring girls' skirts to enforce a four-inch-above-the-knee rule. Four hundred students were told to change their clothes on opening day, and mothers of tall girls complained that stores did not sell skirts long enough for their daughters to comply."

Even with dress codes and uniforms, students managed to impart personal and conventional style into their wardrobes. In 1999, it was reported that the average parent was spending $455 per child on back-to-school items, and that obviously wasn't all scented erasers, mechanical pencils, and Lisa Frank goodies. That was a 12% increase from the previous year, and a slew of celebrity-endorsed advertisements and must-have status brands were part of the shift.

Everybody Loves Kim

Kimberly Denise Jones was the original hip-hop fashion risk-taker. While her peers were known to be more androgynous—think Queen Latifah and Da Brat— Kim embodied sex appeal and confidence. "Everybody wanted to dress her, photograph her, put makeup on her. Annie Leibovitz, Bruce Weber," said Christina Murray, an executive at Atlantic Records. Many of her outfits were styled by Misa Hylton.

Instead of leaning into quiet luxury and minimalism, Kim was all about logos and maximalism, like the time she wore a catsuit with 965,000 crystals and a bejeweled headcage. Kim referred to herself as "The Black Madonna." Her lyrics were laced with designer, and she regularly switched up her hairstyles during a time when lace fronts and custom wigs were pricey. For her 1996 debut album *Hardcore,* the leopard print bikini she wore for the cover was designed by Patricia Field, the soon-to-be *Sex and the City* costume designer.

Kim signed to Wilhelmina Models in 1998, promoted the brand Candie's with Brandy, and appeared as Versace's guest at the 1999 Met Gala, when it was still a super exclusive event. She donned a pink fur coat, a bra, and hot pants that caused a sensation. The matching shoes she wore were too big, but she still made it up the famous stairs of the Metropolitan Museum. Later that year, Kim's purple look at the Video Music Awards, featuring an exposed breast and matching pasty, was cemented into style history.

Kim's glamorous and expensive lifestyle was as much a part of her image as the raw sexual bravado and criminal fantasy. Said Jacob York, then-president of her label Undeas Entertainment: "[Kim] wasn't the wife. She was the high-end side chick to drug dealers. We placed her in a world that we were living in, and it was: You wear all of the finest things because the number one drug dealer, you're his side chick, and he buys you everything. It's all driven by the male hormones, the male ego, the fantasy. It's not about love. It's about being nasty."

Yikes. While Kim was a fashion girl through and through, and she will always be revered for the risks she took in the nineties, her sartorial choices can't be viewed without examining her mindset. She said in a 2000 interview, "All my life men have told me I wasn't pretty enough, even the men I was dating. And I'd be like, 'Well, why are you with me, then?' It's always been men putting me down just like my dad. To this day when someone says I'm cute, I can't see it. I don't see it no matter what anybody says."

By the late nineties, she was rocking blue contacts, which came into fashion just as brightly colored weaves, particularly 613, were gaining popularity. Kim also opened up about her breast implants, just the beginning of her journey with plastic surgery: "That surgery was the most pain I've ever been in in my life. But people made such a big deal about it. White women get them every day. It was to make me look the way I wanted to look. It's my body." In the same interview, she admitted, "I have low self-esteem and I always have. Guys always cheated on me with women who were European-looking. You know, the long-hair type. Really beautiful women that left me thinking, 'How can I compete with that?' Being a regular Black girl wasn't good enough."

Before Biggie died in 1997, he was physically and emotionally abusive to Kim in their toxic relationship. It's hard to say what Kim's legacy would be if he had not died. Speaking with bell hooks in a 1997 *Paper* magazine interview, she alluded to Biggie's emotional abuse, saying, "[He said] you ain't shit without me. You always goin' to need me." She continued, "Till this day I need that person, so they say, 'You need me. You can't fucking make it without me. You're ugly.'" It's upsetting that while Kim thrived in the spotlight, this is what the stylish Queen Bee was subjected to behind the scenes, and worse.

Fashion Conspiracies and "Fast" Fashion

In 1991, Spike Lee referenced an episode of *The Oprah Winfrey Show* that doesn't exist. He said, "Last week, Oprah Winfrey had Liz Claiborne on the show. I guess she wears Liz Claiborne's clothes all the time. Claiborne got on and said she didn't make clothes for Black people to wear. Oprah stopped the show and told her to get her ass off the set... How you gonna get on Oprah's show and say you don't make clothes for Black women? It definitely happened. Get the tape. Every Black woman in America needs to go to her closet, throw that shit out, and never buy another stitch of clothes from Liz Claiborne." This proposed boycott obviously didn't go according to plan because I remember a lot of women in my life wearing Curve perfume. This wasn't the only fashion conspiracy.

By the mid-nineties, Tommy Hilfiger had allegedly appeared on *Oprah* and told her he didn't want Black women in his clothes. Another rumor claimed he didn't like Asians wearing his brand. A Filipino newspaper latched onto the story and published a piece titled *Eat Your Clothes, Mr. Racist Designer* in November 1996. The rumor became so pervasive on the internet that the company issued a statement in March 1997: "Tommy Hilfiger did not make the alleged inappropriate racial comments... Hilfiger wants his clothing to be enjoyed by people of all backgrounds and his collections are put together with the broadest cross-section of individuals in mind. To reinforce this, he features models of all ethnic backgrounds in his fashion shows and advertisements."

Slate Magazine emphasized how beneficial the Black consumer and celebrity was to Tommy Hilfiger's business model, writing: "Tapping his friend and Def Jam Music Group head Russell Simmons for contacts, the designer pursued the rap crowd aggressively. Snoop Doggy Dogg wore Hilfiger on *Saturday Night Live* in 1994. The Fugees, TLC, and Doctor Dre have all donned the free threads Tommy has sent their way." So a conspiracy that he hated Black people in his clothes? Laughable. But the conspiracy theories reflected real feelings of animosity— and critique.

As documented by Paul Smith in *Tommy Hilfiger in the Age of Mass Customization*, internet message boards were filled with black users calling other users derogatory terms for wearing Hilfiger. In particular, they objected to his use of black celebrities and models threaded into American propaganda imagery. But the admonishment and conspiracy theories did not stop the Hilfiger brand. Continued *Slate*: "And the corporation has thrived. Its shares have risen sevenfold since it went public in 1992; its sales are expected to rise 40 percent in fiscal year '97 and a further 30 percent in fiscal year '98."

Numbers were driving fashion more than ever before. In 1995, executives in the nation's top apparel companies were enlisted to divulge the challenges and trends facing the industry heading into the next century. Described Paul Smith, "They saw the need, in essence, to speed up the industry's process of product design, manufacture, and distribution in order to satisfy the ever changing and accelerating demands of retail outlets and their customers." This cleared the way for fast fashion to thrive in the future, especially when the transition of the world's garment and manufacturing industries from the Global North to the Global South was complete. Added Smith, "Simultaneously, the place of consumption - and, of course, capital concentration becomes ever more centralized in the North itself, opening up new channels of product distribution, marketing, and retailing."

Three years before the survey of executives, *The Los Angeles Times* marveled over the new Express business model. The store, originally launched as a cheaper version of The Limited in 1980, had rebranded in the nineties as a more upscale brand, earning $1 billion in sales by 1991. "The formula? Fashion that appeals to women who have outgrown neon but refuse to dress like matrons, knockoffs of European styles, good service and price tags that are usually $50 or less." Bragged an analyst about the company's team of buyers: "One of the advantages Express has over its competitors is speed, the ability to spot a trend and get it on the floor within six weeks after they've seen it." There were a number of lawsuits over this fast and imitative fashion, but it was here to stay.

Grunge, The Gap, and Guess

Thanks to the rapid rise of Seattle bands *Nirvana* and *Pearl Jam*, grunge was quickly turned into a trend, commercialized on the high-fashion runways of Perry Ellis by Marc Jacobs, and covered in magazines and on TV. Think plaid shirts, thick Doc Martens, and jeans, durable stuff. Marc also included Birkenstocks in the 1993 show, making the shoes trendy, but the show got him fired. Before the tastemakers of high fashion got their hands on it, grunge "style" had not been intentional.

"It wasn't like somebody said, 'Let's all dress like lumberjacks and start Seattle chic.' This stuff is cheap, it's durable, and it's kind of timeless. It also runs against the grain of the whole flashy aesthetic that existed in the 80s," said a Seattle resident of the era. Even still, the clothing of Kurt Cobain was especially impactful. Wrote Paul Edgerton Stafford, "It was the visual power of seeing a skinny white kid with stringy hair wearing baggy jeans, a striped T-shirt and tennis shoes belting out choruses with a ferociousness typically reserved for black-clad heavy metal headbangers." The editor of *Details* magazine called it "Unfashion" in 1992, for people who liked "the waif-like look of put-on poverty."

If you wanted stylish basics in the style of "normcore" with questionable labor attached, then you wanted The Gap. The company decided to offer more dresses, blouses, and wardrobe staples for middle class adults who weren't old and stuffy like their parents. Company President Millard "Micky" Drexler described The Gap as "not high-risk fashion, but good taste, good style; not too far to the left, not too far to the right." When competitors wanted to open a lower cost The Gap, Drexler opened 'Gap Warehouse' in 1993, which became Old Navy the following year. Within four years, it was making over one billion in annual sales, thanks to nearly 80% of the items being priced below $22. In The Gap's *Khaki Swing* commercials of 1998, fun young people sprinkled with diversity wore similar outfits and attracted Middle America, capitalizing on the swing revival brought by movies like *Swingers* and bands like Big Bad Voodoo Daddy and Cherry Poppin' Daddies.

For those who craved a bit more luxury, still at a moderately affordable price, they reached for Guess. In the nineties, the brand launched a popular campaign starring Anna Nicole Smith, the atypically curvy *Playboy* Bunny blonde bombshell and former stripper, in a series of glossy black-and-whites. While the boss at her old strip club forced her to work the day shift because she was considered "too fat" for the night shift, Anna's 140-pound, 5'11" physique helped propel her career in Hollywood… along with her marriage to an elderly billionaire on the cusp of death. The Guess campaign also led to other modeling jobs and hosting opportunities, including sexy shots with the then-little-known Swedish brand H&M.

Hair, Home Decor, and Hype

From the braids on superstar Brandy's head to the bevy of manes worn by Lil Kim, Janet Jackson, and the ladies of *Living Single*, and the intricate looks donned by R&B and hip-hop's favorite women, Black hairstyles of the era were Afrocentric and futuristic. Brandy's braids, particularly her super-thin micros, reflected an evolution of the hairstyle: it was now common to use extensions, making the concept of them being "natural" a little murky. In 1992, the popular *Hype Hair* magazine was founded.

Grammy award–winning Lauryn Hill, who rapped about silly girls selling their souls and rocking European weaves (with fake nails done by Koreans), proudly wore dreadlocks on the cover of her album and on the red carpet. Hair, as always, remained political. In the season two episode of *Sister, Sister* titled *Hair Today*, Tamera gets her hair straightened and is treated better by the popular clique at school. That same year, Angela Davis wrote about the watering down of the Afro in an article that expressed her discomfort with a March issue of *Vibe* magazine featuring actress Cynda Williams dressed as her.

Davis was particularly unsettled by Williams recreating her widely publicized FBI wanted poster, writing, "…my legal case is emptied of all content so that it can serve as a commodified backdrop for advertising." The afro was definitely attached to radical politics in the nineties. Wrote Davis, "A young woman who is a former student of mine has been wearing an Afro during the last few months. Rarely a day passes, she has told me, when she is not greeted with cries of "Angela Davis" from total strangers." Such hair was often attacked in schools and the work place.

In 1998, a white teacher in Bushwick, Brooklyn, then described by *The Washington Post* as "a gritty Black and Hispanic neighborhood... notorious for drugs and graffiti", outraged Black parents when she read the book *Nappy Hair* to her third-grade students. Written by Carolivia Herron, the book affirmed "nappy hair" and sought to destigmatize kinky tresses. It would go on to sell over 100,000 copies. The white teacher resigned before the outrage died down. The next year, two of 19-year-old tennis player Venus Williams' signature beads came off her braids during a match at the Australian Open. The umpire penalized Williams a point after the second bead, saying it caused a disturbance, prompting her to yell at him, "There's no disturbance. No one's being disturbed!" She was booed by the crowd and, frustrated and unfocused, lost the match. The beaded hair of Serena and Venus Williams had been contentious in the WASP-y world of tennis since they entered the scene in the mid-nineties.

Nearly every Black person had a mom, cousin, or aunt who rocked super short cuts with intricate curls and waves, the kind of style that had to be adoringly maintained monthly, or even bi-weekly. This meant the relationship between hairstylist and client was strong. For Black men in the early nineties, the hi-top fade still carried weight, and more heads were rocking cornrows like Allen Iverson. But no matter the style, for most Black men, crispy edges were usually a must, continuing the important tradition of black barbershops.

For white men, the mullet was out of style by 1993, and the Caesar haircut was popularized by Antonio Banderas and George Clooney. We can't forget the curtains on teenage heartthrobs like *Boy Meets World*'s Rider Strong, or the appropriated dreadlocks, either. They also rocked a lot of highlights, gel, and frosted tips. Popular styles for women of all colors included bangs, pixie cuts, super cute butterfly clips, and crimped hair à la Christina Aguilera. And who can forget chunky highlights, claw clips, and Hairagami?

White women weren't exempt from the politics of hair, either. Big and blonde manes were often associated with bimbos, gold diggers, and ditzes. The perfectly sculpted coif of Texas Governor Ann Richards symbolized the wise and tough Southern grandma. Wrote *Texas Monthly* in 1992: "Although Republican critics... keep trying to portray her as a shrill feminist liberal, they can't quite keep her in that ideological box because her hairstyle, washed, curled, teased, and sprayed, is straight out of the fifties, the last era of good feeling in America. Her hair makes her a permanent member of the carhop generation, a throwback to small-town values, which is why she appeals to both men and women."

When Paula Jones—the Arkansas woman who accused Bill Clinton of sexual harassment—debuted a new look in 1998, it generated widespread news coverage. She looked especially chic at the White House Press Correspondents Dinner in 1998 she was mysteriously invited to. She had elevated her style from what was often mocked as "white trash" by removing her perm and changing her makeup. Said historian Steven Zdatny at the time, "It's amazing how quickly people recognize social class in hair. There's a haircut that belongs on Wall Street and a different one that belongs in Hollywood." The taming of her hair was accompanied by a completely new wardrobe, akin to the makeover in *Clueless*. Wrote Robin Givhan: "Enough with the dowdy short skirts, cheesy dresses, horrific accessories. A few trips to Nordstrom and Macy's and a couple of suits later… goodbye, Paula. Hello, Ms. Jones."

Paula Jones alleged that Bill Clinton propositioned her while he was serving as Governor of Arkansas, something several people attempted to dispute by attacking her looks. The makeover was, sadly, seen as necessary. Wrote *The Los Angeles Times*, "Any woman suddenly in the glare of TV cameras and news photographers would want to look her best. But in this case, the more attractive Jones looks, the more credible her claim that a public figure would have been willing to risk the kingdom, so to speak, to dally with her. And when she presents herself as an attractive, sophisticated woman instead of a ditzy Southern babe, she has a better chance of being taken seriously." Makeup artist Cydbe Watson added, "She did it all. She maxed out her capacity for beauty."

Marcia Clark, the lead prosecutor in the O.J. Simpson murder trial, faced similar criticism during the mid-nineties. She was frequently labeled as unsophisticated and unattractive, largely due to her curly, un-styled hair. Clark was advised to appear more "feminine" and "soft," and she received a notable boost in favorable news coverage after debuting a shorter and straighter hairstyle. Her hairstylist, Allen Edwards, who charged the prosecutor $150 to break out his scissors, claimed to have received thirty interview requests for the same cut by the end of that news day.

Not all haircuts went over so well, like the 1999 shearing of Keri Russell's voluminous and curly mane after the first season of The WB's *Felicity*. The resulting pixie cut was blamed for a plunge in ratings, despite the fact that the show had been moved to a new time slot. Said an executive for The WB, "We got a lot of emails and letters and feedback from our friends in the industry who were fans of the show. People were disappointed and angry at us and at Keri for cutting off her hair. 'Who made that decision?' they asked." The show's creators, J.J. Abrams and Matt Reeves, did, but everyone seemed to blame Russell.

Over on NBC, The Rachel, seen on Jennifer Aniston's character in *Friends*, was wildly popular for a brief period. It first appeared in the season one episode *The One With the Evil Orthodontist*. The style was created by Chris McMillan, who convinced the actress to shed her long, damaged locks for something new. While Aniston only wore the style through Season 3, it was a hit for most of the rest of the decade. Apparently, it was hard to replicate, but McMillan charged just $60 for it, if you could meet him at his salon in LA. Honestly, I preferred Dana Scully's little bob in *The X-Files*, but that's just me. The bob was also popular on stars like Victoria "Posh Spice" Beckham and Cameron Diaz. One last iconic hair moment? Demi Moore shaved her head bald for her role in 1997's *G.I. Jane*.

Home decor evolved in the nineties. First of all, people had more space to decorate. The house of the decade was certainly the McMansion, featuring a mash-up of architectural styles and prizing columns, arched windows, huge rooms, master bedroom suites, gourmet kitchens, chandeliers, and foyers. Plenty of homes now featured computer rooms and big desks, with oak wood cabinets in upgraded kitchens. At new stores like the TJX-owned HomeGoods, cycles of decor were brought in at relatively low prices. The 1992 grand opening in Boston was noteworthy because there wasn't yet a chain offering "200,000 brand-name items, from place mats to Waterford crystal, at 30 to 70 percent off the usual retail prices," with one analyst saying it was a combination of other stores. People were hungry for deals, still wincing from the end of a recession.

Detailed *The New York Times*, "Items ranged in price from 69 cents for an artificial flower to $300 for [porcelain art]. A set of percale twin sheets that might sell in a department store for $25 will be offered at Home Goods for $9.99." People were becoming accustomed to styling their homes on the cheap. Other big-box and department stores expanded their offerings to capitalize on the desire for self-expression. For instance, Bed Bath and Beyond opened its 200th superstore in August 1999 and reached $1 billion in sales. Thanks to these chains, it was easy to find brightly colored inflatable furniture, clear electronics, folding screens, wicker items, glow-in-the-dark ceiling stickers, and fake fruit and plants. Minimalism was also a major trend following the lush maximalism of the eighties. Still, others embraced animal print, loud wallpapers, sponge painting, and color blocking.

While the fashion, music, design, and cinematography of Hype Williams' only movie, *Belly*, were influential on their own, his work as a music video director also left an indelible mark on the culture. He worked with Mary J. Blige, Usher, Biggie, DMX, Adina Howard, Brandy, Tupac, LL Cool J, Missy Elliott, and more. His cinematography style made hip-hop and R&B videos a treat to watch.

Influential Costume Design

One of the most memorable parts of the 1995 film *Clueless* was Cher's closet computer with the dry-cleaner style automatic racks. The costumes in the film were designed by Mona May, who called the plaid skirt set "a nod to a Catholic schoolgirl uniform, but taken to another level and turned designer." Cher (Alicia Silverstone) wore a total of 59 outfits in the movie, most of which weren't the actual style of teens in 1994, when the film was being made. May said, "The goal was to make it very feminine because, at the time, it was all about grunge. When we went scouting at high school, everybody was wearing big, baggy clothes and you couldn't tell a girl from a boy. We wanted to go against that."

With a $200,000 budget, Mona had to dress every character from lead to extra. Plenty of characters, like Christian, were dressed in thrift store pieces. When Cher gets robbed in the Valley, she mentions to the gun-wielding thief (who takes her bag and fancy cell phone) that she can't lie on the ground because she's wearing an Alaïa party dress. "It's like a totally important designer," she says, voice dripping with condescension. "And I will totally shoot you in the head," he replies. Divulged Mona, "We had to find someone connected to Alaïa and worry about if we could get the dress for free, if we could alter the dress to fit Alicia. Amy wrote the lines for it. I designed the jacket she wore over it, the red and black with the boa trim on the sleeves." Mona also designed the costumes for *Never Been Kissed*, *The Wedding Singer*, and *Romy and Michele's High School Reunion*.

Fictional high school fashion was also a visual treat in 1999's *Jawbreaker*, which featured a trio of mean girls covering up the accidental murder of their best friend. Explained costume designer Vikki Barrett on the movie's fun reimagined pin-up style, "We wanted it to be sweet and sugary-looking. And then it takes a turn. We tried not to use any dark or moody colors at all, and keep it really light, festive and fun, so that the element of darkness would be a surprise." Good costuming could make a movie. In 1990's *Pretty Woman*, Marilyn Vance won a BAFTA for Best Costume Design for her skillful dressing of Vivian Ward (Julia Roberts). People loved Vivian's transition from streetwalker to sugar baby, shown by the discarding of the blue and white hooker ensemble for the red opera dress and a $1.3 million diamond necklace. The dress was made by Marilyn Vance herself. She told *Vogue* later, "Before the decision was made, we ended up creating three different dresses. Poor Julia had to endure so many photos [and] color testing for this dress."

While Roger Ebert may have hated the 1997 film *B.A.P.S.* so much that he gave it a no-star rating, and it was dragged by a bunch of other critics, it's a Black cult classic. Halle Berry and Natalie Desselle showed their comedic chops and looked good while doing it. Costume designer Ruth E. Carter, who had worked on Spike Lee films and would go on to design for *Black Panther*, said, "I was really young. B.A.P.S. was only maybe my third movie. I felt like if I were to do it now, I would probably be more sensitive to my Atlanta sisters. But I looked at it like it was satire, and coming out of theater, I was very much accustomed to satire, and when we think about our history of Vaudeville, and how we really did know slapstick, and it was very funny."

The movie's ghetto fabulous styles, which were inspired by the types of outfits seen in nineties party pictures from the South at Freaknik, Black Bike Week, and the club have since been remixed and recycled into fashion. In 1993's *Poetic Justice*, Janet Jackson and Tupac Shakur were outfitted by costume designers John Lemons and Sharlene Williams. Jackson's look perfectly encapsulated the early nineties sporty tomboy era made famous by rappers.

The Nanny starring Fran Drescher wasn't for everybody, but it was personally one of my late night favorites by the time I was catching reruns on Nick at Nite as a teenager. The costume design was by former actress and model Brenda Cooper, who sourced a bevy of iconic looks preserved on a variety of social media pages and websites. Explained Cooper to *Shondaland* in 2023, "I didn't want the show to have a time stamp. I wanted to create a look that 30 years into the future, the look of that show would be as popular today as it was back then." Fran was draped in fluffy robes and various designers, from Vivienne Westwood to Moschino to Versace, and pieces were repeated in earlier seasons before the budget was increased. Because Fran had so many outfit changes, explained Cooper, "Every week, I had to come up with six outfits that are top to toe tailored with accessories, so I came up with formulas. One formula was the turtleneck under a dress."

In 1992's *Death Becomes Her*, Joanna Johnston designed the glamorous and sexy looks fitting for a highly visual dark comedy magic film about death and aging, starring Meryl Streep and Goldie Hawn. Johnston also did costume design for *Hellraiser* and *Forrest Gump*. For 1996's *The Craft*, costume designer Deborah Everton did a lot of thrifting and altering to create one-of-a-kind wardrobes for parochial school witches. Explained Everton in 2016 to *Dazed Magazine*, "The film still looks good today. I watched it not too long ago and, do you know what, it doesn't look like a 20-year-old film. The clothes are clothes people today still wear." For the Spice Girls film *Spice World*, explained costume designer Kate Carin, "I told the girls in my first meeting that I wanted the movie to look like a cartoon, *Scooby-Doo* on acid, and like a big, luscious bowl of the most exotic and colorful fruit. They loved that."

In 1996's *Evita*, Madonna's 85 costume changes as the Argentinian leader Eva Perón not only broke a Guinness World Record, but caused style experts to predict a desire for 1940s vintage, luxe, and feminine fashion. Remarked Victor Cosa for *The Los Angeles Times*, "Very feminine clothes with a Spanish feel by Karl Lagerfeld, John Galliano and others appeared recently on runways at the spring collections in Europe and New York." The ambitious sartorial smorgasbord that anchored *Evita* was created by Penny Rose, the future mastermind behind *Pirates of the Caribbean* costumes.

Rose was granted special access to Eva's archives and dressed over 40,000 extras with 55,000 costumes, sourced from costume houses and vintage shops, but also produced by seamstresses. Said Victor Cosa, who was over the era's minimalism, "The youth of today hasn't experienced glamour at all." But other fashion experts mused that people jumped the gun, and that nobody was going back to the "New Look" of yore. Said Bill Glass, after he wrongly predicted the outfits would catch on, "That was before I saw the pictures of Madonna in those clothes. She looks much older. Honey, nobody wants to look matronly."

Any tour of costume designers in the nineties isn't complete without Patricia Field, who was responsible for the memorable and influential looks on HBO's *Sex and the City*. Field first met Sarah Jessica Parker on the set of a movie, and the actress introduced her to *Sex and the City*'s creator, Darren Star. Field dressed four distinct characters with so much verve that they set trends off-screen, causing frenzies for Manolo Blahniks, the Fendi Baguette

Bag, the five-dollar tutu worn in the opening sequence, and more. Even Carrie's worst outfits have a sense of charm. The crew gave Field tremendous pushback over Carrie's picnic-time Heidi outfit in a season two episode. Darren Star's vision originally included the kind of safe and sexy outfits more at home on his old show, *Melrose Place*. Said Patricia in 1999, "We had to say to the guys, 'Look, the girls in this show just aren't going to wear miniskirts with high heels. No one in New York dresses like that. Period. That really was a blow to a lot of people.'"

Patricia Field's underground store of eclectic fashions, known since the 1970s to a vibrant LGBT community in West Broadway and NoHo, was suddenly overwhelmed with visitors wanting to shop with the *Sex and the City* stylist. Explained Simon Noonan, "Shows like this do a good job of raising people's threshold for what is acceptable. Maybe they themselves will never wear something that aggressively groovy, but if they watch, they find ways to translate it."

In 1999's *Fight Club*, Tyler Durden's outfits were intentionally selected by Michael Kaplan to appear to be from thrift stores. Susan Lyall did a lot of thrift shopping and collaborating for 1995's cult classic *Empire Records*. She said, on giving Liv Tyler's character a Madonna–Whore vibe, "I remember we shortened the mohair sweater a little bit because it was kind of sexy to reveal her stomach. But she also had to look virginal, like a ripe piece of fruit. I believe those boots were hers."

The short skirts put on the fictional *Ally McBeal* by various costume designers were supposed to be "rebellious." Criticized one Brooklyn attorney to *Entertainment Weekly*, "I wear skirts but nothing thigh length, even if it's beautiful. I don't think jurors care one way or another. [But] you don't get something five or six inches above the knee… You want to look professional." The editor of *Jane* magazine, Jane Pratt, said, "Women find themselves emulating her, feeling OK wearing shorter skirts to the office because of her. She's freeing women up." One TV critic saw the short skirts as a method of the series' absurdist humor, saying, "That sense of absurdity is expressed in the clothes she wears. There's a comic aspect to her dressing. Her clothes are so skimpy and so unprofessional."

In 1996's *Romeo and Juliet*, starring Leonardo DiCaprio and Claire Danes, Kym Barrett added to the dreamy and opulent landscapes of Verona Beach with religious imagery and baroque-inspired pieces on loan from Dolce & Gabbana. She said, "Everything was touched by a human hand. Everything was painted, everything was embellished, everything was aged." Barrett went in an entirely different direction for the futuristic designs in *The Matrix*. She used a variety of techniques to keep the airborne actors stylish and on point while being attached to harnesses and wires. When designing Christian Dior's Fall 1999 couture collection, John Galliano admitted to being "deeply inspired" by *The Matrix*.

Speaking of fashion designers, for the 1997 film *The Fifth Element*, starring Bruce Willis and Milla Jovovich, Jean-Paul Gaultier spent a year drawing 8,000 sketches, eventually creating over 1,000 designs for the film. Marianne Eloise explored the fashion in the futuristic movie, documenting Leeloo's sexy bandage dress, meant to convey naivety; the super-cute McDonald's uniform; and the bold leopard print costume for Ruby Rhod (Chris Tucker). There were also the sexy flight attendant uniforms, which Gaultier described as, "a little change from what they are wearing on Air France." Another film that predicted the style of the future was Hype Williams' *Belly*, starring Nas, DMX, and T-Boz. Costume designer and hip-hop stylist June Ambrose was tasked with designing looks that would "forecast what the hip-hop genre's gonna look like in the millennium."

Jewelry

Popular jewelry of the decade included mood rings, toe rings, custom nameplates, and hip-hop bling. Another major trend was chokers, in everything from lace to velvet to chains. Not everyone was a fan. Rapped Big Boi on 1996's *2 Dope Boyz in a Cadillac*, "I'm sick of these wack ass rappers like I'm tired of hoes in chokers." Ear piercings were on trend in the nineties because it was easier than ever before to get the destigmatized procedure. All it took was a trip to your local mall and a little bravery. There were 1,000 Claire's jewelry stores at the top of the decade, ready to provide the procedure.

For men, having two pierced ears was often considered to be "gay," so it was common for men to stick to one earring if they got the piercing at all. An earring on the right ear was considered the "gay ear" and could be a discreet signal in a homophobic environment. But, reported *The New York Times* in 1991, "So many heterosexual men have begun wearing earrings, often in both ears, that the placement no longer suggests anything about sexual preference." Added *Deseret News* in 1995, "Jewelry stores report that the number of middle-aged men getting their ears pierced is doubling and quadrupling." There was also a rise in multiple piercings in one ear. Other types of body jewelry were catching on too, like tongue piercings, labrets, genital piercings, and Tupac's nose piercing. My own mother had a tongue piercing, labret, and eyebrow piercing.

In 1993, Christy Turlington and Naomi Campbell appeared on runways wearing belly piercings after getting them done together, and the trend caught on. In a 1995 article, one woman described her acceptance of one daughter's cheek piercing and another daughter's belly piercing this way: "At first I was a little dismayed. Then I remembered I really loved the hippie aesthetic. This feels better to me, when it's not profoundly extreme, than acrylic nails and lacquered hair."

Kinderwhore

In 1994, Courtney Love, lead singer of Hole, was catapulted into the spotlight after Kurt Cobain's suicide. She and former roommate Kat Bjelland of Babes in Toyland used to share clothes, and their outfits featured a rotation of baby doll dresses, ripped tights, lingerie, heavy makeup, and Mary Jane shoes meant to, in Love's words, evoke a sense of "irony." In the midst of the Riot Grrrl movement and third-wave feminism, the "kinderwhore" look caught on in the early nineties and found coverage in teen magazines like *Sassy* and *Seventeen*. Reported *Entertainment Weekly* in 1994, "Her popularity is growing. In fact, she may finally be transcending her reputation as the rebellious punk-rocker/druggie mama everyone loves to hate. Her so-called 'kinderwhore' dresses (Love's word) are the uniform du jour on L.A.'s club-lined Sunset Boulevard, as well as in the pages of *Vogue*."

Logomania

In hip-hop, logos were flourishing as much as jewelry. Thanks to the designs of Harlem-based Daniel "Dapper Dan" Ray, luxurious clothing decked out in repeating designer logos was highly coveted by drug dealers and rappers. Fendi successfully sued Dan for copyright infringement in 1992, leading him to close his store and go underground. But logos, whether repeating or simply highly visible (think Polo Ralph Lauren), were here to stay. Tommy Hilfiger's logo was a hip-hop staple, especially for spokeswoman Aaliyah. Karl Kani's scrawled signature logo on your pants was confirmation that you were wearing the same expensive jeans as Diddy and Tupac. The North Face expanded its clientele to hip-hop, and its neat breast logo made a big splash. The expensive clothes were originally for snow sports enthusiasts. Remarked a store manager in 1997, "At the beginning, about 80 percent of the people buying The North Face were technical types, and the rest were wannabes. Now it's about 50-50."

Makeup and Misa

Compared to the 1980s, the beauty looks of the nineties were generally much more pared back. One popular look, personified by Kate Moss and Jennifer Aniston, was minimal, barely-there makeup, sometimes with a bright pop of blush. But there was still plenty of experimentation. Brown lipstick. Frosty lipstick. Brown liner. Metallic eyeshadow. Smokey eyes. Thin eyebrows that took forever to grow back and were reminiscent of 1920s flappers. There was also blue and purple eyeshadow, sometimes with risky red lips! Matte skin was in, though finding the perfect shade was difficult for Black women, whose options were often limited to drugstore aisles, Avon, and Fashion Fair. One of the original supermodels, Iman, launched Iman Cosmetics in 1994. She spent her time in the fashion industry combining makeups to suit her skin, and wanted to corner the market that neglected Black, Asian, and Latina women.

In 1994, the increasingly popular brand MAC established their AIDS Fund to help impoverished people grappling with the consequences of HIV/AIDS. The first spokesperson for the fund's line of Viva Glam lipsticks was RuPaul. In 1998, Brandy signed on to be a spokeswoman for CoverGirl. At the turn of the century, makeup trends included glitters, body sparkles, sparkly or metallic eyelids with nothing else, plus glittery nail polish.

For many Black women, acrylic nails with some curve, like on SWV's Coko, were definitely in. My mother's own two-inch talons endeared me to them for life. For white women, tanning and self-tanner for a perfect (or orange) glow wasn't uncommon. This era was also the blossoming of the celebrity makeup artist, with Kevyn Aucoin making millions as he promoted contouring on the faces of Janet, Madonna, Whitney, and more. Much of this technique had been cultivated from drag performers and trans women.

Japanese and Jamaican-American Misa Hylton was 17 years old when she visited her boyfriend Sean Combs at his internship at Uptown Records in 1991. She ended up styling Jodeci. She also styled Mary J. Blige, whose look was originally tomboyish before Misa teased out more sensual styles, and later, the western looks for *All That I Can Say*. She also styled Faith Evans shortly after she married Biggie, and created looks for Foxy Brown, Dru Hill, Missy Elliott, and more. Her most iconic accomplishments would be with Lil' Kim, whom she styled most frequently.

Misa said about the vision for Lil' Kim's looks for *Crush on You*, "When you talk about changing hair colors and the videos, you really can't push creativity further than that, especially at that time. Today, everyone is walking around with a different wig in different colors. But that wasn't normal back then and to do her *Crush on You* video was a big-time risk. People were telling us we shouldn't do it, but I stood my ground and the director backed me up. We created a masterpiece, and that's when Lil' Kim made her crossover to MTV." As for the 1999 VMA look that prompted Diana Ross to forget where she was and jiggle Lil' Kim's breast, Misa said, "The idea stemmed from a conversation I had with Missy Elliott, who suggested that if she were Lil' Kim, she'd bare one breast." While Misa was the brainchild behind a huge chunk of hip-hop fashion in the nineties and remains on the mood board of many, she was ignored by mainstream fashion and found it hard to build relationships with luxury brands until Lil' Kim found broader success at the turn of the century.

Naomi Campbell and The Supermodel

In January 1990, Naomi Campbell was called the "reigning mega-model of them all" when appearing in *British Vogue* with her fellow supermodels Christy Turlington, Linda Evangelista, Cindy Crawford, and Tatjana Patitz. They were known as the Big Five, until Claudia Schiffer replaced Patitz. George Michael selected the models for his 1990 *Freedom!* video. While all of the supermodels had reputations for being divas, Naomi was saddled with the racism of the British press. Remarked one columnist, "She comes from a very rough part of South London, and to me that says it all. You can take the girl out of Streatham, but you can't take Streatham out of the girl."

Meanwhile, Naomi was paid less than her peers. In 1991, the year it was reported that top supermodels earned $15,000 to $25,000 a day, Naomi said, "I may be considered one of the top models in the world, but in no way do I make the same money as any of them." Claudia Schiffer was making $20,000 a show by 1992. *Time* magazine said, "Campbell must keep an eye on Beverly Peele, 16, who some are calling the 'next Naomi.'" Tyra Banks was also called a Naomi Campbell lookalike, showcasing how willing the industry was to discard and replace its token black models. Another outlier Black model in terms of clout was Tyson Beckford, who appeared as the lead model for Ralph Lauren Polo in 1993. He was the most visible Black male model of the era.

Most models needed endorsement deals and frequent work to be successful. For instance, Cindy Crawford hosted the fashion show *House of Style* on MTV for six seasons. Claudia posed for *Playboy*, signed a contract with L'Oréal, and acted in movies. While Naomi didn't get a makeup contract until 1999, she allegedly made $1.5 million in 1992. In addition to runway shows, she filled her plate with a plethora of roles, from walking the hottest runways, to appearing in Michael Jackson's *In the Closet* video in 1991, Madonna's *Erotica* video and *SEX* coffee table book in 1992, and starring in the 1996 film *Girl 6*.

In 1993, Naomi appeared on *Vogue* twice, including a solo cover in June. Even though it's a major accomplishment to be on a magazine with a 1.5 million circulation, *Vogue* paid roughly $300 for a cover. In between dalliances with Mike Tyson and Robert De Niro, and dropping an album named *Baby Woman* that was popular only in Japan, Naomi was a socialite whose beauty and off-duty fashions were highly influential. Ford and Elite Models got into tiffs over her representation, and a 1993 tumble on a Vivienne Westwood runway didn't stop her grind. To top off her status, Nelson Mandela called her his honorary granddaughter, as she had begun doing charity work in South Africa in 1993.

In the early nineties, when the heroin chic look surged in, Kate Moss made the Big Five the Big Six. But something changed at the end of the decade, when Linda Evangelista said, "The term 'supermodel' is a press-induced word. We have never called ourselves supermodels." Declared the editor of *Allure* magazine in 1999, "Nobody cares about models anymore." Anna Wintour said, "They *were* celebrities. The paparazzi *were* chasing them. Everyone cared what they were having for breakfast and who they were having affairs with." Suddenly, celebrities were becoming models for runways, print advertisements, and magazines, so there was much more competition for jobs among the small-scale models hoping to break into the industry.

The diva reputations and expensive fees of the Big Six also ended momentum for another generation of big names to rise to the top at the same rate and pay scale. The 1997 murder of Gianni Versace was yet another factor in the decline of supermodels. Increasingly, casting directors for fashion shows hired plain, thin, and white models from Eastern Europe in the mid to late nineties. These models were idealized because they didn't "take away" from the clothes. While Naomi Campbell and a handful of other Black models would continue to get work, the whiteness of fashion, and pay inequity, would remain a problem going into the next decade.

Ode to Fabio

In 1991, a chiseled 31-year-old model named Fabio Lanzoni came into prominence when he was profiled on the TV program *A Current Affair*. Why? Because he had appeared on a slew of romance novels by Avon Books, so many that by 1992, over 55 million copies featuring his image had been sold. Fabio was so in style that he sold $25 life-size Fabio cutouts, hosted a hotline where people could call in and speak for $1.99 a minute, and released a 1993 album. In 1994, he became the I Can't Believe It's Not Butter spokesman. His long hair and muscles would remain in style for many white women for the rest of the decade.

Princess Diana and Porno Chic

Before her untimely death in 1997, Princess Diana was a style icon. As a divorcée of the royal family, her every move was under scrutiny. While facing pressure in almost every area of her life, her style seemed effortless. From sprinting away from paparazzi in casual and sporty outfits, to her charity ensembles that she later auctioned for philanthropy, to the infamous revenge dress she wore in 1994 to the Serpentine Gallery while Prince Charles admitted to cheating on her in a television broadcast, she set trends. For many fashion historians, the little black revenge dress (designed by Christina Stambolian) marked a shift in Diana's sartorial choices, as she moved away from royal expectations and embraced a more modern, chic fashion identity.

Quality Magazines

Magazine readership was booming in the nineties. The launch of *Allure* in 1991 was lauded for its focus on makeup, along with critiques of plastic surgery and fad diets. It had 700,000 readers by 1994, the same year that *Vibe* began doling out fashion advice for a hip hop crowd with a penchant for luxury and new technology. discernment. *InStyle* also launched in 1994. *Essence* grew in circulation so much that the *Essence* Music Festival launched in New Orleans in 1995. Style bible *Vogue* continued to be all the rage, and long time creative director Andre Leon Talley became the first black editor-at-large in 1998.

Sassy magazine, published between 1988 and 1994, was feminist and zany, with topics like "The Sassiest Boys in Communist China." Fashion editor Andrea Linett spotted a 17-year-old Chloë Sevigny and appointed her as an intern and model, leading to her eventual stint as a nineties 'It Girl'. *Sassy* was eventually bullied and boycotted by an evangelist group called Women Aglow because of its frank discussions about sex.

Sassy editor Jane Pratt would go on to create *Jane* magazine in 1997, the same year it was reported that 37 percent of the average teen magazine was about appearance, 35 percent about dating, and 32 percent about clothing. Teen girls were ravenous for publications, especially White ones, who often saw themselves reflected on the pages. A 1997 survey found that 42 percent of 12–15-year-old White girls looked to magazines for trends. As such, *Teen People* and *CosmoGirl* were launched to compete with *Seventeen*, *Teen*, and *YM*. *Nylon*, featuring eclectic avant-garde fashion and indie culture, launched in 1999.

Raves and RuPaul

Mark Ehrman summed up the fashions of ravers in 1997 thusly: "Twentysomethings gyrate on the dance floor decked out in candy-colored outfits, Dr. Seuss hats, Bert and Ernie backpacks, Hello Kitty paraphernalia and whistles. And just about everybody has a pacifier dangling from the neck on a string of plastic beads, when they're not sucking on it, that is."

R also stands for RuPaul, who was everywhere in the nineties. After stunning drag performances in the early nineties in Atlanta and New York, Ru dropped a 1993 album, *Supermodel of the World*, which featured the dance single *Supermodel (You Better Work)*. Ru's personality, style, and flair led to a contract with MAC Cosmetics, becoming the first drag queen with an endorsement deal. Ru also made appearances in *Sister, Sister*, *To Wong Foo, Thanks for Everything! Julie Newmar*, *Sabrina the Teenage Witch*, and his own VH1 production, *The RuPaul Show*, showcasing interviews with some of the hottest entertainers of the era and bringing drag and non-binary representation further into the mainstream. Wrote Ru in a 1995 autobiography, "You can call me he. You can call me she. You can call me *Regis and Kathie Lee*; I don't care!"

Starters, Streetwear, and Sportswear

In the early nineties, Starter jackets were all the rage after a campaign featuring DJ Jazzy Jeff, perfect for the new crop of football and basketball teams gaining their footing. Like expensive Air Jordans, they were a status symbol that sometimes came with a hefty price tag. Wrote Jamie Cooper, "In 1990, 17-year-old Uland Tiggs was shot and killed after he gave up his New Orleans Saints Starter jacket to a pair of robbers. In 1993, 17-year-old Karla M. Benner was gunned down in Youngstown, Ohio, for her Starter jacket. In 1992, 14-year-old Dewayne Williams Jr. was killed for his Raiders Starter jacket. In Chicago, four separate teens were murdered for their Starter jackets in 1990 alone."

In 1989, Carl Jones and T.J. Walker started Cross Colours, a fashion line that became popular in 1990 and was seen on everyone from the backwards outfit wearing rappers Kris Kross to Mary J. Blige, Heavy D, Will Smith, and Arsenio Hall. Known for red, black, green, and yellow garments, the company shipped $15 million in merchandise by 1992. Though it would fade into the background due to changes in design and frequent counterfeiting, Cross Colours was responsible for boosting the career of Karl Kani, who started his own company known for its baggy jeans.

In 1994, Supreme was founded in New York City by James Jebbia, the name taken from the John Coltrane song *A Love Supreme*. With $12,000, Jebbia created a store where people could shop and even skate inside, becoming a hub of style and socializing. From the beginning, it was closely tied to the fashion and social scene of the Lower East Side, selling skateboard products and apparel, like cut-and-sew tiger-stripe cargo pants. Graffiti artists went around tagging other advertisements with Supreme stickers, even leading to Calvin Klein nearly suing the company for defacement. Several members of the store's skate team appeared in the 1995 film *Kids*. By the end of the decade, Supreme opened a location in Japan. Other streetwear brands established during the decade include A Bathing Ape, Enyce, and Ecko Unltd.

In 1998, Sean Combs launched Sean John at Bloomingdale's, just one of many hip-hop-adjacent fashion endeavors that blew up in the nineties. There had been Phat Farm, founded by Russell Simmons in 1992. That company would lead to the 1999 launch of Baby Phat by Simmons' then-wife, Kimora Lee. Baby Phat would be instrumental in the Y2K style. FUBU, or For Us, By Us, had also been established in 1992 by Daymond John. While it was intended to be for Black people and was originally on sale at a clothing store on Jamaica Avenue, Macy's began stocking the line in the mid-nineties, and it became a phenomenon.

Reported Sheryl Nance Nash, "John asked his Queens neighborhood friend L.L. Cool J to wear a T-shirt in a photograph for a FUBU promotional campaign in 1993. The trick worked, and eventually... his clothes were being featured in videos for Mariah Carey, Biggie Smalls, and Busta Rhymes. The brand started to gain so much momentum that John and his mother mortgaged the home they jointly owned for $100,000 in start-up capital to pay for a factory and office space." Because plenty of white teenagers wanted to dress akin to the style of music they bought more than anybody else, the brands most closely linked with hip-hop were coveted.

At its peak, FUBU earned $350 million in 1998. Said Douglas Century in an op-ed entitled *Fubu's Move to the Suburbs*, "Can a white consumer really get away with wearing a product designed and marketed by a youthful African-American company whose very name is a rallying cry of racial solidarity and economic empowerment?" But the company's increasing inclusivity led to a decline, and it was also facing new competition, like Jay-Z and Damon Dash launching RocaWear in 1999. Reported *The Source*, "Hip-hop fashion has exploded into the second-fastest growing segment of the apparel business (beat out only by lingerie), earning more than $5 billion in 1997."

Tattoos

It may be hard to imagine, but before the 1990s, tattoos really weren't that common or accepted. They were still stigmatized during the era, but they were increasingly legal and showing up in the mainstream. In New York, tattoo parlors popped up after tattooing became legal in 1997. Shops had been mostly underground since being banned in 1961. By 1996, over half of the people getting tattoos in America were women, who got everything from butterflies to hearts to roses to stars to all the Tweety Birds I saw growing up. Random words in Japanese and Chinese were also trendy. Permanent makeup was also on the menu.

Other popular tattoo trends included tribal designs, popularized by Filipino American artist Leo Zulueta, who inked numerous tastemakers including Dennis Rodman and Tommie Lee. His contemporary designs spread like wildfire, especially because the proliferation of the Internet meant tattoos were no longer localized. The appropriation of such sacred cultural art was lost on people in the nineties.

Famous tattoo included Tupac's THUG LIFE stomach tattoo, which he received at Dago's Tattoo in Houston in 1992. Pamela Anderson got her highly visible barbed wire tattoo because she didn't feel like sitting through daily makeup while filming the title role in the 1996 film *Barb Wire*. Lastly, tattoo removal technology improved in this decade, with Cher successfully starting the process to remove pieces of ink she had received in the seventies. She said in 1999, "I had my first tattoo at 27, and at that time it was a statement," she said. "Now, just about everyone has one, and it's boring."

United Colors of Benneton

In the 1990s, no fashion brand's advertisements stirred controversy quite like the Italian-based United Colors of Benetton, which originally made waves with its diverse campaigns, often subverting expectations of advertising by removing its products from the ads. The campaigns were masterminded by photographer and creative director Oliviero Toscani. His decisions highlighted diversity, HIV/AIDS, famine, war, homosexuality, and more. For instance, he licensed the use of a 1990 image of a man named David Kirby dying of AIDS, surrounded by his family, for Benetton's 1992 campaign. Complained a representative of Gay Men's Health Crisis, "They're exploiting AIDS to make a buck. It does raise an issue, to a certain degree, but it doesn't follow through. There's no copy in this ad except for their logo and a line telling you what number to call for the nearest store."

Responded a Benetton executive, "We seized an opportunity to publicize AIDS to create greater compassion. Would people rather have us show pretty girls in sweaters?" Toscani's work also included ending the nineties with contextless snapshots of men on death row, including one of the transphobic murderers of Brandon Teena. Said Toscani, "This campaign is not about victims. It is about the death penalty. The death penalty is unreligious. The Ten Commandments say 'Thou shalt not kill.' It is against the law." The outrage led to boycotts of the company in America and lawsuits from states whose prisoners had been photographed.

Vera Wang and Victoria's Secret

In 1990, after years of working for *Vogue* and Ralph Lauren, Vera Wang opened her own bridal gown boutique and immediately became a hit. She'd design costumes for ice skating stars Nancy Kerrigan and Michelle Kwan, and also created Posh Spice's wedding gown.

If I close my eyes and think really hard, I can catch a whiff of Victoria's Secret Pear Glacé. The lingerie company was struggling in the early nineties, but in 1991 it launched a fragrance line. In 1993, it started selling the Miracle Bra, and in 1995 it introduced its extremely popular Victoria's Secret Fashion Show in New York. Beverly Peele walked the runway that year. But none of the models, not yet called Angels, received wings until 1998. The Victoria's Secret Fashion Show reached new heights in 1999 when the brand announced a 72-hour countdown during the Super Bowl, hosted by models Tyra Banks and Heidi Klum, who would later walk in the show.

Millions of people were disappointed due to internet connection problems. Regardless, extreme Super Bowl advertising was in style, as was online commerce. Explained journalist Lisa Napoli, "Victoria's Secret was able to reach customers in countries where the company doesn't have stores or doesn't distribute the 350 million catalogues that it mails annually— that's the value of the Web. So are the company's early numbers indicating that men seem more willing to buy online than in Victoria's Secret stores."

White Party

In 1998, Sean Combs began hosting his infamous white parties in the Hamptons. He'd later remark to Oprah, "I wanted to strip away everyone's image and put us all in the same color, and on the same level." What began as a small-ish, A-list gathering eventually became a corporate-sponsored event bringing together multiple segments of Hollywood, marking a new era in hip hop. Diddy's publicist at the time, Cheryl Fox, encouraged the young mogul to invite white celebrities to be in pictures and court mainstream attention. This included Leonardo DiCaprio. These white parties gave Diddy influence, and according to columnist Toby Young, "the seduction of Puffy signals the neutralizing of rap music as a threat to the status quo."

Not only was hip hop the most controversial music of the decade, but it was now the most profitable and the most stylish. When profiling the party and detailing Diddy's sterling reputation in the Hamptons, Monique P. Yazigi wrote, "Women on chairs extended their arms to him as they danced and mouthed the words to Will Smith's *Gettin' Jiggy Wit It*. Men downed shots and danced on the floor. Through all the hysteria, which lasted for nearly four hours, Mr. Combs maintained his nearly asexual detachment." The pretty, fun, and highly publicized gilding, like the fancy white party, covered up whatever monstrosities and excesses lurked beneath.

X-Rated Fashion

During an era when supermodels dabbled in *Playboy*, *Playboy* models became fashion fixtures, and porn stars dotted the red carpet, it's no wonder that fashion houses like Alexander McQueen, Gucci, and Versace incorporated themes of sexuality and BDSM into their designs. In 1992, the same year Madonna delighted and baffled the world with the bestselling coffee table book of all time, *SEX*, Versace's Fall collection, titled Miss S+M, doled out chains and leather.

"We showed a similar collection in Dallas 15 years ago, and they turned the lights up on us. They were disgusted. They said these clothes belonged only in a leather bar. And now, last night, there were 200 socialites in bondage!"

said a delighted Gianni Versace. The looks were polarizing. Said one fashion insider, "There were people who loved it, who thought it was brilliant, the greatest thing he had ever done. And others of us, mostly women, could barely evaluate the design aspect of it because we were so offended. I have to say that I hated it." Remarked Susan Faludi, "These are fantasy clothes, yeah. But whose fantasy? I doubt Versace polled 3,000 women before he sat down to draw them." By the end of the decade, red carpet looks and runway fashion would only become edgier. Relatedly, on the topic of red carpets, Joan Rivers and her daughter Melissa began hosting *E! Entertainment's* pre-award red carpet shows in 1995, leading to the medium becoming much more important in fashion and celebrity PR. The predominant question? "Who are you wearing?"

Y2K

In the three years leading up to the new millennium, futuristic fashion that would set the tone began emerging in films, music videos, and TV. Think of electrified and recycled disco fashion from the seventies, shiny leathers, metallics, latex, and galactic colors.

Zapatos

What would this decade have been without platform flip-flops, Manolo Blahnik strappy sandals, Birkenstocks, Steve Madden slinky slides, chunky loafers, Doc Marten combat boots, and the massive footwear seen on the likes of the Spice Girls? In 1993, the same year that Vivienne Westwood's platform sandals made a splash, Pleasers hit the market, giving women of the world (and sex workers!) the sexy shoes they craved.

On The X-Files

During Thanksgiving of 1999, my immediate family took a trip from Charlotte to Rutherford County, North Carolina. It's my first memory of visiting my nana's family "up in the country," as we called it. My great aunt and uncle lived with their children in an ancient and cavernous two-story home in the middle of nowhere. In the tint of childhood, the house appears in my mind as a horror movie destination where all visitors die violently before the credits roll. At some point during that trip, I have a vague memory of watching a ghastly creature attack someone on television before the screen faded to black. The details are elusive. But I've never forgotten what came next —the spooky and sinister synth of *The X-Files* theme song.

For the greater part of my childhood, I was terrified to sleep without a nightlight, and I dreaded returning to visit my cousins in that creepy home "up in the country." I was convinced that something would unfurl itself from the gap between my bed and the wall to attack me in my sleep, so I enlisted my stuffed animals to straddle the dark unknown. I blame the Fox primetime drama. For years, the theme song of *The X-Files* would send me into a nervous panic while my mind flooded with frightening vignettes of monsters, aliens, and corpses. Even as I grew older and began my foray into horror films, I avoided *The X-Files*. When I finally watched the show in college, I loved it. It was still terrifying, but not because of monsters, aliens, and corpses.

The X Factor

When *Twin Peaks* began airing on ABC in 1990, the surrealist mystery was not appealing to the average viewer. An analyst named Paul Schulman said, "I don't think it has a chance of succeeding. It is not commercial, it is radically different from what we as viewers are accustomed to seeing. There's no one in the show to root for." Creators Mark Frost and David Lynch did not originally want to do a television show, but were convinced by Lynch's agent to write something about "real life in America." They conjured an idea: a high school homecoming queen named Laura Palmer (Sheryl Lee) who lived a double life in the fictional Twin Peaks, Washington.

The 94-minute pilot opened with Laura's plastic-wrapped corpse being discovered by a local logger. Coffee and cherry pie-loving FBI agent Dale Cooper (Kyle MacLachlan) is brought in to investigate. But *Twin Peaks* was not a simple police procedural— it was surreal. Something darker than your average killer lurked underneath the interesting characters, scenic views, and doughnuts. The show's weird plot and atmosphere found some fans and critical acclaim from reviewers. *Entertainment Weekly*'s Ken Tucker recognized the merit in the show but said, "Will *Twin Peaks* be a hit? Not a chance in hell. (Well, maybe in hell.) Soaked corpses, sobbing deputies, and muttering G-men, it's all very unsettling, as is Lynch's refusal to signal the emotion he wants the viewer to feel in any given scene."

Indeed, *Twin Peaks* would be canceled the following year after two seasons and a made-for-TV movie. Critics at the time guessed that the show's cinematography had changed the course of television, but it was missing a crucial special ingredient needed to draw more viewers. *Twin Peaks* had an extremely niche viewership during a time when networks wanted broad audiences to maximize profitability. However, the critical reception of *Twin Peaks* demonstrated that networks could go darker than before in their programming.

Screenwriter Chris Carter had loved eerie shows like *The Twilight Zone, Night Gallery,* and *Kolchak: The Night Stalker* as a child. He had also witnessed scandals like Watergate and the Pentagon Papers. This all served as inspiration when he was called by Fox executive Peter Roth to create material for the channel. Fox spent $2 million to film the pilot of *The X-Files* over fourteen days.

Carter was also inspired by a 1991 poll claiming that 3.7 million people believed they had been abducted by aliens. The Roper polling association surveyed 5,947 people with 11 questions, including: "Have you ever woken up paralyzed and sensing a strange presence in the room? Have you ever 'lost' an hour or more you can't account for? Have you ever felt as if you were flying? Have you ever seen balls of light in your room? Have you ever found scars on your body you could not explain?" Out of those nearly 6,000 surveyed, 119 answered yes to at least four of those questions. The methodology and sample size were questionable, but the concept intrigued Carter.

The X-Files debuted on Fox on September 10, 1993, to an audience of roughly 12 million viewers. Raved Ken Tucker, "*The X-Files* is the most paranoid, subversive show on TV right now." The show was a gradual hit, with its praise and viewership growing stronger after the first season. The plot, atmosphere, and cinematic pacing only boosted the show's X factor: the dynamic between two FBI agents, the ardent believer Fox Mulder (David Duchovny) and the hardened skeptic Dana Scully (Gillian Anderson). Duchovny had impressed both Fox executives and Chris Carter during his appearance as trans FBI agent Denise Bryson in *Twin Peaks*, but the 5'3" Anderson was a hard sell.

Twenty-four-year-old Gillian Anderson was not the Fox Network's ideal candidate, because they wanted someone "taller, leggier, and breastier" than her. Revealed Carter in 2024, "Where's the sex appeal [they asked]. Even though Gillian's beautiful, she wasn't their idea of sexy. First, because they didn't understand what I was trying to do with the show. And she was an unknown, so that never helps." Thankfully, Anderson went on to portray the skeptical Dana Scully in the primetime phenomenon. The "Will They or Won't They" trope played a major part in the show's success. While the pair kept it mostly professional, Scully's ability to tolerate (and even laugh at) Mulder's abysmal jokes throughout the series told me that she was eventually going to spread her legs for him.

Scully's intelligence and scientific expertise contributed to the Scully Effect, in which scores of young girls and women found themselves inspired to pursue careers in Science, Technology, Engineering, and Mathematics (STEM). In a 2018 study of 2,021 women in STEM, 81% found Dana Scully to be a role model. Sixty-three percent of them agreed that she "increased their belief in the importance of STEM" as youth in the nineties. Scully's skepticism and scientific prowess weren't the only influential aspects of the show. The writers weren't afraid to throw large words and complex concepts at the audience, who either needed to grasp for context clues or make a mad dash for their dictionaries during commercial breaks. As discussed in *Lexual Does The 90s*, the series also influenced a wave of science fiction media.

The X-Files' initial airing included 202 episodes and a 1998 blockbuster film. At the height of the show's popularity, Gillian Anderson and David Duchovny were everywhere. They might have been the first "Work Wife and

Work Husband" scenario trotted through the media, exhibited by Anderson kissing Duchovny before she kissed her boyfriend when accepting an award at the 1997 Emmys. The actors even embodied Y2K fashion in a series of 1997 photographs by David LaChapelle, who captured everyone from Drew Barrymore to Tupac Shakur.

In addition to turning Duchovny and Anderson into stars, *The X-Files* also served as a sharpening tool for future titans of television, like *Breaking Bad* showrunner Vince Gilligan, who wrote thirty episodes for the series and executive-produced over eighty. Additionally, while there was a broader mythology that the writers were only somewhat careful about evolving over the series' nine seasons, there were a number of "Monster of the Week" episodes that were unconnected to the main conspiracy. These were often created by guest writers or based on spec scripts. The 2000 film *Final Destination* was based on a spec script by Jeffrey Riddick, who was encouraged to turn it into a feature film. *X-Files* writers Glen Morgan and James Wong helped write the final product.

The Truth Is Out There

The initial central plot of *The X-Files* is that FBI profiler Fox Mulder believes his sister Samantha was abducted by aliens when he was 12 years old. The mystery behind her disappearance leads him to become an expert on alien abductions and an investigator of paranormal activity. During his work prior to Scully's arrival, he deduces that there is a government conspiracy hiding the existence of aliens. Eventually, through the "mytharc" episodes, viewers learn about an overarching plot involving a liaison of powerful men called the Syndicate, who have been facilitating an alien invasion since the 1940s. One of these humans is Bill Mulder, Fox's father.

The aliens, known as the Colonists, abandoned Earth during the last ice age and left behind their genetic material in black oil deposits around the globe. The oil functions as a virus that the Colonists claim will turn humans into a controlled slave race. Instead of permitting the entire human species to be enslaved, the Syndicate brokers a deal with the Colonists in 1973 to allow a small group of humans to become alien hybrids. The aliens give the Syndicate alien embryos in exchange for a few humans as collateral. These include family members of the Syndicate, like Fox Mulder's sister, Samantha. With the alien invasion set for 2012, the Syndicate secretly works on a vaccine for the alien virus, unaware that they are being double-crossed by their co-conspirators. The black oil will not merely infect humans and render them slaves, it will make them hosts for a new alien species.

Conspiracy comes from the Latin word *conspirare*, meaning "to breathe together." Theories about nefarious entities "breathing together" to accomplish sinister goals have flourished throughout history, leading to repression, rebellion, rebirth, violence, and in the worst-case scenarios, genocide.

During the height of the Enlightenment era in 1776, the Order of the Illuminati was established in Bavaria by a law professor named Adam Weishaupt. Made up of philosophers and free thinkers, the Illuminati's goal was to destroy ignorance, superstition, abusive authority, and the power of the Christian clergy. Because monarchs and clergy cohabitated in power, the Illuminati posed a threat to both. As a result, the illuminati was characterized as operating through the Freemason fraternal order to orchestrate the French Revolution that destroyed the monarchy. Allegedly, the illuminati would be coming for other governments too.

In America in 1798, the country teetered on the edge of full-blown war with France due to its neutrality toward Britain during the French Revolutionary Wars. Federalists, who controlled Congress, desired a strong central government and feared that Democratic-Republican criticism of their policies would make Americans sympathetic to the French. That year, Congress passed a series of four laws that would come to be known as the Alien and Sedition Acts. President John Adams, a Federalist, controversially signed the acts into law, making recent immigrants, especially the French, targets. Those foreign rabble-rousers, and anyone who spoke against Federalists, were labeled traitors and aliens.

In addition to raising residency requirements for citizenship from five to fourteen years, the acts authorized the arrest of any foreigner committing "treasonable or secret machinations against the government," including if they "print, utter, or publish... any false, scandalous, and malicious writing" about America. Ultimately, the acts vitalized the Republican Party and helped lead to Thomas Jefferson becoming president, as he accused Federalists of being secretly loyal to the British monarchy. The Federalists were now the conspiratorial traitors and aliens.

Alien comes from the Latin word *alius*, meaning "other" or "another." It evolved into *alienus*, meaning "belonging to another," and eventually came to mean "strange," "foreign," and "different" in fourteenth-century Europe. Humans tend to fear what is unfamiliar to us. Things that are alien carry exponential possibilities for danger.

From the violent witch hunts of Europe to the witch hunts of communist-hater Joseph McCarthy and beyond, at every twist and turn in the wild ride of human history, people have pondered why and how things happen, eventually blaming an alien people, especially when outcomes aren't in their favor. Wishing to make sense of chaos, people connect real and perceived dots to create conspiracy theories. In *Conspiracy Theories in American History: An Encyclopedia*, editor Peter Knight detailed how the Illuminati, Freemasons, and other alien entities were often lumped in with any group that threatened nativist Protestants in the 19th and 20th centuries, including Mormons, Catholics, enslaved people, Jewish people, abolitionists, and immigrants. Conspiracies were also blamed for the civil rights movement, labor movements, and anything else that threatened the status quo.

Not all conspiracy theories are the same. In his libertarian-leaning *The United States of Paranoia: A Conspiracy Theory*, Jesse Walker identified five types of conspiracy theories. The 'enemy outside' plots against a group of people. The 'enemy within' plots against a group from within the group itself. The 'enemy below' is made up of the lower class, who scheme to overthrow the social order, while the 'enemy above' is made up of the powerful minority who maintain the social order for their own benefit. Benevolent conspirators are people who work clandestinely to better the world. As *The X-Files* evolved and Scully and Muller became more informed, their continued work (and unpublicized findings) could be described as benevolently conspiratorial.

At the end of the 20th century, conspiracy theorists of all stripes were given new tools to spread their beliefs, such as through tabloid news. *The Weekly World News* began publishing in 1979, but became popular in the late eighties and early nineties. Wrote Peter Carlson, "*The Weekly World News* was not one of those sleazy tabloids that cover tawdry celebrity scandals. It was a sleazy tabloid that covered events that seemed to occur in a parallel universe, a fevered dream world where pop culture mixed with urban legends, conspiracy theories and hallucinations. Maybe *WWN* played fast and loose with the facts, but somehow it captured the spirit of the age."

From introducing the fictional "Batboy" in 1992 and Hillary Clinton's alien baby in 1993 to reporting that twelve U.S. Senators were aliens, *The Weekly World News* leaned on political satire and the supernatural to sell its papers. Editors also included reprinted stories from local papers that were actually true, muddying the line between fact and fiction. There's no doubt that some Americans took some of the false stories as true. The internet offered another avenue for conspiracy theorists to proselytize. With these pillars in place, the possibilities for proposed perfidy by those in positions of power were endless.

When Fox first aired the pilot of *The X-Files* for focus groups, Chris Carter was amazed at the lack of pushback to the premise. He said, "The thing that was amazing to me in that test marketing was that… everyone believed that the government was conspiring [to cover things up]." The focus group didn't need to suspend any disbelief, they already didn't believe in their government. For Black Americans who routinely traded conspiracy theories (Snapple is owned by the KKK) and facts mistaken for conspiracy theories (the government allowed the proliferation of cocaine into Black neighborhoods), mistrusting the government was not new or novel. But white Americans? It was a big deal.

For older and mostly white generations of Americans raised on the teat of nationalism, many had served their country in the military or worked in the public, federal sector, where most of the jobs were. To accept the worst facts about America and the strangest-yet-most-plausible conspiracy theories would mean acknowledging complicity in a brutal system of oppression. In an episode entitled *Travelers*, the show depicted the raging anti-communist J. Edgar Hoover, who initiated a series of conspiracies (like the destruction of Martin Luther King Jr.) and pushed false theories about his enemies. Frank Spotnitz recalled:

> "We hired a retired FBI agent to serve as a technical advisor on the script. This was a gentleman who'd been with the Bureau for twenty or thirty years, and he was very offended by our script. He was angry that we would even suggest that J. Edgar Hoover, whom he still calls 'Mr. Hoover', would be involved in any of the plots or take any of the positions that he takes in the script. Then he told me that he'd never actually seen our show. 'But if this is the type of story that you're telling,' he told me, 'I can't imagine that it would be very popular.'"

But it was popular. In season one's *Fallen Angel*, Fox Mulder declares to his superiors, "You can deny all the things I've seen, all the things I've discovered, but not for much longer because too many others know what's happening out there. And no one, no government agency, has jurisdiction over the truth." That resonated with people at the End of History. Many Americans were primed and ready to disbelieve the world as it was presented to them. Why wouldn't they? Lies about American superiority, respect for human rights, and commitment to personal liberty were falling apart in the face of mass incarceration, war, and revelations of CIA activities in Latin America and Asia.

In 1991, Oliver Stone's film *JFK* influenced a new generation of Americans to question the Kennedy assassination. It was based on the 1988 book *On the Trail of Assassins* by ex-FBI agent Jim Garrison, who claimed that John F. Kennedy was killed because he planned to change Cold War policy toward the Soviets. Before the film's release, Stone and the studio were criticized. After the film debuted, critics raved. Wrote Richard Corliss for *Time*:

> "Whatever one's suspicions about its use or abuse of the evidence, *JFK* is a knockout. Part history book, part comic book, the movie rushes toward judgment for three breathless hours, lassoing facts and factoids by the thousands, then bundling them together into an incendiary device that would frag any viewer's complacency. Stone's picture is, in both meanings of the word, sensational: it's tip-top tabloid journalism. In its bravura and breadth, *JFK* is seditiously enthralling; in its craft, wondrously complex."

JFK earned over $200 million globally. New fervor over the death of the 35th president led to the John F. Kennedy Assassination Records Collection Act of 1992. This act declassified the remainder of the files associated with the case and established a review board to assess the impact of government secrecy surrounding the assassination. They ruled that most remaining files would be declassified by 2017. This, obviously, did not placate everyone.

Just twenty years before the John F. Kennedy Assassination Records Collection Act, Jane Heller reported that the U.S. government had intentionally withheld treatment for syphilis from Black farmers for four decades during the Tuskegee Syphilis experiments. Just the year before those revelations, a leak of The Pentagon Papers revealed that between 1945 and 1968, the government had lied about and hidden its activities in Vietnam, Laos, and Cambodia in its attempt to choke the communist threat from China, engaging in a series of war crimes and clandestine operations that ultimately sacrificed approximately three million Asian soldiers and civilians and nearly 60,000 American troops. It's no surprise that the people who watched these revelations in real time were enthralled by *The X-Files*.

The season two episode *Sleepless* fused government experimentation and military coverups together, and featured a guest appearance from Tony Todd. It also marked the introduction of X (Steven Williams), a mysterious Black American official who leaks information to Mulder when it suits his interests. On this occasion, X informs Mulder that, in pursuit of perfect soldiers, a scientist during the Vietnam War developed a lobotomy that removed a person's desire to sleep. The soldiers who agreed to the surgery (and survived Vietnam) have not slept for 24 years when *Sleepless* begins.

The results were disastrous, and the episode reminded the audience that sometimes conspiracies take time to unravel. What may sound implausible today may not remain that way forever.

I Need To Believe

Scully's initial understanding of the world is underpinned and girded by science and God— there is little room for aliens, who are not mentioned explicitly in the Bible or proven by science. Mulder's beliefs often lead him to immediately conclude that "aliens did it!" when investigating cases. In the season one standout *Eve*, two unrelated girls named Teena and Cindy, living across the country from one another, have the exact same face. Both of their fathers have been drained of blood on the same day at the same time. Teena claims that she saw "red lightning" shortly before her father was killed. Mulder immediately believes that aliens did it. Scully rejects this theory but admits something is off.

In actuality, the girls are clones from a Cold War-era program designed to create genetically modified humans with extra chromosomes that make them super smart and psychotic. The first batch of experiments were christened Adam and Eve. Both Teena and Cindy were created by an escaped Eve who tampered with eggs at a fertility clinic. They killed their fathers. It's a great and unsettling episode, especially thanks to the performances of the morbid child actors Erika and Sabrina Krievens. In later seasons, the agents tend to immediately deduce culprits or explanations instead of being wrong and investigating. But the early seasons are ripe with error that leave the viewer guessing.

Season two's *Død Kalm* stroked my intense fear of ghost ships to become one of my favorite episodes. When a surviving sailor fleeing from a naval vessel in the Norwegian Sea returns to base, he has unnaturally aged and dies soon after. Scully and Mulder go to investigate. Mulder, unable to connect aliens to the case, leaps to fantastical government conspiracy: the ship is an experiment deliberately placed at the 65th parallel to suss out a "wrinkle in time." As they get trapped on the ship with an untrustworthy sailor and begin to age, Scully theorizes something more scientifically plausible, theorizing that a meteor featuring metallic properties is buried underneath the ocean and affecting their body chemistry. Both are wrong— they've been drinking contaminated water.

In season three's *The List*, a condemned Florida prisoner named Neech declares before being killed in the electric chair that he will return to take the lives of five men who wronged him in prison. Afterwards, a guard is found dead in Neech's cell. Scully and Mulder arrive at the prison, where everyone is split into two camps: believers and skeptics. Scully and the warden believe Neech coordinated a plan with another prisoner before dying. Multiple prisoners and Mulder believe the opposite. As the case unfolds and the body count rises, a prison guard named Parmelly (Ken Foree) is eventually suspected to be the murderer by both Scully and Mulder.

Parmelly is shot and killed by Neech's widow, with whom he was having an affair. She believes she is seeing Neech when she pulls the trigger. The murders are ultimately attributed to Parmelly, but as the agents close the case and prepare to leave, Mulder is clearly disturbed by the facts. To the audience, it's evident that Neech came back from the dead and killed those who wronged him. But Scully successfully convinces Mulder that the case is closed. Shortly after she does, the prison warden, driving by them on his way to work, sees Neech in his rearview mirror. His car crashes, and he dies instantly. Writer Frank Spotnitz said of the episode, "I think it was brave because there is not a single likable character, nobody you can root for. Mulder and Scully do not solve the case, and that is something I had been interested in doing for some time."

In the real world, Scully is more logical than Mulder, but within *The X-Files* universe, when confronted with the truth of government conspiracies, supernatural phenomena, and aliens, she often becomes illogical, fulfilling traditional stereotypes that men are the more rational gender. In season two's *Excelsis Dei*, the viewers witness an invisible entity rape a worker named Michelle at an elderly home. When Michelle tells her story to her employers, the police, and later Scully and Mulder, nobody believes she was raped except for the skeptical Scully.

She is teased by Mulder, who says that all "ghost rape" is unsubstantiated. Eventually, the pair learns that a Malaysian worker has been giving special herbs to the patients, reversing their dementia and other symptoms of old age. But it also gives them the power to channel violent actions through spirits of angry deceased residents. Mulder's reluctance to believe a ghost rape victim when he believes other phenomenon is telling— as was the lack of conclusion on Michelle's fate.

When science doesn't make sense for Scully and offers more questions than answers, she falls back on her Catholic faith, while Mulder leans into alien conspiracy theories (and his love of porn). Scully's faith is first symbolized by the tiny gold cross she wears around her neck, but this gets teased out further as the series progresses. In the show's mythos, aliens are revealed to be real, but there are also a few moments when the divine, or its evil opposition, are real as well.

In the season two episode *Die Hand Die Verletzt*, a small teacher's committee at Crowley High School in New Hampshire discusses whether or not they should allow a production of *Jesus Christ Superstar*. "I don't think that play is appropriate for this high school," says one teacher. Another suggests *Grease* or *Annie*, before another interjects, "Doesn't *Grease* have the F-word?" The principal, Jim Ausbury, agrees to discuss the matter with the drama teacher before ending the meeting for a prayer. One of the teachers interrupts that "the game" is on, obviously annoyed with the prospect of praying. But the principal insists it will be quick. *What prudes*, the viewer thinks, before watching the group of white professionals break into satanic chanting. "He is the hand that wounds," they pray, translating the title of the episode as the camera pans away from the office.

Drawing on old conspiracy theories of satanic teachers preying on children at *McMartin Pre-School* in California in the eighties, Mulder and Scully are called to investigate the corpse of a mutilated teenager named Jerry in the woods. Everyone blames his fellow teenager friends, saying they were satanists who attracted a demonic force. The viewers saw the teenagers go to the woods to complete a black magic ritual (to impress girls)- but they were not the actual summoners of the demonic force.

Things get confusing when frogs rain from the sky, and Mulder notices that water at a drinking fountain is moving counterclockwise, which both agents say violates the laws of physics (though this isn't scientifically true). Regardless, something demonic is afoot. It's quickly revealed to the audience that a substitute science teacher, Mrs. Paddock, is responsible for the killing of the teenager.

Shannon, the stepdaughter of Principal Jim Ausbury, claims that she was kept as a sex slave by her stepfather and other satanists when she was a child and forcibly made pregnant. She alleges that the babies she birthed were then sacrificed for the cult. Scully, ever the skeptic, sympathizes with the teenager's allegations of sexual abuse but doesn't believe the devil worshipping. When they approach Ausbury for his side of the story, he categorically denies any wrongdoing. Afterward, Mrs. Paddock controls Shannon, making her slit her wrists and die.

Ausbury and the satanists meet and realize that a "dark angel" is among them, angry that they have fallen slack in their faith. They conspire to blame Shannon for Jerry's murder to make the police go away so they can carry out a satanic ritual and stave off the devil's wrath. This plan angers Ausbury, who genuinely cared for his stepdaughter. He confesses to Mulder that the satanic sect is real, showing his home's basement where the rituals took place. "We believe man is nothing better than an animal. No better or no worse than those who walk on four legs… Our faith kept us powerful in our community. Wealthy, good health."

The discerning viewer understands through this monologue that all religions have been used at some point to maintain power, authority, and wealth. Ausbury explains that his disgust with the sect's decision to sacrifice an innocent, his stepdaughter, made him realize that he's better than an animal. At this moment, Mrs. Paddock remotely tricks Mulder into thinking Scully is in danger at the school. He cuffs Ausbury to the stairs of the basement and rushes to the school. Ausbury is eaten by a giant snake.

At the school, the agents are captured by the remaining faculty members, who decide to sacrifice them before the devil's "dark angel" can come for them next. One points out it may already be too late, but they continue. Before they can finish their ritual, Mrs. Paddock, remotely controlling the faculty members, forces them to kill themselves one by one as the agents watch in horror. "You're right, it is already too late," Mrs. Paddock says, blowing out a candle.

When the agents free themselves and go looking for Mrs. Paddock, they don't find her. Instead, they find a scrawled chalkboard message reading: "Goodbye. It's been nice working with you." Scully makes no attempts past this episode to further untangle the mystery and confirm or deny the existence of satan (or find the real identity of Mrs. Paddock), perhaps not wanting to tango with a malevolent force. She's skeptical, not stupid. Even more astutely, Scully is a Roman Catholic— meaning she believes in the literal existence of the devil.

Demons are referenced in at least four other episodes of *The X-Files*, but this episode, the first directed by prolific director Kim Manners, was my favorite. As typical with the show, there were easter eggs and pop cultural references. The high school was named after famed satanist Aleister Crowley, and Mrs. Paddock was named after the toad demon in Shakespeare's *Macbeth*. X-Files expert Robert Shearman found that the episode was mocking organized religion, saying that the primary purpose of *Die Hand Die Verletzt* was "to look at the way religious faith has been so watered down and paid nothing but lip service, its rituals and doctrines reinterpreted so that only what's comfortable is adhered to."

In the mythos of *The X-Files*, if Satan-worshipping teachers are killed off by a malevolent entity, the obvious implication is that he is as real as the aliens the agents attempt to ascertain throughout the rest of the series. So are the monsters, including the Jersey Devil, vampires, succubi, and zombies. When cases with a Christian bent present themselves, Scully's steadfast skepticism melts away in a manner that annoys Mulder (and me, the viewer). In *Revelations*, a boy named Kevin with actual stigmata is hunted by a man who believes the boy will be a valuable tool in the future battle between good and evil. Kevin is tracked down by a physically disfigured man named Owen Jarvis, revealed to be his guardian angel. Jarvis is killed in the process of protecting Kevin. Before he is killed, he chastises Scully for her lack of faith.

When Scully performs an autopsy on Jarvis, she finds that his body is not decaying. Because there is no scientific explanation, Scully grasps for one using her faith. In Catholicism, there is a belief that saints do not decompose. When she tells Mulder her theory, his disdain is clear. He tells her not to let her religious beliefs cloud the investigation, as if he doesn't immediately associate 95% of the cases they investigate with aliens. In Mulder's mind (and probably many of the viewers as well), if Scully can believe in Jesus and the devil, why can't she believe in aliens? Are they both not equally unprovable with science?

In season two's *Irresistible*, a serial killer named Donald Pfaster (Nick Chinlund) is a "death fetishist" who cuts off the hair of corpses he handles at a funeral home. Fox refused the original script that depicted Pfaster as a necrophiliac. Chris Carter told Matt Hurwitz and Chris Knowles in *The Complete X-Files: Behind the Series, the Myths, and the Movies*, "You [could not] do the combination of sex and death on network television." In the episode, Pfaster kidnaps Scully, and she witnesses him morph into a demon.

Added Chris, "There are reports of people who had been under the spell of Jeffrey Dahmer, who actually claimed that he shape-shifted during those hours when they were held hostage; that his image actually changed." I couldn't find a source for this, but Carter used this reasoning to make Pfaster's existence subjective to the viewer. What is the face of evil? Scully, who manages to escape and get the upper hand, doesn't believe her own eyes. His condition was never explained, and Scully makes no effort to find out more, with Mulder noting that he grew up normally in a home with four sisters.

Pfaster returned five seasons later in *Orison* when he escapes prison and comes after her. Scully fatally shoots him when he is cuffed and unarmed, which some critics regarded as a terrible transgression of Scully's ethics. Scully tells Mulder she isn't sure if God is in control of her or "something else." This episode was in the seventh season, when her skepticism had been chiseled away. It took seven seasons of abductions, bright lights, near-death experiences, and close calls before Scully finally recognizes the existence of aliens. The viewer must be patient, as Scully is even resistant after a storyline in which she is abducted by aliens, impregnated, and given cancer in season four!

$x(t)$

The 1996 episode *Musings of a Cigarette Smoking Man* is one of my favorites in the series. The tall, mysterious, and threatening government official (William B. Davis) is always shrouded in a cloud of smoke, compliments of Morley Cigarettes. The Smoking Man was originally an extra in the pilot, but as a member of the Syndicate, he grew to be central to the plot, and oddly, one of my favorite characters. In *Musings*, he surveils Scully and Mulder as they listen to the Lone Gunmen detail what they know about him. The Lone Gunmen are a trio of private investigators and conspiracy theory magazine editors named Richard Langly (Dean Haglund), Melvin Frohike (Tom Braidwood), and John Fitzgerald Byers (Bruce Harwood).

Back in 1962, the Smoking Man, son of an executed communist spy, is an Army captain serving at Fort Bragg, North Carolina, when he is pulled aside by his superiors. They insult the Smoking Man's father for being a virulent communist, but also express their admiration that he was an "extraordinary man" who did anything necessary to abide by his beliefs and accomplish his goals. They ask the Smoking Man, who does not yet smoke at this point, if he is also extraordinary. He, who has already been involved with the Bay of Pigs and the assassinations of Congolese leader Patrice Lumumba and Dominican Republic dictator Rafael Trujillo, assures them he is.

He is tasked with assassinating John F. Kennedy, because the president may be seeking peaceful resolution with the Soviet Union. The Smoking Man shoots the president on that fateful 1963 day in Dallas and frames Lee Harvey Oswald. His patsy had previously given him a pack of cigarettes, and he begins smoking.

In 1968, after Martin Luther King Jr. says in a speech, "communism is a judgment against our failure to make democracy real," he is marked for death by a group of men including the Smoking Man and J. Edgar Hoover. While the Smoking Man admires Martin Luther King Jr. and isn't aggressively racist or opposed to civil rights (well, thank God for small miracles), he is staunchly anti-communist, and he believes that King opposing Vietnam will undermine the draft. So the Smoking Man takes matters (and a rifle) into his own hands and assassinates the civil rights leader. Years later, in 1992, he is implied to be involved with the Clarence Thomas confirmation hearings, the Rodney King trial, and even manipulating the Buffalo Bills into losing the Super Bowl a spectacular four times in a row from 1991 to 1994.

The entire time he has been pulling the world's marionette strings, the Smoking Man has been attempting to become a published writer under the pseudonym Raul Bloodworth. When he receives notice from a magazine that his short story will be published in 1992, he quits smoking and excitedly drafts a resignation letter to the FBI. Unfortunately, when the story is printed, it has been changed. Dejected and miserable, he buys a pack of cigarettes and delivers a chilling monologue to a homeless man.

> "Life is like a box of chocolates. A cheap, thoughtless, perfunctory gift that nobody ever asks for. Unreturnable, because all you get back is another box of chocolates. So you're stuck with this undefinable whipped mint crap that you mindlessly wolf down when there's nothing else left to eat. Sure, once in a while there's a peanut butter cup or an English toffee. But they're gone too fast, and the taste is... fleeting. So, you end up with nothing but broken bits filled with hardened jelly and teeth-shattering nuts. And if you're desperate enough to eat those, all you've got left is an empty box filled with useless brown paper wrappers."

In this soliloquy, we learn what drives the Smoking Man to do what he does: unhappiness and nihilism. Meddling in world affairs gives him a sense of purpose that only fuels his unhappiness and nihilism in a vicious cycle. If he were truly driven to fulfill the goals of the Syndicate— saving the world by double crossing the aliens— he wouldn't have been so ready to quit upon learning that he would be a published writer. But he has nothing else. There are no bestsellers or accolades in his future. So he continues the daily grind with a scowl and a cigarette, knowing that with each conspiracy he is making the world darker and more perilous.

In the show's present, one of the Lone Gunmen, Frohike, says that all of the information he's shared about the Smoking Man came from one of his weekly subscriptions, meaning it isn't substantiated, and likely false. If the Smoking Man's nihilistic monologue was imagined by the Lone Gunmen, it's a projection of the lack of control, purpose, and happiness felt by those who submerge themselves in the deepest waters of conspiracy theory culture. They, like the Smoking Man, have nothing else to live for. Connecting the dots gives conspiracy theorists a sense of purpose and assuages their existential dread.

Not everyone realized the plot of the well-received episode was unreliable. Said writer Frank Spotnitz, "In the closing scene, Frohike tells Mulder and Scully that the whole story was something he read in a crummy magazine. A lot of people didn't pick up on that subtlety. They thought that this was indeed the factual history of the CSM. As far as I'm concerned, it's not. Some of it may indeed be true, and some of it may… well, never mind."

Therein lies the rub with endless conspiracy theories— the inevitable lack of confirmation leads to fatigue. The entire narrative of the Smoking Man was unreliable. If anything can be a conspiracy, no historical narrative is true. If no historical narrative is true, nothing matters— except for the beliefs and biases you already have. If all of your beliefs about the world are placed on a pedestal of clandestine and esoteric wisdom, it not only gives you a sense of importance but also makes you feel endangered. If ruthless entities lurk behind every corner, aiming their rifle at you and waiting to take you down at the right moment, things can feel overwhelming. And if nothing matters, why risk your head to push back against a mountainous status quo? You eventually say, *fuck it*. You choose ignorant bliss.

A number of writers (Cantor, Kinney, Kellner) have pointed out that *The X-Files* is a postmodern, post–nation-state narrative in which humanity's greatest institutions have lost respect and mystery, one reason the show was so appealing to American viewers at the so-called End of History. But this appeal couldn't last. Interest in government corruption, scandals, and other negativity became passé at the turn of the century, a fatiguing symbol of the nineties.

Think about the bevy of Clinton scandals and allegations in the late nineties. The same fatigue happened with *The X-Files*, whose mythology became more convoluted and inconsistent as the show progressed. Season seven of *The X-Files* started airing in Autumn 1999. Frank Spotnitz said about the filming process, "There was a pretty strong sentiment inside and outside the show that it was time to call it a day." David Duchovny jumped ship after season seven due to contractual disputes, only appearing intermittently in season eight and once in the final season during the finale. He also successfully sued the Fox Network for underselling the program to its affiliates and underpaying him. Duchovny's presence was missed.

In March 2001, the pilot episode of *The Lone Gunmen* premiered, starring the characters first introduced in *The X-Files*. It was created and produced by Vince Gilligan. In the plot, malevolent rogues within the American government hijack a plane and plan to crash it into the World Trade Center. The Lone Gunmen avert this atrocity. Though positively received, the series was cancelled due to lackluster ratings, airing its last episode in April. Five months later, the September 11 attacks occurred. Said Frank Spotnitz, "We were really upset, and worried that somehow we had inspired the plot. But we were relieved to discover that the plot predated *The Lone Gunmen*, and that 9/11 had nothing to do with our work." The terrorist attacks would have a profound effect on America, and on *The X-Files*.

The first episode of the final season aired one month after the attacks. The reviews were mixed. The series was cancelled in May 2002 after nine years. "We lost our audience on the first episode [of that last season]," Chris Carter recalled. Joyce Millman wrote in *The X-Files Finds the Truth: Its Time Is Past*, "Without Mulder and Scully at its heart, *The X-Files* is just another middling sci-fi anthology. It was once the champion of its 9 p.m. Sunday time slot (where it moved, from Fridays, in 1996), but its ratings have been soft since Season 7. With HBO's *The Sopranos* and *Six Feet Under* around... *The X-Files* is no longer the hottest show on the Sunday block."

It also didn't help that a nation of people who had low levels of faith and trust in their government in the nineties was suddenly filled with unbridled post-9/11 nationalism. The patriotism wouldn't last forever, but it did make conspiracy-theory-laden content like *The X-Files* seem, at best, out of touch and goofy, or at worst, subversive, and not in the fun way described by reviewers of the pilot in 1993. People who once fit the mythos of *The X-Files* into their worldview, alongside salacious tabloids, Clinton conspiracy theories, and fears of Y2K, had new fears. Their primary concerns were no longer propaganda, scientific experimentation, and aliens, but Muslims, weapons of mass destruction, and "illegal aliens."

Final Thoughts

The X-Files was a critically acclaimed landmark in prestige television, flourishing in an era when the introduction of the internet and technological advances made people believe that life's most pressing questions would soon be answered. It set a new benchmark in fan obsession thanks to dedicated and self-proclaimed "X-Philes", who were active in online forums, crafted fan art, bought merchandise, and indulged in cosplay. The term "shipping" comes from fervent fan wishes to see Scully and Mulder in a relationship. The series was endlessly parodied and referenced in various aspects of pop culture from the mid-nineties onward. It would later be revived for two films and a 2018 continuation series after cancellation, with a plot line that apparently throws everything I've analyzed in this essay into question.

Knowing that there are limits to our understanding of the world will never stop us from attempting to learn about the unknown. We will continue to categorize our knowledge until it makes sense. For some people, that means contriving endless conspiracy theories to make order out of chaos, sliding all the way down a conspiracy iceberg until you're crushed by the weight of the ocean. For others, it means blaming demonic forces waging a war against good, serving as religious reassurance that God will protect you. For many, it means both. Either way, you are granted a sense of purpose. Otherwise, as the Smoking Man pointed out, "All you got left is an empty box filled with useless brown paper wrappers."

But if *The X-Files* hammered home any point, it's that there's much about the world that we will never know. Conspiracies take time to unravel. What may sound implausible today may not remain that way forever. Future generations may one day know some or most of what we don't, but *we* will never know. We can theorize and guess, but in the end we will be dead and ignorant. That is a hard-to-swallow pill for many humans, including myself. That was, and is, the scariest part of *The X-Files* for me.

90s Scandals

From the small television in my nana's kitchen, the whirlwind of scandal was always lurking. To cause national outrage for reprehensible behavior in the nineties wasn't easy. Tabloid magazines only had so many pages. People were competing with philandering politicians, corrupt cops, and howling hypocrites— and yet, average people and celebrities alike became embroiled in juicy plots that unfolded in nationwide media.

1990: Milli Vanilli

In the late eighties, Robert "Rob" Pilatus and Fabrice "Fab" Morvan, two aspiring singers from Munich and Paris, began looking for performance opportunities in Munich. They met producer Frank Farian, who persuaded them to be the face of demo songs, including the track *Girl You Know It's True*. He didn't like the duo's singing, but he liked their performance style and charisma, and christened them *Milli Vanilli*. By 1988, they were touring and released an album titled *All or Nothing*, and no song used their voices. They lip-synched everything.

The album was reissued in America by Arista Records as *Girl You Know It's True*, with their names falsely listed as the vocalists in the album inserts. In July 1989, while on a Club MTV Tour hosted by VJ Downtown Julie Brown, faulty equipment caused a track to skip in the background. The audience was confused, and in a panic, Pilatus ran off stage. Despite growing industry rumors that the pair were frauds, they continued to perform and release music videos.

In a March 1990 feature titled *Two Scoops of Vanilli*, journalist Jay Cocks wrote, "Milli Vanilli, a dance-music duo that sounds like Alvin and the Chipmunks and speaks English like the two Teutonic muscle heads on

Saturday Night Live, has done something boggling. The group, scorned by critics and adored by club-goers and devotees of MTV, has scored three No. 1 singles off its debut album, *Girl You Know It's True*. It has also sold 10 million copies worldwide… and copped three American Music Awards in January." They also won a Grammy for Best New Artist.

Cocks claimed that Pilatus said, "Musically, we are more talented than any Bob Dylan. Musically, we are more talented than Paul McCartney. Mick Jagger, his lines are not clear. He don't know how he should produce a sound. I'm the new modern rock 'n' roll. I'm the new Elvis." The pair would later claim this was taken out of context, but the ridicule followed, on talk shows and the sketch comedy *In Living Color*.

Pilatus and Morvan demanded that Farian allow them to sing on the next album. Instead, Farian dropped the act and revealed that they had been lip-syncing in a public statement on November 14. Said Pilatus, "The last two years of our lives have been a total nightmare. We've had to lie to everybody. We are true singers, but that maniac Frank Farian would never allow us to express ourselves." The public reaction was mostly negative, with Arista dropping the duo and the Grammys formally rescinding their Best New Artist award on November 19. Pilatus and Morvan held a press conference on November 20, where they sang for the assembled reporters and promised to return their Grammy.

Americans who bought the reissued album with liner notes attributing vocals to Pilatus and Morvan were eligible for refunds. Pilatus and Morvan became a punchline for the rest of the decade, and they tried to stage a comeback multiple times. Rob Pilatus became addicted to drugs and got caught up in crime, even being arrested for making terroristic threats at an L.A. apartment complex. The next year, he was dead from a mix of drugs and alcohol.

1991: City College Stampede

On December 28, 1991, over 5,000 people were excited to attend the Heavy D and Puff Daddy Celebrity Charity Game at City College of New York in Harlem. The event was sponsored by a student organization called Evening Student Government and promoted by Kiss-FM. Big Daddy Kane, Ed Lover, Jodeci, Michael Bivins, and Run-DMC were scheduled to play, with proceeds going to HIV/AIDS prevention.

The gym had a legal capacity of 2,730, and video would later show that over

2,000 extra people were packed inside. This was worsened by the fracas outside the gym. Reported Laurie Goldstein for *The Washington Post*:

> "Some fans, who began arriving for the scheduled 6PM game as early as 2PM, said they were shocked to see so few security personnel to manage the bulging throng. As many as 700 people arrived without tickets, police said...When the crowd broke through glass exterior doors, it surged with such force that it bent a lamppost in the rush to enter the building's foyer and hurry down the stairwell to the gym. Doors between the stairwell and the gym that had been closed were opened too late to relieve the pressure of the scores of people on the stairs. When the doors finally opened, people tumbled into the gym over the bodies of those who had been crushed."

Someone foolishly announced over the intercom, "Three people are dead because you didn't listen," leading to a second stampede and more chaos. Recalled a witness, "People started running. People were pushing down other people. People on the bottom were getting trampled. People jumped off the bleachers and crushed them." Some people, amidst the chaos and death, were demanding their money back.

Robert D. McFadden wrote for *The New York Times*, "Some witnesses said the rap stars pitched in to help the victims, while some of the disappointed fans interrupted them from time to time, seeking their autographs." EMS didn't arrive on the scene for thirty minutes after the first call was made at 7:17 PM. In addition to a variety of injuries, including a broken neck, nine people, ages 15 to 28, were killed in the stampede. Blame was placed everywhere, but by most of the mainstream press, it was placed on the people. There were nearly 700 so-called "gatecrashers" who were accused by witnesses of cutting lines, flaring chaos, pushing people, and getting rowdy, some allegedly even starting fights before the stampede began.

Said Al Sharpton, "We are ashamed of those young Black people [who], despite a lack of security, conducted themselves in a way that hurt innocent people." The conservative columnist Heather MacDonald leaned on "personal responsibility" in a 1992 assessment of media coverage of the scandal titled *Spreading the Blame Too Thin*, writing, "The denial of individual responsibility places ever-increasing burdens on institutions. If people are not expected to control themselves, these institutions must control them, and be blamed when things go wrong."

Over 1,400 people had died in the Mecca tunnel tragedy in Saudi Arabia due to a blockage in 1990, and 42 more were killed in a religious sanctuary in Mexico in 1991. The onus of responsibility being placed solely on teenagers and young adults at a mismanaged venue was irresponsible, but it helped bolster ongoing criticism of Black American youth and hip hop culture.

On *Geraldo* in 1992, the mustachioed and sneaky host asked his audience if they had ever been afraid to attend a rap concert because of the threat of violence and chaos. Sister Souljah claimed that the youth who attended the concert didn't have enough self-respect because they stayed at an overcrowded venue, placing blame on the victims and celebrity idolatry. One white woman countered, telling *Geraldo* she had been to a rowdy and violent, mostly white, Grateful Dead concert and that rap was not the problem.

Just twelve years earlier, eleven people had been killed during a concert for *The Who* in Cincinnati, Ohio. The culprit? Poor crowd control. It was the same at City College. Explained a 16-year-old named Lori Grant, "At Madison Square Garden when there's a concert, the cops come in the hundreds, on motorcycles, in cars, in vans, like a parade of cops. Here, I only saw one cop, and only one cop car outside." There were actually 66 police officers on hand at City College, but none had been inside the venue when the stampede began. Survivors recalled being stuck under and on top of other people for twenty minutes or more before police moved to evacuate the stairway leading to the gym.

Reported Michael Specter, "A Fire Department official who insisted on anonymity criticized the police, saying, 'If they had problems getting into the place, why wouldn't they call us? Why wouldn't they utilize all emergency services?'" The lack of crowd management was blamed on the game's sponsors and promoters, who hired 38 campus guards and 20 Nation of Islam guards. Additionally, despite knowing the gym's legal capacity was 2,730, the greedy promoters, namely Diddy, had sold at least 5,000 tickets. Diddy issued a statement: "I am sorry for being the promoter of the event. I just pray for the families and pray for the children who lost their lives every day. It's a tragic event, and my heart goes out to the families." The scandal deepened, though.

Reported Specter on the inquiries, "For every fact that emerged during the day, there were at least two new questions. It remained unclear who sold the advance tickets to the game and why more were on sale at the door. City and state officials said they had no record of the organization that was supposed to benefit from the event, The AIDS Education Outreach Program. They said it was not registered with the Secretary of State, as required by law." A series of lawsuits followed throughout the rest of the decade. The families of the nine victims settled out of court with the event's sponsors and promoters. Diddy and Heavy D were responsible for half of the settlement payments, and the college was responsible for the other half.

1991: Pee-wee's Peewee

In July 1991, Paul Reubens, also known as Pee-wee Herman, the host of the popular children's television program *Pee-wee's Playhouse*, was arrested during a sweep of an adult movie theater named XXX South Trail Cinema in Sarasota, Florida. He was in town visiting his parents and decided to treat himself to a triple feature at the theater. Police witnessed him masturbating.

After being arrested for indecent exposure, Reubens reportedly offered to perform at a Pee-wee Herman children's benefit to make the whole thing go away. The offer was denied. A journalist recognized Reubens' name in the arrest reports and publicized the story. Reubens faced one year in jail and a $1,000 fine. His career immediately suffered. Reported Mark Harris and Ty Burr for *Entertainment Weekly*,

> "On July 29, CBS announced that it was pulling the five remaining reruns of *Pee-wee's Playhouse*. The same day, Disney-MGM Studios in Florida suspended from its studio tour a tape in which Pee-wee explains how voice-over tracks are made. On July 30, it was reported that Toys 'R' Us was removing Pee-wee toys from its stores, but as the Herman fad had peaked three years ago, few were left on the shelves. 'It's not like something happened with Cabbage Patch,' said Toys 'R' Us spokeswoman Angela Bourdon. 'Then we'd have a problem.'"

Numerous celebrities came to Reubens' defense, including Bill Cosby and Cyndi Lauper. Hundreds of his fans gathered in Los Angeles, New York, and San Francisco in "Hands Off Our Pee-wee" rallies. In a poll of 500 parents commissioned by *Entertainment Weekly*, they found that "fewer than one-third think that Pee-wee's movies and TV series should be off-limits to children, and by a 3-to-2 margin, the parents we asked have no problem with letting their kids watch his shows."

Reubens pleaded no contest to the charge of indecent exposure after initially denying it, avoiding jail and a fine. Instead, he was sentenced to 75 hours of community service. He appeared in character at the 1991 MTV Music Awards and received a standing ovation. His career would continue, though it would again come under scrutiny in 2002 when he was found to be in possession of nude images of children.

1992: Marge Schott and the Cincinnati Reds

The Cincinnati Reds had swept the World Series in 1990 in four games, miffing the team's owner because she wanted more games and more revenue. That owner was 63-year-old Marge Schott, a trust fund kid and Cincinnati native. She didn't throw a party for the team, who went out by themselves for burgers. When Schott first became majority owner of the Reds in 1983, it was losing money. Under her leadership, the Reds turned a $15 million annual profit by 1992. She was somewhat popular for keeping ticket and hot dog prices low during a period of recession.

Former employee Tim Sabo filed a failed lawsuit against Schott and the Reds, claiming he had been fired in 1991 for testifying in a separate lawsuit that the company had an unwritten policy of not hiring Black people. Charles "Cal" Levy, who once served as marketing director for the team, said in a deposition that he had heard Schott refer to former players Eric Davis and Dave Parker as "million-dollar n-words." He also alleged that Schott had been antisemitic and showed him, a Jewish man, a Nazi swastika armband that a former employer had given her as a gift.

When asked about playing with Nazi dolls as a child and owning the swastika armband as an adult, Schott said, "Figures a Jewish guy would find it, huh, honey... What's a Jewish guy looking through my drawers for anyway? Right, honey?" Schott admitted to calling her players the slur, saying, "Of course, 'nigger' is a demeaning word. But I know that Blacks call it to each other, too. I've been in the business world for 24 years and never had any problem with discrimination." In the same interview where she was accused of calling Martin Luther King Jr. Day "Nigger Day," she also remarked, "Hitler was good in the beginning, but he went too far." She used the J-word referring to Asians multiple times, among other extremely racist comments.

Baseball legend Hank Aaron publicly called for her suspension, while the Anti-Defamation League stated that she had "tainted and sullied baseball." Al Sharpton, Jesse Jackson, and others generated more press coverage that embarrassed Cincinnati city boosters and baseball fans. Local news anchor Jerry Springer reported on the scandal. Cincinnati's reputation for racism was well known. This was where a chapter of the Ku Klux Klan had received city permits to erect a cross, which was later torn down by angry citizens. Some sports observers noted that the scandal surrounding Marge Schott would become a watershed moment, much like the 1987 firing of Dodgers executive Al Campanis for his racist remarks about Black people.

A committee was formed to investigate the racism claims and determine whether Schott should be fired. In February 1993, she was fined $250,000 and banned from anything not behind the scenes until November. Said Schott, "In fairness to me, I wish to add that while I am not without blame in this matter, I am also not the cause of the problem. Minority issues have been present in baseball long before I came to the game." Wrote *The Oklahoman*, "Schott's behavior and remarks warrant a suspension under that huge umbrella known as 'the best interest of baseball.' But to what degree? And is she alone? How many other racist owners are out there, and will they be equally punished? Is all this simply the owners' best chance to get rid of the major league's only female owner?"

In 1996, when ticket sales were falling and Schott had a 37% approval rating among Cincinnatians, *Sports Illustrated* published an article by Rick Reilly that exposed her alcoholism, lack of baseball knowledge, and severe loneliness as a childless widow, in addition to her racist beliefs and her stated preference not to hire women of "childbearing age." Some critics called the writing against her a misogynistic "cheap shot" meant to oust her from the male-dominated world of baseball. But Marge herself said, "Some of the biggest problems in this city come from women wanting to leave the home to work. I don't really think baseball is a woman's place, honey. I really don't. I think it should be left to the boys."

Because Marge's deceased husband had cheated on her, Rick Reilly described that "she has waged a one-woman war for fidelity. Her goal is to rid baseball of 'cutesy-poos,' as she calls them: the groupies who end up in ballplayers' hotel rooms. She says she has hired private investigators to videotape her players getting on and off buses and going in and out of hotels, to make sure there is no cutesy-pooing going on." Players complained about their mail being opened. The powers that be wanted her gone and pressured her to resign. She finally relented.

On April 20, 1999, the same day as the Columbine shooting and Adolf Hitler's birthday, Schott agreed to sell her controlling stake in the Reds for $67 million.

1993: Jerry Seinfeld

In 1993, the NBC show *Seinfeld* dominated ratings in its fifth season. Shortly after the famed comedian Jerry Seinfeld turned 38, he met 17-year-old Shoshanna Lonstein in Central Park and gave her his number. She was a wealthy Upper East Side prep girl, destined for George Washington University the following year. Her parents were cool with the relationship. She turned eighteen a few weeks after meeting him, and Seinfeld went public with her. Tabloids of the era, like *People*, referred to the relationship as an "unlikely romance." Said one of his close friends, "I think it's serious between them. She's beautiful and mature. She's good for him." Added his manager, George Shapiro: "I've never seen him happier." They dated for four years, breaking up in 1997. And, of course, in an era of R. Kelly and Woody Allen, Seinfeld faced no consequences.

1994: Tyke The Elephant

On August 20, 1994, a 21-year-old, 8,000-pound African bush elephant named Tyke refused to continue performing at the Circus International at the Neal Blaisdell Center in Kakaako, Honolulu, Hawaii. Tyke had previously been in trouble three times for rampaging and destroying property in Pennsylvania and North Dakota, but this time was worse.

Tyke crushed and killed a zookeeper and elephant trainer named Allen Campbell. Campbell, who had cocaine and alcohol in his bloodstream at the time of his death, had a reputation for abusing animals and had been fired from the Denver Zoo in 1990 for mistreatment. After trampling Campbell, Tyke stormed the arena as the audience fled in a scene of chaos caught on camera. She nearly killed a publicist who tried to stop her from fleeing the circus grounds and made it outside to the streets of Kakaako. Police shot Tyke 86 times before she collapsed and died.

Dozens of people, including Animal Rights Hawaii, filed lawsuits against Circus International and Tyke's owner, Jon Cuneo, based on the fact that Tyke had acted out previously and was known to be dangerous. They settled out of court. Allen Campbell's wife, Ginger, received $5 million. Cuneo was fined $12,500 by the U.S. Department of Agriculture. The USDA hit him with 19 violations that were mitigated by his agreement to a suspended license and the relocation of his herd of elephants to approved locations and sanctuaries, plus another $200,000 fine. One of those elephants would end up in Casper, Wyoming, at a circus in 1996, where it would knock down and repeatedly kick its trainer.

The scandal reignited interest in the treatment of circus and zoo animals. In particular, people began to question if these intelligent mammals— who were involved in at least thirty other violent incidents between 1990 and 1994— were rebelling. Ringling Bros. and Barnum & Bailey scrambled to differentiate themselves as responsible elephant caregivers. The following year, they established the Center for Elephant Conservation in Florida. Many zookeepers were weighing the risks. Wrote Louis Sahagún, "Federal laws banning importation of elephants have pushed the average cost of pachyderms, which are frequently traded among zoos, circuses and private owners, to $100,000. Liability insurance for an elephant runs about $25,000 a year, double the annual insurance for a 1994 Rolls-Royce Corniche in Los Angeles County."

1995: Hugh Grant Gets Arrested

In 1995, a Black woman named Estella Marie Thompson, a sex worker calling herself "Divine Brown," was caught giving a $50 blow job to actor Hugh Grant on L.A.'s Sunset Boulevard. At the time, Grant was dating British sex symbol Elizabeth Hurley, who was a tabloid darling because she was Grant's girlfriend. When cops knocked on the white BMW's window, the cheapskate Grant said, "What about my money?" Divine replied, "Honey, we're going to jail." They were both arrested. Grant received a fine, two years' probation, and was ordered to take a mandatory AIDS education program. Estella also received a fine and was enrolled in the same AIDS course, but was additionally sentenced to 180 days in jail for violating her parole.

In the long run, the oral sex scandal actually helped Estella's life. She became a minor 15-minute celebrity and was even impersonated. *The Sun* allegedly offered Brown $150,000 for an interview about the encounter with Grant, posting *WANTED* posters around Sunset Boulevard. *News of the World* either paid more or got to her first, as they ultimately broke her story. She was flown to Brazil to appear in a lingerie commercial and made appearances on various Brazilian TV shows. Described one reporter of her somewhat high-profile appearance at a Mike Tyson fight: "She flitted about in a brown leather ensemble with fingernails like exotic weaponry. She sipped Rémy Martin from a gold-painted souvenir goblet."

Estella later did a re-creation of the incident in a porn film and earned a reported $1.6 million in the years that followed, appearing on radio shows, strip club stages, softcore editorials, and hosting gigs. On her transition from street-based survival sex work to the budding world of online sex work, she said in 2007, "Everything worked out for the better. It helped me turn it into something positive... I was blessed that it could get me out of that lifestyle." Estella also proudly reported that she had sent her three children to private school.

Hugh Grant, known for his romantic roles, was splashed across tabloids but ultimately emerged unscathed after a widely viewed *Tonight Show* interview with Jay Leno, where he laughed off the incident, saying, "I think you know in life what's a good thing to do and what's a bad thing, and I did a bad thing. And there you have it." While television host Larry King and others wanted to plumb the depths of Hugh Grant's mind to understand why he would cheat on Elizabeth Hurley with a Black street worker, he remained mostly vague and charmingly self-deprecating in his statements. But as we all know, Hugh Grant getting caught with his pants down on Sunset Boulevard wasn't the biggest oral sex–related scandal of the decade.

1995: TLC's Bankruptcy

On July 3, 1995, the group TLC filed for bankruptcy. The previous year, Lisa "Left Eye" Lopes had accidentally burned down the home of her abusive boyfriend, Andre Rison, when she set his sneakers on fire in a bathtub. While it led to legal consequences and gave Left Eye a reputation for being volatile, the incident didn't dampen the success of their album *CrazySexyCool*, which was released to critical acclaim. It ultimately reached diamond status, and the women were everywhere. But behind the scenes, they were locked into a bad contract. Each member was living on $50,000 or less per year, and they were approximately $3.5 million in debt. They weren't broke from flagrant overspending like early nineties sensation MC Hammer.

Some of this debt came from the spike in Left Eye's insurance premiums after the arson, and from paying Andre's restitution. But most of it stemmed from their exploitative contract. Their 1991 agreement with LaFace Records gave them 56 cents, split three ways, per album. Pebbitone, their management company, charged them for various expenses and took further cuts from their earnings. LaFace was owned by Babyface and L.A. Reid, whose wife, Perri "Pebbles" Reid, owned Pebbitone. The scandal sparked renewed interest in exploitative record contracts, exposing the oily nature of the music industry, especially for Black artists.

At the 38th Annual Grammy Awards on February 28 1996, Chilli said: "We are the biggest selling female group ever... 10 million albums worldwide... we have worked very hard! We have been in this business for five years, and we are broke as broke can be." A few months later, the women renegotiated their contracts and settled with their management. They also bought the rights to their name from Pebbles. TLC's financial struggles contributed to the eventual collapse of Pebbles and L.A. Reid's marriage. Pebbles filed for divorce and later sued LaFace.

Two years after TLC's bankruptcy, Toni Braxton also filed for bankruptcy, despite having sold millions of albums, and ultimately sued Arista and LaFace. Like TLC, Toni was stuck in a deeply unfavorable deal. Her lawsuit was unsuccessful, and she was forced to file for bankruptcy.

1996: Jessica Dubroff

In 1996, seven-year-old Jessica Whitney Dubroff of Pescadero, California became a minor celebrity when it was reported that she was attempting to become the youngest pilot to fly a plane across the United States in a journey dubbed Sea to Shining Sea. She had thirty-three hours of flight training from an instructor named Joe Reid. The flight was planned in three legs using Reid's light aircraft, and he would accompany her while she piloted the plane. The trip cost her father, Lloyd Dubroff, who would also be on the flight, $15,000, which he said was "less than I'd pay for private school."

Lloyd created merchandise, contacted the media, and promoted Jessica's journey as a record-setting event, though no official aviation authority was tracking such records. Some speculated they were trying to keep up with tween pilot Vicki Van Meter, who had flown a plane from Maine to California at age 11 in 1993. Jessica was homeschooled, not allowed to watch television, and her parents were unconventional to say the least. Wrote Richard Stengel for *Time*:

> "For all their New Age patter, Jessica's mother and father seemed to be stage parents of the old school, pushing their daughter in front of the curtain, hoping she would become a star, Macaulay Culkin *in a cockpit*. The week before the flight, Jessica handed out signed photographs to members of the Half Moon City Council. Dubroff spent $1,300 on custom-made baseball caps to distribute to friends and the media. They read: *JESSICA WHITNEY DUBROFF, SEA TO SHINING SEA, April 1996.* He also primed her to write a letter to President Clinton, inviting him along for a ride. "To visit you at the White House would be wonderful," she wrote in her simple, child's hand, "and clearly to pilot an airplane that you would be in would bring me even greater joy." (The White House did not accept.)"

Jessica was also interviewed on all of the big three networks, and *ABC* even gave Lloyd a Hi8 camera to capture footage of the journey. The trio took off on April 10 from Half Moon Bay, California, and successfully completed their first leg to Cheyenne, Wyoming. Jessica spoke to a flock of cameras and journalists, and you could see the brittle nervousness in her smile and body language. Described Stengel, "I enjoyed it," she said, forcing a smile, sounding, as always, like she was imitating adult speech. "I had two hours' sleep last night."

Despite being warned that the weather was unsuitable, the trio left on April 11 with 96 pounds of excess weight. The plane crashed, and everyone on board died. Wrote Stengel, "Overnight [Jessica] became the poster child of parental and media exploitation, of an ethos that granted children too much freedom rather than too little, of a parental drive not content to let children be children. Many wondered whether the freedom to pursue personal identity had been pushed too far." An investigation by the National Transportation Safety Board blamed poor conditions and the heavy plane, stating: "Contributing to the pilot in command's decision to take off was a desire to adhere to an overly ambitious itinerary, in part, because of media commitments." They also made it clear that, because a child cannot legally man a flight, the actual pilot was Reid.

This was a clear example of the dangers of media sensationalism. Said J. Max McClellan, the editor of *Flying Magazine*, "Jessica's flight is the kind of thing that, absent media coverage, would never have happened. [So-called flying records by youngsters are a bogus concept]... We've intentionally ignored attempts like this here at *Flying* because we didn't want to promote the activity. It has no validity from an aviation sense; the pilot in reality is the certified pilot." Said Ted Koppel on ABC, "We need to begin by acknowledging our own contribution... We feed one another: those of you looking for publicity and those of us looking for stories."

Jessica's 59-year-old father, Lloyd, had been going broke and raising a newborn with his 19-year-old new wife, and another newborn with his ex-wife, Jessica's mother, Lisa. When he agreed to be on the fated Sea to Shining Sea flight, he took out four life insurance policies worth $3 million that the two women fought over after the crash. Declared Lisa, when asked if she regretted allowing her 7-year-old daughter to pilot a plane, "I'd have her do it again in a second. You have no idea what this meant to Jess." Lisa also said she hoped the legal status of youth aviation did not change.

Bill Clinton signed the Federal Aviation Reauthorization Act of 1996 into law on October 9, including legislation that made it illegal for young pilots to attempt to fly and set records by requiring age-restricted medical certification and a private pilot's license.

1997: Infidelities

Kelly Flinn

This 27-year-old First Lieutenant was the first female B-52 pilot in the Air Force, providing good public relations for the military during a period of ongoing gender inequity. The military hoped to move past negative press from the Tailhook scandal in 1991 and various high-profile rape cases discussed in *Lexual Does the Nineties*. A 1995 promotional television spot highlighted Flinn's status as the first of her gender to fly a B-52 for the Air Force. Bragged the report, "[Her future] may one day include becoming squadron commander and a shuttle astronaut."

In North Dakota, a young airwoman named Gayla Zigo was stationed at the Minot Air Force Base, where Flinn was her superior. Zigo's husband, a discharged Navy sailor and soccer coach named Marc, met Kelly Flinn and struck up an affair. According to Flinn, Marc told her that he was legally separated from his wife. According to Gayla, Flinn was the nefarious seducer, saying, "I thought she was simply being a friend to my husband, not trying to break up my marriage. Less than a week after we arrived to the base, Lieutenant Flinn was in bed with my husband having sex."

Of course, Marc, who was voted "class flirt" at his Catholic high school and had once been arrested for assaulting Gayla, was lying to both women. Gayla found a love letter after several months and reported Flinn. The military had begun to take adultery prosecutions more seriously, with reports showing that such cases increased from 16 in 1987 to 67 in 1996, curiously around the same time more women were being admitted into combat ranks.

Flinn was ordered to end the affair, but she didn't, and she lied to senior officers about it. When a different officer faced his own investigation for misconduct and assault, he reported Flinn. She faced one year in prison for several offenses, including disobeying a lawful order, perjury, and fraternization. The case became headline news because of Flinn's previous status as a press and recruitment darling. Some people saw hypocrisy in the intense focus on her adultery. Wrote one reader to the *Minot Daily News*, "I would like to see you print an article about the very next male pilot who is charged with adultery, print his name and ruin his life before he has been found guilty."

While civilians and the media zeroed in on the adultery aspect, General

Ronald Fogleman said, "In the end, this is not an issue of adultery. This is an issue about an officer, entrusted to fly nuclear weapons, who lied." Others disagreed. Journalist Elaine Sciolino noted Republican Senator Slade Gorton saying, "I'm no flaming feminist by any stretch of the imagination. I'm very pro-military. But a supportive command structure would have treated this quite differently. This is an injustice to her and a black eye on the Air Force."

Flinn's lawyer was the same man who represented Army Staff Sergeant Delmar Simpson, a sergeant and drill instructor convicted of raping six women in Aberdeen, Maryland. Ultimately, Flinn resigned with a general discharge from the Air Force. Reported the *Associated Press*, "The future for the 26-year-old first lieutenant is far from bleak. Her celebrity status is already attracting talk of book deals and movies. Mr. Spinner says she has received offers to fly for commercial airlines."

The Honey Trap

Frank Gifford, a 66-year-old former Giants player and football announcer in 1997, had been married to his 23-years-younger wife, the television host Kathie Lee, since October 1986. Though Kathie Lee had once declared in her autobiography that "cheating is out of the question," Frank was rumored to be in the streets. In 1997, the tabloid *The Globe* paid a 46-year-old woman named Suzen Johnson to meet and seduce Gifford at the Regency Hotel in New York City. Suzen was a former flight attendant who narrowly missed being on the ill-fated TWA Flight 800 in 1996 because she switched her shift the day before.

It took Suzen three attempts to get Frank back to her room, which was outfitted with recording equipment. *The Globe* published the transcribed tapes of the tryst first, prompting the Giffords to deny that the affair had ever taken place, calling the transcript a lie. It was an especially rough era for Kathie Lee, who faced mounting public backlash from her sweatshop labor scandal the previous year. *The Globe* was an especially low tabloid, having previously published the autopsy photos of Selena and JonBenét Ramsey. They then released photos of the honeypot tryst, forcing Frank to come clean.

Said a smug *Globe* editor named Tony Frost, "Initially we had no intention of using that video. Our hands were forced... after the Giffords and their lawyer attacked us and ridiculed our initial story and threatened to sue us. In the face of such strenuous denials and attempts to discredit our information, we had to prove we were telling the truth." While it was true that Frank cheated on the wholesome Kathie Lee, the bigger scandal was the lengths a publication would go to in order to generate scandal. Bill O'Reilly called the trap an outrage. The *National Enquirer*'s Steve Coz said, "It's one thing to catch a celebrity cheating and another to induce or entrap them. Without *The Globe*, there would be no story here. I'm in the tabloid industry, and this is way over the top. It's downright cruel."

While Frank was demoted by ABC in the wake of the affair, Suzen soaked up her fifteen minutes of fame by posing for *Playboy*. Wrote Marcus Errico in 1997, "Johnson received a six-figure sum for the spread. Add that to the reported $75,000 she picked up from *The Globe* for luring Frank to the Regency, and the curvy blonde has turned a nifty profit on her dalliance." Suzen was possibly paid up to $125,000, depending on different sources. Of course, she launched her own unsuccessful lawsuit in 1999, alleging that *The Globe* never informed her that the hotel room had cameras.

The Bill Cosby Extortion Plot

1997 was the year that a 22-year-old aspiring filmmaker named Autumn Jackson threatened to tell the world that Bill Cosby was her father if he didn't pay her $40 million. She made the demand on the same day that Bill Cosby's son, Ennis, had been murdered in a carjacking, January 16. Autumn expected the grieving father to pay up. Instead, Autumn and two co-conspirators were arrested for extortion, and during the trial, Cosby admitted to having an affair with Autumn's mother, Shawn Upshaw, in Las Vegas and paying her $100,000 for her silence.

Cosby denied Autumn was his daughter, saying that when he met her as a youth, he told her, "I will be for you a father figure, but I am not your father." The issue of paternity was ruled irrelevant to the extortion charge. Autumn was convicted and sentenced to 26 months in prison. The extortion conviction was overturned on appeal after fourteen months and then reinstated in 1999. A blood test revealed that Cosby was not the father.

Eddie Murphy

36-year-old box office draw Eddie Murphy was married to Nicole Mitchell and shared three children with her. At the time, Eddie was being paid $17.5 million for his role in the film *Dr. Dolittle*. On May 2, 1997, Shalimar Seiuli, a Samoan trans sex worker, was being surveilled by police when she was picked up by Eddie Murphy on Santa Monica Boulevard. Police pulled Murphy over and questioned him for thirty minutes. He claimed that he was giving Shalimar a ride, not attempting to pay her for sex. Murphy was allowed to leave, while Shalimar was arrested for an outstanding prostitution warrant.

The National Enquirer paid Shalimar $15,000 bond in exchange for her story. She insisted that Eddie Murphy picked her up for sex. The story went international and generated transphobic jokes, as other trans sex workers were solicited for their alleged hookups with Eddie Murphy. Shalimar unfortunately died the following year after falling from her apartment, and it was ruled an accident, though rumors persisted among her friends and family that she may have been killed.

1998: Karl Malone

In 1998, Utah Jazz player Karl Malone continued to cement his legacy as one of the greatest power forwards of all time. In conservative and religious Utah, Malone had a positive and family-friendly reputation, sharing four children with his wife, Kay. In July, the tabloid The Globe broke the news that the father of four had three extramarital children. Two, a pair of twins named Cheryl and Daryl, were born in 1981 to Bonita "Rita" Ford. Bonita and Karl were both 17 years old when she gave birth to them. Malone alluded to them in a 1989 interview, saying, "You'd have to be an absolute nut to get married your first or second year in the league. Unless you banged her up in high school and y'all got a set of twins." At the time, he was earning $1.4 million a year. Bonita took care of his children with $40 a month from a housecleaning job and $259 in monthly welfare payments. She sued for $3,500 a week and eventually settled out of court in the eighties.

The other extramarital child was with a woman named Gloria Bell of Summerfield, Louisiana, who was 13 when she gave birth in 1983. She named her son Demetress. At the time, Malone was a 20-year-old player at Louisiana Tech. Malone gave Gloria $125 a week in child support and covered health expenses, after her parents, Ola Mae and Tommie, sought $200 per week in a paternity suit. Eventually, Malone argued that $6,500 a year was excessive and reached a confidential one-time settlement with his formerly underage victim and her family in 1989. Ola Mae testified that Malone told her, "[I] wasn't trying to get no baby, I wasn't in love with her, I was just doing something." Cheryl and Daryl remembered seeing Malone around Summerfield, and he would ignore them.

When this was reported in 1998, it didn't stop Malone's career. Declared Jazz President Frank Layden, "When people start casting stones at Karl Malone, they better live in a brick house." Coincidentally, Salt Lake City was wrapped up in its own scandal, bribing a member of the Olympics Committee to become the host city for the Winter Games in 2002. As for Malone, very little coverage zeroed in on the age gap as a serious transgression, though a few pointed out that Bell and her family could have asked to prosecute under Louisiana's laws. In the Pelican State, where the age of consent was 17, there was a ten-year statute of limitations for sex crimes that began when Gloria turned 17, which expired on June 7 1997.

Gloria Bell said her parents never considered having Malone prosecuted because he was a "neighborhood kid" and hero. The sign welcoming people to Summerfield in the late eighties and nineties read, "Welcome to Karl Malone Country." They also felt he wouldn't be able to provide financial assistance from jail. The same year the statute of limitations expired, and Malone was crowned his team's Most Valuable Player, he reflected on his own father's suicide when he was three. He told *The New York Times*, "I've got three kids of my own, and never will I do anything to leave them to fend for themselves. It was kind of like hanging over my head, my father not being around, and I was always upset that he wasn't, and that it was his own decision that he wasn't. And I didn't accept that, and that's what drives me now, because I'm motivated as a man, as a father and as a person."

But Karl "The Mailman" Malone failed to deliver as a father, only publicly embracing the twins Cheryl and Daryl in 1997, and rejecting Demetress, whom he didn't meet until 2008 or have a relationship with until 2014. Cheryl became a member of the WNBA's Detroit Shock, and Demetress was an offensive lineman for various NFL teams.

1998: George Michael

On April 7, 1998, the singer George Michael was arrested in Beverly Hills, California, for "engaging in a lewd act" in a public restroom at Will Rogers Memorial Park. Beverly Hills was in the middle of cracking down on the sexual practice of "cruising" by gay and bisexual men in an undercover sting operation. The park was known for cruising activities, even being listed on a webpage of notable U.S. cruising spots. Wrote *The Los Angeles Times*: "[Recreation and Parks Department] Stephen Miller has a little warning for lunch-hour visitors to his Beverly Hills parks who have an appetite for anything beyond a sandwich or a summer salad: Stay away. Don't even think about it. Read his lips, his parks are havens for families and little old ladies and folks who want a little peace and quiet. So no cruising for sex partners allowed."

George Michael was one of the sting operation's casualties, and in the process, he was outed as a queer man. He pleaded no contest to the charge, was sentenced to counseling, fined $810, and ordered to complete 80 hours of community service. He later released a song and video titled *Outside*, spoofing the incident. The undercover police officer who arrested him, a man named Marcelo Rodriguez, was so angered by the portrayal that he launched a failed lawsuit the following year for emotional distress.

1999: Hillsdale College

In 1999, Hillsdale College was a small, private, conservative institution in Michigan with about 1,200 students. The 64-year-old president, George C. Roche III, was a conservative celebrity who had been employed there for almost thirty years. Under his leadership, the school had increased its endowment from $4 million to $184 million, becoming what William F. Buckley Jr. called "the most prominent conservative college in the country." That same year, Roche divorced his wife of 44 years while she had cancer and remarried five months later.

In November, Roche's son, George IV, a history professor, told *National Review* that his wife of 21 years, Lisa, had ended her life on the family gazebo after informing him that she had been having an affair with his father. The elderly Roche denied the allegations but promptly stepped down from his $188,000-a-year job with a $3 million settlement. The scandal generated discussion about Roche's ruthless tenure as president, the hypocrisy of conservatives, and corruption in higher education. Some students were quoted as being worried that the scandal would taint their degrees or that the endowment money would stop flowing, critical concerns for a private school that rejected federal regulations. In fact, students with federal aid money had not been allowed to attend since 1985, keeping the school lily white and staunchly conservative. Other students were simply disappointed that their so-called celebrity principal had done something so depraved, with one student saying, "It is the same with Newt falling."

That same year, Senator Newt Gingrich had divorced his second wife, Marianne, shortly after she was diagnosed with multiple sclerosis, intending to marry his staffer Callista Bisek, with whom he had been having an affair since 1993. Keep in mind that he had also divorced his former high school geometry teacher and first wife, Jackie, while she was being treated for uterine cancer in 1980. What a scumbag. Both the Hillsdale and Newt headlines were circulating while conservatives were attempting to remove

Bill Clinton from office because of his lies and infidelities.

Notes on Methodology and Sources

I narrowed the scope of this project after reading the illuminating and diverse works of historians cited in the bibliography, creating a chronological yet thematic narrative with room for my own interpretations, investigations, and research. This book was a medley of primary and secondary sources including newspapers, journals, speeches, video, interviews, memos, and other mediums— many of which only exist on the internet, ready to be ripped down at any time.

The disappearing internet is a significant issue with cataloging modern history, despite the popular adage "the internet is forever." I have saved many of these sources in my own growing physical archive, but revising this list for publishing made me realize a few sources needed to be replaced because of disappearing pages.

I discussed the nineties with friends, family, and strangers, while also reading through online message boards for people's most unfiltered (and unhinged) opinions and stories, finding ways to connect broader trends with cultural and regional niches. I discovered that I shared a birthday with several nineties subjects, including Ellen Degeneres, Anita Baker, Kirk Franklin, Ricky 'Freeway' Ross, and Scott Amedure.

I soaked myself in nineties films and TV shows throughout the duration of this project, listening for references and regional stories that I could dig into. Regional history was important to this narrative, so I spent a lot of time reading random newspaper archives and watching a lot of old local news reports. Major shoutout to the people who cared to record things in the nineties and upload them decades later on YouTube!

As main characters of the nineties die and this book ages (hopefully like wine), it will be updated incrementally as new information becomes available. The beauty of studying history is the way our interpretations of past events evolve with time. History is always a living and breathing thing!

Bibliography
Main Texts

- *90s Bitch: Media, Culture, and The Failed Promise of Gender Equality* (Allison Yarrow)
- *1995: The Year The Future Began* (W. Joseph Campbell)
- *A People's History of The United States* (Howard Zinn)
- *America In The Nineties* (Nina Esperanza Serrianne)
- *Backlash* (Susan Faludi)
- *Bring the War Home: The White Power Movement and Paramilitary America* (Kathleen Belew)
- *Conservatives in Power: The Reagan Years, 1981-1989, A Brief History With Documents* (Meg Jacobs and Julian E. Zelizer)
- *Fault Lines: A History of The United States Since 1974* (Kevin Kruse and Julian E. Zelizer)
- *Jesus and John Wayne: How White Evangelicals Corrupted a Faith and Fractured a Nation* (Kristin Kobes Du Mez)
- *Girls To The Front: The True Story of The Riot Grrl Movement* (Sara Marcus)
- *Lexual Does The 90s* (Elexus Jionde)
- *Living In The Eighties* (Edited by Gil Troy and Vincent J Cannato)
- *Morning In America: How Ronald Reagan Invented The 1980s* (Gil Troy)
- *Official Negligence: How Rodney King and the Riots Changed Los Angeles and the LAPD* (Lou Cannon)
- *Partisans: The Conservative Revolutionaries Who Remade American Politics in the 1990s* (Nicole Hemmer)
- *Stiffed: The Roots of Modern Male Rage* (Sudan Faludi)
- *Superpredator: Bill Clinton's Use and Abuse of Black America* (Nathan J. Robinson)
- *The 1970s: A New Global History From Civil Rights to Economic Inequality* (Thomas Borstelmann)
- *The Age of Clinton: America in the 1990s* (Gil Troy)
- *The Age of Reagan: A History, 1974-2008* (Sean Wilentz)
- *The Culture of Fear: Why Americans Are Afraid of The Wrong Things* (Barry Glassner)
- *The Naughty Nineties: Triumph of The American Libido* (David Friend)
- *The Nineties* (Chuck Klosterman)
- *The Other Eighties: A Secret History of America in the Age of Reagan* (Bradford Martin)
- *The Postmodern Presidency: Bill Clinton's Legacy in US Politics* (Steven Schier)
- *The Red and The Blue: The 1990s and the Birth of Political Tribalism* (Steve Kornacki)
- *The Roaring Nineties: The History of The World's Most Prosperous Decade* (Joseph E Stiglitz)
- *The Seventies: The Great Shift in American Culture, Society, and Politics* (Bruce J Schulman)
- *The Shock Doctrine: The Rise of Disaster Capitalism* (Naomi Klein)

A 90s Baby

- Applebome, Peter. *Charlotte's Downtown Manages To Stay Up Late for*

- *Tournament*. The New York Times, 2 Apr. 1994, https://www.nytimes.com/1994/04/02/us/charlotte-s-downtown-manages-to-stay-up-late-for-tournament.html.
- "ATF Probes Arson at Black Church in N.C." Los Angeles Times, 8 June 1996, www.latimes.com/archives/la-xpm-1996-06-08-mn-12791-story.html.
- Blackmon, Chyna. "Charlotte's Oldest LGBTQIA+ Nightclub Is Temporarily Closing Its Doors. What's Next?" The Charlotte Observer, 6 Oct. 2023, www.charlotteobserver.com/charlottefive/c5-around-town/c5-development/article280203939.html.
- Boiling, Christina. "A Former Panther Paid for Her Degree. Now She's Using It to Teach History – but with Twitter and Lively..." Charlotte Observer, 14 June 2017, www.charlotteobserver.com/living/article156185474.html.
- Brachey, Nancy. "Its a Fun Way to Focus on Learning." The Charlotte Observer, 23 Jan. 2000, www.newspapers.com/image/629803704/.
- Burkins, Glenn H. "'The Hardest Year of My Life': At High-Poverty Garinger High School, a Student Works to Overcome Covid-Related Hardships." *QCity Metro*, 12 Dec. 2020, https://qcitymetro.com/2020/12/12/garinger-high-school.
- Butler, Isaac, and Dan Kois. "How a Southern Theater Won Its Battle to Stage Angels in America but Lost the Culture Wars." Slate Magazine, Slate, 13 Feb. 2018, slate.com/culture/2018/02/the-world-only-spins-forward-excerpt-about-angels-in-america-and-charlotte-repertory-theatres-1996-production.html.
- Charlotte Urban Institute. NoDa Perceived: Past, Present and Future of a Mill Village. 28 Oct. 2020, https://ui.charlotte.edu/story/noda-perceived-past-present-and-future-mill-village.
- Comer, Matt. "20 Years of Charlotte Pride." *Charlotte Pride History Project*, 2021, https://charlottepride.org/history/20years.
- Crowe, Jerry. "CHARLOTTE HITS THE BIG TIME : A Dream Comes True When City Is Awarded NBA Franchise." *Los Angeles Times*, 7 Jun. 1987, https://www.latimes.com/archives/la-xpm-1987-06-07-sp-801-story.html.
- Dodd, Scott, and Ted Mellnick. "CHARLOTTE'S POPULATION BALLOONED IN 1990S | THE SPIKE IN POPULATION MAKES THE QUEEN CITY THE 26TH-LARGEST IN THE NATION." *Greensboro News and Record*, 31 Mar. 2001, https://greensboro.com/charlottes-population-ballooned-in-1990s-the-spike-in-population-makes-the-queen-city-the-26th/article_0d976e33-c74f-5005-a9d3-5e4bf185e558.html.
- "Excelsior Club." *Levine Museum of the New South*, https://www.museumofthenewsouth.org/digital/excelsior-club.
- "First Family Dollar." Levine Museum of the New South, https://www.museumofthenewsouth.org/digital/first-family-dollar.
- Funk, Tim. "5 Things to Know about Charlotte's 1996 "Angels in America" Controversy." Charlotte Observer, 16 May 2017, www.charlotteobserver.com/living/religion/article150751257.html.
- "Gay Bars and Clubs: A Look at Charlotte's History." *QnotesCarolinas.Com*, 9

- Aug. 2019, https://qnotescarolinas.com/gay-bars-and-clubs-a-look-at-charlottes-history.
- Gibbs, Stephanie, et al. "Race Day Put to the Test." The Charlotte Observer, 14 Mar. 1997, www.newspapers.com/image/628440181/.
- Graham, David A. "Shattering Charlotte's Myth of Racial Harmony." The Atlantic, 22 Sep. 2016, https://www.theatlantic.com/politics/archive/2016/09/charlotte-race-history/501221.
- Griffin, Willie. Street Name Historical Documentation. Charlotte Legacy Commission, 2020, https://www.charlottenc.gov/files/sharedassets/city/v/1/city-government/leadership/documents/legacy-commission/street-name-historical-documentation.pdf.
- Hagwood, Kayland. *"Challenges Keep Pushing You to Be Stronger" | 25 Years of Mert's Heart and Soul in Uptown.* WCNC, 29 Aug. 2023, https://www.wcnc.com/article/money/business/merts-heart-and-soul-celebrates-25th-anniversary/275-76a5b853-e4c0-4d97-b71f-e2d9e8a562e8.
- "Horizons Blurb." The Charlotte Observer, 29 July 2001, www.newspapers.com/image/630305942/.
- Jameson, Tonya. Paid to Party: What Was It like Covering Charlotte Nightlife in the '90s and Early 2000s? 9 Nov. 2023, www.charlotteobserver.com/charlottefive/c5-worklife/article279892389.html.
- Kohn, Bernie. "Early Departures Jam Airport." The Charlotte Observer, 6 Apr. 1994, www.newspapers.com/image/627003387/.
- Kurzeja, Paul. "The History of Banking in Charlotte." Charlotte Museum of History, charlottemuseum.org/learn/articles/the-history-of-banking-in-charlotte/.
- Leggett, Page. "Baring Our Souls: The Return of Angels in America." Creative Loafing Charlotte, 7 May 2014, clclt.com/charlotte/baring-our-souls-the-return-of-angels-in-america/Content?oid=3396444.
- "Levine Museum of the New South." *NCpedia*, https://www.ncpedia.org/levine-museum-new-south.
- Lunsford, Brandon. "Vibrant Mural at Northwest School of the Arts Sheds Light on History of West Charlotte." *CLTure*, 19 Nov. 2019, https://clture.org/northwest-school-of-the-arts.
- McCurry, Doug. "Closet Racism: White America's Dirty Little Secret." The Charlotte Observer, 8 Aug. 1996, www.newspapers.com/image/628419285/.
- McShane, Chuck. "The Story of Charlotte, Part 12: Blotting out the Sun" Charlotte Magazine, 24 Mar. 2015, www.charlottemagazine.com/the-story-of-charlotte-part-12-blotting-out-the-sun/.
- Morrill, Jim. "Clinton Here Today; Monday, Tuesday Too?" The Charlotte Observer, 2 Apr. 1994, www.newspapers.com/image/626989458/.
- Muccigrosso, Catherine. "How Excelsior Club Became a Hub for Charlotte's Black Community over the Years." The Charlotte Observer, 22 Feb. 2024, www.charlotteobserver.com/news/business/article285494727.html.
- Newsome, Melba. "There's Something About Ballantyne." *Charlotte*

- *Magazine*, 19 Nov. 2012, https://www.charlottemagazine.com/theres-something-about-ballantyne.
- *North Carolina Community Profile: Charlotte, Mecklenburg County [1990]*. N.C. Dept. of Commerce, Economic Development Office, 1990.
- *Our School / About Us*. Northwest School of The Arts, https://www.cmsk12.org/domain/939.
- Perlmutt, David. "Glory Bound: Only Two Survive Tonight." The Charlotte Observer, 2 Apr. 1994, www.newspapers.com/image/626989305/.
- Pitkin, Ryan. "Elexus Jionde Is a New Kind of Black History Teacher." Creative Loafing Charlotte, Mar. 2017, clclt.com/charlotte/elexus-jionde-is-a-new-kind-of-black-history-teacher/Content?oid=4022986.
- Romero, Dennis. "New Club a Sleek Addition to Uptown's Nightlife." The Charlotte Observer, 24 Dec. 1993, www.newspapers.com/image/626982874/.
- Rothacker, Jennifer Wing. "With New Choices Come Big Changes." The Charlotte Observer, 2 Dec. 1999, www.newspapers.com/image/629798789/.
- Sack, Kevin. *Play Displays a Growing City's Cultural Tensions*. The New York Times, 22 Mar. 1996, https://www.nytimes.com/1996/03/22/us/play-displays-a-growing-city-s-cultural-tensions.html.
- Smith, Dean. "The Future Is Wow." The Charlotte Observer, 21 Nov. 1999, www.newspapers.com/image/629718535/.
- Smith, Doug. "They Built the Street-- and the People Came." The Charlotte Observer, 6 Apr. 1994, www.newspapers.com/image/627003387/.
- Soloff, Katie Peralta. "Charlotte Was an 'Eager-to-Please Town' Back When We Last Hosted the Final Four." Axios, 5 Apr. 2022, https://www.axios.com/local/charlotte/2022/04/05/charlotte-was-an-eager-to-please-town-back-when-we-last-hosted-the-final-four-293531.
- Toner, Robin. "An Underdog Forces Helms into a Surprisingly Tight Race." The New York Times, 31 Oct. 1990, www.nytimes.com/1990/10/31/us/an-underdog-forces-helms-into-a-surprisingly-tight-race.html.
- Way, Emma. "A Condensed (and Brutally Honest) History of Creative Loafing." *Charlotte Magazine*, 19 Dec. 2018, https://www.charlottemagazine.com/a-condensed-and-brutally-honest-history-of-creative-loafing.
- WFAE. "Tough Choices Ahead As Charlotte Nears End Of Annexation Road." WFAE 90.7 - Charlotte's NPR News Source, 22 Jan. 2013, https://www.wfae.org/local-news/2013-01-22/tough-choices-ahead-as-charlotte-nears-end-of-annexation-road.
- "Where Are They Now?: The Gang of Five ." Charlotte Magazine, 20 July 2010, www.charlottemagazine.com/where-are-they-now-the-gang-of-five/.

On The Spice Girls

- "A Dash of Success." The Knoxville News-Sentinel, 19 Mar. 1997, https://www.newspapers.com/image/775982350.
- "Chris Evans Weighs in on the Spice Girls." YouTube, 15 Mar. 2021,

Bibliography

- www.youtube.com/watch?v=Pbq7LaHSWE4.
- "Cool Britannia Turns on Blair as Musicians Voice Their Disillusionment with Government Pop Goes PM's Street Cred." *The Herald*, 11 Mar. 1998, https://www.heraldscotland.com/news/12302410.cool-britannia-turns-on-blair-as-musicians-voice-their-disillusionment-with-government-pop-goes-pms-street-cred.
- Dockterman, Eliana. "The True Story Behind Charles and Camilla's Phone Sex Leak." *TIME*, 9 Nov. 2022, https://time.com/6226657/crown-charles-camilla-tampongate.
- Ebert, Robert. "Spice World Movie Review & Film Summary (1998)." Roger Ebert, https://www.rogerebert.com/reviews/spice-world-1998.
- Gupta, Alisha Haridasani, and Jennifer Harlan. How the Spice Girls' Manufactured Girl Power Became Real. 28 Apr. 2022, https://www.nytimes.com/2022/04/28/arts/music/spice-girls-girl-power.html.
- Harding, Luke. "Meet John Major's Last Hope." The Guardian, 13 Dec. 1996, https://www.newspapers.com/image/260596867.
- Heath, Chris. "Spice Girls: Too Hot to Handle." Rolling Stone, 10 Jul. 1997, https://www.rollingstone.com/music/music-news/spice-girls-too-hot-to-handle-63901.
- "How the Spice Effect Still Packs Punch." BBC News, 6 Jul. 2016, https://www.bbc.com/news/entertainment-arts-36714177.
- Jolly, Nathan. "Your Guide to the Very Best Spice Girls Merch (Once) Available." The Brag, 5 Apr. 2018, thebrag.com/the-very-best-spice-girls-merch/.
- Kenner, Rob. "Neneh Cherry Talks 'Blank Project,' 'Buffalo Stance,' And..." Complex, 18 Feb. 2014, https://www.complex.com/music/a/rob-kenner/neneh-cherry-interview-blank-project-buffalo-stance-and-biggie.
- Lemish, Dafna. "Spice World: Constructing Femininity the Popular Way. Popular Music and Society 26(1), 17-29." Popular Music and Society, 1 Jan. 2003, https://www.academia.edu/es/930780/Lemish_D_2003_Spice_World_Constructing_femininity_the_popular_way_Popular_Music_and_Society_26_1_17_29.
- *LONDON SWINGS! AGAIN!* Vanity Fair, Mar. 1997, https://archive.vanityfair.com/article/1997/3/london-swings-again.
- Low, Valentine. "Bad News Mr Blair. Spice Say You're Nice but You Won't Get Their Vote." Evening Standard, 12 Dec. 1996, https://www.newspapers.com/image/726190418.
- Lownie, Andrew. "The inside Story of Sarah Ferguson's "Toe Sucking" Scandal": Daily Mail, 18 Aug. 2024, www.dailymail.co.uk/news/royals/article-13710231/Sarah-Ferguson-toe-sucking-John-Bryan-1992.html.
- Maskell, Emily. "Mel C Confirms Margaret Thatcher Was 'Absolutely Not' the First Spice Girl." Attitude, 21 Sep. 2022, https://www.attitude.co.uk/culture/music/melanie-c-confirms-margaret-thatcher-was-absolutely-not-the-first-spice-girl-386027.
- The Hot Press Newsdesk. "FROM THE ARCHIVE: The Spice Girls 1997 Cover Story." Hotpress, https://www.hotpress.com/music/archive-spice-

- girls-1997-cover-story-22773597.
- Vincent, Alice. "When the Spice Girls Hit Cannes: The inside Story of Spice World, 'the Worst Film Ever Made.'" The Telegraph, 29 Sep. 2017, https://www.telegraph.co.uk/films/2017/09/29/spice-world-20-spice-girls-made-movie-history.
- "Mel B of the Spice Girls Says She Was Target of Racial Slurs While Growing Up." The Straits Times, 8 Jun. 2020, https://www.straitstimes.com/lifestyle/entertainment/mel-b-of-the-spice-girls-says-she-was-target-of-racial-slurs-while-growing.
- "Mel B Says Dad Carried Her as a Baby to Avoid Being Targeted in Racist Attacks." Daily Mirror, 25 May 2021, https://www.mirror.co.uk/3am/celebrity-news/mel-b-says-dad-carried-24179793.
- "Mel B Shares Her Experience of Racism in the Spice Girls." Red Online, 8 Jun. 2020, https://www.redonline.co.uk/red-women/news-in-brief/a32795826/mel-b-racism-interview.
- Myers, Randy. "Girls Just Wanna Have Fun in Wacky 'Spice World.'" The State, 19 Jun. 1998, https://www.newspapers.com/image/753076179.Palmer, Alasdair. "Focus." Sunday Telegraph, 15 Dec. 1996, https://www.newspapers.com/image/752092017.
- Patterson, Sylvia. "The 1990s Were the Best of Times ... until the Spice Girls Ruined Everything." The Guardian, 4 Jul. 2016, https://www.theguardian.com/commentisfree/2016/jul/04/1990s-spice-girls-celebrity-culture.
- Pisa, Nick. "MY MARTINI SPICE...; Emma made love any time, any place, anywhere." The Free Library 20 April 1997. <https://www.thefreelibrary.com/MY MARTINI SPICE...; Emma made love any time, any place, anywhere.-a061141824>
- Mitchell, Thomas. "Seven Unexpected Revelations in Netflix's David Beckham Documentary." The Sydney Morning Herald, 4 Oct. 2023, https://www.smh.com.au/culture/tv-and-radio/seven-unexpected-revelations-in-netflix-s-david-beckham-documentary-20231004-p5e9n7.html.
- Montefiore, Simon Sebag. "SPICE GIRLS BACK SCEPTICS ON EUROPE." The Spectator Archive, 14 Dec. 1996, https://archive.spectator.co.uk/article/14th-december-1996/14/spice-girls-back-sceptics-on-europe.
- ---. "Time to Add a Bit of Spice to Politics." The Daily Telegraph, 12 Dec. 1996, https://www.newspapers.com/image/752088933.
- Nielsen Business Media. Billboard. Nielsen Business Media, Inc., 9 Jan. 1999, https://archive.org/details/bub_gb_Fw0EAAAAMBAJ.
- Posh and Becks Tie the Knot. BBC News, 4 Jul. 1999, https://news.bbc.co.uk/2/hi/special_report/1999/07/99/the_posh_wedding/385535.stm.
- Rose, Lydia Naomi. "6 Black British Tracks of My Childhood." Medium, 19 Dec. 2017, https://medium.com/@justlydz_/6-black-british-tracks-of-my-childhood-b8da6adf9a13.
- Soteriou, Stephanie. "Spice Girls Reaction to Blackface Performers Resurfaces Online." BuzzFeed News, 19 Dec. 2023, www.buzzfeednews.com/article/stephaniesoteriou/spice-girls-blackface-

- performers-mel-b-response.
- Spice Girls: Taking on the Brit Pop Boys. musicweek.com, 1995, https://www.musicweek.com/files/IMG_5662.JPG.
- "Spicy Talk: A Male-Female Dialogue about the 'Girls.'" *The Kansas City Star*, 28 Jan. 1996, https://www.newspapers.com/image/685001688.
- SPICE GIRLS SITE GETS SLAPPED BY PC CRITICS. Tech Monitor, 17 Jul. 1997, https://techmonitor.ai/technology/spice_girls_site_gets_slapped_by_pc_critics_1.
- Spice World. Directed by Bob Spiers, PolyGram Filmed Entertainment, 1997.
- *Sun Pips OK! To Posh Wedding Photos.* BBC News, 6 Jul. 1999, https://news.bbc.co.uk/2/hi/special_report/1999/07/99/the_posh_wedding/387126.stm.
- Thomas, Cal. "Why Do Parents Support Cultural Rape of Their Girls by Acts like Spice Girls?" *The Arizona Republic*, 25 Jun. 1998, https://www.newspapers.com/image/124041348.
- Twigger, Will. "Spice Girls Could Have Been without Geri Halliwell as Memo Shows Plan to Axe Her." *Daily Mirror*, 28 Oct. 2019, https://www.mirror.co.uk/3am/celebrity-news/spice-girls-could-been-without-20740388.
- Vassell, Nicole. "Mel C Says She Was Sexually Assaulted the Night before First Spice Girls Gig." *The Independent*, The Independent, 15 Sep. 2022, https://www.independent.co.uk/arts-entertainment/music/news/mel-c-sexual-assault-spice-girls-b2167151.html.
- Weaver, Caity. The Rise of the Spice Girls Generation (Published 2019). 19 Jul. 2019, https://www.nytimes.com/2019/07/19/style/spice-girls-reunion.html.
- Wright, Lindsay. *Do-It-Yourself Girl Power: An Examination of the Riot Grrrl Subculture.* James Madison Undergraduate Research Journal, 2016, https://commons.lib.jmu.edu/cgi/viewcontent.cgi?article=1018&context=jmurj&httpsredir=1&referer=.

90s Food
General

- "'90s Promise to Stir Up Food Industry." *Los Angeles Times*, 27 Mar. 1991, https://www.latimes.com/archives/la-xpm-1991-03-27-fi-918-story.html.
- BEVERLY BUNDY Fort Worth Star-Telegram. "1990S PUT BRAKES ON '80S EXCESS\ FOOD IN THE CENTURY'S FINAL DECADE WAS ALL ABOUT SAVING TIME AND HEALTHFUL CHOICES." *Greensboro News and Record*, 21 Dec. 1999, https://greensboro.com/1990s-put-brakes-on-80s-excess-food-in-the-centurys-final-decade-was-all-about/article_d287073d-6c2b-5497-9adb-6ca2eea98f04.html.
- Hezel, Anna. "The 1990s Moments That Changed the Way We Think About Food." *TASTE*, 24 Apr. 2019, https://tastecooking.com/1990s-moments-changed-way-think-food.
- Schlosser, Eric. Fast Food Nation: *The Dark Side of the All-American Meal*. Houghton Mifflin, 2001

1990

- "A TASTE TEST OF LOONEY TUNES, OTHER KIDS MEALS." *Chicago Tribune*, 14 Mar. 1991, https://www.chicagotribune.com/news/ct-xpm-1991-03-14-9101230579-story.html.
- Burros, Marian. "EATING WELL; the Slimming of Fat Fast Food." *The New York Times*, 25 July 1990, www.nytimes.com/1990/07/25/garden/eating-well-the-slimming-of-fat-fast-food.html?smid=url-share.
- "Bush's Broccoli Bashing Steams Vegetable Producers." *Great Falls Tribune*, 28 Mar. 1990, https://www.newspapers.com/article/91229950/bushs-broccoli-bashing-steams/https://www.latimes.com/archives/la-xpm-1990-03-27-mn-263-story.html.
- Carman, Tim. "As President, George H.W. Bush Never Wavered from His Hard Line on Broccoli." *The Washington Post*, 5 Dec. 2018, https://www.washingtonpost.com/news/food/wp/2018/12/05/as-president-george-h-w-bush-never-wavered-from-his-hard-line-on-broccoli.
- "Come on, George! Give Broccoli Another Try." *Tampa Bay Times*, 29 Aug. 1991, https://www.tampabay.com/archive/1991/08/29/come-on-george-give-broccoli-another-try.
- dadsoldtapes. "Doritos "Soviet Union" Commercial ." YouTube, 1990, www.youtube.com/watch?v=YqYcKd8EILs.
- Dowd, Maureen. *"I'm President," So No More Broccoli!* 23 Mar. 1990, https://www.nytimes.com/1990/03/23/us/i-m-president-so-no-more-broccoli.html.
- Hotchkiss, Michael. "Princeton Researcher Digs into the Contested Peanut-Allergy Epidemic." *Www.Princeton.Edu*, 25 Jul. 2013, https://www.princeton.edu/news/2013/07/25/princeton-researcher-digs-contested-peanut-allergy-epidemic.
- "How to Get George Bush to Eat Broccoli Recipe Contest." The Desert Sun, 8 Nov. 1990, www.newspapers.com/image/748832944/.
- "McDonalds to Open in School Cafeteria." *UPI*, 21 Aug. 1990, https://www.upi.com/Archives/1990/08/21/McDonalds-to-open-in-school-cafeteria/7380651211200.
- "MINIATURE MEALS PACKAGED DINNERS FOR CHILDREN FEED GROWING HUNGER FOR CONVENIENCE." *The Morning Call*, 17 Apr. 1991, https://www.mcall.com/1991/04/17/miniature-meals-packaged-dinners-for-children-feed-growing-hunger-for-convenience.
- "New Test for Peanut Allergies." Baraboo News Republic, 22 Dec. 1991, www.newspapers.com/image/871175361/.
- Ostermeier, Eric. "George H.W. Bush: Hater of Broccoli." *Smart Politics*, 9 Jul. 2013, https://smartpolitics.lib.umn.edu/2013/07/09/george-hw-bush-hater-of-brocco.
- Pascual, Psyche. "Students Want More Fast Food in School Cafeterias : Nutrition: Restricted to Campus at Lunchtime, Youths in Norwalk-La Mirada District Want to Dump Usual Fare, Leaving a Bad Taste in Mouths of Worried Kitchen Employees." *Los Angeles Times*, 24 Oct. 1993, https://

Bibliography

- www.latimes.com/archives/la-xpm-1993-10-24-hl-49098-story.html.
- Ramirez, Anthony. "Soviet Pizza Huts Have Local Flavor." *The New York Times*, 11 Sept. 1990, www.nytimes.com/1990/09/11/business/soviet-pizza-huts-have-local-flavor.html.
- Rummel, Rachel. "The Original McDonald's French Fry." *Atlas Obscura*, https://www.atlasobscura.com/foods/original-mcdonalds-french-fry.
- "School Systems Are Turning to Fast-Food Outlets." *Tampa Bay Times*, 17 Sep. 1990, https://www.tampabay.com/archive/1990/09/17/school-systems-are-turning-to-fast-food-outlets.
- Shapiro, Laura. *The Zap Generation*. Newsweek, Feb. 1990, https://www.myownmeals.com/wp-content/uploads/2020/08/1990-Newsweek-February-26.pdf.
- The Associated Press. "New Foods Have Kid Appeal." *News.Google.Com*, 9 May 1990, https://news.google.com/newspapers?id=bjkdAAAAIBAJ&sjid=6KUEAAAAIBAJ&pg=5797,2752139&dq=looney-tunes-meals&hl=en.
- The Associated Press. "KFC Hot Wings Are a Hot Item." *The San Francisco Examiner*, 24 Mar. 1990, www.newspapers.com/image/462135522/.
- The Associated Press. "Peanut Allergies Studied in Arkansas." *The Springfield News-Leader*, 7 June 1993, www.newspapers.com/image/207801751/.
- "When the Hell Did Everyone Become Allergic to Peanuts?" *Mic*, 29 Sep. 2015, https://www.mic.com/articles/125970/when-the-hell-did-everyone-become-allergic-to-peanuts.
- Yasuda, Gene. "Companies See Cold Cash in Courting Young Taste Buds." *Los Angeles Times*, 17 Jul. 1990, https://www.latimes.com/archives/la-xpm-1990-07-17-fi-263-story.html.

1991

- Bannister, Laura. "Dinner at the End of America by Laura Bannister." *The Paris Review*, 7 Feb. 2018, https://www.theparisreview.org/blog/2018/02/07/dinner-end-america.
- "Catfish Platter Part of McDonald's Menu." The Greenwood Commonwealth, 24 May 1992, www.newspapers.com/image/237792799/.
- Hays, Constance L. "From out of the Gym, into the Grocery Store; Energy Bars Jump into the Mainstream." *The New York Times*, 22 Nov. 1997, www.nytimes.com/1997/11/22/business/from-out-of-the-gym-into-the-grocery-store-energy-bars-jump-into-the-mainstream.html?pagewanted=all.
- HERNANDEZ, GREG. "Planet Hollywood to File for Bankruptcy Reorganization." Los Angeles Times, 18 Aug. 1999, www.latimes.com/archives/la-xpm-1999-aug-18-fi-1222-story.html.
- "It's part cafe, part sports bar and all show biz." St. Petersburg Times, CITY ed., sec. BUSINESS, 17 Dec. 1995, p. 1H. NewsBank: Access World News, https://infoweb.newsbank.com/apps/news/openurl?ctx_ver=z39.88-2004&rft_id=info%3Asid/infoweb.newsbank.com&svc_dat=AWNB&req_dat=1028A39C75C2B899&rft_val_format=info%3Aofi/.

fmt%3Akev%3Amtx%3Actx&rft_dat=document_id%3Anews/
0EB52DCD576F3E53.
- JOEKthePANDA. "Dan Quayle Misspells "Potato."" YouTube, 27 Jan. 2010, www.youtube.com/watch?v=Wdqbi66oNuI.
- "MCDONALD'S CASTS FOR CATFISH CUSTOMERS." *Scholar.Lib.vt.Edu*, Roanoke Times, 15 Feb. 1991, https://scholar.lib.vt.edu/VA-news/ROA-Times/issues/1991/rt9102/910215/02150696.htm.
- "Planet Hollywood Opens in San Antonio - Scenes from the Grand Opening (1996)." Directed by Jim Ruddy, Texas Archive, 1996.
- Smothers, Ronald. *Company Ousts Gay Workers, Then Reconsiders (Published 1991)*. 28 Feb. 1991, https://www.nytimes.com/1991/02/28/us/company-ousts-gay-workers-then-reconsiders.html.
- Storey, Kate. "The Rise and Fall of Planet Hollywood." *Esquire*, 9 Jun. 2021, https://www.esquire.com/entertainment/a36439327/planet-hollywood-origin-story-history-interview.
- Taylor, Elise. "The Rise and Fall of Fashion Cafe." *Vogue*, 23 Aug. 2023, https://www.vogue.com/article/the-rise-and-fall-of-fashion-cafe.
- The Associated Press. "McDonalds to Test Catfish Sandwich." Tucscon Citizen, 1 Mar. 1991, www.newspapers.com/image/579293741/.
- "The Snack That Was the Chip of the '90s." *Snack Stack*, 4 Dec. 2021, https://www.snackstack.net/p/the-snack-that-was-the-chip-of-the.
- Yasuda, Gene. "HOTEL IS NEW VENTURE for PLANET HOLLYWOOD." Orlando Sentinel, 26 Sept. 1997, www.orlandosentinel.com/1997/09/26/hotel-is-new-venture-for-planet-hollywood/.

1992
- "ALL THE PRESIDENT'S MENUS." *Sun Sentinel*, 14 Jan. 1993, https://www.sun-sentinel.com/1993/01/14/all-the-presidents-menus.
- Applebome, Peter. "THE 1992 CAMPAIGN: Death Penalty; Arkansas Execution Raises Questions on Governor's Politics." The New York Times, 25 Jan. 1992, www.nytimes.com/1992/01/25/us/1992-campaign-death-penalty-arkansas-execution-raises-questions-governor-s.html.
- Burros, Marian. *Bill Clinton and Food: Jack Sprat He's Not*. 23 Dec. 1992, https://www.nytimes.com/1992/12/23/garden/bill-clinton-and-food-jack-sprat-he-s-not.html.
- ---. *Now Is the Time to Come to the Aid of Your Favorite Cookies*. 15 Jul. 1992, https://www.nytimes.com/1992/07/15/garden/now-is-the-time-to-come-to-the-aid-of-your-favorite-cookies.html.
- Chicago Tribune. McDonalds to Serve New Pie. 6 May 1992, www.newspapers.com/image/744057694/.
- Doyne, Shannon. "In Praise of Marcella Hazan." *East Fork Pottery*, https://www.eastfork.com/journal/in-praise-of-marcella-hazan.
- ewjxn. "1992 MC Hammer KFC Popcorn Chicken TV Commercial." YouTube, 18 Sept. 2017, www.youtube.com/watch?v=vGWjYEqW1f8.
- Fisher, Lawerence M. *Market Place; A Coffee Trend Is Going Public (Published 1992)*. 28 May 1992, https://www.nytimes.com/1992/05/28/business/market-place-a-coffee-trend-is-going-public.html.

Bibliography

- Fuetsch, Michele. "'Coffee's the Drug of the '90s . . . the New, Safe Drug.' : Tasting a Different Kind of Brew : Food: A Growing Number of Americans Are Choosing Gourmet Java and Coffeehouses over Alcohol and Bars." *Los Angeles Times*, 22 Jul. 1993, https://www.latimes.com/archives/la-xpm-1993-07-22-me-15752-story.html.
- Graedon, Joe. "The Unwanted Perks of the '90s Coffee Craze." *Tampa Bay Times*, 21 Jan. 1997, https://www.tampabay.com/archive/1997/01/21/the-unwanted-perks-of-the-90s-coffee-craze.
- Bryant, Adam. "COMPANY NEWS; Coke Adds a Clear Cola to Its "New Age" Stable." Archive.org, 15 Dec. 1992, web.archive.org/web/20200209033208/www.nytimes.com/1992/12/15/business/company-news-coke-adds-a-clear-cola-to-its-new-age-stable.html.
- "How Marcella Hazan Became a Legend of Italian Cooking." The New Yorker, 15 Nov. 2021, www.newyorker.com/culture/kitchen-notes/how-marcella-hazan-became-a-legend-of-italian-cooking.O'Neill, Molly. "New Mainstream: Hot Dogs, Apple Pie and Salsa." The New York Times, 11 Mar. 1992, www.nytimes.com/1992/03/11/garden/new-mainstream-hot-dogs-apple-pie-and-salsa.html.
- Plotnikoff, David. "1993 Could Be Remembered as the Year of the Clear." The Daily Herald, 30 Mar. 1992, www.newspapers.com/image/470782548/?fcfToken=eyJhbGciOiJIUzI1NiIsInR5cCI6IkpXVCJ9.eyJmcmVlLXZpZXctaWQiOjQ3MDc4MjU0OCwiaWF0IjoxNjg2Mjk1OTA5LCJleHAiOjE2ODYzODIzMDI9.iLeZkkXMG6XePnxPhBe4xXSSyYBm6EPdjGFhYte9-DM.
- The Fattening - Did the Low-Fat Era Make Us Fat? | Diet Wars | FRONTLINE | PBS. 8 Apr. 2004, www.pbs.org/wgbh/pages/frontline/shows/diet/themes/lowfat.html.
- Willett, Walter C., and Meir J. Stampfer. "Rebuilding the Food Pyramid." Scientific American Sp, vol. 16, no. 4, Dec. 2006, pp. 12–21, www.scientificamerican.com/article/rebuilding-the-food-pyramid/, https://doi.org/10.1038/scientificamerican1206-12sp. •
- Harlan, Bill. "USDA's Food Pyramid for Colossal Eaters." Rapid City Journal, 3 May 1992, www.newspapers.com/image/527585036/.
- MacVean, Mary. "The Importance of Cooking Italian." *Valley News*, 18 Nov. 1992, https://www.newspapers.com/image/833939471.
- Marx, Rebecca Flint. "When SnackWell's Was the Flavor of Permissible Indulgence." *TASTE*, 23 Apr. 2019, https://tastecooking.com/snackwells-flavor-permissible-indulgence.
- Purdy, Chase. "The Blatantly Sexist Cookie Bake-off That Has Haunted Hillary Clinton for Two Decades Is Back." *Quartz*, 21 Aug. 2016, https://qz.com/762881/the-blatantly-sexist-cookie-bake-off-that-has-haunted-hillary-clinton-for-two-decades-is-back.
- Robinson, Nathan. "The Death of Ricky Ray Rector." Jacobin.com, 5 Nov. 2016, jacobin.com/2016/11/bill-clinton-rickey-rector-death-penalty-execution-crime-racism.
- Sagon, Candy. "DOESN'T CLINTON DESERVE A BREAK TODAY?" *The*

- *Washington Post*, 16 Dec. 1992, https://www.washingtonpost.com/archive/lifestyle/food/1992/12/16/doesnt-clinton-deserve-a-break-today/677bafc3-a9b9-4929-b9a5-a84162245ee9.
- Scovern, Linda. "Food Pyramid Offers New Teaching Tool." The Newark Advocate, 22 Oct. 1992, www.newspapers.com/image/289240136/.
- White, Daniel. "A Brief History of the Clinton Family's Chocolate-Cookies." *TIME*, 19 Aug. 2016, https://time.com/4459173/hillary-bill-clinton-cookies-history.

1993

- Burros, Mariasn. *Eating Well: The Debate Over Milk and an Artificial Hormone; More Milk, More Confusion: What Should the Label Say? (Published 1994)*. 18 May 1994, https://www.nytimes.com/1994/05/18/garden/eating-well-debate-over-milk-artificial-hormone-more-milk-more-confusion-what.html.
- Dinner Is Served at Burger King (Advertisement). 3 Feb. 1993, www.newspapers.com/image/579840774/.
- Grady v. Frito-Lay. 2001, cases.justia.com/pennsylvania/superior-court/e02007_01.pdf?ts=1396142159.
- Grady v. Frito-Lay. 2003, caselaw.findlaw.com/court/pa-supreme-court/1114692.html.
- Heyl, Eric. "Doritos Lawsuit Crumbles in Court." *TribLIVE.Com*, TribLIVE.com, https://archive.triblive.com/news/doritos-lawsuit-crumbles-in-court.
- Kardashian, Kirk. "The End of Got Milk?" *The New Yorker*, 28 Feb. 2014, https://www.newyorker.com/business/currency/the-end-of-got-milk.
- Kasper, Rob. "Down-Home Food Is a Big Hit at Mall Gathering." The Baltimore Sun, 18 Jan. 1993, www.newspapers.com/image/170774446/.
- Koerner, Brendan. "The Long, Slow, Torturous Death of Zima." *Slate*, 26 Nov. 2008, https://slate.com/human-interest/2008/11/the-long-slow-torturous-death-of-zima.html.
- Mason, Margaret. "MILK? IT MAY NOT DO A BODY GOOD." *The Washington Post*, 7 Mar. 1994, https://www.washingtonpost.com/archive/lifestyle/1994/03/07/milk-it-may-not-do-a-body-good/8720490e-65c8-42cb-995f-21b9e85d2dee.
- Paybarah, Azi. *Lon Adams, Who Gave the Slim Jim Its Flavor, Dies at 95 (Published 2020)*. 3 Dec. 2020, https://www.nytimes.com/2020/12/03/us/lon-adams-dead.html.
- "Restoring Sanity to Legal System." *POLITICO*, https://www.politico.com/story/2011/03/restoring-sanity-to-legal-system-051095.
- Richman, Phyllis C. "HAIL TO THE CHIEF FROM CHEFS." *The Washington Post*, 29 Jan. 1993, https://www.washingtonpost.com/archive/lifestyle/1993/01/29/hail-to-the-chief-from-chefs/72468f0e-392d-4605-a952-891b3c6c77a2.
- Salkin, Allen. From Scratch: The Uncensored History of the Food Network. G.P. Putnam's Sons, 1 Oct. 2013.
- "Snapple Tries to Cap the Rumors." *Los Angeles Times*, 2 Sep. 1993, https://

Bibliography

- www.latimes.com/archives/la-xpm-1993-09-02-fi-30895-story.html.
- Sugar, Rachel. "How Food Network Turned Big-City Chef Culture Into Middle-America Pop Culture." *Grub Street*, 30 Nov. 2017, https://www.grubstreet.com/2017/11/early-days-food-network-oral-history.html.
- *THE MEDIA BUSINESS: ADVERTISING; Once Again, Burger King Shops for an Agency.* 21 Oct. 1993, https://www.nytimes.com/1993/10/21/business/the-media-business-advertising-once-again-burger-king-shops-for-an-agency.html?sec=&spon=&pagewanted=print.
- ?"?url=https%3A%2F%2F
- *YOU ARE THERE;Slim Jim: Present at the Creation (Published 1996)*. 28 Jul. 1996, https://www.nytimes.com/1996/07/28/magazine/sunday-july-28-1996-you-are-there-slim-jim-present-at-the-creation.html?scp=4&sq=slim%20jim&st=cse.

1994

- All Things Considered. "Coke Hopes to Sell New Drink on How It Feels Not Tastes." Wayback Machine, NPR, 27 May 1994, web.archive.org/web/20041016183939/home.pacifier.com/~ntierney/npr.htm.
- "ARCH SUPPORTS: MCDONALD'S SAYS HOMESTYLE IS WHERE THE HEARTH IS." *Sun Sentinel*, 27 Sep. 1994, https://www.sun-sentinel.com/1994/09/27/arch-supports-mcdonalds-says-homestyle-is-where-the-hearth-is.
- Bartlett, Tom. "Step Away From the Coke Machine." *The Chronicle of Higher Education*, 4 Apr. 2010, https://www.chronicle.com/article/step-away-from-the-coke-machine.
- Brownell, Kelly D. *Get Slim With Higher Taxes*. 15 Dec. 1994, https://www.nytimes.com/1994/12/15/opinion/get-slim-with-higher-taxes.html.
- Burros, Marian. *Former Surgeon General Begins Push for Americans to Slim Down (Published 1994)*. 5 Dec. 1994, https://www.nytimes.com/1994/12/05/us/former-surgeon-general-begins-push-for-americans-to-slim-down.html.
- Collins, Glenn. *Pepsico Pushes a Star Performer*. 3 Nov. 1994, https://www.nytimes.com/1994/11/03/business/pepsico-pushes-a-star-performer.html.
- Crenson, Matt. "A Toxic Fast-Food Environment Afflicts U.S., Crusader Says." *Los Angeles Times*, 1 Dec. 2002, https://www.latimes.com/archives/la-xpm-2002-dec-01-adna-food1-story.html.
- Edwards, Cliff. "Fast Food, Down Home Cooking." The Capital Times, 30 Sept. 1994, www.newspapers.com/image/521491152/.Eiselle, Stella M. "Welcome to Mexico." The Charlotte Observer, 20 Nov. 1994, www.newspapers.com/image/627449265/.
- "Food Scandal: Chronology." *The Guardian*, 12 Feb. 1999, https://www.theguardian.com/news/1999/feb/12/food.science1.
- Gerlin, Andrea. "Spilled Coffee Worth 2.9 Million." *Tampa Bay Times*, 2 Sept. 1994, www.newspapers.com/image/324270442/.
- Giaimo, Cara. "The Rise and Fall of Fruitopia, the Trippiest Beverage of the

- '90s." *Atlas Obscura*, 12 Sep. 2016, https://www.atlasobscura.com/articles/the-rise-and-fall-of-fruitopia-the-trippiest-beverage-of-the-90s.
- Greenaway, Twilight. "How Did Avocados Become the Official Super Bowl Food?" *Smithsonian Magazine*, 1 Jan. 2013, https://www.smithsonianmag.com/arts-culture/how-did-avocados-become-the-official-super-bowl-food-8332793.
- Greenwald, John. "Will Teens Buy It?" Wayback Machine, Time, 30 May 1994, web.archive.org/web/20130602032514/www.time.com/time/magazine/article/0,9171,1101940530-164486,00.html.
- "HEARTH EXPRESS CLOSED." *Www.Supermarketnews.Com*, https://www.supermarketnews.com/archive/hearth-express-closed.
- Koerner, Brendan. "The Long, Slow, Torturous Death of Zima." Slate Magazine, Slate, 26 Nov. 2008, www.slate.com/id/2204596/.
- MacGuill, Dan. "Did Rush Limbaugh Say Nicotine Wasn't Proven To Be Addictive?" *Snopes*, 7 Feb. 2020, https://www.snopes.com/fact-check/rush-limbaugh-nicotine-addictive.
- "MCDONALD'S SCRAPS HEARTH EXPRESS." *Chicago Tribune*, 8 Jul. 1995, https://www.chicagotribune.com/news/ct-xpm-1995-07-08-9507080039-story.html.
- Mayer, Jean, and Jeanne Goldberg. "CHEFS BOYCOTT GENETICALLY ALTERED FOOD." Deseret News, 25 Jan. 2024, www.deseret.com/1992/10/6/19008834/chefs-boycott-genetically-altered-food/.
- Meikle, James. "Journal to Publish GM Food Hazards Research." The Guardian, 5 Oct. 1999, www.theguardian.com/science/1999/oct/05/gm.food.Montgomery, Scott. "Call Us Irresponsible." St. Louis Post-Dispatch, 26 Dec. 1994, www.newspapers.com/image/142385289/.
- Mozes, Alan. "The Fat Tax: A Controversial Tool in War Against Obesity." *Www.Healthday.Com*, 11 Jan. 2006, https://www.healthday.com/health-news/public-health/the-fat-tax-a-controversial-tool-in-war-against-obesity-530229.html.
- Penenberg, Adam L. *Snapple Challenged in Wide Market (Published 1994)*. 10 Jul. 1994, https://www.nytimes.com/1994/07/10/nyregion/snapple-challenged-in-wide-market.html.
- Saladino, Emily. "The Unlikely Origins of Tableside Guacamole." *Saveur*, 2 Nov. 2022, https://www.saveur.com/culture/food-history-tableside-guacamole.
- Sheu, Wendy. "The Evolution of the Modern Snack Tax Bill: From World War I to the War Against Obesity." *Dash.Harvard.Edu*, 2006, https://dash.harvard.edu/bitstream/handle/1/8846753/Sheu06.html?sequence=2&referrer=&lastReferrer=www.taxrates.com.
- Simmons, Andy. "Here's What Really Happened in McDonald's Hot Coffee Lawsuit." *Reader's Digest*, 25 Sep. 2019, https://www.rd.com/article/hot-coffee-lawsuit.
- *Snapple Escapes the Grip of Rumors (Published 1993)*. 19 Jan. 1993, https://www.nytimes.com/1993/01/19/business/snapple-escapes-the-grip-of-rumors.html.

Bibliography

- The Associated Press. California's Snack Tax Taxes Mind. 24 July 1991, www.newspapers.com/image/573589301/.
- "'Twinkie Tax' Marketing to Kids." *Wilmington Star-News*, 13 Nov. 2002, https://www.starnewsonline.com/story/news/2002/11/13/twinkie-tax-marketing-to-kids/30499994007.
- Wall Street Journal. "It's A Fruity Fallout: New Age Beverages Losing Sales Fizz Last Year's Trendy Drinks Are Seeing Slower Growth As Carbonated Soft Drinks Make A Comeback." *Wayback Machine*, 14 Oct. 1995, https://web.archive.org/web/20170222054118/https://articles.orlandosentinel.com/1995-10-14/business/9510130929_1_coca-cola-beverages-new-age.
- Winerip, Michael. "You Call That a Tomato?" The New York Times, 24 June 2013, www.nytimes.com/2013/06/24/booming/you-call-that-a-tomato.html.

1995

- Bloomberg Business News. "Fruit-Drink Makers on Lookout for next Exotic Flavor." *The Los Angeles Times*, 29 Aug. 1995, www.newspapers.com/image/155477056.
- Kornblut, Anne E. "The $1.7 Billion Snapple Drinker." *Daily News*, 6 Nov. 1994, www.newspapers.com/image/474364060/.
- Feder, Jody. CRS Report for Congress the Pigford Cases: USDA Settlement of Discrimination Suits by Black Farmers Tadlock Cowan Analyst in Natural Resources and Rural Development. 29 May 2013.
- Fullwood III, Sam. "Black Farmers Reap a Harvest of Anger." Los Angeles Times, 28 June 1998, www.latimes.com/archives/la-xpm-1998-jun-28-mn-64524-story.html.
- Marks, Peter. "AT WORK WITH: Wendy Kaufman; Snapple! Cackle! Pop! A Star Is Born." *The New York Times*, 4 Jan. 1995, www.nytimes.com/1995/01/04/garden/at-work-with-wendy-kaufman-snapple-cackle-pop-a-star-is-born.html.
- "A Letter to Clinton and Gore by Alice Waters." *Earthlight.Org*, 9 Dec. 1995, https://earthlight.org/alicewaters23.html.
- *Blue Gets Most Votes In M&M Color Contest*. SFGATE, https://www.sfgate.com/news/article/blue-gets-most-votes-in-m-m-color-contest-3038671.php.
- "Bottled Up Profits Aren't Flowing like They Used to at Packaged-Goods Companies." *CNN*, 18 Sep. 2000, https://web.archive.org/web/20130208082640/https://money.cnn.com/magazines/fortune/fortune_archive/2000/09/18/287706.
- Fulwood, Sam, Iii. "Black Farmers Reap a Harvest of Anger." *Los Angeles Times*, 28 Jun. 1998, https://www.latimes.com/archives/la-xpm-1998-jun-28-mn-64524-story.html.
- Gillin, Eric. "The Oral History of the Launch of Epicurious." *Epicurious*, 18 Aug. 2015, https://www.epicurious.com/about/epicurious-oral-history-article.
- Meister, Ever. "The Birth of the Frappuccino." *Saveur*, 1 Dec. 2022, https://

- www.saveur.com/recipes/history-of-the-frappuccino.
- Pratt, Steven. "Many Of US Are Fat, So Shape Up, America -- First Lady, Former Surgeon General Everett Koop Launch Drive To Point Out Health Risks Of Obesity." *The Seattle Times*, 5 Dec. 1994, https://archive.seattletimes.com/archive/?date=19941205&slug=1945531.
- Saxena, Jaya. "Strawberry and Kiwi: Why?" *TASTE*, 23 Apr. 2019, https://tastecooking.com/strawberry-and-kiwi-why.
- The Center For Consumer Freedom Team. *Seinfeld's "Soup Nazi" Stars as Food Cop in New Ad.* 28 Sep. 2004, https://consumerfreedom.com/press-releases/70-seinfelds-soup-nazi-stars-as-food-cop-in-new-ad.

1996

- Babineck, Mark. "Ranchers Are Mad at Oprah." *Times Record News*, 17 June 1997, www.newspapers.com/image/778447270/.
- BRUCE, BONNIE, and DENISE WILFLEY. "Binge Eating Among the Overweight Population." *Journal of the American Dietetic Association*, vol. 96, no. 1, Elsevier BV, Jan. 1996, pp. 58–61, doi:10.1016/s0002-8223(96)00016-8.
- Elliott, Stuart. "THE MEDIA BUSINESS: ADVERTISING; "Gump" Sells, to Viacom's Surprise." The New York Times, 7 Oct. 1994, www.nytimes.com/1994/10/07/business/the-media-business-advertising-gump-sells-to-viacom-s-surprise.html.
- Glass, Jeremy. "The Man Behind the Arch Deluxe, McDonald's Biggest Flop, Is Still Proud of His Work." *Eater*, 23 Jul. 2021, https://www.eater.com/22584033/mcdonalds-arch-deluxe-burger-discontinued-marketing-flop-andrew-selvaggio.
- Negin, Elliot. Columbia Journalism Review, https://www.pbs.org/tradesecrets/docs/alarscarenegin.html.
- "See the hit movie, buy the shrimp: Meridian Products' Gump spin-off.." The Free Library. 1995 E.W. Williams Publications, Inc. https://www.thefreelibrary.com/See+the+hit+movie%2c+buy+the+shrimp%3a+Meridian+Products%27+Gump+spin-off.-a016582015
- "Two Decades Ago, Taco Bell Convinced America That It Had Bought the Liberty Bell." *PhillyVoice*, 30 Mar. 2018, https://www.phillyvoice.com/two-decades-ago-taco-bell-convinced-america-it-had-bought-liberty-bell.

1997

- Bauer, Scott. "Burgerless King." *The Times*, 23 Aug. 1997, www.newspapers.com/image/305732541/.
- ---. "MEATPACKER, 2 EMPLOYEES INDICTED in 1997 RECALL." *The Washington Post*, 17 Dec. 1998, www.washingtonpost.com/archive/politics/1998/12/17/meatpacker-2-employees-indicted-in-1997-recall/2aa17c8e-fb69-4a43-a103-84d685f38c71/.
- "Chocolate Toy Withdrawn." *The New York Times*, 2 Oct. 1997, www.nytimes.com/1997/10/02/us/chocolate-toy-withdrawn.html.
- Collins, Glenn. "As Summer Ends, a Burger War." *Nytimes.com*, The New

York Times, 31 Aug. 1997, www.nytimes.com/1997/08/31/weekinreview/as-summer-ends-a-burger-war.html.
- Hays, Constance L. "Burger King Campaign Is Promoting New Fries." *The New York Times*, 11 Dec. 1997, www.nytimes.com/1997/12/11/business/burger-king-campaign-is-promoting-new-fries.html.
- Janofsky, Michael. "25 Million Pounds of Beef Is Recalled." *The New York Times*, 22 Aug. 1997, www.nytimes.com/1997/08/22/us/25-million-pounds-of-beef-is-recalled.html.
- Lehndoff, John. "Burger King's New `Fries' Are Tasty but Aren't Real." *Deseret News*, 19 Apr. 1998, www.deseret.com/1998/4/19/19375403/burger-king-s-new-fries-are-tasty-but-aren-t-real.
- Lewis, Neil A. "Giants in Candy Waging Battle over a Tiny Toy." *The New York Times*, 28 Sept. 1997, www.nytimes.com/1997/09/28/us/giants-in-candy-waging-battle-over-a-tiny-toy.html.
- Pioneer Press. "Chipotle's Secret: Never Show the Burrito." *Twin Cities*, 23 Nov. 2007, www.twincities.com/2007/11/23/chipotles-secret-never-show-the-burrito/.
- Press, Associated. "BURGER KING TARGETS FRIES of ARCH RIVAL." *The Washington Post*, 18 Nov. 1997, www.washingtonpost.com/archive/business/1997/11/18/burger-king-targets-fries-of-arch-rival/0fdb0a3d-18c1-4b8c-a3e8-e164002a49ed/. Accessed 25AD.
- Pressley, Sue Anne. "OPRAH WINFREY WINS CASE FILED by CATTLEMEN." *Washington Post*, 27 Feb. 1998, www.washingtonpost.com/archive/politics/1998/02/27/oprah-winfrey-wins-case-filed-by-cattlemen/dd4612f5-ccbf-4e3d-a1c1-f84d1f4fd23c/.
- Reyes, David. "An Old Activist Resumes the Fight for Latino Rights." *The Los Angeles Times*, 2 Aug. 1998, www.newspapers.com/image/160025163/.
- ---. "Latino Leader Calls for Taco Bell Boycott." *Los Angeles Times*, 14 July 1998, www.latimes.com/archives/la-xpm-1998-jul-14-fi-3450-story.html.
- The Associated Press. "Ice Cream Linked to Salmonella in 15 States." *The New York Times*, 16 Oct. 1994, Ice Cream Linked to Salmonella in 15 States.
- Vasquez, Tina. "The 1990s Boom of California's Mexican Supermarkets." *TASTE*, 23 Apr. 2019, tastecooking.com/1990s-boom-californias-mexican-supermarkets/.
- Vets, Elaine. "Hot under Collar over Spiced-up Macaroni and Cheese." *Evansville Courier and Press*, 5 Apr. 1997, www.newspapers.com/image/762935871/.
- "Whose Food Is It Anyway?" *Newsweek*, 11 Mar. 1996, www.newsweek.com/whose-food-it-anyway-175912.

1998

- Colloff, Pamela. "How the West Was Won Over." *Texas Monthly*, Mar. 1998, www.texasmonthly.com/food/how-the-west-was-won-over.
- Hayes, Constance L. "Fickle Finger of Fat; Nabisco Gives in as Consumers Shun Snackwell's, Demanding Taste." *The New York Times*, 1 May 1998, www.nytimes.com/1998/05/01/business/fickle-finger-fat-nabisco-gives-consumers-shun-snackwell-s-demanding-taste.html.

- Gabaccia, Donna R. We Are What We Eat : Ethnic Food and the Making of Americans. Cambridge (Mass.) ; London, Harvard University Press, 2000.
- "International Cuisine Reaches America's Main Street.." The Free Library. 2000 Frozen Food Digest, Inc. https://www.thefreelibrary.com/International+Cuisine+Reaches+America%27s+Main+Street.-a066762987
- Klein, Karen E. "To Make Dough, Try a New Mix." Los Angeles Times, 7 Oct. 1998, https://www.latimes.com/archives/la-xpm-1998-oct-07-fi-29998-story.html.
- Lubow, Arthur. "Steal This Burger." *The New York Times*, 19 Apr. 1998, www.nytimes.com/1998/04/19/magazine/steal-this-burger.html.
- Painter, Bryan. "Amarillo Weathering Worldwide Attention Oprah Lawsuit Brings Spotlight." The Oklahoman, 8 Feb. 1998, https://www.oklahoman.com/story/news/1998/02/08/amarillo-weathering-worldwide-attention-oprah-lawsuit-brings-spotlight/62292267007.
- "QUAKER GETS READY TO HATCH NEW OATMEAL LINE." Chicago Tribune, 27 Mar. 1998, https://www.chicagotribune.com/news/ct-xpm-1998-03-27-9803270049-story.html.
- Verhovek, Sam Howe. "Talk of the Town: Burgers v. Oprah." *The New York Times*, 21 Jan. 1998, www.nytimes.com/1998/01/21/us/talk-of-the-town-burgers-v-oprah.html.
- Verhovek, Sam Howe. Word for Word / Last Meals; For the Condemned in Texas, Cheeseburgers Without Mercy. 4 Jan. 1998, https://archive.ph/20220204173134/https://www.nytimes.com/1998/01/04/weekinreview/word-for-word-last-meals-for-the-condemned-in-texas-cheeseburgers-without-mercy.html.

1999
- Bourdain, Anthony. "'Don't Eat Before Reading This" *The New Yorker*, 19 Apr. 1999, https://www.newyorker.com/magazine/1999/04/19/dont-eat-before-reading-this.
- Canedy, Dana. "Food Lion to Acquire Hannaford Brothers." *The New York Times*, 19 Aug. 1999, www.nytimes.com/1999/08/19/business/food-lion-to-acquire-hannaford-brothers.html.
- "Coming to Terms With Martha Stewart -- New York Magazine - Nymag." New York Magazine, 26 Jun. 2008, https://nymag.com/news/media/48253.
- Fabricant, Florence. "For a Thirsty City, It's a Cocktail Summer." *The New York Times*, 21 July 1999, www.nytimes.com/1999/07/21/dining/for-a-thirsty-city-it-s-a-cocktail-summer.html.
- *Food Lion to Acquire Hannaford Brothers (Published 1999)*. 19 Aug. 1999, https://www.nytimes.com/1999/08/19/business/food-lion-to-acquire-hannaford-brothers.html.
- *Fabricant, Florence. For a Thirsty City, It's a Cocktail Summer*. 21 Jul. 1999, https://www.nytimes.com/1999/07/21/dining/for-a-thirsty-city-it-s-a-cocktail-summer.html.
- Gallup Inc. "In U.S., 5% Consider Themselves Vegetarians." *Gallup.Com*, 26 Jul. 2012, https://news.gallup.com/poll/156215/consider-themselves-vegetarians.aspx.

Bibliography

- "How 'Sex and the City' Ruined the Cosmo." *VICE*, 29 Nov. 2017, https://www.vice.com/en/article/mb9q58/how-sex-and-the-city-ruined-the-cosmo.
- "INNOVATIONS IN FOOD FOR THE '90S." *Greensboro News and Record*, 21 Dec. 1999, https://greensboro.com/innovations-in-food-for-the-90s/article_19c61fb4-baec-5a49-91e3-615a74ceede2.html.
- Knudson, Max B. "Albertson's Closing on Its Huge Merger." *Deseret News*, 23 Jun. 1999, https://www.deseret.com/1999/6/23/19452165/albertson-s-closing-on-its-huge-merger.
- "Supermarket Squeeze: The Real Costs of the Kroger-Albertsons Deal." *American Economic Liberties Project*, https://www.economicliberties.us/our-work/supermarket-squeeze.
- "The History of Vegetarianism in the U.S." *ArcGIS StoryMaps*, 10 Dec. 2023, https://storymaps.arcgis.com/stories/6cdcd8a7b87f4d24972f338e08a28d5e.
- "Vegetarian Journal Sep/Oct 97 How Many Vegetarians Are There? -- The Vegetarian Resource Group." *Www.Vrg.Org*, https://www.vrg.org/journal/vj97sep/979poll.htm.
- cnn.com, https://www.cnn.com/CNN/Programs/people/shows/stewart/profile.html.
- time.com, https://content.time.com/time/magazine/article/0,9171,393733-1,00.html.

On King Of The Hill

- Associated Press. "Texas Candidate's Comment about Rape Causes a Furor." *The New York Times*, 26 Mar. 1990, www.nytimes.com/1990/03/26/us/texas-candidate-s-comment-about-rape-causes-a-furor.html.
- Bai, Matt. ""King of the Hill" Democrats?" *The New York Times*, 26 June 2005, www.nytimes.com/2005/06/26/magazine/king-of-the-hill-democrats.html.
- Brownfield, Paul. "Deep in the Heart of Arlen, Texas." *Los Angeles Times*, 20 Oct. 2002, www.latimes.com/archives/la-xpm-2002-oct-20-ca-brown20-story.html.
- Burka, Paul. "1993: The Best and Worst Legislators." *Texas Monthly*, July 1993, www.texasmonthly.com/news-politics/the-best-and-worst-legislators-1993/.
- Butterfield, Fox. "Bush's Law and Order Adds up to Tough and Popular." *The New York Times*, 18 Aug. 1999, archive.nytimes.com/www.nytimes.com/library/politics/camp/081899wh-gop-bush.html.
- Carpenter, Dale, and Bryan Wildenthal. "When Democrats Do Bad Things -Response." *Glapn.org*, 14 Feb. 2005, www.glapn.org/sodomylaws/usa/texas/txeditorial06.htm.
- Casriel, Erika. "Bush and the Texas Death Machine." *Rolling Stone*, 3 Aug. 2000, www.rollingstone.com/politics/politics-news/bush-and-the-texas-death-machine-189483/.
- Dore Perkins, Kathryn. "To Spank or Not to Spank, Great Debate Goes On." *Daily Times-Advocate*, 1994, www.newspapers.com/image/571952706/.

- Draper, Robert. "Tough Love Story." *Texas Monthly*, Oct. 1996, www.texasmonthly.com/news-politics/tough-love-story/.
- Duggan, Paul. "George W. Bush: The Texas Record." *Washingtonpost.com*, 9 Nov. 1999, www.washingtonpost.com/wp-srv/WPcap/1999-11/09/075r-110999-idx.html.
- Fielding, Jonathan. "To Spank or Not to Spank." *Los Angeles Times*, 8 July 2002, www.latimes.com/archives/la-xpm-2002-jul-08-he-ourbox8-story.html.
- Fitzgibbons, Ruth Miller. "George Bush, TOO." *D Magazine*, Apr. 1992, www.dmagazine.com/publications/d-magazine/1992/april/george-bush-too/.
- Gamino, Denise. "Raids Reveal Nursing Care Problems." The Tampa Tribune, 26 May 1992, www.newspapers.com/image/339097409/.
- GRACZYK, MICHAEL. "American Indian Tribe Fights Texas to Keep Bingo Center Open." *The Seattle Times*, 10 May 2017, www.seattletimes.com/business/american-indian-tribe-fights-texas-to-keep-bingo-center-open/.
- Huff, Neil. "The Cost of Comfort: Racial Hierarchies in "King of the Hill", PopMatters." PopMatters, 15 July 2019, www.popmatters.com/racial-hierarchies-king-of-hill-2639191612.html.
- Ivins, Molly. "A-Men. A-Women. A-Ann." *The Texas Observer*, 6 Oct. 2006, www.texasobserver.org/2309-a-men-a-women-a-ann-10-years-difference-and-ann-richards-couldve-been-president/.
- Judge, Mike, et al. King of the Hill. Seasons 1-13. Beverly Hills, Calif.: Twentieth Century Fox Home Entertainment, 1997-2009.
- Lyman, Rick. "Ann Richards, Plain-Spoken Texas Governor Who Aided Minorities, Dies at 73 ." *The New York Times*, 14 Sept. 2006, www.nytimes.com/2006/09/14/us/14richards.html.
- McCaig, Steven, et al. "1990s: Spotlight on Texas." *Texas Film Commission*, gov.texas.gov/film/page/1990s.
- Morning, Dallas. " Richards Courts Black Voters." *The Portal to Texas History*, 5 Mar. 1990, texashistory.unt.edu/ark:/67531/metadc916215/, local-cont-no: UNTA_AR0789-01-0082-006.
- Ndubuisi, Yvonne. "Cutting close to Home." *Fort Worth Star-Telegram*, 1990, www.newspapers.com/image/642290242/.
- O'Hare, Peggy. "Kesler vs. Brazoria County." *The Facts*, 26 June 1999, www.newspapers.com/image/27007253/.
- O'Neal 0, Sean. "Walkers and Lone Rangers: How Pop Culture Shaped the Texas Rangers Mythology." *Texas Monthly*, 16 Nov. 2022, www.texasmonthly.com/arts-entertainment/how-pop-culture-shaped-texas-rangers-myth/.
- O'Neal, Sean. "Texas Could Sure Use a Man like Hank Hill, I Tell You What." *Texas Monthly*, 9 Dec. 2021, www.texasmonthly.com/arts-entertainment/texas-needs-a-man-like-hank-hill/.
- Pressley, Sue Anne. "A NEW RESIDENCE and a TRAGEDY." *The Washington Post*, 3 Sept. 1993, www.washingtonpost.com/archive/politics/1993/09/03/a-new-residence-and-a-tragedy/40806717-7d3e-4540-

Bibliography

be53-7602edbfe1f8/.

- "Prints and Photographs Collection | Texas State Library." *Texas.gov*, 2021, www.tsl.texas.gov/governors/modern/richards-p05.html.
- Service, Cox News. "MIKE JUDGE'S `KING' HAS a REAL TEXAS AIR." *Chicago Tribune*, 8 Feb. 1997, www.chicagotribune.com/1997/02/08/mike-judges-king-has-a-real-texas-air/.
- Sills, Ed. "Senate Plan Kills Sodomy Law." *The Portal to Texas History*, 23 Apr. 1993, texashistory.unt.edu/ark:/67531/metadc1823032/, local-cont-no: UNTA_AR0756-049-46-051.
- Spencer, Jason. "County Eyes New Jail Deal." *The Facts*, 21 June 1998, www.newspapers.com/image/13813150/.
- Staff, Newsweek. "Born on the Border." *Newsweek*, 23 Oct. 1995, www.newsweek.com/born-border-184270.
- Suro, Roberto. "THE 1990 ELECTIONS: Texas; RICHARDS PROMISES a NEW DIRECTION." *The New York Times*, 8 Nov. 1990, www.nytimes.com/1990/11/08/us/the-1990-elections-texas-richards-promises-a-new-direction.html.
- Swartz, Mimi. "Meet the Governor: Ann Richards." *Texas Monthly*, 1 Oct. 1990, www.texasmonthly.com/news-politics/meet-the-governor-ann-richards/.
- Teague, Michael. "George W. Bush and the "Texas Solution."" *Criminal Justice Matters*, vol. 44, no. 1, June 2001, pp. 38–40, https://doi.org/10.1080/09627250108552906.
- "The Film and Video Archive of Texas." *Texasarchive.org*, 2025, texasarchive.org/1990s?page=4.
- "The Struggle to Preserve the Black Experience in Houston | Kinder Institute for Urban Research." *Kinder Institute for Urban Research | Rice University*, 2021, kinder.rice.edu/urbanedge/struggle-preserve-black-experience-houston.
- Tinsley, Anna M. "Governor Proclaims Sunday Selena Day." *Corpus Christi Caller-Times*, 14 Apr. 1995, www.newspapers.com/image/759064758/.
- Verhovek, Sam Howe. "Houston Elects Lee Brown as Its First Black Mayor." *The New York Times*, 8 Dec. 1997, www.nytimes.com/1997/12/08/us/houston-elects-lee-brown-as-its-first-black-mayor.html.
- ---. "THE 1994 CAMPAIGN: IN TEXAS; Rock-Star Appeal or Not, Governor Faces Tough Race in Lone Star State." *The New York Times*, 25 Sept. 1994, www.nytimes.com/1994/09/25/us/1994-campaign-texas-rock-star-appeal-not-governor-faces-tough-race-lone-star.html.
- ---. "THE 1994 CAMPAIGN: TEXAS; Governor and Her Rival Meet in Debate." *The New York Times*, 22 Oct. 1994, www.nytimes.com/1994/10/22/us/the-1994-campaign-texas-governor-and-her-rival-meet-in-debate.html.
- ---. "Unusual Leader in a Dallas Campaign." *The New York Times*, 5 May 1995, www.nytimes.com/1995/05/05/us/unusual-leader-in-a-dallas-campaign.html.
- "Videotaped Prison Beating in Texas Spurs FBI Probe." *Los Angeles Times*, 20 Aug. 1997, www.latimes.com/archives/la-xpm-1997-aug-20-mn-24207-

- story.html.
- Walker, Jesse. "Animated Discourse." *Reason.com*, 14 Dec. 2003, reason.com/2003/12/14/animated-discourse/.
- Weinman, Jaime. "A Brief History of King of the Hill ." *Macleans*, 31 Oct. 2008, macleans.ca/uncategorized/a-brief-history-of-king-of-the-hill/.
- Wootson Jr., Cleve R. "Profiting from Prisoners." *Washington Post*, 19 Oct. 2020, www.washingtonpost.com/graphics/2020/national/george-floyd-america/criminal-justice/.

90s True Crime
1990- Art Heist

- Beam, Alex. " Mrs. Gardner's Annual Claim on Heaven." *MCNS Articles*, 19 Apr. 1995, mcnsarticles.blogspot.com/2003_11_09_archive.html.
- Boston, Associated Press in. "FBI Says Two Suspects Who Stole $500m in Art from Boston Museum Are Dead." *The Guardian*, 7 Aug. 2015, www.theguardian.com/artanddesign/2015/aug/07/fbi-isabella-stewart-gardner-museum-art-theft-suspects-dead.
- Butterfield, Fox . "Boston Thieves Loot a Museum of Masterpieces." *The New York Times*, 19 Mar. 1990, www.nytimes.com/1990/03/19/arts/boston-thieves-loot-a-museum-of-masterpieces.html.
- Canellos, Peter S. "Security Experts Say Guards Erred in Opening Door." *The Boston Globe*, 21 Mar. 1990, www.newspapers.com/image/439386880/.
- FBI. "FBI Provides New Information Regarding the 1990 Isabella Stewart Gardner Museum Art Heist." *FBI*, 18 Mar. 2013, archives.fbi.gov/archives/boston/press-releases/2013/fbi-provides-new-information-regarding-the-1990-isabella-stewart-gardner-museum-art-heist.
- "Gardner Museum Art Heist." *The Boston Globe*, www.bostonglobe.com/metro/Gardner-Museum-art-heist/.
- "Historic Footage Connected to Gardner Museum Burglary Released, Public Assistance Sought ." *FBI*, 6 Aug. 2015, www.fbi.gov/contact-us/field-offices/boston/news/press-releases/historic-footage-connected-to-gardner-museum-burglary-released-public-assistance-sought.
- Isabella Stewart Gardner Museum. "The Theft." *Www.gardnermuseum.org*, www.gardnermuseum.org/about/theft-story.
- Murphy, Shelley. "Man Suspected in Gardner Museum Heist Set Free - the Boston Globe." *BostonGlobe.com*, 13 Nov. 2016, www.bostonglobe.com/metro/2019/11/13/man-linked-gardner-museum-heist-set-free/HHwDXfUA13gcBZmdKXLrkJ/story.html?event=event12.
- National Public Radio. "Former Security Guard Reflects on What He Lost One Fateful Night." *NPR*, 13 Mar. 2015, www.npr.org/2015/03/13/392567024/former-security-guard-reflects-on-what-he-lost-one-fateful-night.
- Risen, Clay. "Richard Abath, Guard at Center of Boston Art Museum Heist, Dies at 57." *The New York Times*, 29 Feb. 2024, www.nytimes.com/2024/02/29/us/richard-abath-dead.html.
- Suddath, Claire. "The Case of the Empty Frames Remains Art World's

Biggest Mystery." *Bloomberg.com*, 30 June 2020, www.bloomberg.com/news/features/2020-06-30/gardner-museum-theft-remains-art-world-s-biggest-mystery.

1991- Happyland Fire
- Blumenthal, Ralph. "FIRE in the BRONX; 87 DIE in BLAZE at ILLEGAL CLUB; POLICE ARREST EJECTED PATRON; WORST NEW YORK FIRE since 1911." *The New York Times*, 26 Mar. 1990, www.nytimes.com/1990/03/26/nyregion/fire-bronx-87-die-blaze-illegal-club-police-arrest-ejected-patron-worst-new-york.html.
- Lueck, Thomas J. "Slide from Riches for Landlord in Happy Land Case." *The New York Times*, 8 July 1995, www.nytimes.com/1995/07/08/nyregion/slide-from-riches-for-landlord-in-happy-land-case.html?pagewanted=all&src=pm.
- Roberts, Sam. "Julio Gonzalez, Arsonist Who Killed 87 at New York Club in '90, Dies at 61." *The New York Times*, 15 Sept. 2016, www.nytimes.com/2016/09/15/nyregion/julio-gonzalez-arsonist-who-killed-87-at-new-york-club-in-90-dies-at-61.html.
- Sennott, Charles M. "FIRE in the BRONX; 7 Victims: Their Stories, Struggles and Dreams of Better Lives." *The New York Times*, 29 Mar. 1990, www.nytimes.com/1990/03/29/nyregion/fire-in-the-bronx-7-victims-their-stories-struggles-and-dreams-of-better-lives.html.
- Tomasson, Robert E. "Shock Lingers as Happy Land Trial Starts." *The New York Times*, 9 July 1991, www.nytimes.com/1991/07/09/nyregion/shock-lingers-as-happy-land-trial-starts.html.
- TREADWELL, DAVID. "Blaze Kills 87 in N.Y. Social Club : Fire: An Employee's Ex-Boyfriend Is Arrested on Arson and Murder Charges." *Los Angeles Times*, 26 Mar. 1990, www.latimes.com/archives/la-xpm-1990-03-26-mn-61-story.html.

1991— Father's Day Massacre
- Arias, Ron. "A Bloody Sunday." *People*, 5 Aug. 1991, people.com/archive/a-bloody-sunday-vol-36-no-4/.
- "Ex-Officer Cleared in Heist." *The Cincinnati Post*, 18 June 1992, www.newspapers.com/image/765230464/.
- "Inside the Investigation into the 1991 Colorado Father's Day Bank Massacre." *Denver 7 Colorado News (KMGH)*, 16 June 2021, www.denver7.com/news/local-news/denver7-archive-inside-the-investigation-into-the-colorado-fathers-day-bank-massacre.
- Mitchell, Kirk. "James King, Key Figure in Mystery of Denver Father's Day Massacre, Dies." *The Denver Post*, 10 June 2013, www.denverpost.com/2013/06/10/james-king-key-figure-in-mystery-of-denver-fathers-day-massacre-dies/.
- The Associated Press. "Ex-Policeman Held in Slayings." *Democrat and Chronicle*, 8 July 1991, www.newspapers.com/image/137399987/.

1992- Shanda Sharer
- Goodlad Heline, Marti. "Madison Teen Gets 50-Year Term." *The South Bend Tribune*, 3 June 1993, www.newspapers.com/image/520249594/.
- Grant, Richard. "Bored to Death." *The Age*, 19 Sept. 1992, p. 7, www.newspapers.com/image/120618695/.
- Grossman, Ron. "On July 29, Tempo Reported a Case...." *Chicago Tribune*, 8 Jan. 1993, www.chicagotribune.com/1993/01/08/on-july-29-tempo-reported-a-case/.
- Jones, Aphrodite. *Cruel Sacrifice*. Pinnacle Books, 1994, archive.org/details/cruelsacrifice00aphr/page/46/mode/2up.
- Lewis, Bob. "Thinking the Unthinkable: What Led 4 Teens to Torture, Murder Child?" *Los Angeles Times*, 31 Jan. 1993, www.latimes.com/archives/la-xpm-1993-01-31-mn-1053-story.html.
- Lohr, David. "All about Shanda Sharer, ." *Archive.org*, web.archive.org/web/20070822035659/www.crimelibrary.com/notorious_murders/young/shanda_sharer/5c.html.
- Pillow, John C. "Fate of Loveless Sex-Abuse Case Unclear Two Years after Arrest." *The Courier-Journal*, 3 Feb. 1995, p. 4, www.newspapers.com/image/110577008/.
- "Shanda Sharer's Mother and Murderer Form Unlikely Alliance." *Https://Www.wave3.com*, WAVE 3, 21 May 2012, www.wave3.com/story/18573121/shanda-sharers-mother-and-murderer-form-unlikely-alliance/.

1993- Lorena Bobbit
- "Battle of Sexes Joined in Case of a Mutilation." *The New York Times*, 8 Nov. 1993, www.nytimes.com/1993/11/08/us/battle-of-sexes-joined-in-case-of-a-mutilation.html.
- Chozick, Amy. "You Know the Lorena Bobbitt Story. But Not All of It." *The New York Times*, 30 Jan. 2019, www.nytimes.com/2019/01/30/arts/television/lorena-bobbitt-documentary-jordan-peele.html.
- "Judge Declares Mistrial in Castration Case." *SFGATE*, 10 Feb. 1995, www.sfgate.com/news/article/judge-declares-mistrial-in-castration-case-3045368.php.
- "Lorena Bobbitt Meets Ecuador President ." *UPI*, 17 Oct. 1996, www.upi.com/Archives/1996/10/17/Lorena-Bobbitt-meets-Ecuador-president/3574845524800/.
- Odum, Maria E. "MARINE RECORDS on ABUSE MAY FIGURE in BOBBITT TRIAL." *Washington Post*, The Washington Post, 7 Jan. 1994, www.washingtonpost.com/archive/local/1994/01/07/marine-records-on-abuse-may-figure-in-bobbitt-trial/c2a834e8-6a9e-4223-b8d9-56cc924d293f/.
- Pershing, Linda. ""His Wife Seized His Prize and Cut It to Size": Folk and Popular Commentary on Lorena Bobbitt." *NWSA Journal*, vol. 8, no. 3, 1996, pp. 1–35. *JSTOR*, https://doi.org/10.2307/4316459.
- Staff, Post Features. "Why Was John Wayne Bobbitt at a Palm Beach Gardens Hot Dog Contest?" *The Palm Beach Post*, Palm Beach Post, 23 June 2017, www.palmbeachpost.com/story/lifestyle/2017/06/23/why-was-

Bibliography

- john-wayne-bobbitt/7342293007/.
- Tousignant, Marylou, and Bill Miller. "LORENA BOBBITT DETAILS DEMISE of MARRIAGE." *The Washington Post*, 13 Jan. 1994, www.washingtonpost.com/archive/politics/1994/01/13/lorena-bobbitt-details-demise-of-marriage/1b1487f0-769f-4d13-a85e-4670b722f1b0/.
- Tousignant, Marylou, and Carlos Sanchez. "LORENA BOBBITT RELEASED from MENTAL HOSPITAL." *Washington Post*, 1 Mar. 1994, www.washingtonpost.com/archive/local/1994/03/01/lorena-bobbitt-released-from-mental-hospital/a3017782-19a4-47ae-a6c2-316f0d0f776d/.

1993— Taco Bell Strangler

- Bryant, Erica. "Mothers of Murdered Offspring Founder Reflects after 30 Years, Talks about Expansion of Organization." *WSOC TV*, 29 Mar. 2023, www.wsoctv.com/news/local/mothers-murdered-offspring-founder-reflects-after-30-years-talks-about-expansion-organization/SU6QZASHKVH5VIZYWPVOPSEWHA/.
- "Crime Stoppers Notice about Michelle Stinson." *The Charlotte Observer*, 21 Sept. 1993, www.newspapers.com/image/626589294/.
- DeAngelis, Mary Elizabeth. "Clues Sought in Strangling of Woman." *The Charlotte Observer*, 8 Mar. 1993, www.newspapers.com/image/626566248/.
- ---. "Victom's Mother Starts Support Group." *The Charlotte Observer*, 28 Mar. 1993, www.newspapers.com/image/626546020/.
- Garfield, Ken, and Henry Eichel. "Man Charged with 10 Murders." *The Charlotte Observer*, 14 Mar. 1994, www.newspapers.com/image/626982064/.
- Gordon, Michael. "11 Victims in Two States: A Timeline of Henry Wallace's Killings in Charlotte and SC." *Charlotte Observer*, 26 July 2023, www.charlotteobserver.com/news/local/crime/article277173683.html.
- ---. "As a Serial Killer Moved like a Shadow across Charlotte, One Woman Made a Promise." *Charlotte Observer*, 26 July 2023, www.charlotteobserver.com/article277172618.html.
- ---. "Henry Wallace Killings Exposed Flaws in CMPD Homicide Investigations, Sparked Changes." *Charlotte Observer*, 27 July 2023, www.charlotteobserver.com/article277525813.html.
- "Man Charged with Slayings in N.C. Sought in Kitsap Case." *Seattle Times*, 14 Mar. 1994, archive.seattletimes.com/archive/?date=19940314&slug=1900185.
- McCollum, Brian. "Anatomy of an Investigation." *The Charlotte Observer*, 18 Mar. 1994, www.newspapers.com/image/626994054/.
- Rogers, John. "Man Called Most Prolific Serial Killer in US History Dies." AP NEWS, 20 Apr. 2021, apnews.com/article/us-news-california-samuel-little-3b63489aa94bebe08120a3b76393d7ee.
- Wiliams, Ed. "A Violent Place." *The Charlotte Observer*, 7 May 1994, www.newspapers.com/image/627001650/.
- Wright, Angela. "Body Found in June Identified as Missing Charlotte Woman's." *The Charlotte Observer*, 6 Aug. 1992, www.newspapers.com/image/626578625/.

- ---. "Mom Found Slain; Children Witnessed Killing, Police Say." *The Charlotte Observer*, 16 Sept. 1993, www.newspapers.com/image/626567227/.
- ---. "Mothers of Children Who Were Murdered Launch Campaign." *The Charlotte Observer*, 8 Sept. 1993, www.newspapers.com/image/626578625/.

1994— Tonya Harding
- Brennan, Christine. "Washingtonpost.com: Tonya Harding Remains the Public Enigma." *Washington Post*, 23 Jan. 1994, www.washingtonpost.com/wp-srv/sports/longterm/olympics1998/history/timeline/articles/time_012394.htm.
- Chicago Tribune. "THREAT ADDS to HARDING'S LIST of WOES." *Chicago Tribune*, 7 Nov. 1993, www.chicagotribune.com/1993/11/07/threat-adds-to-hardings-list-of-woes/.
- Crossman, Matt. "Harding-Kerrigan 20 Years Later: Remembering the Stunning, Life-Changing Attack." *Bleacher Report*, 19 Dec. 2013, bleacherreport.com/articles/1887592-harding-kerrigan-20-years-later-remembering-the-stunning-life-changing-attack.
- "Figure Skater Tries Baseball." *The Naples Daily News*, 12 Mar. 1992, www.newspapers.com/image/801458670/.
- Gormley, Shannon. "In 1994, Garbage Dumped at a Portland Bar Helped Solve a Notorious FBI Case." *Willamette Week*, 23 May 2018, www.wweek.com/culture/2018/05/22/in-1994-garbage-dumped-at-a-portland-bar-helped-solve-a-notorious-fbi-case/.
- Harvey, Randy. "On Thin Ice." *Los Angeles Times*, 5 Jan. 1992, www.newspapers.com/image/177282966/.
- Koberstein, Paul. "The Tonya Harding Story Brought out the Best—and Worst—in the News Media." *Willamette Week*, 7 Jan. 2024, www.wweek.com/archive/2024/01/06/the-tonya-harding-story-brought-out-the-bestand-the-worstin-the-news-media/.
- Kovaleski, Serge F. "PORTLAND: CITY under SEIGE." *The Washington Post*, 9 Feb. 1994, www.washingtonpost.com/archive/sports/1994/02/09/portland-city-under-seige/90e1cfc6-3b86-40a6-9934-6b50c9c0e9ae/.
- Krause, Elizabeth. *The Bead of Raw Sweat in a Field of Dainty Perspirers": Nationalism, Whiteness and the Olympic-Class Ordeal of Tonya Harding*. 1996.
- "Not Your Average Ice Queen." *Sports Illustrated Vault | SI.com*, 13 Jan. 1991, vault.si.com/vault/1992/01/13/not-your-average-ice-queen-a-troubled-past-hasnt-stopped-tonya-harding-from-becoming-a-figure-skating-champion.
- Oregonian/OregonLive, Katy Muldoon | The. "Tonya Harding-Nancy Kerrigan 20 Years Later: The Highlights in a Timeline." *Oregonlive*, 6 Jan. 2014, www.oregonlive.com/tonya-harding/2014/01/tonya_harding-nancy_kerrigan_2.html.
- Orlean, Susan. "The Tonya Harding Fan Club." *The New Yorker*, 14 Feb. 1994, www.newyorker.com/magazine/1994/02/21/tonya-harding-fan-club-susan-orlean.
- Smolowe, Jill. "Figure Skater Tonya Harding: Tarnished Victory." TIME,

- nextgen, 24 Jan. 1994, time.com/archive/6724627/figure-skater-tonya-harding-tarnished-victory/.
- Swift, E. M. "Anatomy of a Plot." *Sports Illustrated Vault | SI.com*, 14 Feb. 1994, vault.si.com/vault/1994/02/14/anatomy-of-a-plot-even-in-their-version-of-events-which-differs-from-tonya-hardings-the-confessed-conspirators-in-the-nancy-kerrigan-assault-were-at-once-goons-and-buffoons.
- ---. "On Thin Ice." *Sports Illustrated Vault | SI.com*, 24 Jan. 1994, vault.si.com/vault/1994/01/24/on-thin-ice-as-the-olympics-loomed-nancy-kerrigan-was-back-on-skates-and-tonya-harding-was-under-siege.
- Swift, E.M. "Stirring." *Sports Illustrated Vault | SI.com*, 2 Mar. 1992, vault.si.com/vault/1992/03/02/stiring.
- The Associated Press. "FIGURE SKATING; Kerrigan Attacker and Accomplice Sent to Jail." *The New York Times*, 17 May 1994, www.nytimes.com/1994/05/17/sports/figure-skating-kerrigan-attacker-and-accomplice-sent-to-jail.html.
- "WORLD JUDGES SMILE on U.S. SKATERS." *Chicago Tribune*, 29 Mar. 1992, www.chicagotribune.com/1992/03/29/world-judges-smile-on-us-skaters/.
- Zimmerman, Rachel. "FIGURE SKATING; the Harding Fan Club Has a Song in Its Heart." *The New York Times*, 24 Jan. 1994, www.nytimes.com/1994/01/24/sports/figure-skating-the-harding-fan-club-has-a-song-in-its-heart.html.

1995- Freddy's Fashion Mart
- Barry, Dan. "DEATH on 128TH STREET: THE DISPUTE;Plans to Evict Record-Shop Owner Roiled Residents." *The New York Times*, 9 Dec. 1995, www.nytimes.com/1995/12/09/nyregion/death-128th-street-dispute-plans-evict-record-shop-owner-roiled-residents.html.
- GOLDMAN, JOHN J. "8 Die as Gunman Sets Afire N.Y. Store Tied to Dispute : Violence: Harlem Shop Had Been Target of Protests Ove." *Los Angeles Times*, 9 Dec. 1995, www.latimes.com/archives/la-xpm-1995-12-09-mn-12115-story.html.
- Kleinfeld, N.R. "DEATH on 125th STREET: The Dispute;from a Quiet Beginning, a Volatile Brew Explodes in Harlem." *The New York Times*, 10 Dec. 1995, DEATH ON 125th STREET: The Dispute;From a Quiet Beginning, a Volatile Brew Explodes in Harlem.
- McFadden, Robert D. "Giuliani and Bratton See Racism in Harlem Fire." *The New York Times*, 10 Dec. 1995, www.nytimes.com/1995/12/10/nyregion/giuliani-and-bratton-see-racism-in-harlem-fire.html.
- Purdy, Matthew. "For Owner of Harlem Clothing Store, a Collision of Two DifferentWorlds." *The New York Times*, 16 Dec. 1995, www.nytimes.com/1995/12/16/nyregion/for-owner-of-harlem-clothing-store-a-collision-of-two-differentworlds.html.
- Sexton, Joe. "A Life of Resistance: A Special Report;Gunman's Ardent Credo: Black Self-Sufficiency." *The New York Times*, 18 Dec. 1995, www.nytimes.com/1995/12/18/us/life-resistance-special-report-gunman-

s-ardent-credo-black-self-sufficiency.html?pagewanted=all.

1995— Tracie McBride
- Hargrave, Kacee. "McBrides Talk about Pain, Loss, Anger." *Https:// Www.newspapers.com/Image/789569237/*, 5 Nov. 1995.
- Miller, Mark. "Should Louis Jones Die?" *Newsweek*, 13 Mar. 2003, www.newsweek.com/should-louis-jones-die-132259.
- Serrano, Richard A. "A War Hero, a Condemned Killer." *Los Angeles Times*, 14 Jan. 2003, www.latimes.com/archives/la-xpm-2003-jan-14-na-clemency14-story.html.
- ---. "Gulf War Veteran Executed for 1995 Murder." *Los Angeles Times*, 19 Mar. 2003, www.latimes.com/archives/la-xpm-2003-mar-19-na-execute19-story.html.
- "United States of America, Plaintiff-Appellee, v. Louis Jones, Defendant-Appellant, 132 F.3d 232 (5th Cir. 1998)." *Justia Law*, 1998, law.justia.com/cases/federal/appellate-courts/F3/132/232/469339/.

1996- Jeffrey Epstein
- Baker, Mike. "The Sisters Who First Tried to Take down Jeffrey Epstein." *The New York Times*, 26 Aug. 2019, www.nytimes.com/2019/08/26/us/epstein-farmer-sisters-maxwell.html.
- Davis, Ben. "Jeffrey Epstein Accuser Maria Farmer Says the New York Academy of Art Helped Enable the Disgraced Financier." *Artnet News*, 27 Aug. 2019, news.artnet.com/art-world/maria-farmer-new-york-art-academy-1610506.
- Ellison, Sarah, and Jonathan O'Connell. "Epstein Accuser Holds Victoria's Secret Billionaire Responsible, as He Keeps His Distance." *The Washington Post*, 5 Oct. 2019, www.washingtonpost.com/business/economy/epstein-accuser-holds-victorias-secret-billionaire-responsible-as-he-keeps-his-distance/2019/10/05/1b6baf6c-d0d3-11e9-b29b-a528dc82154a_story.html.
- Hong, Nicole, and Rebecca Davis O'Brien. "Following Epstein's Arrest, Spotlight Shifts to Financier's Longtime Associate." *The Wall Street Journal*, 11 July 2019, www.wsj.com/articles/following-epsteins-arrest-spotlight-shifts-to-financiers-longtime-associate-11562881299.
- Small, Zachary. "Disgraced Billionaire Jeffrey Epstein's Art World Connections." *Hyperallergic*, 10 July 2019, hyperallergic.com/508823/jeffrey-epstein/.
- Steel, Emily, et al. "How Jeffrey Epstein Used the Billionaire behind Victoria's Secret for Wealth and Women." *The New York Times*, 25 July 2019, www.nytimes.com/2019/07/25/business/jeffrey-epstein-wexner-victorias-secret.html.

1996- JonBenet Ramsey
- 9News. "9NEWS Interviews John and Patsy Ramsey." *Www.youtube.com*, 13 Oct. 2016, www.youtube.com/watch?v=lyPfM2xizXg.
- ---. "A Tour of the Ramsey House." *Www.youtube.com*, 26 Oct. 2016,

Bibliography

- www.youtube.com/watch?v=ZQV-amyVl7c.
- "Bungled JonBenet Case Bursts a City's Majesty." *The New York Times*, 5 Dec. 1997, www.nytimes.com/1997/12/05/us/bungled-jonbenet-case-bursts-a-city-s-majesty.html.
- Dean, Michelle. "American Obsession: How JonBenét Ramsey Gave Rise to the Online Detective." *The Guardian*, The Guardian, 9 Sept. 2016, www.theguardian.com/us-news/2016/sep/09/jonbenet-ramsey-murder-20-year-anniversary-online-detectives.
- "Experts Dissect JonBenet Ramsey Ransom Note." *ABC News*, 27 Sept. 1998, abcnews.go.com/US/video/9271998-experts-dissect-jonbenet-ramsey-ransom-note-29249678.
- Janofsky, Michael. "JonBenet's Mother Was Killer, Detective Says." *The New York Times*, 10 Apr. 2000, www.nytimes.com/2000/04/10/us/jonbenet-s-mother-was-killer-detective-says.html.
- Jerome, Richard. "Mystery Couple." *Peoplemag*, 6 Oct. 1997, people.com/archive/cover-story-mystery-couple-vol-48-no-14/.
- "JonBenét: The Door the Cops Never Opened." *Newsweek*, 23 Sept. 2016, www.newsweek.com/jonbenet-ramsey-door-cops-never-opened-501705.
- Maloney, J.J. "The Murder of JonBenét Ramsey ." *Crime Magazine*, 7 May 1999, web.archive.org/web/20141129041656/www.crimemagazine.com/murder-jonben%C3%A9t-ramsey.
- Reuters. "Gov. Owens Gets Strong Support in JonBenet Case." *Los Angeles Times*, 29 Oct. 1999, www.latimes.com/archives/la-xpm-1999-oct-29-mn-27420-story.html.
- Roberts, Michael. "John Mark Karr/Alexis Valoran Reich: "My Passion Is My Work with Children."" *Westword*, 9 June 2010, www.westword.com/news/john-mark-karr-alexis-valoran-reich-my-passion-is-my-work-with-children-5889469.
- Rosenberg, Howard. "A Clear Case of Media Mayhem." *Los Angeles Times*, 28 Sept. 1998, www.latimes.com/archives/la-xpm-1998-sep-28-ca-27182-story.html.
- Staff, Newsweek. "No Justice for Jonbenet." *Newsweek*, 25 Oct. 1999, www.newsweek.com/no-justice-jonbenet-168028.

1997—Sherrice Iverson
- Bandow, Doug. "The Power of Shame." *Cato Institute*, 14 Feb. 2000, www.cato.org/commentary/power-shame.
- Banks, Sandy. "A Murdered Child and Our Moral Deficiency." *Los Angeles Times*, 2 Oct. 1998, www.latimes.com/archives/la-xpm-1998-oct-02-ls-28380-story.html.
- Dahlberg, Tim. "TEEN PLEADS GUILTY to KILLING 7-YEAR-OLD." *The Washington Post*, 9 Sept. 1998, www.washingtonpost.com/archive/politics/1998/09/09/teen-pleads-guilty-to-killing-7-year-old/e244b87b-3b6c-4368-9953-7adac8218d50/.
- Lee, Henry K. "David Cash Is Spat upon off Campus." *SFGATE*, 19 Sept. 1998, www.sfgate.com/news/article/David-Cash-Is-Spat-Upon-Off-Campus-2989895.php.

- Press, The Associated. "Killer of Girl in Casino Gets Life Term." *The New York Times*, 15 Oct. 1998, www.nytimes.com/1998/10/15/us/killer-of-girl-in-casino-gets-life-term.html.
- Reuters. "Friend of Defendant Is Target of Protest." *The New York Times*, 27 Aug. 1998, www.nytimes.com/1998/08/27/us/friend-of-defendant-is-target-of-protest.html.
- ---. "Youth Is Held in Slaying of Girl at Nevada Casino." *The New York Times*, 30 May 1997, www.nytimes.com/1997/05/30/us/youth-is-held-in-slaying-of-girl-at-nevada-casino.html.
- SALTER, STEPHANIE. "Who Can Possibly Reach David Cash's Heart of Darkness?" *SFGATE*, 4 Oct. 1998, www.sfgate.com/bayarea/article/Who-can-possibly-reach-David-Cash-s-heart-of-3066518.php.
- Terry, Don. "Mother Rages against Indifference." *The New York Times*, 24 Aug. 1998, www.nytimes.com/1998/08/24/us/mother-rages-against-indifference.html.
- The Associated Press. "Campus Peers Shun Student Who Did Not Report Child's Killing." *The New York Times*, 4 Oct. 1998, www.nytimes.com/1998/10/04/us/campus-peers-shun-student-who-did-not-report-child-s-killing.html.
- Yan, Michael . "Cashing in on Tragedy Illuminates Society's Problems - Daily Bruin." *Daily Bruin*, 10 Aug. 1998, dailybruin.com/1998/08/09/cashing-in-on-tragedy-illumina.
- ZAMICHOW, NORA. "The Fractured Life of Jeremy Strohmeyer." *Los Angeles Times*, Los Angeles Times, 19 July 1998, www.latimes.com/archives/la-xpm-1998-jul-19-mn-5552-story.html.

1997— Mary Kay Letourneau
- Anderson, Rick. "Mary Kay Letourneau Always Seems Ready for Her Close-Up. From Mocking Her." *Seattle Weekly*, 12 Apr. 2015, www.seattleweekly.com/news/mary-kay-letourneau-always-seems-ready-for-her-close-up-from-mocking-her/.
- Basheda, Lori. "Teacher's Family Tries to Move Past Scandal." *The San Bernardino County Sun*, 24 Aug. 1997, p. 9.
- Bunn, Austin. "Prisoner of Love - Salon.com." *Salon.com*, 27 Jan. 2000, www.salon.com/2000/01/27/letourneau/.
- Dickson, E. J. "How the Media Turned Child Rape into a "Tryst" for Mary Kay Letourneau." *Rolling Stone*, 8 July 2020, www.rollingstone.com/culture/culture-features/mary-kay-letourneau-vili-fualauu-relationship-media-child-rape-tryst-1025466/.
- Press, Associated. "Groupies Swarm around Letourneau Case Strangers' Advice May Have Influenced Her Decisions after She Gained Notoriety." *Spokesman.com*, The Spokesman-Review, 13 Feb. 1998, www.spokesman.com/stories/1998/feb/13/groupies-swarm-around-letourneau-case-strangers/.
- The Associated Press. "Ex-Lawmakers Daughter Guilty of Child Affair." *The San Francisco Examiner*, 11 Aug. 1997, www.newspapers.com/article/the-san-francisco-examiner/98110567/.
- ---. "PAROLE REVOKED, EX-TEACHER SENT to PRISON in TEEN SEX

Bibliography

- CASE." *The Washington Post*, 7 Feb. 1998, www.washingtonpost.com/archive/politics/1998/02/07/parole-revoked-ex-teacher-sent-to-prison-in-teen-sex-case/ed36067d-b2b7-49f6-962e-241b15ff579b/.
- "Vili Fualaau Saw "Things Clearly" after Split from Mary Kay Letourneau: Source." *People*, 2020, people.com/crime/vili-fualaau-split-mary-kay-letourneau-he-sees-things-clearly/.
- Warrick, Pamela. "The Fall from Spyglass Hill." *Los Angeles Times*, 29 Apr. 1998, www.latimes.com/archives/la-xpm-1998-apr-29-ls-45407-story.html.

1998— Thurston High School
- Cyr, Miranda. "25 Years Later: Healing from the Thurston High Shooting." *The Register-Guard*, Register-Guard, 20 May 2023, www.registerguard.com/story/news/local/2023/05/20/25-years-thurston-high-school-mass-shooting-springfield-mikael-nickolauson-benjamin-walker-kinkel/70232948007/.
- Erdely, Griffin. "Archives: 17-Year-Old Disarms High School Shooter in Oregon." *Carnegie Hero Fund Commission*, 8 June 2023, www.carnegiehero.org/from-the-archives-17-year-old-disarms-high-school-shooter-in-oregon/.
- Gonnerman, Jennifer. "What Happens to a School Shooter's Sister?" *The New Yorker*, 27 Nov. 2023, www.newyorker.com/magazine/2023/12/04/what-happens-to-a-school-shooters-sister.
- Merritt, Nancy, et al. *The Author(S) Shown below Used Federal Funds Provided by the U.S. Department of Justice and Prepared the Following Final Report: Document Title: Oregon's Measure 11 Sentencing Reform: Implementation and System Impact*. 2055.
- Schulberg, Jessica. "Kip Kinkel Is Ready to Speak." *HuffPost*, 12 June 2021, www.huffpost.com/entry/kip-kinkel-is-ready-to-speak_n_60abd623e4b0a2568315c62d.
- Taylor, Bill. *Background Brief on Measure 11*. May 2004.
- The Associated Press. "Teenage School Gunman Gets 112 Years." *Los Angeles Times*, 11 Nov. 1999, www.newspapers.com/image/161441399/?clipping_id=31142578&fcfToken=eyJhbGciOiJIUzI1NiIsInR5cCI6IkpXVCJ9.eyJmcmVlLXZpZXctaWQiOjE2MTQ0MTM5OSwiaWF0IjoxNzExNzY3ODkwLCJleHAiOjE3MTE0NTQyOTB9.w3U_fAebZL8oNLG1XIJJySrk21GdWWkZuK5AEZNDjbI.

1999— Barry Winchell
- Becker, Elizabeth. "Pentagon Orders Training to Prevent Harassment of Gays." *The New York Times*, 2 Feb. 2000, www.nytimes.com/2000/02/02/us/pentagon-orders-training-to-prevent-harassment-of-gays.html.
- Clines, Francis X. "For Gay Soldier, a Daily Barrage of Threats and Slurs." *The New York Times*, 12 Dec. 1999, www.nytimes.com/1999/12/12/us/for-gay-soldier-a-daily-barrage-of-threats-and-slurs.html.
- France, David. "An Inconvenient Woman." *The New York Times*, 28 May 2000, www.nytimes.com/2000/05/28/magazine/an-inconvenient-

woman.html.
- Hackett, Thomas. "The Execution of Private Winchell (Rolling Stone)." *Wayback Machine*, Rolling Stone, 2 Mar. 2000, web.archive.org/web/20060213230320/www.davidclemens.com/gaymilitary/rolstobarry.htm.
- Prichard, James. "Soldier Gets Life with Chance of Parole." *The Greenville News*, 12 Aug. 1999, www.newspapers.com/image/1015381550/.
- ---. "Soldiers Life Ended Violently in Barracks." *The State Journal*, 12 Aug. 1999, www.newspapers.com/image/1015381550/.
- Rowe, Michael. "Love in a Dangerous Time." *People*, 27 May 2003, books.google.com/books?id=s2QEAAAAMBAJ&pg=PA40-IA7&#v=onepage&q&f=false.

1999- Rae Carruth
- Assael, Shaun. "Ex-Panther Wideout Rae Carruth Is at the Center of Scandal in Charlotte, N.C. -- ESPN the Magazine Archives - ESPN." *ESPN.com*, ESPN, 10 July 2012, www.espn.com/espn/story/_/page/Mag15nightgames/ex-panther-wideout-rae-carruth-center-scandal-charlotte-nc-espn-magazine-archives.
- Bamberger, Michael. "First-Degree Tragedy Rae Carruth Was a Gifted but Unassuming Wide Receiver for the Panthers. Now He Stands Accused of Ordering the Murder of His Pregnant Girlfriend--a Horrific Crime That, like Carruth Himself, Remains Shrouded in Mystery." *Wayback Machine*, Sports Illustrated, 27 Dec. 1999, web.archive.org/web/20210410215945/vault.si.com/vault/1999/12/27/firstdegree-tragedy-rae-carruth-was-a-gifted-but-unassuming-wide-receiver-for-the-panthers-now-he-stands-accused-of-ordering-the-murder-of-his-pregnant-girlfrienda-horrific-crime-that-like-carruth-himself-remains-shrouded-in-my.
- "Cherica Adams 911 Call Transcript." *Https://S3.Documentcloud.org/Documents/5001924/Transcript-of-911-Call-From-Cherica-Adams.pdf*, 16 Nov. 1999.
- "Fmr. NFL Player Rae Carruth Moves to Pennsylvania after Prison Term for Girlfriend's Murder." *6abc Philadelphia*, 24 Oct. 2018, 6abc.com/rae-carruth-son-released-cherica-adams-net-worth/4548020/.
- "Former NBA Player Testifies against Carruth." *ABC News*, 5 Dec. 2000, abcnews.go.com/Sports/story?id=100123&page=1.
- Fowler, Scott. ""I Want Him Dead": Hitman Hired to Kill Cherica Adams Will Never Forgive Carruth." *Charlotte Observer*, 16 Oct. 2018, www.charlotteobserver.com/sports/spt-columns-blogs/scott-fowler/article219417845.html.
- ---. "Chancellor Lee Adams, the Son Rae Carruth Tried to Kill, Is Now a Man Graduating High School." *Charlotte Observer*, 26 May 2021, www.charlotteobserver.com/sports/spt-columns-blogs/scott-fowler/article251584383.html.
- ---. "Hitman Who Killed the Pregnant Girlfriend of Former Panther Rae Carruth Dies in Prison." *Charlotte Observer*, 11 Dec. 2023, www.charlotteobserver.com/sports/article282906678.html.

Bibliography

- Frazier, Eric. "Carruth's Bond Stays at $3 Million." The Charlotte Observer, 2 Dec. 1999, www.newspapers.com/image/629798789/.
- Hemphill, Beth. "83-NC v. Carruth: Cindy Gresham, Barbara Turner & Tiffany Adams." *Court TV*, 24 Nov. 2020, www.courttv.com/title/83-nc-v-carruth-cindy-gresham-barbara-turner-tiffany-adams/.
- Lake, Thomas. "The Boy They Couldn't Kill: How Rae Carruth's Son Survived and Thrives." *Sports Illustrated*, 7 Jan. 2015, www.si.com/nfl/2015/01/07/si-60-the-boy-they-couldnt-kill-rae-carruth-son.
- "Mother Contradicts Daughter in Carruth Trial." *ABC News*, 9 Jan. 2001, abcnews.go.com/Sports/story?id=99973&page=1.
- "NC v. Rae Carruth: Carolina Panther on Trial ." *Court TV*, www.courttv.com/trials/nc-v-carr.
- RaeCarruthDidIt. "Cherica Adams 911 Call." *YouTube*, 5 Oct. 2012, www.youtube.com/watch?v=KrV2vgI7r-A.
- Richmond, Peter. "Rae Carruth, the Women Who Loved Him, and the One He Wanted Dead." *Deadspin*, 11 July 2013, web.archive.org/web/20220108231043/deadspin.com/rae-carruth-the-women-who-loved-him-and-the-one-he-wa-747347792.
- Siner, Jeff. "Chancellor Lee Adams Continues to Beat Odds as He Turns 21." *Charlotte Observer*, 12 Nov. 2020, www.charlotteobserver.com/sports/article247114257.html.
- "Wiggins v. Boyette ." *CourtListener*, 15 Feb. 2011, www.courtlistener.com/opinion/204834/wiggins-v-boyette/?q=%22Rae%20Carruth%22.

90s Serial Killers

- Bonn, Scott. "Serial Killer Myth No. 5: All Victims Are Female." *Psychology Today*, 2014, www.psychologytoday.com/us/blog/wicked-deeds/201411/serial-killer-myth-no-5-all-victims-are-female.
- "Boys, Girls & Bundyphiles—Fans, Followers of Serial Killers Often "Condemned" for Interest." *The Columbia Chronicle*, 24 Oct. 2016, columbiachronicle.com/bc9649e6-99f5-11e6-aaea-ffba1999cc26.
- Bradshaw, Paul. "Blood, Bodies and the Box: How "Seven" Changed Film and TV Forever." *NME*, 23 Sept. 2020, www.nme.com/features/seven-brad-pitt-morgan-freeman-david-fincher-2759534.
- Bruini, Frank. "Hack by Popular Demand." Saint John Times Globe, 19 Sept. 1994, www.newspapers.com/image/1115083423/.
- Cassel, David. "A Killer Site ." *Salon.com*, 3 Oct. 1997, www.salon.com/1997/10/03/news_384/?fbclid=IwAR3vzA1o64v5qXk7eL6aRAHYUktR9yo-20IrkUtcuzN6DO9pzbmdkn0O26c.
- Chicago Tribune. "OWNER WILL TURN GACY'S ART to ASHES." *Chicago Tribune*, 18 May 1994, www.chicagotribune.com/1994/05/18/owner-will-turn-gacys-art-to-ashes/.
- Craven, Wes. Scream. Dimension Films, 1996.
- Cullins, Ashley. ""Faster, Better and More Blood": A "Scream" Oral

History." The Hollywood Reporter, 29 Oct. 2021, www.hollywoodreporter.com/movies/movie-features/scream-movie-cast-stories-1235038248/.
- "DAHMER ESCAPEE TELLS of CLOSE CALL." *Chicago Tribune*, Feb. 1992, www.chicagotribune.com/1992/02/01/dahmer-escapee-tells-of-close-call/.
- Delgado, Michelle. "How "Scream" Explored the Exploitative Nature of the Nightly News." *Smithsonian Magazine*, 29 Oct. 2021, www.smithsonianmag.com/arts-culture/how-scream-explored-the-exploitative-nature-of-the-nightly-news-180978960/.
- Demme, Jonathan. The Silence of the Lambs. Orion Pictures, 1991.
- DeSANTIS, JOHN. "Accused Lived on the Fringe of Two Worlds." *Houma Today*, 4 Dec. 2006, web.archive.org/web/20210128012212/www.houmatoday.com/article/DA/20061204/News/608089983/HC.
- *Dismay over Big-Budget Flops*. The New York Times, 17 Oct. 1995, www.nytimes.com/1995/10/17/movies/dismay-over-big-budget-flops.html.
- Fincher, David. "Se7en", New Line Cinema, 2001.
- "Gacy Artwork to Go up in Smoke." *Los Angeles Times*, 15 May 1994, www.latimes.com/archives/la-xpm-1994-05-15-mn-58010-story.html.
- Gilstrap, Peter. "Was Ted Bundy Framed." *Phoenix New Times*, 23 May 1996, www.phoenixnewtimes.com/news/was-ted-bundy-framed-6423916.
- "Guard Suspected in Dahmer Auction." *Trentonian*, 6 Jan. 2001, www.trentonian.com/2001/01/06/guard-suspected-in-dahmer-auction/.
- Hallemann, Caroline. "Gianni Versace's Funeral." Yahoo Life, 17 Jan. 2018, www.yahoo.com/lifestyle/gianni-versace-apos-funeral-232528650.html.
- HILLINGER, CHARLES. "Blind Couple See Only Good, Not the Guilt of the Helpers." *Los Angeles Times*, 29 Jan. 1987, www.latimes.com/archives/la-xpm-1987-01-29-mn-2252-story.html.
- Johnson, Dirk. "Bid to Auction Killer's Tools Provokes Disgust." *The New York Times*, 20 May 1996, www.nytimes.com/1996/05/20/us/bid-to-auction-killer-s-tools-provokes-disgust.html.
- Levitt, Steven. Chapter 4, Where Have All the Criminals Gone? 12 Apr. 2005. https://ir101.co.uk/wp-content/uploads/2018/11/Levitt-Where-Have-all-the-Criminals-Gone.pdf
- Margaritoff, Marco. "Doreen Lioy Was a Successful Editor — but She Gave It All up to Marry a Serial Killer." *All That's Interesting*, 16 Jan. 2021, allthatsinteresting.com/doreen-lioy.
- Martin, Andrew, et al. "THE MANY FACES of ANDREW CUNANAN." Chicago Tribune, 16 May 1997, www.chicagotribune.com/1997/05/16/the-many-faces-of-andrew-cunanan/.
- Martin, Phillip. " Serial Killers Are so 1990.", Arkansas Democrat Gazette. 2 Feb. 2021, www.arkansasonline.com/news/2021/feb/02/serial-killers-are-so-1990/.
- Maslin, Janet. "FILM REVIEW: NATURAL BORN KILLERS; Young Lovers with a Flaw That Proves Fatal." *The New York Times*, 26 Aug. 1994, www.nytimes.com/1994/08/26/movies/film-review-natural-born-killers-

young-lovers-with-a-flaw-that-proves-fatal.html.
- Mikulec, Sven. ""Se7en": A Rain-Drenched, Somber, Gut-Wrenching Thriller That Restored David Fincher's Faith in Filmmaking • Cinephilia & Beyond." *Cinephilia & Beyond*, 27 May 2017, cinephiliabeyond.org/se7en-rain-drenched-somber-gut-wrenching-thriller-restored-david-finchers-faith-filmmaking/.
- Milwaukee Journal Sentinel. "A Look Back at Serial Killer Jeffrey Dahmer through Photos." *Www.jsonline.com*, 23 Sept. 2022, www.jsonline.com/picture-gallery/news/2022/09/23/look-back-milwaukee-serial-killer-jeffrey-dahmer-monster-jeffrey-dahmer-story-ohio/8091203001/.
- Mitchell, Molli. "What Happened to Glenda Cleveland? Woman Who Tried to Stop Jeffrey Dahmer." *Newsweek*, 21 Sept. 2022, www.newsweek.com/glenda-cleveland-jeffrey-dahmer-neighbor-what-happened-1744813.
- Molloy, Dan. "Woman Who Called 911 on Dahmer Reacts to Netflix Series." *Spectrum News*, 30 Sept. 2022, spectrumnews1.com/wi/milwaukee/news/2022/09/30/key-witness-reacts-to-renewed-attention-to-dahmer-case.
- Montesano, Anthony. "Seven's Deadly Screenwriter:Andrew Kevin Walker on His Masterpiece." *Cinefantastique*, vol. 27, no. 6, Feb. 1996, pp. 48–50, archive.org/details/cinefantastique_1970-2002/Cinefantastique%20Vol%2027%20No%206%20%28Feb%201996%29/page/n47/mode/2up.
- Naraharisetty, Rohitha. "What Pop Culture Misunderstands about Serial Killers." *Www.theswaddle.com*, 2 May 2022, www.theswaddle.com/what-pop-culture-misunderstands-about-serial-killers.
- O'Brein, Maureen . "The ""American Psycho"" Controversy." *EW.com*, 8 Mar. 1991, ew.com/article/1991/03/08/american-psycho-controversy/.
- Oates, Joyce Carol. ""I Had No Other Thrill or Happiness" | Joyce Carol Oates." *Www.nybooks.com*, 24 Mar. 1994, www.nybooks.com/articles/1994/03/24/i-had-no-other-thrill-or-happiness/.
- Perry, Tony. "Fugitive's Death Leaves a Trail of Contradictions." Los Angeles Times, 25 July 1997, www.latimes.com/archives/la-xpm-1997-jul-25-mn-16212-story.html.
- Petty, Michael John. "You Have "Se7en" to Thank for the Rise of Faith-Based Horror." *Collider*, 14 Oct. 2022, collider.com/seven-david-fincher-faith-based-horror-movies/.
- Press, From Associated. "Police-Racial Issue Arises in Wake of Mass Murders : Crime: Milwaukee Activists Are Concerned over High Propo." *Los Angeles Times*, 29 July 1991, www.latimes.com/archives/la-xpm-1991-07-29-mn-187-story.html.
- Ramsland, Katherine, and Karen Pepper. "Serial Killer Culture: Art, Souvenirs about Serial Killers - Crime Library - Crime Library on TruTV.com." *Wayback Machine*, 2009, web.archive.org/web/20090601230703/www.trutv.com/library/crime/criminal_mind/psychology/s_k_culture/7.html.
- Rosenblatt, Roger. *Snuff This Book! Will Bret Easton Ellis Get Away with Murder?* The New York Times, 16 Dec. 1990, nytimes.com/1990/12/16/

- books/snuff-this-book-will-bret-easton-ellis-get-away-with-murder.html.
- "Serial Killers Have Piled up Victims in Screen and in Books." *Detroit Free Press*, 28 Aug. 1994, www.newspapers.com/image/98326749/.
- "Shooting Suspect Is from Area." *Asbury Park Press*, 21 Apr. 1993, www.newspapers.com/image/145877220/.
- Slee, Amruta. "Once upon a Time in America." *The Age*, 1 Oct. 1994, www.newspapers.com/image/122968446/.
- Sorrentino, Christopher. ""American Psycho."" *The New York Times*, 20 Jan. 1991, www.nytimes.com/1991/01/20/books/l-american-psycho-956391.html.
- Staff, Wired News. "AOL to Take down Serial-Killer Site." *WIRED*, 12 Sept. 1997, www.wired.com/1997/09/aol-to-take-down-serial-killer-site/.
- Stingl, Jim. "Cleveland Tried to Stop Dahmer from Killing." *Www.jsonline.com*, 4 Jan. 2011, archive.jsonline.com/news/milwaukee/112910479.html.
- Stone, Oliver, director. Natural Born Killers. Warner Bros., 1994.
- Strum, Charles. "Paroled Rapist Charged with Killing 5 Women in New Jersey." *The New York Times*, 14 Apr. 1992, www.nytimes.com/1992/04/14/nyregion/paroled-rapist-charged-with-killing-5-women-in-new-jersey.html.
- Taubin, Amy. "Wolves, Lambs – and Clarice Starling: The Rise of the Serial Killer in 1990s Cinema." *BFI*, 29 Jan. 2021, www.bfi.org.uk/sight-and-sound/features/clarice-starling-rise-movie-serial-killer-twin-peaks-silence-lambs-henry-portrait.
- Terry, Don. "Jeffrey Dahmer, Multiple Killer, Is Bludgeoned to Death in Prison." *The New York Times*, 29 Nov. 1994, www.nytimes.com/1994/11/29/us/jeffrey-dahmer-multiple-killer-is-bludgeoned-to-death-in-prison.html.
- ---. "Serial Murder Case Exposes Deep Milwaukee Tensions." *The New York Times*, 2 Aug. 1991, www.nytimes.com/1991/08/02/us/serial-murder-case-exposes-deep-milwaukee-tensions.html.
- The Associated Press. "Dahmer Apartment Demolition Begins." *The Bulletin*, 17 Nov. 1992, news.google.com/newspapers?id=4BcpAAAAIBAJ&pg=4771.
- Venant, Elizabeth. "An "American Psycho" Drama : Books: The Flap Surrounding Bret Easton Ellis' Third Novel Flares Again. NOW Is Seeking a Boycott of His New Publisher. Other Observers Raise Questions of Censorship." *Los Angeles Times*, 11 Dec. 1990, www.latimes.com/archives/la-xpm-1990-12-11-vw-6308-story.html.
- Walters, Laurel Shaper. "Dahmer Case Unleashes Black Anger in Milwaukee." *Christian Science Monitor*, 16 Aug. 1991, www.csmonitor.com/1991/0816/16041.html.
- Westervelt, Eric. "More People Are Getting Away with Murder. Unsolved Killings Reach a Record High." *NPR*, 30 Apr. 2023, www.npr.org/2023/04/29/1172775448/people-murder-unsolved-killings-record-high.
- Wiest, Julie. *Creating Cultural Monsters: A Critical Analysis of the Creating Cultural Monsters: A Critical Analysis of the Representation of Serial Murderers in America Representation of Serial Murderers in America*. 2009.

Bibliography

90s Halloween
- ""I Could Move in There": When Jane Byrne Moved into Cabrini-Green | Jane Byrne | Chicago Stories." *WTTW Chicago*, 22 Mar. 2022, interactive.wttw.com/chicago-stories/jane-byrne/i-could-move-there-when-jane-byrne-moved-into-cabrini-green.
- "1000 Halloween Arrests in Isla Vista." *The Sacramento Bee*, 2 Nov. 1992, www.newspapers.com/image/626093164/.
- "Acquittal in Doorstep Killing of Japanese Student." *The New York Times*, 24 May 1993, www.nytimes.com/1993/05/24/us/acquittal-in-doorstep-killing-of-japanese-student.html?pagewanted=all.
- Alter, Ethan. "Inside "and Then There Was Shawn," the Scary-Funny "Boy Meets World" Halloween Episode." *Yahoo Entertainment*, 26 Oct. 2016, www.yahoo.com/entertainment/boy-meets-world-halloween-episode-and-then-there-was-shawn-130029292.html.
- "An Oral History of the Infamous "Boy Meets World" Horror Parody Episode." *Hollywood*, 31 Oct. 2012, www.hollywood.com/tv/an-oral-history-of-the-infamous-boy-meets-world-horror-parody-episode-57239771.
- Associated Press. "Michigan Youth Taken for Vandal Fatally Shot." Los Angeles Times, 3 Nov. 1992, www.latimes.com/archives/la-xpm-1992-11-03-mn-1095-story.html.
- Aydin, Diana. "A Halloween Mystery." *Guideposts*, 30 Oct. 2015, guideposts.org/angels-and-miracles/miracles/gods-grace/a-halloween-mystery/.
- "BELLE SUED over HALLOWEEN INCIDENT." *Chicago Tribune*, 6 Jan. 1996, www.chicagotribune.com/1996/01/06/belle-sued-over-halloween-incident/.
- Belle, Albert. "Albert Belle Agrees to Settle a Lawsuit - UPI Archives." *UPI*, 24 Oct. 1997, www.upi.com/Archives/1997/10/24/Albert-Belle-agrees-to-settle-a-lawsuit/6133877665600/.
- "BLACK SLASHER `CANDYMAN` DRAWS FIRE over `RACIST` DEPICTIONS." *Chicago Tribune*, 29 Oct. 1992, www.chicagotribune.com/1992/10/29/black-slasher-candyman-draws-fire-over-racist-depictions/.
- Booth, William. "MAN ACQUITTED of KILLING JAPANESE EXCHANGE STUDENT." *Washington Post*, 24 May 1993, web.archive.org/web/20180305202556/www.washingtonpost.com/archive/politics/1993/05/24/man-acquitted-of-killing-japanese-exchange-student/34a75a09-0a7b-468d-89c5-d6d8d7504f7c/.
- Bragg, Rick. "Psychiatrist for Susan Smith's Defense Tells of a Woman Desperate to Be Liked." *The New York Times*, 22 July 1995, www.nytimes.com/1995/07/22/us/psychiatrist-for-susan-smith-s-defense-tells-of-a-woman-desperate-to-be-liked.html.
- Candyman. Directed by Bernard Rose, TriStar Pictures, 16 Oct. 1992.
- Caprilozzi, Christine. "Twenty Year Retrospective of Candyman with Virginia Madsen." *Horror News Network*, 14 Dec. 2012, www.horrornewsnetwork.net/twenty-year-retrospective-of-candyman-

with-virginia-madsen/.
- Chavez, Tim. "Fine Tuning." *The Daily Oklahoman*, 4 Nov. 1990, www.newspapers.com/image/452470769/.
- "Childhood Pedestrian Deaths during Halloween -- United States, 1975-1996." *Www.cdc.gov*, 24 Oct. 1997, www.cdc.gov/mmwr/preview/mmwrhtml/00049687.htm.
- Cohen, Roger. "Journal: A Treat or U.S. Trick? Whatever, Halloween's Here." *Nyu.edu*, 31 Oct. 1997, pages.stern.nyu.edu/~nroubini/Emu/france-halloween.html.
- "Conundrum at Cornell: Pumpkin's Lofty Perch." *The New York Times*, 27 Oct. 1997, www.nytimes.com/1997/10/27/nyregion/conundrum-at-cornell-pumpkin-s-lofty-perch.html.
- Cooper, Mariah. "Best Halloween TV Episodes of All Time: "Modern Family" and More." *Us Weekly*, 24 Oct. 2024, www.usmagazine.com/entertainment/pictures/best-halloween-tv-episodes-of-all-time-modern-family.
- Cooper, Michael. "Egg Thrown on Halloween Sparks Fatal Fight." *The New York Times*, 2 Nov. 1998, www.nytimes.com/1998/11/02/nyregion/egg-thrown-on-halloween-sparks-fatal-fight.html.
- "Cornell Library's PumpkinCam." *Cornell.edu*, 2017, pumpkin.library.cornell.edu/.
- "Defense Depicts Japanese Boy as "Scary."" *The New York Times*, 21 May 1993, www.nytimes.com/1993/05/21/us/defense-depicts-japanese-boy-as-scary.html.
- Deverell, John. "Bart Simpson and the Turtle Gang Ready to Make Halloween Calls." The Toronto Star, 27 Oct. 1990, www.newspapers.com/image/946125134/.
- Domonoske, Camila. "After 20 Years, Can Cornell Finally Bust Open Its Great Pumpkin Mystery?" *NPR*, 31 Oct. 2017, www.npr.org/sections/thetwo-way/2017/10/31/561217424/after-20-years-can-cornell-finally-bust-open-its-great-pumpkin-mystery.
- "DYING WOMAN MISTAKEN for HALLOWEEN ACT." *Hartford Courant*, 4 Nov. 1997, www.courant.com/1997/11/04/dying-woman-mistaken-for-halloween-act/.
- Ebert, Roger. "Hocus Pocus Movie Review & Film Summary." Https://Www.rogerebert.com/, 16 July 1993, www.rogerebert.com/reviews/hocus-pocus-1993.
- Ewinger, James. "4 to Do Community Work for Belle Egging." *The Plain Dealer*, 6 Apr. 1996, www.newspapers.com/image/1071250047/.
- FLORENCE, MAL. "Belle Is up to Old Tricks on Halloween." *Los Angeles Times*, 2 Nov. 1995, www.latimes.com/archives/la-xpm-1995-11-02-sp-63899-story.html.
- Garvey, Megan. "Tainted Candy No Longer a Halloween Worry." *Los Angeles Times*, 31 Oct. 1998, www.latimes.com/archives/la-xpm-1998-oct-31-mn-37952-story.html.
- George, Carmen. "Hangtree and Spook Lanes in Madera County May Be

Renamed. But Not Everyone Agrees." *Fresno Bee*, 11 July 2020, www.fresnobee.com/news/local/article244101492.html.
- Grace, Julie. "STANDOFF at ROBY RIDGE." *TIME*, nextgen, 27 Oct. 1997, time.com/archive/6731694/standoff-at-roby-ridge/.
- "HALLOWEEN HOOPLA CONVENIENCE, SAFETY CONCERNS LEAD to a NUMBER of CHANGES in TRADITIONAL CELEBRATIONS." *Sun Sentinel*, 24 Oct. 1990, www.sun-sentinel.com/1990/10/24/halloween-hoopla-convenience-safety-concerns-lead-to-a-number-of-changes-in-traditional-celebrations/.
- "HALLOWEEN IS NEARING. TIME to DRESS up as YOUR FAVORITE SERIAL KILLER." *Chicago Tribune*, 20 Oct. 1996, www.chicagotribune.com/1996/10/20/halloween-is-nearing-time-to-dress-up-as-your-favorite-serial-killer/.
- "Halloween Past and Present." *The New York Times*, 17 Nov. 1994, www.nytimes.com/1994/11/17/garden/l-halloween-past-and-present-850543.html.
- "Halloween Seen as Threat to Sacred Mexican Holiday." *Latinamericanstudies.org*, 29 Oct. 1999, www.latinamericanstudies.org/culture/halloween.htm.
- "Halloween's No Treat for Coveted Black Cats." *New York Daily News*, 23 Oct. 1999, www.nydailynews.com/1999/10/23/halloweens-no-treat-for-coveted-black-cats/.
- HEFFLEY, LYNNE. "They're Just in Time for Halloween: Seasonal Treats to Delight Kids." *Los Angeles Times*, 29 Oct. 1998, www.latimes.com/archives/la-xpm-1998-oct-29-ca-37166-story.html.
- "INTERVIEW / the Sweet Smell of Excess: Bernard Rose Has an Oral." *The Independent*, 13 Mar. 1993, www.independent.co.uk/arts-entertainment/interview-the-sweet-smell-of-excess-bernard-rose-has-an-oral-fixation-kevin-jackson-talked-to-him-about-the-appetites-behind-his-new-horror-film-candyman-1497390.html.
- "Isla Vista Quiets after Halloween." *The Lompoc Record*, 1 Nov. 1993, www.newspapers.com/image/540656775/.
- "Japen Warns Its U.S.-Bound Students "Freeze" Means Stop - UPI Archives." *UPI*, 12 June 1993, www.upi.com/Archives/1993/06/12/Japen-warns-its-US-bound-students-freeze-means-stop/6474739857600/.
- Judd, Terry, and Lynne Boezaart. "Years Haven't Healed Wounds." The Muskegon Chronicle, 13 Nov. 1994, https://www.newspapers.com/image/1081799615/.
- Lovell, Glen. "Critics Say Horror Film "Candyman" Mixes Veiled Racism with Fright." *Hartford Courant*, 7 Nov. 1992, www.newspapers.com/image/242166202/.
- Manjoo, Farhad. "How the Pumpkin Got on the Tower." *Github.io*, 2025, cornelldailysun.github.io/pumpkin-feature/.
- Marriott, Laura. "Welcoming the Mayor to Hell | the Story of Jane Byrne and Cabrini Green." *HeadStuff*, 15 Jan. 2017, headstuff.org/culture/history/cabrini-green-mayor-jane-byrne/.

- Milke, Jean, and Patricia Miller. "Hayride Reopens as Victim Mourned." *Asbury Park Press*, 27 Oct. 1990, www.newspapers.com/image/148217717/.
- Morgenstern, Roger, et al. "Sentence in Slaying : Two Years or Less." The Muskegon Chronicle, 18 Mar. 1993, www.newspapers.com/image/1081424942/.
- Mura, Bob. "Suit over Accidental Hanging Settled." *Asbury Park Press*, 18 June 1994, p. 4.
- Musgrave, Paul. "The Politics of Trunk or Treat." *Substack.com*, Systematic Hatreds, 31 Oct. 2023, musgrave.substack.com/p/the-politics-of-trunk-or-treat.
- Narcisse, Evan. ""Candyman": Why This Racially Charged Horror Movie Is Scarier than Ever." *Rolling Stone*, 31 Oct. 2018, www.rollingstone.com/tv-movies/tv-movie-features/why-candyman-is-scarier-than-ever-749776/.
- "NATION : Teen Dies in Halloween Accident." *Los Angeles Times*, 29 Oct. 1990, www.latimes.com/archives/la-xpm-1990-10-29-mn-2730-story.html.
- Nichols, Peter M. "Home Video; Fall Zombies and Ghosts." *The New York Times*, 18 Sept. 1998, www.nytimes.com/1998/09/18/movies/home-video-fall-zombies-and-ghosts.html.
- Pandell, Lexi. ""The Biggest College Party in California": A History of Isla Vista's Halloween." *The Daily Nexus | the University of California, Santa Barbara's Independent, Student-Run Newspaper.*, 25 Oct. 2010, dailynexus.com/2010-10-25/biggest-college-party-california-history-isla-vistas-halloween/.
- ---. "The Biggest College Party in California: A History of Isla Vista's Halloween Pt. 2." *The Daily Nexus | the University of California, Santa Barbara's Independent, Student-Run Newspaper.*, 26 Oct. 2010, dailynexus.com/2010-10-26/biggest-college-party-california-history-isla-vistas-halloween-pt-2/.
- "PICK 3 TURNS up 666 on HALLOWEEN." *Chicago Tribune*, 1 Nov. 1996, www.chicagotribune.com/1996/11/01/pick-3-turns-up-666-on-halloween/.
- "Playing the Bart: It's a Simpsons Halloween." Daily News, 24 Oct. 1990, www.newspapers.com/image/466802574/.
- "Prank Leads to Accidental Shot and a Teenager Is Dead." *Tampa Bay Times*, 12 Oct. 2005, www.tampabay.com/archive/1992/11/26/prank-leads-to-accidental-shot-and-a-teenager-is-dead/.
- ""Roby Ridge."" WIRED, 31 Oct. 1997, www.wired.com/1997/10/roby-ridge/.
- Rose, Bernard, director. Candyman. TriStar Pictures, 1992
- Ruane, Michael. "Fears Prompt Shelters to Suspend Cat Adoptions for Halloween." *Washingtonpost.com*, 27 Oct. 1997, www.washingtonpost.com/wp-srv/local/daily/oct99/cats27.htm.
- Rubenstein, Carin. "PARENT & CHILD; Halloween: A Big Boom in Boos." *The New York Times*, 27 Oct. 1994, www.nytimes.com/1994/10/27/garden/parent-child-halloween-a-big-boom-in-boos.html.
- Scheer, Robert. "The River of Hypocrisy Runs Wide and Deep : The Smith Case Is Remarkable, Too, for Its Rank Immorality." *Los Angeles Times*, Aug. 1995, www.latimes.com/archives/la-xpm-1995-08-01-me-30101-story.html.

Bibliography

- Steinberg, Jacques. "Fed by Rumors, Fears of Gangs Keep Pupils Home on Halloween." *The New York Times*, 1 Nov. 1997, www.nytimes.com/1997/11/01/nyregion/fed-by-rumors-fears-of-gangs-keep-pupils-home-on-halloween.html.
- "TEEN WHO POSED as VICTIM of HANGING IS FOUND DEAD." *Orlando Sentinel*, 23 Oct. 1990, www.orlandosentinel.com/1990/10/23/teen-who-posed-as-victim-of-hanging-is-foun.
- "Temporary Retailers Fight over Space as Holidays Approach ." *The Seattle Times*, 22 Oct. 2000, archive.seattletimes.com/archive/?date=20001022&slug=4049449.
- The Associated Press. "15 Year Old Dies in Halloween Gag." *The Island Packet*, 29 Oct. 1990, www.newspapers.com/image/840659750/.
- ---. "Cocaine-Laced Treat Sends Kid to Hospital." *The Odessa American*, 2 Nov. 1996.
- ---. "Teen-Agers Win Prizes for K.K.K Costumes." *The New York Times*, 31 Oct. 1993, www.nytimes.com/1993/10/31/us/teen-agers-win-prizes-for-kkk-costumes.html.
- Tucker, Cynthia. "A Tragic Shooting No Slogan Explains." *Sarasota Herald-Tribune*, 29 May 1993, obits.theadvocate.com/us/obituaries/theadvocate/name/webb-haymaker-obituary?id=33656123.
- UPI. "More Simpson "Merchandising" ." Sentinel Tribune, 25 Oct. 1990, www.newspapers.com/image/922194295/.
- WAX, ROBERTA G. "Halloween's Big Business at Boo-Tiques." *Los Angeles Times*, 24 Oct. 2000, www.latimes.com/archives/la-xpm-2000-oct-24-me-41250-story.html.
- Weakley, Teresa. "#AdamsAct: Grand Haven Family Turns Grief during Halloween into Kindness Challenge." Wood TV, 7 Oct. 2022, www.woodtv.com/news/ottawa-county/adamsact-grand-haven-family-turns-grief-during-halloween-into-kindness-challenge/.
- Wilson, Marshall. "Loose Mask, Not Drugs, Caused Boy to Pass Out." *SFGATE*, 2 Nov. 1996, www.sfgate.com/bayarea/article/loose-mask-not-drugs-caused-boy-to-pass-out-2960925.php.
- WOODYARD, CHRIS. "Universal Has Frightful Plans : Halloween: Studio/Park's Horror Nights Will Compete with Knott's Scary Farm." *Los Angeles Times*, 15 Sept. 1992, www.latimes.com/archives/la-xpm-1992-09-15-fi-758-story.html.

Boy Meets World
- Aguiton, Rafael Motamayor. "Dinosaurs: The Making of TV's Saddest, Strangest Sitcom Finale." *Vulture*, 7 Aug. 2018, www.vulture.com/2018/08/dinosaurs-tvs-saddest-sitcom-finale.html.
- Boy Meets World. Created by Michael Jacobs, ABC Productions, 1993–2000. University of Wisconsin–Madison.
- Davis, Madison. "The Surprisingly Conservative Core of Boy Meets World." *Episodes*, 22 Sept. 2021, episodes.ghost.io/boy-meets-world-conservative-angela/.

- Davis, Trina McGee. "Trina's Tweets." *Twitter*, 12 Jan. 2020, x.com/realtrinamcgee/status/1216319034842468352?ref=episodes.ghost.io.
- ---. "TV Can Help World Erase Color Lines." *Los Angeles Times*, 22 Feb. 1999, www.latimes.com/archives/la-xpm-1999-feb-22-ca-10422-story.html?ref=episodes.ghost.io.
- Forward, Devon. ""Boy Meets World" Cast Recalls "Damaging" Set Environment on Sitcom." *Parade*, 22 July 2022, parade.com/news/boy-meets-world-cast-recalls-damaging-set-environment-showrunner.
- Kupfer, Lindsey. ""Boy Meets World" Creator Reveals Why Shawn and Angela Couldn't End up Together." *Page Six*, 15 June 2018, pagesix.com/2018/06/15/boy-meets-world-creator-reveals-why-shawn-and-angela-couldnt-end-up-together/?ref=episodes.ghost.io.
- Perkins, Ken Parish. "Boy Meets World Has Cute Kid Charm." *The Huntsville Times*, 23 Sept. 1993, www.newspapers.com/image/1186348465/.
- Rowles, Dustin. "Revisiting "the Wonder Years" Sexual Harassment Lawsuit during the MeToo Movement." *Pajiba*, 29 Jan. 2018, www.pajiba.com/tv_reviews/whats-the-deal-with-the-the-wonder-years-sexual-harassment-lawsuit.php.
- Schildhause, Chloe. ""Dream, Try, Do Good": The Oral History of "Boy Meets World."" *UPROXX*, 31 Jan. 2017, uproxx.com/tv/boy-meets-world-oral-history/.
- Soteriou, Stephanie. ""Boy Meets World's" Rider Strong Was "Very Upset" Filming Banned Ep." *BuzzFeed News*, 3 Nov. 2022, www.buzzfeednews.com/article/stephaniesoteriou/boy-meets-world-rider-strong-upset-irresponsible-sex.
- ---. "The "Boy Meets World" Cast Addressed Trina McGee's Racism Accusations." *BuzzFeed News*, 16 Aug. 2022, www.buzzfeednews.com/article/stephaniesoteriou/boy-meets-worlds-will-friedle-racism-trina-mcgee.
- ---. "The Cast of "Boy Meets World" on Their "Unhealthy" Experiences on Set." *BuzzFeed News*, 12 Aug. 2022, www.buzzfeednews.com/article/stephaniesoteriou/boy-meets-world-uncomfortable-kissing-child-actors?bfsource=relatedmanual.
- Spencer, Ashley. "What Happened to Rider Strong?" *VICE*, 21 Aug. 2019, www.vice.com/en/article/where-is-boy-meets-worlds-rider-strong-now-2019/.
- Stone, Jamie. *Acting like a Kid*. 21 Sept. 1999, www.newspapers.com/image/238954165/?clipping_id=172127782&fcfToken=eyJhbGciOiJIUzI1NiIsInR5cCI6IkpXVCJ9.eyJmcmVlLXZpZXctaWQiOjIzODk1NDE2NSwiaWF0IjoxNzUzMzMxMzUwLCJleHAiOjE3NTM0MTc3NTB9.feDR4G5fZZ2JmsK9rSrQdMm_92zUdOS1zSWwgY3OGWM.
- Trbovich, Tom. Dinosaurs: Changing Nature. ABC, 20 July 1994.
- Wilson, Margo. "Visit the "World" of an 11-Year-Old Boy." *The San Bernardino County Sun*, 24 Sept. 1993, www.newspapers.com/image/81128661/.

90s Christmas
- 6HailMarys. "Tickle Me Elmo Stunt News Coverage." YouTube, KHTY, 21 Apr. 2012, www.youtube.com/watch?v=qnqP66KmfLE.

Bibliography

- "'Santa Clause' Has a Line That Could Invite Trouble | the Seattle Times." *Seattletimes.com*, 19 Oct. 1997, archive.seattletimes.com/archive/?date=19971019&slug=2566882.
- Baca, Maria Elena. "Desperate Shoppers Not Laughing at Tickle Me Elmo." *Archive.org*, Star Tribune (Minneapolis, MN), 10 Dec. 1996, web.archive.org/web/20140714113343/www.highbeam.com/doc/1G1-62644967.html.
- Barry, Dan. "A Christmas Tale of the Gottis and Tickle Me Elmo." *The New York Times*, 18 Dec. 1996, www.nytimes.com/1996/12/18/nyregion/a-christmas-tale-of-the-gottis-and-tickle-me-elmo.html.
- Brandon, Karen. "Office Christmas Party Evolving." *Tulsa World*, 7 Dec. 1993, www.newspapers.com/image/893477920/.
- CBC. "The Tickle Me Elmo Craze That Caused a Walmart Employee to Get Trampled, 1996." YouTube, 25 Dec. 2018, www.youtube.com/watch?v=-ajNOP1UvPU.
- Chatelain, Marcia. "American Historian, Meet American Girl | ." *Perspectives on History | AHA*, Dec. 2015, www.historians.org/perspectives-article/american-historian-meet-american-girl-december-2015/.
- DeChick, Joe. ""Home" Also a Success in Stores." *The Cincinnati Enquirer*, 30 Nov. 1992, www.newspapers.com/image/102017215/.
- Delgado, Michelle. "Keeping Tamagotchi Alive." *Smithsonian Magazine*, 22 Dec. 2021, www.smithsonianmag.com/innovation/keeping-tamagotchi-alive-180979264/.
- GOLDBERG, CAREY. "A Russian Christmas--Better Late than Never : Soviet Union: Orthodox Church Celebration Is the First under Co." *Los Angeles Times*, 7 Jan. 1991, www.latimes.com/archives/la-xpm-1991-01-07-mn-5892-story.html.
- Hansell, Saul. "Amazon's Risky Christmas." *The New York Times*, 28 Nov. 1999, www.nytimes.com/1999/11/28/business/amazon-s-risky-christmas.html.
- ---. "Toys "R" Us Falls behind on Shipping." *The New York Times*, 23 Dec. 1999, www.nytimes.com/1999/12/23/business/toys-r-us-falls-behind-on-shipping.html.
- Henry, James S. "Why I Hate Christmas." *The New Republic*, 31 Dec. 1990, newrepublic.com/article/115994/reasons-why-christmas-terrible-holiday.
- Jesse Coffey. "THE ROSIE O'DONNELL SHOW Clip - Do the Elmo! (1996)." YouTube, 30 Sept. 2018, www.youtube.com/watch?v=3y8tqRVQYso.
- "Just Tickled." *People*, 13 Jan. 1997, people.com/archive/just-tickled-vol-47-no-1/.
- Kalicka, Abby. "An inside Look at Oprah's Favorite Things through the Years." *Oprah Daily*, 13 Nov. 2020, www.oprahdaily.com/life/a34619475/oprahs-favorite-things-through-the-years/.
- "KKK to Erect Cross on Cincinnati Square." *Tampa Bay Times*, 21 Dec. 1992, www.tampabay.com/archive/1992/12/21/kkk-to-erect-cross-on-cincinnati-square/.
- "Klan-Erected Cross Is Knocked Down." *The Los Angeles Times*, 12 Dec. 1992, www.newspapers.com/image/177409285/.
- Lacter, Mark. "Office Christmas Parties Just Aren't the Same." *Santa Cruz Sentinel*, 5 Dec. 1992, www.newspapers.com/image/71408524/.
- McDougall, Deborah. "Surviving the Office Christmas Party: Career and Reputation Could Go down the Drain." *The Windsor Star*, 5 Dec. 1991,

www.newspapers.com/image/503700152/.
- Mistry, Priyansha. "THE EVOLUTION of OFFICE CHRISTMAS PARTY: From Outlandish, Drunken Mixers to a Somber, Unhurried Affair." *The HR Digest*, Dec. 2017, www.thehrdigest.com/evolution-office-christmas-parties-outlandish-drunken-mixers-somber-unhurried-affair/.
- Noble, Greg. "From the Vault: Ku Klux Klan Erected Cross on Cincinnati's Fountain Square in 1992." *WCPO 9 Cincinnati*, 24 Aug. 2017, www.wcpo.com/news/our-community/from-the-vault/from-the-vault-ku-klux-klan-erects-cross-on-cincinnatis-fountain-square-in-1992.
- Porter, Connie. "Addy Joins American Girl Doll Lineup." *Wisconsin State Journal*, 7 Sept. 1993, www.newspapers.com/image/406418469/.
- Press, The Associated. "Klan's Christmas Cross Is Quickly Torn Down." *The New York Times*, 22 Dec. 1992, www.nytimes.com/1992/12/22/us/klan-s-christmas-cross-is-quickly-torn-down.html.
- Reuters. "Christmas Is Put Back in Cuba, This Once." *The New York Times*, 15 Dec. 1997, www.nytimes.com/1997/12/15/world/christmas-is-put-back-in-cuba-this-once.html.
- ---.""Christmas Story" Still a Hit with Cable Viewers." Reuters, 31 Dec. 2007, www.reuters.com/article/lifestyle/christmas-story-still-a-hit-with-cable-viewers-idUSN31537193/.
- Rosenfeld, Megan. "WHOLESOME BABES in TOYLAND." *The Washington Post*, 24 May 1993, www.washingtonpost.com/archive/lifestyle/1993/05/24/wholesome-babes-in-toyland/b4ed92ca-1571-4ec9-9290-4dfb4ded0b7b/.
- Sanchez, Gabriel H. "This Is What Christmas Shopping Looked like in the '90s." *BuzzFeed News*, 3 Dec. 2018, www.buzzfeednews.com/article/gabrielsanchez/this-is-what-christmas-shopping-looked-like-in-the-90s.
- Scheier, Rachel, and Nancy Dillon. "Toysrus.complaints." *Daily News*, 24 Dec. 1999, www.newspapers.com/image/479744210/.
- Silsby, Gillen. "Only 79 Shopping Days..." *Monrovia News-Post*, 7 Oct. 1990, www.newspapers.com/image/606354028.
- Sheldon, Jeff. "A Brief History of the "24 Hours of a Christmas Story" Marathon ." The Retro Network, 22 Dec. 2020, theretronetwork.com/a-brief-history-of-the-24-hours-of-a-christmas-story-marathon/.
- Stanley, Alessandra. "Recession Darkens Christmas Shopping Spirit." *The New York Times*, 17 Dec. 1990, www.nytimes.com/1990/12/17/nyregion/recession-darkens-christmas-shopping-spirit.html.
- Weiss, Joanna M. "Is Santa Claus a Jew? | Opinion | the Harvard Crimson." Thecrimson.com, 15 Dec. 1990, www.thecrimson.com/article/1990/12/15/is-santa-claus-a-jew-pbib/.

On Moesha
- BANKS, SANDY. "Middle-Class Blacks Feel Sense of Betrayal." *Los Angeles Times*, 3 May 1992, www.latimes.com/archives/la-xpm-1992-05-03-mn-1946-story.html.
- Braxton, Greg. "Co-Creator of TV Hit "Moesha" Fired." *Los Angeles Times*, 2 Dec. 1999, www.latimes.com/archives/la-xpm-1999-dec-02-fi-39659-story.html.
- ---. "UPN Will Try to Widen Its Appeal." *Los Angeles Times*, 10 Dec. 1997, www.latimes.com/archives/la-xpm-1997-dec-10-ca-62364-story.html.
- Brown, Evan Nicole. "How UPN Ushered in a Golden Decade of Black TV

- — and Then Was Merged out of Existence." *The Hollywood Reporter*, 16 Feb. 2022, www.hollywoodreporter.com/tv/tv-features/upn-black-tv-the-wb-moesha-the-parkers-1235091212/.
- Carter, Kelley L. "On TV, a Fledgling UPN Tried to Follow NBC and Fox with Black Programming." *Andscape*, 14 May 2020, andscape.com/features/on-tv-a-fledgling-upn-tried-to-follow-nbc-and-fox-with-black-programming/.
- GARDNER, ELYSA. "Next from the Diva Machine." *Los Angeles Times*, 7 July 1998, www.latimes.com/archives/la-xpm-1998-jul-07-ca-1304-story.html.
- Gerston, Jill. "COVER STORY;Brandy, Pop Star, Plays a Teen-Ager, Though Not Just Any Teen-Ager." *The New York Times*, 11 Feb. 1996, www.nytimes.com/1996/02/11/tv/cover-story-brandy-pop-star-plays-a-teen-ager-though-not-just-any-teen-ager.html?pagewanted=2.
- Giorgis, Hannah. "Most Hollywood Writers' Rooms Look Nothing like America." *The Atlantic*, 13 Sept. 2021, www.theatlantic.com/magazine/archive/2021/10/the-unwritten-rules-of-black-tv/619816/.
- Gold, Jonathan. "Day of the Dre." *Rolling Stone*, 30 Sept. 1993, www.rollingstone.com/music/music-news/day-of-the-dre-97921/.
- https://www.pbssocal.org/people/josh-sides. "The Center Can Hold: Leimert Park and Black Los Angeles." *PBS SoCal*, 12 Nov. 2013, www.pbssocal.org/shows/departures/the-center-can-hold-leimert-park-and-black-los-angeles.
- James, Kendra. "It's Possible: An Oral History of 1997'S "Cinderella."" *Shondaland*, 2 Nov. 2017, www.shondaland.com/inspire/a13138172/brandy-whitney-houston-oral-history-cinderella/.
- Johnson, Steve. "CHEERS for BRANDY." *Chicago Tribune*, 23 Aug. 1999, www.chicagotribune.com/1999/08/23/cheers-for-brandy/.
- Kaplan, Don. ""MOESHA" FIRES CREATOR ; BRANDY OUSTS HER, WINS BID to SHIFT HIT'S DIRECTION." *New York Post*, 7 Dec. 1999, nypost.com/1999/12/07/moesha-fires-creator-brandy-ousts-her-wins-bid-to-shift-hits-direction/.
- Max, Daniel. "McMillan's Millions." *The New York Times*, 9 Aug. 1992, www.nytimes.com/1992/08/09/magazine/mcmillan-s-millions.html.
- Mifflin, Lawrie. "TELEVISION/RADIO; UPN's "Moesha," the Nonwhite Hit Nobody Knows." *The New York Times*, 26 Sept. 1999, www.nytimes.com/1999/09/26/arts/television-radio-upn-s-moesha-the-nonwhite-hit-nobody-knows.html?auth=login-google1tap&login=google1tap.
- Moesha. Created by Ralph Farquhar, Sara V. Finney, and Vida Spears, Big Deal Productions / Saradipity Productions / Jump Street Productions, 1996-2001
- Moretti, M Mindy. "TEEN POP STAR IS WELL-TUNED to MOESHA'." *The Washington Post*, 19 May 1996, www.washingtonpost.com/archive/lifestyle/tv/1996/05/19/teen-pop-star-is-well-tuned-to-moesha/b43a6476-f090-47f9-90ad-cb2d5850621b/.
- Perkins, Ken Parish. ""Moesha" Has Suffered but Its Still a Rare Comedy." *Star Tribune*, 5 Jan. 1999, www.newspapers.com/image/194625383/.
- Samuels, Anita M. "UP and COMING: Brandy; at 16, Her Debut Is a Sweet Success." *The New York Times*, 2 Apr. 1995, www.nytimes.com/1995/04/02/

- arts/up-and-coming-brandy-at-16-her-debut-is-a-sweet-success.html.
- "Singer Brandy Turns Actress in New Tv Series "Moesha."" *Jet*, 26 Feb. 1996, pp. 58–62.
- Smith, Erika D. "How to Win the Fight against Gentrification in Leimert Park." *Los Angeles Times*, 27 June 2023, www.latimes.com/california/story/2023-06-27/leimert-park-gentrification-land-trust-black-cultural-destination.
- Sonksen, Mike. "The History of South Central Los Angeles and Its Struggle with Gentrification." *PBS SoCal*, 14 Sept. 2017, www.pbssocal.org/shows/city-rising/the-history-of-south-central-los-angeles-and-its-struggle-with-gentrification.
- "The Myth of Cinderella." *Newsweek*, 3 Nov. 1997, www.newsweek.com/myth-cinderella-171266.
- Tucker, Ken. "Moesha." *Entertainment Weekly*, 19 Apr. 1996, ew.com/article/1996/04/19/moesha/.
- Weiner, Jennifer. "A Star Is Born." Anderson Independent-Mail, 2 Aug. 1995, www.newspapers.com/image/812586295/.

90s Style

- "A Closer Look at Gaultier's Fifth Element Costume Design." *Dazed*, 1 May 2017, www.dazeddigital.com/fashion/article/35459/1/a-closer-look-at-gaultiers-fifth-element-costume-design.
- "A Good Hair Day : Prosecutor Marcia Clark Sheds Curls for a New Look." *Los Angeles Times*, 12 Apr. 1995, www.latimes.com/archives/la-xpm-1995-04-12-mn-53816-story.html.
- Adams, Lorraine. "THE FIGHT of HER LIFE." *Washington Post*, 20 Aug. 1995, www.washingtonpost.com/archive/lifestyle/1995/08/20/the-fight-of-her-life/bc1c8614-336d-4bc5-858c-9cd1b618d405/.
- Allaire, Christian. "How Jawbreaker Delivered Epic Fashions with a Tiny Costume Budget." *Vogue*, 20 Feb. 2024, www.vogue.com/article/jawbreaker-director-costume-designer-interview.
- Anderson, Lisa. '90s America Trying so Hard to Recreate Its Fantasy of the '50s from TV to Fashion, Nation Embracing Ideas It Perceives as Representing a Simpler Time, Trend Watchers Say. The Spokesman-Review, 2 Mar. 1995, www.spokesman.com/stories/1995/mar/02/90s-america-trying-so-hard-to-recreate-its/.
- Barmash, Isadore. "Gap Finds Middle Road to Success." The New York Times, 24 June 1991, www.nytimes.com/1991/06/24/business/gap-finds-middle-road-to-success.html.
- Barrientos, Tanya. "The "Rachel" Is a Cut above the Rest of the Dos." *Anderson Independent-Mail*, 13 Oct. 1995, www.newspapers.com/image/813710577/.
- "BATH & BODY WORKS: "the McDONALD'S of TOILETRIES."" *Web.archive.org*, 4 Aug. 1997, web.archive.org/web/20130527131053/www.businessweek.com/1997/31/b353898.htm.
- Bernstein, Joseph. "Cool Tribal Tattoo. Is It from the '90s?" *The New York Times*, 19 May 2023, www.nytimes.com/2023/05/19/style/tribal-tattoo-90s.html.
- Borrelli-Persson, Laird. "Sarah Jessica Parker Narrates the History of 1990s Fashion in Vogue." *Vogue*, 18 Dec. 2017, www.vogue.com/article/vogue-125-video-fashion-history-sarah-jessica-parker-1990s.

Bibliography

- Brooke, Eliza. "The Eternal Life of the '90s Supermodel." *The New York Times*, 1 Nov. 2023, www.nytimes.com/2023/11/01/magazine/the-supermodels-show.html.
- Capuzzo, Mike. "Fabio Fever." *Southern Illinoisan*, 21 Nov. 1993, www.newspapers.com/image/82474899/.
- Carlin, Shannon. "25 Years after Felicity, It's Time to Revisit TV's Most Infamous Haircut." *TIME*, Time, 29 Sept. 2023, time.com/6318711/felicity-haircut-25-years-premiere/.
- Century, Douglas. "VIEW; Not so Fly (for This White Guy)." *The New York Times*, 31 Jan. 1999, www.nytimes.com/1999/01/31/style/view-not-so-fly-for-this-white-guy.html.
- Cerini, Marianna. "1990s Fashion: A Brief History of What We Wore." *CNN*, 29 Apr. 2020, www.cnn.com/style/article/1990s-fashion-history/index.html.
- "COLORED with CONTROVERSY." *Washington Post*, 13 Feb. 1992, www.washingtonpost.com/archive/lifestyle/1992/02/13/colored-with-controversy/a362eee9-385b-421c-9943-e2dcd8f33fdc/.
- "Courtney Love Comes out of Hiding." *EW.com*, 12 Aug. 1994, ew.com/article/1994/08/12/courtney-love-comes-out-hiding/.
- Davis, Angela Y. "Afro Images: Politics, Fashion, and Nostalgia." Critical Inquiry, vol. 21, no. 1, 1994, pp. 37–45, www.jstor.org/stable/1343885.
- Debroy, Pritha. "Breaking Barriers: Dennis Rodman?S Style Evolution in the 90s." *EssentiallySports*, Oct. 2023, www.essentiallysports.com/category/nba/nba-legends-basketball-news-breaking-barriers-dennis-rodmans-style-evolution-in-the-nineties/.
- Denizet-Lewis, Benoit. "The Man behind Abercrombie & Fitch." *Salon*, Salon.com, 24 Jan. 2006, www.salon.com/2006/01/24/jeffries/.
- Du Lac, J. Freedom. "Abercrombie and Fitch Benefits from Top 40 Hit." *Daily Press*, 17 Sept. 1999, www.newspapers.com/image/237710182/.
- EHRMAN, MARK. "Baby's Night Out." *Los Angeles Times*, 2 Jan. 1997, www.latimes.com/archives/la-xpm-1997-01-02-ls-14776-story.html.
- "Everything You Need to Know about Supreme (2019)." *Shredz Shop Skate*, 2019, shredzshop.com/blogs/news/everything-you-need-to-know-about-supreme-2019.
- Gallagher, Brenden. "How Gap Ruled the '90s." *Grailed*, 1 Sept. 2017, www.grailed.com/drycleanonly/gap-in-the-90s.
- "Gap Launches Old Navy Clothing Co. In Brick Township." *Asbury Park Press*, 6 Oct. 1994, www.newspapers.com/image/148246210/.
- Givhan, Robin. "Paula Jones's About-Face." *Washington Post*, 16 Jan. 1998, www.washingtonpost.com/wp-srv/politics/special/pjones/stories/pj011698.htm.
- Goldman, Andrew. "Atoosa, Former High School Loser, Is Hearst's New Cosmogirl Queen." *Observer*, 14 Feb. 2000, observer.com/2000/02/atoosa-former-high-school-loser-is-hearsts-new-cosmogirl-queen/.
- Gonzalez, Xochitl. "Hip-Hop's Midlife Slump." *The Atlantic*, 3 July 2023, www.theatlantic.com/ideas/archive/2023/07/hip-hop-mainstream-evolution-puff-daddy-hamptons-white-party/674725/.
- Greenhouse, Steven. "Abercrombie & Fitch Bias Case Is Settled." *The New York Times*, 17 Nov. 2004, www.nytimes.com/2004/11/17/us/abercrombie-fitch-bias-case-is-settled.html.

- gscott2012. "Icons of Photography: Bruce Weber." *The United Nations of Photography*, 5 Feb. 2021, unitednationsofphotography.com/2021/02/05/icons-of-photography-bruce-weber/.
- Hall, Trish. "Piercing Fad Is Turning Convention on Its Ear." *The New York Times*, 19 May 1991, www.nytimes.com/1991/05/19/news/piercing-fad-is-turning-convention-on-its-ear.html.
- Hargrove, Channing. "In the History of Hip-Hop Fashion, There's No Ignoring Lil' Kim." *Andscape*, 6 Mar. 2023, andscape.com/features/in-the-history-of-hip-hop-fashion-theres-no-ignoring-lil-kim/.
- Harman, Justine. "Why That Outfit: Corey Mason's Mohair and Plaid in "Empire Records."" *ELLE*, Oct. 2014, www.elle.com/culture/movies-tv/news/a15506/liv-tyler-fashion-empire-records/.
- Harris, James. "From Nike to Nautica, Here Are the 90s Brands That Defined the Decade." *Complex*, 12 Jan. 2022, www.complex.com/style/a/james-harris/the-best-brands-of-the-90s.
- Harrison, Barbara Grizzuti. "Spike Lee Hates Your Cracker Ass." *Esquire*, Oct. 1992, www.esquire.com/news-politics/a20809/spike-lee-1092/.
- Hass, Nancy. ""Sex" Sells, in the City and Elsewhere." *The New York Times*, 11 July 1999, www.nytimes.com/1999/07/11/style/sex-sells-in-the-city-and-elsewhere.html.
- Hassell, Greg. "Retailer Tries Warehousing on for Size." The Houston Chronicle, 11 Aug. 1993, www.newspapers.com/image/1207484230/.
- Hayt, Elizabeth. "For Her: It's a Handbag Moment." *The New York Times*, 18 July 1999, www.nytimes.com/1999/07/18/style/for-her-it-s-a-handbag-moment.html.
- Heckerling, Amy. Clueless. Paramount Pictures, 1995. • Helmore, Edward. ""Heroin Chic" and the Tangled Legacy of Photographer Davide Sorrenti." *The Guardian*, The Guardian, 24 May 2019, www.theguardian.com/fashion/2019/may/23/heroin-chic-and-the-tangled-legacy-of-photographer-davide-sorrenti.
- "Hemlines Play Rising Role on "McBeal" Television: Thigh-High Skirts on the Popular Fox Show Drive a Plot Twist That Lands the Title Character in Hot Water." *Baltimore Sun*, 15 Oct. 1998, www.baltimoresun.com/1998/10/15/hemlines-play-rising-role-on-mcbeal-television-thigh-high-skirts-on-the-popular-fox-show-drive-a-plot-twist-that-lands-the-title-character-in-hot-water/.
- Hlavaty, Craig. "Tupac Shakur Got His Iconic "Thug Life" Tattoo in Houston." *Chron*, 12 Sept. 2017, www.chron.com/culture/celebrities/article/Tupac-Shakur-got-his-iconic-Thug-Life-tattoo-in-12191938.phpjustin.
- Holmlund, Marcus. "Intimate Photos of '90s Hip-Hop's Biggest Stars, from the Woman Who Styled Them." *The New York Times*, 19 May 2016, www.nytimes.com/2016/05/19/t-magazine/entertainment/90s-hip-hop-stylist-misa-hylton.html.
- Hope, Clover. "The Meaning of Lil' Kim." *Pitchfork*, 25 Jan. 2021, pitchfork.com/thepitch/the-meaning-of-lil-kim-motherlode-book/.
- hooks, bell. "bell hooks Goes on the down Low with Lil' Kim." PAPER Magazine, May 1997, www.papermag.com/lil-kim-bell-hooks-cover.
- "Jewelry of the 1990s." *My Jewelry Repair*, 2 Nov. 2023, myjewelryrepair.com/2023/11/1990s-jewelry/.
- Judson, George. "Uncool in School: Dress Code Debate." *The New York*

Bibliography

- *Times*, 5 Oct. 1995, www.nytimes.com/1995/10/05/nyregion/uncool-in-school-dress-code-debate.html.
- Keeps, David A. "POP VIEW; How RuPaul Ups the Ante for Drag." *The New York Times*, 11 July 1993, www.nytimes.com/1993/07/11/archives/pop-view-how-rupaul-ups-the-ante-for-drag.html.
- Killen, Rob. *the Achilles' Heel of Dress Codes: The Definition of Proper Attire the Achilles' Heel of Dress Codes*. Tulsa Law Review, 2000.
- KRIER, BETH ANN. "FASHION : Tapping into an Appetite for Hip Apparel, the Chain Offers Designer Knockoffs and Moderate Price Ta." *Los Angeles Times*, 12 June 1992, www.latimes.com/archives/la-xpm-1992-06-12-vw-262-story.html.
- Kuczynski, Alex. "Trading on Hollywood Magic; Celebrities Push Models off Women's Magazine Covers." *The New York Times*, 30 Jan. 1999, www.nytimes.com/1999/01/30/business/trading-on-hollywood-magic-celebrities-push-models-off-women-s-magazine-covers.html.
- LACHER, IRENE. "Fabio Inc. : A Touch of Talent, a Heap of Hype: He's Not Just a Hunk, He's a Conglomerate." *Los Angeles Times*, 19 Nov. 1993, www.latimes.com/archives/la-xpm-1993-11-19-vw-58639-story.html.
- Lakshmi Gopalkrishnan. "Dirty Linen." *Slate Magazine*, Slate, 11 Apr. 1997, slate.com/culture/1997/04/dirty-linen.html.
- LFO. Summer Girls. Arista, 29 June 1999.
- "Lil Kim Zone-Exclusive Photos of Kim's Abercrombie & Fitch Quarterly Magazine Shoot, 1999." *Lil Kim Zone*, 24 June 2015, www.tapatalk.com/groups/lil_kim_zone/exclusive-photos-of-kim-39-s-abercrombie-fitch-qua-t15899-s40.html.
- Lodi, Marie. "14 Fashion Facts from the 1996 Film "Romeo + Juliet."" *Nylon*, 17 Nov. 2021, www.nylon.com/fashion/romeo-and-juliet-costumes-1996-fashion.
- ---. "How 'Spice World"S Costume Designer Nailed the "Scooby-Doo on Acid" Look." *Nylon*, 20 Feb. 2024, www.nylon.com/fashion/spice-world-fashion-25-anniversary.
- ---. "This Trail-Blazing Female Rapper Has Had the Most Memorable Red Carpet Moments Ever." *The Zoe Report*, 9 Aug. 2023, www.thezoereport.com/culture/lil-kim-fashion.
- London, Lela. "Clueless Designer Mona May Proves Iconic Costume Design Pays off in Hollywood." *Forbes*, 15 Mar. 2021, www.forbes.com/sites/lelalondon/2021/03/15/clueless-mona-may-proves-iconic-costume-design-pays-off-in-hollywood/?sh=16c68254e44e.
- Malone, Maurice. *Designing Men: Maurice Malone's Impact on 90s Hip-Hop Fashion and Urban Mainstream Raise*. 22 Jan. 1999, mauricemaloneusa.com/blogs/news/90s-urban-hip-hop-fashion-designers.
- Marin, Rick. "Grunge: A Success Story ." *The New York Times*, 15 Nov. 1992, www.nytimes.com/1992/11/15/style/grunge-a-success-story.html?pagewanted=all.
- McCord, Brooke. "Creating the (Oc)Cult Fashion That Defined the Craft." *Dazed*, 3 May 2016, www.dazeddigital.com/fashion/article/30973/1/creating-the-cult-fashion-that-defined-the-craft.
- "MEN of the '90S SEND a PIERCING MESSAGE." *Deseret News*, 8 Oct. 1995, www.deseret.com/1995/10/8/19197426/men-of-the-90s-send-a-piercing-message/.

- Menkes, Suzy. "RUNWAYS; Fetish or Fashion?" *The New York Times*, 21 Nov. 1993, www.nytimes.com/1993/11/21/style/runways-fetish-or-fashion.html.
- Moss, Gabrielle. "How the Craft: Legacy's Costume Designer Re-Envisioned the Film's Iconic Costumes." *SYFY*, 19 Oct. 2020, www.syfy.com/syfy-wire/how-the-craft-legacys-costume-designer-re-envisioned-the-films-iconic-costumes.
- Nadra Nittle. "Before Fenty: Over 100 Years of Black Makeup Brands." *Racked*, Racked, 23 Jan. 2018, www.racked.com/2018/1/23/16901594/black-makeup-brands-history.
- Nance-Nash, Sheryl. "FUBU Founder Daymond John Stages His next Act - DailyFinance." *Web.archive.org*, 24 Sept. 2012, web.archive.org/web/20120924141410/www.dailyfinance.com/2010/07/24/fubu-founder-daymond-john-stages-his-next-act/.
- Napoli, Lisa. "THE MEDIA BUSINESS: ADVERTISING; Was the Victoria's Secret Show a Web Failure? Hardly. There's No Such Thing as Bad Publicity." *The New York Times*, 8 Feb. 1999, www.nytimes.com/1999/02/08/business/media-business-advertising-was-victoria-s-secret-show-web-failure-hardly-there-s.html.
- Offman, Craig. "Live from Death Row." *Salon.com*, 17 Apr. 2000, www.salon.com/2000/04/17/benetton.
- Okwodu, Janelle. "Before You See Valerian, Revisit the Fifth Element's Iconic Costumes with Milla Jovovich and Jean Paul Gaultier." *Vogue*, 21 July 2017, www.vogue.com/article/the-fifth-element-jean-paul-gaultier-milla-jovovich-20th-anniversary-valerian.
- ---. "Lil' Kim Shares the Story behind Her Iconic '90s Met Gala Looks." *Vogue*, 4 May 2020, www.vogue.com/article/met-gala-lil-kim-1999-versace-iconic-outfit.
- Outkast. 2 Dope Boyz in a Cadillac. Arista/LaFace, 27 Aug. 1996.
- Peoples, Betsy (1996). "A Serious Sitcom Success". Emerge Magazine. pp.7
- Petter, Olivia. "Patricia Field Interview: Sex and the City Costume Designer on Her New Book, Chris Noth and Dressing Carrie Bradshaw." *The Independent*, 14 Feb. 2023, www.independent.co.uk/life-style/fashion/features/patricia-field-sex-and-the-city-interview-b2281351.html.
- Pressler, M. "Abercrombie & Fitch's Controversial Quarterly." *North Jersey Herald and News*, 31 July 1998, www.newspapers.com/image/528967355/.
- Read, Richard. "Workers Wary of Nike Reforms." *The Oregonian*, 14 May 1998, www.newspapers.com/image/1093164045/.
- Reddy, Karina. "1990-1999 | Fashion History Timeline." *Fashion History Timeline*, Fashion Institute of Technology, 15 Sept. 2020, fashionhistory.fitnyc.edu/1990-1999/.
- Reuters. "U.S. Starts Inquiry into Calvin Klein Ads." *The New York Times*, 9 Sept. 1995, www.nytimes.com/1995/09/09/business/us-starts-inquiry-into-calvin-klein-ads.html.
- Reynaud, Floriane. "The Secrets behind Julia Roberts' Red Dress in Pretty Woman." *Vogue Paris*, 28 Oct. 2020, www.vogue.fr/fashion-culture/article/the-secrets-behind-julia-roberts-red-dress-in-pretty-woman.
- Rifkin, Glenn. "COMPANY NEWS; Housewares, Lots of Them, at a Discount." *The New York Times*, 7 May 1992, www.nytimes.com/1992/05/07/business/company-news-housewares-lots-of-them-at-a-

discount.html.
- Roberts, Vida. "Sold on Evita Women Are Being Bombarded with the Agressive Marketing of a Legendary Woman Who Had No Taste." *Baltimore Sun*, 19 Dec. 1996, www.baltimoresun.com/1996/12/19/sold-on-evita-women-are-being-bombarded-with-the-agressive-marketing-of-a-legendary-woman-who-had-no-taste/.
- ROBINSON, GAILE. "The Allure of Allure : Why Is the Young Magazine a Winner? It Might Have Something to Do with Edito." *Los Angeles Times*, 8 Dec. 1994, www.latimes.com/archives/la-xpm-1994-12-08-ls-6668-story.html.
- Rudolph, Barbara, et al. "Marketing Beauty and the Bucks." *Wayback Machine*, Time Magazine, 7 Oct. 1991, web.archive.org/web/20090419130313/www.time.com/time/magazine/article/0,9171,973984-1,00.html.
- SAJBEL, MAUREEN. "Evita Rules!" *Los Angeles Times*, 27 Nov. 1996, www.latimes.com/archives/la-xpm-1996-11-27-ls-3248-story.html.
- Samuels, Allison. "A Whole Lotta Lil' Kim." *Newsweek*, Newsweek, 26 June 2000, www.newsweek.com/whole-lotta-lil-kim-160903.
- Schmidt, Luella. "Remembering the 90s and the Benetton Ads." *Luella Schmidt*, 25 Aug. 2021, www.luellaschmidt.com/post/remembering-the-90s-and-the-benetton-ads.
- Schollmeyer, Josh. "Sex, Lies and Cheap Cologne: An Oral History of Abercrombie & Fitch's Softcore Porn Mag." *MEL Magazine*, 14 Aug. 2020, melmagazine.com/en-us/story/sex-lies-and-cheap-cologne-an-oral-history-of-abercrombie-fitchs-softcore-porn-mag.
- "SCHOOL DRESS CODES: AN IDEA THAT MAY BE BACK in FASHION." *Chicago Tribune*, 14 Sept. 1990, www.chicagotribune.com/1990/09/14/school-dress-codes-an-idea-that-may-be-back-in-fashion/.
- "SCHOOL DECIDES to DRESS for SUCCESS." Chicago Tribune, 6 Sept. 1990, www.chicagotribune.com/1990/09/06/school-decides-to-dress-for-success/.
- Schulman, Michael. "Patricia Field Hangs up Her Retail Wig." *The New York Times*, 26 Dec. 2015, www.nytimes.com/2015/12/27/fashion/patricia-field-hangs-up-her-retail-wig.html.
- Sebra, Matt. "Why Puff Daddy's White Party Was the Best 4th of July Party of All Time." *GQ*, 4 July 2016, www.gq.com/gallery/puff-daddy-white-party-fourth-of-july-sean-combs.
- Segran, Elizabeth. "Escalating Sweatshop Protests Keep Nike Sweating." *Fast Company*, Fast Company, 28 July 2017, www.fastcompany.com/40444836/escalating-sweatshop-protests-keep-nike-sweating.
- "She Had Style, She Had Flair: The Costume Designer of "the Nanny" Breaks down the Show's Iconic Looks." *Shondaland*, 1 Nov. 2023, www.shondaland.com/inspire/a45628868/she-had-style-she-had-flair-the-costume-designer-of-the-nanny-breaks-down-the-shows-iconic-looks/.
- Souphanh, Boon Mark. "To the Max: How Tokyo Became a Sneaker Mecca." *Www.sneakerfreaker.com*, 15 July 2020, www.sneakerfreaker.com/features/to-the-max-how-tokyo-became-a-sneaker-mecca/.
- Spindler, Amy M. "New "Evita" Look Is Too Alive and Well." *The New York Times*, 10 Dec. 1996, www.nytimes.com/1996/12/10/style/new-evita-look-is-too-alive-and-well.html.

- Spindler, Amy M. "The 90'S Version of the Decadent Look." *The New York Times*, 7 May 1996, www.nytimes.com/1996/05/07/style/the-90-s-version-of-the-decadent-look.html.
- Stables, Paige. "How Tattoos Have Evolved in the Last 30 Years." *Allure*, 20 Feb. 2021, www.allure.com/story/history-of-tattoos-90s-2000s-2010s.
- Stafford, Paul. "The Grunge Effect: Music, Fashion, and the Media during the Rise of Grunge Culture in the Early 1990s." *M/c Journal*, vol. 21, no. 5, 6 Dec. 2018, journal.media-culture.org.au/index.php/mcjournal/article/view/1471, https://doi.org/10.5204/mcj.1471.
- Star, Darren. Sex and the City. HBO, 1998-2004.
- Stein, Jeannine. "When Rumors Are Clothed as Truth." *Los Angeles Times*, 1 Apr. 1997, www.latimes.com/archives/la-xpm-1997-04-01-ls-44002-story.html.
- Stewart, Ian. "Nike Supervisor Gets 6 Months for Abusing Workers." *Www.saigon.com*, 22 June 1997, www.saigon.com/nike/apjun22.html.
- Stuglik, Julie. "School Dress Codes a Balancing Act." *The South Bend Tribune*, 21 Aug. 1995, www.newspapers.com/image/521005443/.
- Sullivan, Robert. "The History of Supreme: From Small Shop to Legendary Cult Status." *Vogue*, Vogue, 10 Aug. 2017, www.vogue.com/article/history-of-supreme-skate-clothing-brand.
- Swartz, Jon, and Chronicle Staff Writer. "Apple Profit up -- IMac Sales Cited." *SFGate*, 14 Jan. 1999, www.sfgate.com/business/article/Apple-Profit-Up-iMac-Sales-Cited-2952619.php.
- Szabo, Julia. "Geared for the Grocery, or Mount Everest ." *The New York Times*, 9 Mar. 1997, www.nytimes.com/1997/03/09/style/geared-for-the-grocery-or-mount-everest.html.
- The Associated Press. "Disgruntled Factory Workers Begin to Speak out in Vietnam." *The Independent-Record*, 22 June 1997, www.newspapers.com/image/392900385/.
- ---. "Justice Department Plans No Charges over Calvin Klein Ads." *Los Angeles Times*, 16 Nov. 1995, www.newspapers.com/image/155451145/.
- "The Fashion Genius behind ""the Fifth Element."" *EW.com*, 23 May 1997, ew.com/article/1997/05/23/fashion-genius-behind-fifth-element/.
- The Henry J. Kaiser Family Foundation. "Teens, Tweens, and Magazines." *Wayback Machine*, 2004, web.archive.org/web/20151208234750/kaiserfamilyfoundation.files.wordpress.com/2013/01/tweens-teens-and-magazines-fact-sheet.pdf.
- Todd, Susan. "Behind the Buzz." *The Morning Call*, 30 Aug. 1999, www.newspapers.com/image/278759576/.
- Usborne, David. "Benetton Death Row Ads Outrage America." *The Independent*, 2 Apr. 2000, www.independent.co.uk/news/world/americas/benetton-death-row-ads-outrage-america-279554.html.
- Wallace, Christopher. Big Poppa. Bad Boy/Arista, Dec. 1994.
- ---. Hypnotize. Bad Boy/Arista, 4 Mar. 1997.
- "Vibe Magazine 1994." Internet Archive, Mar. 1994, archive.org/details/bub_gb_9ysEAAAAMBAJ/page/n53/mode/2up.
- Weinraub, Bernard. "Ratings Grow for a Series, like the Hair of Its Star." *The New York Times*, 4 Dec. 2000, www.nytimes.com/2000/12/04/arts/ratings-grow-for-a-series-like-the-hair-of-its-star.html.
- Wren, Christopher S. "Clinton Calls Fashion Ads' "Heroin Chic"

Deplorable." *The New York Times*, 22 May 1997, www.nytimes.com/1997/05/22/us/clinton-calls-fashion-ads-heroin-chic-deplorable.html.
- Yazigi, Monique P. "A NIGHT out WITH: Puffy; Gettin' Jiggy Wit the Jet Set." *The New York Times*, 23 Aug. 1998, www.nytimes.com/1998/08/23/style/a-night-out-with-puffy-gettin-jiggy-wit-the-jet-set.html.
- Young, Toby. "Rappers Aspire to Nicer Class of Ghetto." *The Observer*, 5 Sept. 1999, www.newspapers.com/image/258645476/.
- Zeman, Ned. "Spike This Story." *Newsweek*, 5 Oct. 1992, www.newsweek.com/spike-story-199860.

On The X-Files
- Alair, Matt. "The X-Files: A History of the Fandom." Den of Geek, 24 Jan. 2018, www.denofgeek.com/tv/the-x-files-a-history-of-the-fandom/.
- "Alien and Sedition Acts ." National Archives, 1798, www.archives.gov/milestone-documents/alien-and-sedition-acts.
- Cantor, Paul A. "This Is Not Your Father's FBI: The X-Files and the Delegitimation of the Nation-State." *The Independent Review*, vol. 6, no. 1, 2001, pp. 113–23. JSTOR, http://www.jstor.org/stable/24562305.
- Carlson, Peter. "All the News That Seemed Unfit to Print." Washingtonpost.com, 7 Aug. 2007, www.washingtonpost.com/wp-dyn/content/article/2007/08/06/AR2007080601293.html.
- Carson, Tom. "Fear Factor: Inside the Paranoia-Entertainment Complex." *The Baffler*, no. 37, 2017, pp. 6–11. JSTOR, http://www.jstor.org/stable/26358579.
- Davis, David Brion. "Conspiracy Theories in America: A Historical Overview." Conspiracy Theories in America, ABC-CILO, Inc., 2003, pp. 1–14.
- Kellner, Douglas. "The X-Files and the Aesthetics and Politics of Postmodern Pop." *The Journal of Aesthetics and Art Criticism*, vol. 57, no. 2, 1999, pp. 161–75. JSTOR, https://doi.org/10.2307/432310.
- KINNEY, KATHERINE. "THE X-FILES AND THE BORDERS OF THE POST-COLD WAR WORLD." *Journal of Film and Video*, vol. 53, no. 4, 2001, pp. 54–71. JSTOR, http://www.jstor.org/stable/20688370.
- Knight, Peter. "Making Sense of Conspiracy Theories." Conspiracy Theories in America, ABC-CILO, Inc., 2003, pp. 15–25.
- Kuhlman, Martha. "The Uncanny Clone: 'The X-Files', Popular Culture, and Cloning." *Studies in Popular Culture*, vol. 26, no. 3, 2004, pp. 75–87. JSTOR, http://www.jstor.org/stable/23414935.
- KYDD, ELSPETH. "DIFFERENCES: THE X-FILES, RACE AND THE WHITE NORM." *Journal of Film and Video*, vol. 53, no. 4, 2001, pp. 72–82. JSTOR, http://www.jstor.org/stable/20688371.
- McLean, Adrienne L. "Media Effects: Marshall McLuhan, Television Culture, and 'The X-Files.'" *Film Quarterly*, vol. 51, no. 4, 1998, pp. 2–11. JSTOR, https://doi.org/10.2307/1213239.
- Mifflin, Lawrie. "Despite Virtues, "Moesha" Ignored." The Cincinnati Enquirer, 27 Sept. 1999, www.newspapers.com/image/102353046/.
- Millman, Joyce. "TELEVISION/RADIO; "the X-Files" Finds the Truth: Its

- Time Is Past." *The New York Times*, 19 May 2002, www.nytimes.com/ 2002/05/19/arts/television-radio-the-x-files-finds-the-truth-its-time-is-past.html.
- Newitz, Annalee. *Chris Carter Says 9/11 Killed X-Files, but America Is Ready for It Again.* 23 Feb. 2008, web.archive.org/web/20120817060221/io9.com/ 360044/chris-carter-says-911-killed-x+files-but-america-is-ready-for-it-again.
- Radio Free Galaxy. "1991 Geraldo Jeffrey Dahmer Episode - Interview with Tracy Edwards." Www.youtube.com, 2023, www.youtube.com/watch? v=iQaTIeVanFg. Accessed 4 Apr. 2024.
- *The X-Files.* Created by Chris Carter, Ten Thirteen Productions / 20th Century Fox Television, 1993–2002.
- Tucker, Ken. "Alien Nation." *Entertainment Weekly*, 10 Sept. 1993, web.archive.org/web/20071221184214/www.ew.com/ew/article/ 0,,308321,00.html.
- Tucker, Ken. "Read EW's Original 1990 Review of "Twin Peaks."" *Entertainment Weekly*, 6 Apr. 1990, ew.com/article/1990/04/06/twin-peaks-3/.
- Walker, Jesse. The United States of Paranoia: A Conspiracy Theory. First edition. Harper, 2013.

90s Scandals
Zuxco, Tom. "The People's Peep Show." Tampa Bay Times, 3 June 1997, pp. D1, D4, www.newspapers.com/image/326294925/.

1990-Mili Vanilli
- Cocks, Jay. "Music: Two Scoops of Vanilli." *TIME*, nextgen, 5 Mar. 1990, time.com/archive/6714303/music-two-scoops-of-vanilli/.
- *Ex-Member of Mili Vanilli Arrested for Terrorist Threat.* Jet Magazine, 19 Feb. 1996, books.google.com/books? id=FzgDAAAAMBAJ&q=rob+pilatus+jail&pg=PA18#v=onepage&q&f=false.
- Pareles, Jon. "Wages of Silence: Milli Vanilli Loses a Grammy Award." *The New York Times*, 20 Nov. 1990, www.nytimes.com/1990/11/20/arts/wages-of-silence-milli-vanilli-loses-a-grammy-award.html.
- PHILIPS, CHUCK. "It's True: Milli Vanilli Didn't Sing : Pop Music: The Duo Could Be Stripped of Its Grammy after Admitting It." *Los Angeles Times*, 16 Nov. 1990, www.latimes.com/archives/la-xpm-1990-11-16-ca-4894-story.html.
- "Rob Pilatus, Member of Defunct Pop Group Mili Vanilli, Dies in Germany." *Jet*, 27 Apr. 1998, p. 57.

1991— City College Stampede
- Gonzalez, David. "STAMPEDE at CITY COLLEGE; 8 Lives That Came Together, Then Were Lost in a Crush." *The New York Times*, 30 Dec. 1991, www.nytimes.com/1991/12/30/nyregion/stampede-at-city-college-8-lives-that-came-together-then-were-lost-in-a-crush.html.
- Goodstein, Laurie. "'THEY JUST KEPT PUSHING ... '." *The Washington Post*, 30 Dec. 1991, www.washingtonpost.com/archive/politics/1991/12/30/

- they-just-kept-pushing/bcde71c5-af0c-4135-aa78-d3b63f2fb571/.
- HellaClassic. "1991 Geraldo Show with Luke of the 2 Live Crew, Doug E. Fresh, Sister Souljah & Young MC." *YouTube*, www.youtube.com/watch?v=ysW5kjolJ_U.
- MacDonald, Heather. "Spreading the Blame Too Thin." *City Journal*, 1992, www.city-journal.org/article/spreading-the-blame-too-thin.
- McFadden, Robert D. "STAMPEDE at CITY COLLEGE; Inquiries Begin over City College Deaths." *The New York Times*, 30 Dec. 1991, www.nytimes.com/1991/12/30/nyregion/stampede-at-city-college-inquiries-begin-over-city-college-deaths.html.
- Mitchell, Jessi. "CCNY Stampede Victims to Be Remembered 33 Years Later on Saturday in Harlem." *Cbsnews.com*, 27 Dec. 2024, www.cbsnews.com/newyork/news/city-college-of-new-york-stampede-harlem-1991/.
- Specter, Michael. "STAMPEDE at CITY COLLEGE; Excess Ticket Sale May Have Caused Fatal Crush at Gym." *The New York Times*, 31 Dec. 1991, www.nytimes.com/1991/12/31/nyregion/stampede-at-city-college-excess-ticket-sale-may-have-caused-fatal-crush-at-gym.html.
- Sullivan, John. "Rap Producer Testifies on Fatal Stampede at City College." *The New York Times*, 24 Mar. 1998, www.nytimes.com/1998/03/24/nyregion/rap-producer-testifies-on-fatal-stampede-at-city-college.html.

1991- Peewee's Peewee
- Burr, Ty. "The Pee-Wee Herman Scandal." *EW.com*, 14 Aug. 1991, ew.com/article/1991/08/16/pee-wee-herman-scandal/.
- Crane, R.J. "The Pee Wee Herman Story." *Vanity Fair*, 1999, web.archive.org/web/20070314153055/peeweestory.tripod.com/article/vf091999.html.
- Feldman, Charles. "Pee Wee Herman Actor Charged." *CNN*, 16 Nov. 2002, www.cnn.com/2002/SHOWBIZ/11/15/reubens.artwork.flap/.
- Rohter, Larry. "`Pee-Wee Herman' Pleads No Contest | the Seattle Times." *Seattletimes.com*, 8 Nov. 1991, archive.seattletimes.com/archive/19911108/1316042/pee-wee-herman-pleads-no-contest.
- Stein, Joel. "Cinema: Bigger than Pee-Wee." *Time*, 9 Apr. 2001, www.time.com/time/magazine/article/0,9171,999636-1,00.html.

1992— Marge Schott
- Berkow, Ira. "BASEBALL; Marge Schott: Baseball's Big Red Headache." *The New York Times*, 29 Nov. 1992, www.nytimes.com/1992/11/29/sports/baseball-marge-schott-baseball-s-big-red-headache.html.
- Chass, Murray. "BASEBALL; Ex-A's Employee Cites Schott Racial Remarks." Archive.org, 26 Nov. 1992, web.archive.org/web/20150526060954/www.nytimes.com/1992/11/26/sports/baseball-ex-a-s-employee-cites-schott-racial-remarks.html.
- Goldstein, Richard. "Marge Schott, Eccentric Owner of the Reds, Dies at 75." The New York Times, 3 Mar. 2004, www.nytimes.com/2004/03/03/sports/baseball/03SCHO.html.
- Klemesrud, Judy. "MARGE SCHOOT, CINCINNATI BOOSTER, IS ROOTING for HER HOME TEAM." *The New York Times*, 8 Mar. 1985, www.nytimes.com/1985/03/08/style/marge-schoot-cincinnati-booster-is-

- rooting-for-her-home-team.html.
- Reilly, Rick. "Heaven Help Marge Schott: Cincinnati's Owner Is a Red Menace ." Sports Illustrated, 20 May 1996, www.si.com/mlb/2014/11/19/heaven-help-marge-schott-rick-reilly-si-60.
- Rohde, John. "Schott's Racism Not Marginal." *The Oklahoman*, Oklahoman, 8 Dec. 1992, www.oklahoman.com/story/news/1992/12/08/schotts-racism-not-marginal/62474171007/.
- The Associated Press. "BASEBALL; Schott Agrees to Sell Reds." The New York Times, 21 Apr. 1999, www.nytimes.com/1999/04/21/sports/baseball-schott-agrees-to-sell-reds.html.

1993— Jerry Seinfeld
- Schneider, Karen. "The Game of Love." *People.com*, 28 Mar. 1994, people.com/archive/cover-story-the-game-of-love-vol-41-no-11/.
- Dini von Mueffling. "Bloomingdale's or Bust! The Rise of Shoshanna Lonstein (Jerry's Ex)." Observer, 18 Jan. 1999, observer.com/1999/01/bloomingdales-or-bust-the-rise-of-shoshanna-lonstein-jerrys-ex/.

1994-Tyke The Elephant
- Bernardo, Rosemarie. ""Shots Killing Elephant Echo across a Decade."" Starbulletin.com, 16 Aug. 2004, archives.starbulletin.com/2004/08/16/news/story2.html.
- Davey, Monica. ""Elephant Incidents in Recent Years."" St. Petersburg Times, 6 May 1993, p. 5.
- Gillingham, Paula. "Tyke's Rampage." *Honolulu Star-Advertiser*, 23 Aug. 1994, www.newspapers.com/image/265843730/.
- Hoover, Will. "Slain Elephant Left Tenuous Legacy in Animal Rights | the Honolulu Advertiser | Hawaii's Newspaper." Honoluluadvertiser.com, 20 Aug. 2004, the.honoluluadvertiser.com/article/2004/Aug/20/ln/ln19a.html.
- Magaoay, Sandi. "Trampled Man Says Trainer Saved His Life." *Honolulu Star-Bulletin*, 24 Aug. 1994, www.newspapers.com/image/273874629/.
- Sahagún, Louis. "Elephants Pose Giant Dangers." Los Angeles Times, 11 Oct. 1994, www.latimes.com/archives/la-xpm-1994-10-11-mn-49101-story.html.
- The Associated Press. "Elephant That Killed Man in Hawaii Also Ran Amok in N.D." *Grand Folks Herald*, 25 Aug. 1994, www.newspapers.com/image/1131842273/.

1995- Hugh Grant
- AP Archive. "USA: PROSTITUTE DIVINE BROWN SENTENCED to 6 MONTHS JAIL." *YouTube*, 30 July 2015, www.youtube.com/watch?v=n4t7K3Mn1wA.
- Associated Press. "Brazil Just Loves Divine Brown." *Times Colonist*, 7 July 1996, www.newspapers.com/image/508269103/.
- "Brown's Life Divine since Arrest with Grant." *The Cincinnati Enquirer*, 18 Mar. 1996, www.newspapers.com/image/102190346/.
- Daily News wire services. "Divine Brown: Hugh Grant's Loss Paid off Handsomely for Her." *Anchorage Daily News*, 12 Mar. 1996, www.newspapers.com/image/1059909233/.

Bibliography

- Divine. "Divine Brown Gets 180-Day Sentence - UPI Archives." *UPI*, 6 Sept. 1995, www.upi.com/Archives/1995/09/06/Divine-Brown-gets-180-day-sentence/2510810360000/.
- "Hugh Grant Arrested for Sex with Prostitute." *Lancaster New Era*, 28 June 1995, www.newspapers.com/image/565347309/.
- "Hugh Grant Interview Jay Leno 1995 Tonight Show." Daily Motion, 1995, www.dailymotion.com/video/x8spcwm.
- "Hugh's Divine Intervention." *The Sydney Morning Herald*, 7 July 2007, www.smh.com.au/entertainment/celebrity/hughs-divine-intervention-20070707-gdqk6l.html.
- Kriegel, Mark. "Bout Crowd Is Too Divine." *Daily News*, 20 Aug. 1995, www.newspapers.com/image/474981115/.
- "TO FORGO IS DIVINE." *TIME*, nextgen, 6 Sept. 1995, time.com/archive/6926103/to-forgo-is-divine/.

1995— TLC
- Cooper, Carol. "TLC's T-Boz: "a Lot of People Have Made Money off of Us, and We Haven't."" *The Guardian*, The Guardian, 1998, www.theguardian.com/music/2015/jul/08/rocks-back-pages-tlc-rolling-stone-1995-t-boz-chilli-left-eye.
- "FALCON RECEIVER'S HOME DESTROYED." *Chicago Tribune*, 10 June 1994, www.chicagotribune.com/1994/06/10/falcon-receivers-home-destroyed/.
- Iqbal, Nosheen. "TLC: "I Will Never Forget the Day We Were Millionaires for Five Minutes."" *The Guardian*, 24 June 2017, www.theguardian.com/music/2017/jun/24/tlc-will-never-forget-day-we-were-millionaires-for-five-minutes.
- Philips, Chuck. "Group Tops Charts but Claims Bankruptcy." *Los Angeles Times*, 28 May 1996, www.latimes.com/archives/la-xpm-1996-05-28-mn-9230-story.html.
- Samuels, Anita M., and Diana B. Henriques. "Going Broke and Cutting Loose;Bankruptcy Has New Appeal for Music Groups Chafing at Their Contracts ." *The New York Times*, 5 Feb. 1996, www.nytimes.com/1996/02/05/business/going-broke-cutting-loose-bankruptcy-has-new-appeal-for-music-groups-chafing.html.
- "SPORTS PEOPLE: FOOTBALL; Rison's Girlfriend Charged in Home Fire." *The New York Times*, 11 June 1994, www.nytimes.com/1994/06/11/sports/sports-people-football-rison-s-girlfriend-charged-in-home-fire.html.
- "TLC Settles Contract Dispute with Label." *Los Angeles Times*, 27 Nov. 1996, www.latimes.com/archives/la-xpm-1996-11-27-fi-3354-story.html.

1996—Jessica Dubroff
- "49 U.S.C. § 44724 - U.S. Code Title 49. Transportation § 44724 ." *Findlaw*, 2024, codes.findlaw.com/us/title-49-transportation/49-usc-sect-44724.html.
- Chamings, Andrew. "A "Child Pilot" Isn't a Thing: The Tragedy of Jessica Dubroff." *SFGATE*, 26 Apr. 2021, www.sfgate.com/local/article/jessica-dubroff-child-pilot-bay-area-history-16113058.php.
- Gathright, Alan. "Dubroff Tragedy Goes On." *Dayton Daily News*, 5 Jan. 1997, www.newspapers.com/image/408625756/.
- Gordon, Rachel. "Record Wasn't at Stake When Jessica Crashed." *SFGATE*,

- 15 Apr. 1996, www.sfgate.com/news/article/Record-wasn-t-at-stake-when-Jessica-crashed-3155289.php.
- Howe, Rob. "Final Adventure." *People.com*, 29 Apr. 1996, people.com/archive/cover-story-final-adventure-vol-45-no-17/.
- McCormick, Erin, and Eve Mitchell. "THE TRAGIC FLIGHT of JESSICA DUBROFF." *Wayback Machine*, San Francisco Gate, 14 Apr. 1996, web.archive.org/web/20120531231912/www.sfgate.com/cgi-bin/examiner/article.cgi?year=1996&month=04&day=14&article=NEWS15677.dtl.
- Mitchell, Eve. "Young Pilot's Survivors Start Court Face-Off." *The San Francisco Examiner*, 15 Dec. 1997, www.newspapers.com/image/462436669/.
- Stengel, Richard. "Fly Til I Die." Wayback Machine, Time Magazine, 22 Apr. 1996, web.archive.org/web/20070509211224/www.time.com/time/magazine/article/0,9171,984431-1,00.html.

1997— Infidelities
- "Autumn Jackson Found Guilty in Bill Cosby Extortion Trial." *Jet*, 11 Aug. 1997, books.google.com/books?id=ScMDAAAAMBAJ&q=autumn+jackson&pg=PA4#v=onepage&q&f=false.
- Errico, Marcus. "Frank Gifford's Mistress Exposed in "Playboy."" *E! Online*, E! News, 9 Aug. 1997, www.eonline.com/news/34987/frank-gifford-s-mistress-exposed-in-playboy.
- "Forever Young: Revisiting the Life & Death of Shalimar Seiuli." *UTOPIA Washington*, 17 Dec. 2021, utopiawa.org/forever-young-revisiting-the-life-death-of-shalimar-seiuli/.
- "From a Love Affair to a Court-Martial." *Nytimes.com*, 14 Dec. 1997, archive.nytimes.com/www.nytimes.com/books/97/12/14/home/airwoman-court-martial.html.
- "Globe Paid Woman to Lure Gifford into Hotel Room | the Seattle Times." *Seattletimes.com*, 18 May 1997, archive.seattletimes.com/archive/?date=19970518&slug=2539829.
- KEMPSTER, NORMAN. "Lying, Not Adultery, Is Female Pilot's Top Crime, AF Says." *Los Angeles Times*, 22 May 1997, www.latimes.com/archives/la-xpm-1997-05-22-mn-61313-story.html.
- O'Neill, Helen. "Flinn Offered Jobs, to Request Waiver." *New Bedford Standard-Times*, Standard-Times, 24 May 1997, www.southcoasttoday.com/story/news/nation-world/1997/05/24/flinn-offered-jobs-to-request/50609963007/.
- ---. "Pilot's Dream Ends with General Discharge." *The Kalamazoo Gazette*, 23 May 1997, www.newspapers.com/image/1152462572/.
- Schwartz, John. "The Art of Blackmail." *The New York Times*, 3 Oct. 2009, www.nytimes.com/2009/10/04/weekinreview/04schwartz.html?_r=1.
- Smith, Kyle. "Double Trouble." *People.com*, 19 May 1997, people.com/archive/double-trouble-vol-47-no-19/.
- "Tabloid Gets Snared in Gifford Affair." *Tribunedigital-Orlandosentinel*, 18 May 1997, web.archive.org/web/20150826080205/articles.orlandosentinel.com/1997-05-18/news/9705171005_1_kathie-lee-

Bibliography

- gifford-frank-gifford-globe.
- Weiser, Benjamin. "Judges Reinstate Conviction in Extortion of Bill Cosby." *The New York Times*, 16 Nov. 1999, www.nytimes.com/1999/11/16/nyregion/judges-reinstate-conviction-in-extortion-of-bill-cosby.html.

1998- Karl Malone

- FANTIN, LINDA. "KARL'S KIDS." *The Albuquerque Tribune*, 30 July 1998, www.newspapers.com/image/786243660/.
- Gee, Andre. "The NBA Shouldn't Have Creepy Karl Malone at All-Star Weekend." *Rolling Stone*, 18 Feb. 2023, www.rollingstone.com/culture/culture-sports/karl-malone-creepy-nba-ban-all-star-weekend-utah-gloria-bell-rape-vanessa-bryant-harassment-1234682580/.
- Hill, Jemele. "Hill: Karl Malone's Shameful Secret." *ESPN*, 12 May 2008, www.espn.com/espn/page2/story?page=hill/080507.
- "Malone Paternity Revealed." *Philly-Archives*, 23 July 1998, web.archive.org/web/20160304093706/articles.philly.com/1998-07-23/sports/25738724_1_karl-malone-cheryl-and-daryl-bonita-ford.

1998-George Michael

- Glionna, John M. "Beverly Hills Steps up Patrols to Stop Cruising." *Los Angeles Times*, 29 May 1998, www.latimes.com/archives/la-xpm-1998-may-29-me-54502-story.html.
- McALLISTER, SUE. "Pop Singer George Michael Arrested in Restroom of Beverly Hills Park." *Los Angeles Times*, 9 Apr. 1998, www.latimes.com/archives/la-xpm-1998-apr-09-me-37715-story.html.
- Sim, Bernardo. "Remembering the Time George Michael Was Arrested for Cruising in 1998." *Out Magazine*, 2 Mar. 2023, www.out.com/gay-music/george-michael-cruising.

1999-Hillsdale

- Drummond, Dee. "Son Trying to Cope with Wife's Death and Father's Role." Pittsburgh Post-Gazette, 1999, www.newspapers.com/image/91125953/.
- Ellis, Jonathan. "Sex, Lies and Suicide." *Salon.com*, 19 Jan. 2000, www.salon.com/2000/01/19/hillsdale/.
- Juzwiak, Rich. "From Pamela Anderson to Tonya Harding: The Decade That Turned the Sex Tape Mainstream." *Jezebel*, 2021, www.jezebel.com/from-pamela-anderson-to-tonya-harding-the-decade-that-1846282676.
- Meredith, Robyn. "Scandal Rocks a Conservative Campus." *The New York Times*, 15 Nov. 1999, www.nytimes.com/1999/11/15/us/scandal-rocks-a-conservative-campus.html.
- Miller, John J. "Horror at Hillsdale." *National Review*, 13 Nov. 1999, www.nationalreview.com/1999/11/horror-hillsdale-john-j-miller/.
- Rapoport, Roger. "Hillsdale." *Internet Archive*, 2000, archive.org/details/hillsdalegreektr00rapo/page/n9/mode/2up.

Index

A

Abath, Ricky, 72–75
Abercrombie & Fitch, 176–77
Adams, Cherica, 104–6
Adams, Victoria, 14–16, 20–21, 24, 189, 203
Air Jordans, 176, 178, 200
aliens, 206–7, 209–11, 214–16, 218–20, 222
American Psycho (Book), 109–10
Anderson, Gillian, 208
Anderson, Pamela, 202
Angelou, Maya, 174
Aniston, Jennifer, 189, 196
apples, 42, 44, 176
Arista Records, 224–25, 234
Arkansas, 4, 31, 34, 188
Asians, 64, 184, 229
Asian serial killers, 118
Atlanta, 32, 95, 97, 191, 200
Atlantic Records, 163, 182

B

baseball, 101, 230
Batman, 63, 128, 155, 164
beauty, 19, 80, 126, 159, 180, 188, 196, 198
Beckford, Tyson, 197
Bentley, Lamont, 167, 174
Bezos, Jeff, 160
bin Laden, Osama, 127
Birkenstocks, 185, 205
black men, 66, 119, 169, 187
Black serial killers, 87
black women, 66, 85, 87, 112, 118, 124, 162, 183, 196
Blair, Tony, 17–18, 22–23, 25
Bobbitt, John, 81–82

Bobbitt, Lorena, 81–82, 91
Bojangles, 83, 85
Bourdain, Anthony, 49
Braxton, Toni, 234
British culture, 18, 21, 26
Brown, Melanie, 14–17, 20, 22–24
Bryant, Kobe, 174
Bunton, Emma, 14–15
Burger King, 28–29, 36, 45, 47
Bush, George H.W., 33, 155
Bush, George HW, 30
Bush, George W, 53, 68–71

C

California, 41, 66, 98–99, 125–26, 137, 143, 163, 171, 216, 234, 240
Calvin Klein, 179–80, 201
Campbell, Naomi, 31, 118, 195, 197–98
cancer, 38, 44, 70, 95, 130, 219, 241
Candyman, 122–25
Carey, Mariah, 157, 201
Carolina Panthers, 5, 103, 105–6
Carruth, Rae, 103–7
Carter, Chris, 208, 212, 218, 222
Carter, Sean, 76, 202
Castro, Fidel, 159
Catholicism, 160, 211, 218, 236
Charlotte, North Carolina, 2–11, 20, 83–84, 87, 103, 120, 206
Charlotte Hornets, 5, 106
Charlotte-Mecklenburg Police Department (CMPD), 84, 86–87, 117
China, 176, 213
Chipotle, 36, 47
chips, 37, 43
Chisholm, Melanie, 14–15, 23–24
chocolates, box of, 30, 220

Christmas, 95, 125–26, 129, 132, 153–60
class, 22, 25, 61, 137–38, 140–41, 147
Cleveland, Glenda, 112
Clinton, Bill, 4, 32–33, 35, 41, 59, 61, 71, 132, 140, 158, 160, 180, 188, 221, 234–35, 242
Clinton, Hillary, 30, 32, 53, 91, 211
CMPD (Charlotte-Mecklenburg Police Department), 84, 86–87, 117
Cobain, Kurt, 185, 195
coffee, 40, 53, 118, 207
Colorado, 12, 36, 47, 76, 95, 97, 103, 126
Columbine, 70, 98, 100, 115, 181, 230
Combs, Sean, 195, 201, 204, 227–28
comic books, 114, 121, 128, 213
communism, 57, 199, 211, 219
conspiracy theories, 59, 63, 184, 211–12, 215–16, 221, 223
cookies, 37, 53, 133, 154
Cool Britannia, 17–18, 25
Cosby, Bill, 228, 238
CourtTV, 2, 72, 76, 78, 81, 106, 140
crack, 61, 85–86, 112, 126
Cuba, 45, 75, 160, 181
cult, 52, 62, 143, 149, 152, 193, 216
Cunanan, Andrew, 118

D

Dahmer, Jeffrey, 112–14, 218
Davis, Angela, 186–87
death penalty, 61, 68, 86, 93, 106, 127, 203
Democratic National Convention, 52, 60
Democrats, 35, 51, 53–54, 59, 61, 71
Depp, Johnny, 31, 125
DiCaprio, Leonardo, 100, 193, 204
dinosaurs, 134–35, 151
Disney Channel, 134, 147–48
Doc Martens, 181, 185, 205
Dole, Bob, 70

Doritos, 27, 35, 37, 47
Douglas, John, 110–11, 115
drag queens, 142, 196, 200
Drescher, Fran, 191
Duchovny, David, 208, 221

E

eating disorders, 20, 24, 62, 174, 179
Ebert, Roger, 18, 20, 26, 111, 125, 191
Eckardt, Shawn, 88–90
Edwards, Tracy, 113
Elliot, Missy, 190, 196–97
Ellis, Brett Easton, 109, 177
End of History, 2, 14, 67, 134, 162, 178, 212, 221
Epstein, Jeffrey, 93–95
Evangelista, Linda, 118, 197–98

F

Faludi, Susan, 137, 205
Farquhar, Ralph, 165–66
fast fashion, 183–84
FBI, 8, 74–75, 78, 84, 87, 89–90, 94, 110, 112, 117–18
Finney, Sara V., 165, 169
Fishel, Danielle, 135–36, 139, 148
Food Lion, 8, 50, 84
Food Network, 35, 46
football, 4, 21, 55, 58, 103, 200, 237
Foreman, George, 37, 66
Forrest Gump, 43, 192
Fox Network, 55, 59, 162, 206–8, 212, 218, 221
Fresh Prince of Bel-Air, 162, 178
Friedle, Will, 131, 135–36, 144–45
Friends (Television Show), 18, 39, 63, 173, 189

G

Gantt, Harvey, 5, 7

Gifford, Kathie Lee, 200, 237–38
Gilligan, Vince, 208, 222
Gingrich, Newt, 158, 241
Giuliani, Rudolph, 67, 92, 177
Grant, Hugh, 232
Grant,Hugh, 232–33
Gulf War Syndrome, 93
guns, 70, 88, 100–101, 122–23, 192

H
Haliwell, Geri, 17, 19–24
Halloween, 57, 81, 120–22, 125–33
Harding, Tonya, 7, 87–91
Harry Potter, 18
Hartman, Phil, 159
Harvard, 73
Hattori, Yoshihiro "Yoshi," 122–23
Hawk, Shawna, 83–86
HBO, 48, 192, 222
Heavy D, 201, 225, 228
Hill, Hank, 54–56, 60, 71
Hill, Peggy, 56, 59, 65
hip-hop, 37, 178, 181, 186, 190, 195, 202
HIV/AIDS, 7, 44, 172, 179, 196, 203, 225, 227, 232
homophobia, 6–7, 11, 103, 113, 135
Hoover, J. Edgar, 212, 220
horror, 11, 108, 111, 116, 123, 206, 217
Houston, 52, 55, 67, 202
    Whitney, 19, 164
Hussein, Saddam, 132
Hylton, Misa, 182, 196–97

I
Idaho, 44, 130
Illinois, 40, 114, 123, 127, 130, 177
illuminati, 210–11
immigrants, 65, 119, 210–11
Indigenous culture, 63
In Living Color, 162, 225

internet, 10, 42, 151, 184, 202, 211, 222
Iraq, 29, 132
Israeli, 94
Italian, 34, 48, 118, 134, 144, 203
Iverson, Sherrice, 97, 99

J
Jackson, Janet, 186, 191
Jacobs, Michael, 135, 144–45, 147, 151
Jameson, Jenna, 177
January 26, 2, 89, 178
Japan, 39, 64, 93, 114, 123, 164, 178, 201
Jewish people, 154–55, 211
Jones, Paula, 91, 188
Judge, Mike, 55–56, 71
Jumper, Valencia, 84, 86

K
Kani, Karl, 195, 201
Kelly, Robert, 171, 231
Kennedy, John F., 105, 213, 219
Kentucky Fried Chicken, 27–28, 32, 34, 40–41
Kerrigan, Nancy, 87–89, 91, 138
King, Rodney, 168
King Jr., Martin Luther, 41, 66, 219–20, 229
King of the Hill, 51–69, 71
Kiwi Strawberry, 42
Ku Klux Klan, 39, 67, 124, 131, 155, 212, 229
Kwan, Michelle, 90, 203

L
labor, sweatshop, 176
Laos, 64, 112, 213
Latifah, Queen, 162–63, 182
Latina women, 196
Latinos, 9, 65–66, 69, 92, 169
Latino serial killers, 118

Latino vote, 54, 67
Lee, Spike, 125, 177, 183
Leimert Park, 163, 165–66, 170, 175
Leno, Jay, 233
Letourneau, Mary Kay, 99–100
LGBTQ, 7, 103
Liebeck, Stella, 39
Lil Kim, 174, 177, 186, 196–97
Lillard, Matthew, 115–16
Limbaugh, Rush, 38–39
liquor, 48, 147, 154
Living Single, 162, 186
LL Cool J, 163, 190
London, 3, 13–14, 18, 116
Love, Caroline, 83, 86
Loveless, Melinda, 78–80
Lucas, Henry Lee, 68, 108
Lynch, David, 108, 207

M

Mac, Bernie, 66, 174
Macaulay Culkin, 153, 155, 234
Madonna, 180, 192, 198, 204
Major, John, 23
Malone, Karl, 239
Mandela, Nelson, 17, 31, 198
Massachusetts, 72, 87, 121
Maxwell, Ghislaine, 94–95
McBride, Tracie, 92–93
McDonald's, 27–31, 33, 40, 43–45, 47, 79, 194
McGee-Davis, Trina, 144–46, 151
McMillan, Terry, 166–67, 189
McQueen, Alexander, 18, 204
McVeigh, Timothy, 47
Michael, George, 197, 240–41
military, 93, 102–3, 212–13, 236
militiamen, 130–31
Milli Vanilli, 224
Moss, Kate, 18, 179, 196, 198

MTV, 55, 154, 197, 225
Murphy, Eddie, 123, 238–39

N

NAFTA, 41, 47
Najimy, Kathy, 57, 125
Nance, Sharon, 83, 86
Nazi, 42, 131, 229
NBA, 5, 174
necrophilia, 111, 114, 118, 218
New Jersey, 32, 117, 120
New Orleans, 4, 35, 106, 132, 199–200
New York, 2, 4, 8, 48, 67, 92, 104–5, 151, 153, 155, 158, 160, 200, 202–3, 228
Nike, 89, 178
North Carolina, 2, 5, 13, 20, 26, 60, 83, 103, 120–21, 206, 219
Norwood, Brandy, 162–65, 173–75, 182, 186, 190, 196
Notorious BIG, 14, 183, 190, 201

O

O'Donnell, Rosie, 158
Ohio State University, 2, 93, 112
Olympics, 26, 89–91, 240

P

Parker, Sarah Jessica, 125, 192
Pentagon Papers, 59, 93, 207, 213
Philadelphia, 43, 67, 74, 135–36, 151
pies, 32–33, 35, 154
pizza, 13, 27–29, 34, 41
Planet Hollywood, 31, 159
Playboy, 82, 181, 186, 197, 204, 238
police brutality, 67, 168
porn, 35, 82, 114, 150, 177, 204, 215
Power Rangers, 157
Prince Charles, 20–21, 23, 199
Princess Diana, 21, 118, 199

Q

Quayle, Dan, 32
Quintanilla, Selena, 65–66, 237

R

Ramsey, JonBenét, 95–97, 237
rape, 81, 84, 100, 109, 114, 119
republicans, 8, 51, 53–54, 59, 71, 99, 158
Ressler, Robert, 110
Reubens, Paul, 228
Richards, Ann, 51, 54, 67–70, 187
Rivera, Geraldo, 113, 227
Rodman, Dennis, 180, 202
Ruby Ridge, 130–31
RuPaul, 196, 200
Russ, William, 131, 135
Rwanda, 141

S

sandwich, 29, 36, 81, 240
San Francisco, 4, 118, 128, 228
satan, 133, 216–17
Saturday Night Live, 184, 225
Savage, Ben, 135, 151
Schiffer, Claudia, 31, 197
Schwarzenegger, Arnold, 31, 159
Scientology, 143
Scooby-Doo, 131–32, 153, 192
Seattle, 34, 161, 185
Seinfeld, 42, 230–31
  Jerry, 230
Seiuli, Shalimar, 238
serial killers, 84–85, 87, 108–12, 115, 117–19, 218
  interracial crime, 118
sex, 22, 48, 62, 65, 137, 147, 171–72, 178, 182, 192–93, 198, 204, 239
Sex and the City, 48, 178, 182, 192–93
sex workers, 56, 61, 83, 86, 116–18, 205, 232, 239

Shakespeare, 3, 100, 135, 217
Shakur, Tupac, 190–91, 194–95, 202, 209
Shanda Sharer, 78–80
Short, Clare, 23
Simpson, O.J., 72, 106, 117, 188
The Simpsons, 39, 42, 55, 121
Sister Souljah, 227
Smith, Anna Nicole, 186
Smith, Susan, 126–27
Snackwells, 33, 49
Snapple, 39, 42, 212
Snoop Dogg, 61, 86, 165, 184
South Africa, 16, 89, 198
South Carolina, 5, 83, 86, 120, 126
Soviet Union, 27, 154, 219
Spears, Vida, 165, 169–70, 174
Spice Girls, 13–26, 205
Spice World, 13, 17–20, 192
Spotnitz, Frank, 212, 221–22
Springer, Jerry, 62, 229
Star, Darren, 192–93
Starbucks, 34, 39
starter jackets, 5, 200
Stern, Howard, 118
Stewart, Martha, 48, 111
strip clubs, 103, 106, 186, 232
Strohmeyer, Jeremy, 97–98
Strong, Rider, 135–36, 138, 142, 144–47, 187
suicide, 60, 143, 195, 240
supermodels, 196–98, 200

T

Taco Bell, 28, 41, 43, 45, 47, 83–85
Tarantino, Quentin, 37, 115
tattoos, 170, 180, 202
taxes, 38, 53, 56, 59, 68, 94, 103
Texas, 44, 47, 51–55, 63, 65, 67–71, 92, 123
TGIF, 134, 136, 151–52

Thanksgiving, 104, 141, 206
Thatcher, Margaret, 22–23
Thomas, Clarence, 220
Thompson, Estella Marie, 232
TLC, 184, 233–34
tobacco, 2, 47, 219
Todd, Tony, 123, 213
Tommy Hilfiger, 183–84, 195
tort reform, 40, 54
Toys"R"Us, 154, 158
transphobia, 103, 203
trans women, 102, 142, 196, 208, 238–39
Treehouse of Horror, 121
Triangle Shirtwaist Fire, 75–76
Trump, Donald, 31, 155, 177
Turlington, Christy, 31, 195
Twin Peaks, 108, 122, 206–8

V

vampires, 108, 126, 218
Vanity Fair, 18, 46, 94
vegan, 181
vegetarian, 42, 44, 49, 166
Versace, Gianni, 118, 198, 205
Vibe Magazine, 173, 186, 199
Victoria's Secret, 93, 203–4
Vietnam, 64, 178, 213, 220
virginity, 24, 62, 171–72

W

Wallace, Henry Louis, 83, 87, 117
Walmart, 49, 158
Washington, Denzel, 115
Weaver, Randy, 130
Weber, Bruce, 177, 182
Wendy's, 29–30, 32, 34, 44
white trash, 61, 90, 136–37, 188
white women, 117, 183, 187, 196, 199
Williams, Hype, 163, 190, 194
Wilson, Yvette, 169, 174

Winfrey, Oprah, 44, 47, 159, 183, 204
World Trade Organization, 161, 178

X

X-Files, 189, 206–23

Y

Y2K, 160, 201, 205, 209, 222
Yamaguchi, Kristi, 87

Z

Zima, 35, 39
zombies, 112, 131–32, 218

Acknowledgements

This book has been my passion for so long that it is hard to believe it is finally complete. It was a culmination of not just hard work and vision, but of support and life changing moments.

My mother Tamara Arevia Peake and my nana Patricia Ann Peake were two early supporters and champions of this project, though their involvement stretches back further than seven years. Thank you mother for teaching me to read and putting a pen in my hand by the age of three. You very intentionally fostered my love for writing and reading and it has paid off in dividends. I am endlessly curious and expressive because of you! Thank you nana for taking me to thrift stores and book stores frequently as a child. You were always sliding me money for books and typewriters, which never went unappreciated. To my best friend in the whole world, Kwaneshia Patterson, thank you for supporting me and helping me shoot the marketing materials for this project.

My gratitude extends to people who were only briefly in my life as well. To my ninth grade English teacher, Ms. Williams, who skipped standard curriculum to give us a college-level seminar steeped in research, annotations, and crisp packets of juicy essays on popular culture that I hoped to one day craft— thank you! To my 12th grade history teacher who shall remain nameless, thanks for getting so fed up with the rowdiness of my fourth period U.S. History classmates that you sat at your desk, pulled out your iPhone, and told me to teach the class. Everyone settled down and paid attention while I discussed the Progressive Era using your notes, my own factoids, and the overhead projector (remember those?!). I know it ate you up inside but seeing others take notes and respond to my on-the-spot lesson awakened something in me!

Acknowledgements

To Brittany Penland Jennings, a former writer at The Charlotte Observer, thank you so much for doing a feature on me in the 12th grade that changed my life in two significant ways. First, you allowed me to take a book titled *The Sexual History of London: From Roman Londinium to the Swinging City---Lust, Vice, and Desire Across the Ages* from the *Observer* review library. That book, by Catherine Arnold, was an early introduction to the type of historical writing I wanted to do, ultimately influencing me to pursue a history degree at The Ohio State University so I could learn how to properly research and write compelling narratives. Secondly, the article that Ms. Jennings wrote led to a totally free scholarship to OSU by NFL player Steve Smith Sr. To Steve and his family, thank you for seeing my potential and believing in me. I am doubtful that I would be where I am now without your generosity. Because of the things I learned at school for free, my life became centered around making knowledge accessible for those not fortunate enough to be seen in a newspaper article and gifted with $160,000 by a multi-millionaire.

To my Patreon members at every tier, I appreciate your belief in me, your patience with me, and your loving feedback. I also want to give a special thanks to Angelica Knight, Cherise Everett, Sydney, Jordan Guinn, Simply J, Girl Back There, Sophia Regalo, Amanda De La Cruz, Brigette, Brianna Cheri, Sara Grack, LaShane, Sinna, and MeaResea Homer for being Patreon Associate Producers on this project.

Lastly, thank you to whoever is reading this book. There were many caffeine-fueled nights where I was hunched over my notes, sources, and keyboard, tired and in need of a vacation, thinking of the eventual book on the nineties that I knew would follow my YouTube series. *Keep going*, I'd tell myself, picturing a stranger holding my labor of love in their hands. Now, here you are. Thank you.

About The Author

Elexus 'Lexual' Jionde has loved history all her life. From an early age she was enchanted by the idea of creating her own media— assembling books and magazines on thrifted typewriters from the age of five onward— filling the pages with essays, poems, and short stories. After earning her degree in History from The Ohio State University in 2016, she made it her mission to make accurate, challenging, and esoteric research accessible to everyone. Her work has focused on modern social history, black people, black women, and sexuality, creating a wealth of public scholarship not bogged down by jargon. Her work crucially covers aspects of history often overlooked or ignored in mainstream narratives. Since launching Intelexual Media in January 2017, Elexus has spent countless time researching, writing, and editing YouTube videos that have been viewed over 20,000,000 times. She lives in Atlanta, Georgia in an all-pink apartment with her two dogs, Butters and Brownie. She enjoys video games, running, iced coffee, and letting loose her frustrations on the dance floor. You can keep up with her projects and writing at IntelexualMedia.com.

COMPLETE

YOUR COLLECTION!

www.ingramcontent.com/pod-product-compliance
Lightning Source LLC
Chambersburg PA
CBHW050102170426
43198CB00014B/2431